THE NEW AMERICAN CRISIS

Also available from The New Press

Open Fire: The Open Magazine
Pamphlet Anthology

THE NEW AMERICAN CRISIS

Radical Analyses of the Problems Facing America Today

EDITED BY

GREG RUGGIERO AND STUART SAHULKA

THE NEW PRESS
New York

LIBRARY OF CONGRESS CATALOGING-IN-PUBLICATION DATA

The new American crisis: radical analyses of the problems facing America today /
edited by Greg Ruggiero and Stuart Sahulka.
    p.   cm.
  ISBN 1-56584-317-7
  1. United States—Politics and government—1993–
    I. Ruggiero, Greg. I. Sahulka, Stuart.
E885.N48   1996
973.929—dc20   95-22646
CIP

PUBLISHED IN THE UNITED STATES BY THE NEW PRESS, NEW YORK
DISTRIBUTED BY W. W. NORTON & COMPANY, INC., NEW YORK

Established in 1990 as a major alternative to the large, commercial
publishing houses, The New Press is the first full-scale nonprofit American
book publisher outside of the university presses. The Press is operated
editorially in the public interest, rather than for private gain; it is committed
to publishing in innovative ways works of educational, cultural, and
community value that, despite their intellectual merits, might not normally
be commercially viable. The New Press's editorial offices are located at the
City University of New York.

Book design by Paul Chevannes
Composition by Jean Poderos

Production management by Kim Waymer
Printed in the United States of America

95 96 97 98   9 8 7 6 5 4 3 2 1

This book is dedicated to our parents,
for all their encouragement,
guidance, and love

THE LOW ROAD

MARGE PIERCY

What can they do
to you? Whatever they want.
They can set you up, they can
bust you, they can break
your fingers, they can
burn your brain with electricity,
blur you with drugs till you
can't walk, can't remember, they can
take your child, wall up
your lover. They can do anything
you can't stop them
from doing. How can you stop
them? Alone, you can fight,
you can refuse, you can
take what revenge you can
but they roll over you.

But two people fighting
back to back can cut through
a mob, a snake-dancing file
can break a cordon, an army
can meet an army.

Two people can keep each other
sane, can give support, conviction,
love, massage, hope, sex.
Three people are a delegation,
a committee, a wedge. With four
you can play bridge and start
an organization. With six
you can rent a whole house,
eat pie for dinner with no
seconds, and hold a fund raising party.
A dozen make a demonstration.
A hundred fill a hall.
A thousand have solidarity and your own newsletter;
ten thousand, power and your own paper;
a hundred thousand, your own media;
ten million, your own country.

It goes on one at a time,
it starts when you care
to act, it starts when you do
it again after they said no,
it starts when you say *We*
and know who you mean, and each
day you mean one more.

CONTENTS

Preface

The slogan at the beginning of the twentieth century was progress.
The cry at the end of the twentieth century is survival.
The call for the next century is hope.
—MUTO ICHIYO from *Global Visions, Beyond The New World Order*

Over the past five years the Open Magazine Pamphlet Series has struggled to express the political agitation and progressive vision of Americans who are unhappy with the destructiveness of American power and the deterioration of the country's social conditions. Founded originally as "an emergency broadcast effort" during the Gulf War, the Pamphlet Series voiced progressives' calls for the removal of George Bush and an end to the deregulating and destabilizing conservative regime of Reganomics.

Thus, when Clinton's election ousted Bush and ended twelve years of Republican control, we were ready to switch gears, readjust our focus, and concentrate more on putting forth proposals than fomenting protest. Clinton's procorporate agenda, however, has been almost identical to that of his predecessors. With GATT and NAFTA, Clinton was prepared to cut any amount of pork to get his way; yet, when affordable health care came to the table, the average citizen's hopes were dashed on the rocks of profiteering and partisan politics. After almost four years in office it is clear that neither an administration of Democrats nor the two-party system itself is going to take steps toward developing a sustainable economy or a socially conscious agenda.

Increasingly, Americans are waking up to the fact that even the liberal wing of the two-faction business party ignores the needs of common people. As Juliet Schor writes:

> The debate between Republicans and Democrats has narrowed to a marginal one. Both sides now worship at the altar of the market, differing mainly on whether it should be marginally regulated in the public interest or not regulated at all. Both defend the sanctity of the existing distribution of income, wealth, and power. And both Republicans and Democrats turn their backs on democracy and genuflect to twin gods of "growth" and "free-trade."

In a country that touts democracy to the rest of the world, why do we have such an amazingly narrow political spectrum? Why should Americans accept such a paltry set of choices? The alternative of organizing ourselves, creating new alliances, and even forming completely new parties with new ideas and policies is the hope that guides us into the twenty-first century.

What is *The New American Crisis*? It is a collection of pamphlets and essays that documents the current crisis of democracy, the hegemony of corporate influence, the privatization of society and commercialization of public life, and advances progressive challenges to it. The new American crisis entails the struggle to preserve and expand the public good, increase democratic participation, and utilize government for the benefit of the entire citizenry, not just the corporate sector.

One may well ask, what is new about this crisis? For Native Americans this is a five-hundred-year-old story of intrusion and assault. However, it may be the progressives who ultimately have the upper hand in the long struggle against the managers of capital. Winona LaDuke reminds us that "a society based on conquest cannot survive when there's nothing left to conquer." As Newt Gingrich and his Republican cohorts lead the way in a scorched earth campaign for the "free" market, the ensuing material and moral poverty will serve as constant reminders of missed opportunities to rebuild and restore community in America. At that point, progressive plans for investing in America's social infrastructure will sound the clarion call for a long overdue overhaul of the existing democracy.

Developing an autonomous, noncommercial, public information media will be a major first step in empowering the citizenship and establishing a sound foundation for democratic renewal. In the years ahead, as the Internet integrates more fluidly into our preexisting television and radio technology, we may find ourselves with the tools not only to bypass corporate programming, but with the means to launch petitions, initiate referendums, and pass legislation. Such ability would mark true breakthroughs in democratic participation. However, these hopes are only technological pipe dreams if the primary information needs of society are unmet, and urgent action isn't taken to ensure that the new technology doesn't create yet another barrier between information "Haves" and "Have-nots."

Any solution to this crisis requires open debate and grass-roots policy initiatives independent of the two-party system. It is for this reason that the

Open Magazine Pamphlet Series has recently forged a solidarity with the progressive New Party. Instead of merely reacting to the depravity of the corporate agenda or hoping that someday someone will bring them under democratic control for us, we must organize *now* to create our own options and alternatives. We believe the New Party is one such option.

In the meantime, we must persist with our challenges to the two-party system, debate the role of government in securing the welfare of the people, and look to changing our own lives in ways that will have an impact on corporations and improve the quality of public and private life. If democracy is to be revived and made to flourish, we the American people must restore it ourselves, formulate and administer our own social policies, take the responsibility to live peacefully with our international neighbors, and freely live out our highest hopes for the future.

Acknowledgments

We would like to express our appreciation and thanks to the contributors to this volume who have helped to make the Open Magazine Pamphlet Series a critical success; to Harvey Kaye for his invaluable friendship, energy, and ideas as advisor to the series; to Robert Ruggiero for his generous guidance and support; to Steve Hatch for his computer wizardry and patient coaching on the Internet; to Falcon Printing for their excellent work in printing all of our pamphlets; to Peter Meyer and friends at the *Nation* for their solidarity and research assistance; to William Parker and Daniel Carter for their visionary jazz and soulful inspiration; to Barbara Pillsbury for her diligent commitment in translating and posting volumes of Zapatista communiques on the Internet; to Noam Chomsky for his prolific and unrelenting service to democratic struggle; and to our friends and readers for five years of encouragement and support.

"The Low Road" was published originally in *The Moon is Always Female* (New York: Alfred A. Knopf, Inc).

"Hope for the Nineties" was published originally in *Covert Action*, no. 27 (Winter 1993–94), pp. 32–36.

"Rollback" is an edited and revised edition of a four-part article that was published originally in *Z Magazine* (Jan., Feb., Mar., Apr. 1995).

"After the Summit" is an updated edition of an article that was published originally in *Socialist Review*, vol. 22, no. 4 (Oct.-Dec. 1992), pp. 57–92.

"NAFTA, GATT, and the World Trade Organization: The New Rules for Corporate Conquest" was published originally in *Open Magazine Pamphlet #29* (Apr. 1994).

"Notes on NAFTA" was published originally in the *Nation* (29 Mar. 1993) and in *Open Magazine Pamphlet #24* (June 1993).

"Global Village or Global Pillage?" was published originally as "After NAFTA" in the *Nation* (6 Dec. 1993) and in *Open Magazine Pamphlet #29* (Apr. 1994).

"Power History, & Warfare" was published originally in *Open Magazine Pamphlet #7* (1991).

"Rebuilding America: A New Economic Plan for the 1990s" was published originally in *Open Magazine Pamphlet #21* (Oct. 1992).

"Starting from Chiapas: The Zapatista Fire the Shot Heard Around the World" is an expanded version of an article that was published originally as "The Mayan Revolution, the Zapatistas Fire the Shot Hear 'Round the Global Market" in the *Village Voice* (Feb. 1, 1994) and in *Open Magazine Pamphlet #30* (Feb. 1994).

"Original Declaration of War from the Lacandon Jungle by the Zapatistas to the People of Mexico" and "Zapatista Communique, Statement of January 6, 1994" were translated by Barbara Pillsbury, posted on the Internet, and published widely, including in *Open Magazine Pamphlet #30* (Feb. 1994).

"Zapatista Communique" was translated by Barbara Pillsbury, posted on the Internet, and published widely, including in *Open Magazine Pamphlet #30* (Feb. 1994).

"Statement of the Zapatista Insurgents" was published originally in a limited edition *Open Magazine Pamphlet* by William Parker entitled "Music Is" (June 1994).

"Who Is Marcos?" was originally published in *Covert Action Quarterly*, no. 52 (Spring 1995).

"Learning from Native Peoples" was the Thirteenth Annual E. F. Schumacher Lecture presented at Yale University (Oct. 23, 1993) and was published originally by the E. F. Schumacher Society (1994).

"The Information Superhighway: 500 Ways to Pave Over the Public" is an interview conducted by the Open Magazine Pamphlet Series that which appeared in *Z Magazine* (March 1994).

"On Malcolm X: His Message and Meaning" was published originally in *Open Magazine Pamphlet* #22 (Nov. 1992).

"Breaking Bread: A Dialogue Among Communities in Search of a Common Ground" is an edited transcript of a discussion at the High School of Fashion Industries auditorium, New York City (June 21, 1994).

"This Is War!" was published originally in the *Chicago Reader* (20 Jan. 1995).

"A Sustainable Economy for the Twenty-first Century" was published originally in *Open Magazine Pamphlet #31* (April 1995).

"How Divided Progressives Might Unite" was published originally in the *New Left Review*, no. 210 (March-April 1995).

THE OPEN MAGAZINE PAMPHLET SERIES is being archived by the Tamiment Institute Library, 70 Washington Square South, New York, NY 10012; email: elmer1.bobst.nyu.edu; Tel. (212) 998-2630.

INTRODUCTION:
THE NEW AMERICAN CRISIS

HARVEY J. KAYE

> These are the times that try men's souls. The summer soldier and the sun-
> shine patriot will, in this crisis, shrink from the service of their country; but
> he that stands it *now,* deserves the love and thanks of man and woman.
> Tyranny, like hell, is not easily conquered; yet we have this consolation with
> us, that the harder the conflict, the more glorious the triumph.

So wrote Tom Paine in December 1776. Not even a year had passed since he
had penned *Common Sense,* brashly announcing that "We have it in our
power to begin the world over again" and effectively transforming the ram-
bunctious and rebellious political sentiment of colonial America into a struggle for national independence. And it had been only several months since the
democratic ideals he had begun to articulate were translated into the
Declaration of Independence, the first modern revolutionary manifesto
asserting the essential equality of humanity and a people's right to self-determination and "Life, Liberty and the pursuit of Happiness."

Now, however, with winter taking hold, the Revolution seemed to be in
full retreat on the battlefield and doomed to collapse. Nevertheless, Paine
would not surrender to despair. Hoping to reenergize the cause and further
mobilize his fellow citizens-in-the-making against British imperialism and its
Tory supporters, he set himself to producing a new series of pamphlets, to be
known as *The American Crisis.* Seven years later, after many a campaign military, political, and ideological, independence was won.

But, of course, the struggle for freedom, equality, and democracy in
America had only begun. Generation after generation of Americans were to
find themselves confronting the power and ambitions of the propertied and
the privileged who have always been ready to declare the Revolution over
and eager to get on with the business of the day. Yet, as much as the power
elites past and present would attempt to declaim otherwise, the promise and
possibility of America was neither inscribed nor to be comprehended in
finite terms.

There is no evading the tragic character of the American experience: the genocidal treatment of native peoples; the slave trade and the slave regime; the repeated exploitation of immigrants young and old; the corporate devastation of working-class communities and the environment; imperial interventions and the suppression of popular revolutions abroad; persistent oppressions of class, race, ethnicity, and gender...

Yet, the exploitation, inequality, and injustice have not gone unchallenged. America's revolutionary foundations empowered a radical tradition that has made the nation's history—however contradictory, tragic, or ironic the record—a narrative of struggle, more often progressive than not, to expand both the *we* in "We, the People" and the process by which "the people" can genuinely govern.

From the outset, family farmers contested governments dominated by gentry landowners and urban financial and mercantile interests, and radical artisans and industrial mechanics—Tom Paine's own ilk—organized working men's parties in efforts to control both their own labor and those who would govern them. These may read like experiences of defeat, but they clearly registered that America's working people were prepared to continue the fight to secure and defend their democratic rights—even if it now meant battling their fellow citizens.

In the southern states, African-American men and women resisted and, occasionally, in the face of overwhelming odds, rebelled against a social order that sought to reduce them to being merely the property of their masters. In the process, they undermined the regime that held them in bondage and crafted cultural practices and institutions that have not only enabled them to endure and pursue a long and continuing struggle for justice and equality, but that have deeply enriched other movements for freedom in America and globally.

In 1848 American women and a smaller number of men, in many cases veterans of the ongoing antislavery movement (including the great African-American orator and abolitionist, Frederick Douglass), met in Seneca Falls, New York, for the first women's rights convention. Composing their manifesto in the very language of the Declaration of Independence, the conventioneers proclaimed the equality of men and women and demanded that women be secured the same rights as male citizens. The women's suffrage amendment entered the Constitution seventy years later; though here, too, securing the franchise, however long the conflict and fundamental the right, was merely the first of many contests for gender equality.

The prophetic memory of America's promise and possibility, and the struggle for liberty, equality, and democracy, were refreshed again and again both by native-born and immigrant generations of radicals—agrarianists, populists, laborists, feminists, socialists, anarchists, pacifists, environmentalists, and campaigners for the civil and social rights of minorities.

The struggle continues and, once again, as so many times before, "These are the times that try men's [and women's] souls… "

Stated bluntly, for the past twenty years we have been subjected to what can only be described as "class war from above" against the achievements of the New Deal, postwar liberalism and social democracy, and the progressive changes wrought by the diverse struggles of the sixties.

The corporate powers-that-be were quite clear about it. They were convinced that the several campaigns of the day were on the verge of merging into a broad radical-democratic movement and that the reforms already secured in the struggles for the civil rights of racial and ethnic minorities, the social rights of the poor, the equal rights of women, the cessation of imperial wars, and the much less celebrated but no less remarkable working-class insurgency for changes in the workplace and a greater share of the national product portended even greater and more profound upheavals in the years ahead.

In reaction, the corporate and political elites mobilized and, in many a public statement and manifesto, pronounced themselves ready to respond. Among the most original and impressive of such initiatives was the Trilateral Commission, an organization bringing together the chieftains of multinational capital and a host of the leading "centrist" political figures from Western Europe, Japan, and the United States. Launched by the head of the Chase Manhattan Bank, David Rockefeller, the commission included presidential aspirants Jimmy Carter and George Bush.

In their first major report, *The Crisis of Democracy* (1975), the Trilateralists declared that the United States and the other Western polities were facing "governmental overload," more specifically, a "crisis" in which the problems of "governance" stemmed from "an excess of democracy." The report readily acknowledged the threat as coming from below, that is, from minorities, women, public-interest groups, and labor unions. But, in their elitist worldview, the most immediate danger was perceived to be that posed by the spreading "adversary culture" of media and university intellectuals, specifically, "value-oriented intellectuals who [in contrast to the "technocrats and policy-oriented intellectuals"] often devote themselves to the derogation of leadership, the challenging of authority, and the unmasking and delegitimation of established institutions."

What was to be done? Bluntly stating that the "effective operation of a democratic political system usually requires some measure of apathy and noninvolvement on the part of some individuals or groups," the Trilateral report called for an abatement of popular democratic politics and the possible "regulation of the media" and "retrenchment and rationalization of higher education." And this was just the leading edge of the "revolution from above"—in fact, the Trilateralists were considered moderates compared to the conservative forces marshalling further to the right.

Lucratively financed by both the "*Fortune* 500" and small business associations, in the course of the 1970s a *New* Right alliance was formed of right-wing single-interest groups (from anti–gun control and antitax to anti–women's rights groups), Protestant fundamentalists (recruited to the "Moral Majority" and similar organizations by a new breed of televangelists), and conservative and neoconservative intellectuals (free-marketeers and supply-siders, opponents of affirmative action, and cold warriors regularly holding down extraacademic appointments in corporate-funded Washington thinktanks).

Truly, it was a strange coalition. Yet, however diverse and even contradictory the respective parties seemed, they were all hostile to liberal reformism and the persistent struggles for class, race, and gender justice and equality; and their respective but mutual hostilities were brilliantly and effectively harnessed by the Republican cadres gathered around actor-turned-politician Ronald Reagan. Fortified in their quest for power by both the global recession of the late seventies and the apparent ineffectiveness of the Carter administration, the rapid ascent of this New Right was registered in the Reagan and Bush administrations (1980–1992), permitting the class war from above to command public policy even more directly.

Reaganism, as the new political and economic regime came to be called, was pursued under the guise of restoring America's greatness, its industrial robustness and military prowess, and redeeming the supposedly traditional values of family, law and order, and the work ethic. However, behind a rhetoric of patriotism and shared values, Reaganism inaugurated a period of blatant greed and profiteering in which the American economy was further deindustrialized and corporate capital was empowered to intensify its ongoing assault on organized labor—thereby speeding up the process by which the rich got richer and working people and the poor were made poorer. Also, it instituted a policy of "military Keynesianism" in which tax rates for the upper classes were cut and domestic programs were defunded while billions of dollars more were spent on the military in pursuit of a Second Cold War— thereby providing for the further decay of the country's infrastructure and for the streets and alleyways of America's cities to become home to hundreds of thousands of the nation's citizens.

If these acts, and the hardship and despoliation they wrought, were themselves not enough to warrant criminal charges, elements within and without the Reagan administration proceeded to aid state and guerrilla terrorism in Central America and to conspire against constitutional government in the United States, as demonstrated in the Iran-Contra affair.

At the same time, the New Right politicos were determined to drive the surviving remnants of the New Left of the 1960s from the public arena *and* to fabricate a new postliberal conservative political hegemony. Cultural and ideological campaigns against liberals and progressives alike were enthusiastically pursued by Republican officeholders from their bully pulpits, and their attacks were broadcast ever more widely by growing numbers of right-wing radio talkshow hosts (the champion among them, Rush Limbaugh, even garnered a late-night television slot).

Portraying everyone from "unionized schoolteachers" and "leftist and feminist college professors" to "single mothers on AFDC" as somehow subversive of American life, the New Right made public education and social welfare the major targets of their ideological "culture wars" and succeeded in shaping the public discourse on those subjects.

Sadly, the prominence of the Right was further enhanced by the apparent retreat of the political and intellectual left. The Democrats, the so-called people's party, offered limited opposition and, even more often, deferred to the political-economic agenda of Reaganism. The more progressive segments of the political left, which, unfortunately, had failed to create the fearfully imagined radical-democratic coalition, was marked by division and feebleness in the face of the conservatives' political juggernaut. And the intellectual left contributed to its own marginalization from public debate by transforming itself into an "academic left" and becoming self-absorbed in scholarly debates, debates made all the more incomprehensible, politically irrelevant, and (rightly) subject to ridicule because of the importance given to the ideas and language of postmodernism and poststructuralism.

Moreover, the corporate news media regularly treated the Republican presidential victories as prime indicators that a conservative consensus was actually taking hold across the country, thereby reinforcing the New Right politicians' claims to possession of a mandate for their plans and projects.

The apparent defeat of the Left in all its varieties *and* the concurrent dissolution of the Soviet Empire and closing of the Cold War signalled the *global* triumph of capital. Thus, the intellectuals of the New Right proceeded to do what the agents of ruling classes have always been wont to do: they announced the "end of history." They declared that America and the world had arrived at the terminus of world-historical development, the culmination of universal history. In short, we were informed that radical-democratic possibilities are finished, that the further progress and development of liberty and equality is foreclosed, forever. To think otherwise was pronounced not just utopian but dangerous.

The powers-that-be may be keen to declare victory, but they are well aware—far more so, it often seems, than those of us constituting the intellectual left—that the struggle for liberty, equality, and democracy is not exhausted. The persistence of exploitation and oppression continues to generate social antagonisms and conflict, and America's radical traditions and historical ideals stand in inspiring contrast to the reality of contemporary experience. Indeed, however quiescent "the people" may seem, the majority of Americans are unpersuaded that the democratic promise and possibility of America is fulfilled. They remain anxious about the future, wary of their governing elites, committed to the values of social justice and equality and, even, prepared to support public action to address the nation's economic and social problems. The powerful realize these things.

Nevertheless, lacking a serious and organized opposition capable of presenting a truly alternative and comprehensive radical-democratic vision and project, popular anxieties and aspirations continue to be weighed down in cynicism and despair, expressing themselves in ways ranging from the determined passivity of refusing to vote or get involved in any fashion whatsoever, to supporting eccentric and demagogic populisms such as Ross Perot's presidential campaign and the more recent Republican Party "Contract With America," to desperate acts of uprising and riot, as witnessed in Los Angeles in the spring of 1992. Philip Mattera describes it well in *Prosperity Lost:* "These days there is not much collective dreaming in America. The erosion of living standards and the increase in economic insecurity have brought about a climate of quiet frustration and cynicism. People have been caught between official pronouncements that these are the best of times and their personal realization that life is getting tougher every day."

For a brief moment it did seem likely that the politics of progressivism might be returned to the public political agenda. While "New Democrat" Clinton never pretended to be a radical or, for that matter, even an old-style liberal, in the 1992 elections he did succeed in defeating the conservative Republican candidate and incumbent president, George Bush, by issuing a call for "change" and running on a platform that promised, for starters, a reduction in the military budget in favor of rebuilding the nation's infrastructure from highways and bridges to housing and public schools; the establishment of a national, universal health-care system; and the recommitment of the federal government to efforts to both ensure and extend the civil and social rights of all citizens. But, as we know, the only major changes legislated have been the NAFTA and GATT world-trade pacts so ardently sought by multinational capital.

Admittedly, the Clinton administration did attempt the enactment of the more popular initiatives. However, in the absence of coherent and engaged political agencies pressuring from the left, retreat, compromise, collapse became the orders of the day. Perhaps this was to be expected, for there was little chance that Clinton and his cohort were themselves going to mobilize the popular support necessary to confront the handsomely endowed forces of conservatism and reaction. Think back to the long-since-celebrated Clinton inauguration, whereat the new president urged Americans to "be bold, embrace change and share the sacrifices needed for the nation to progress."

It should be recalled that William Jefferson Clinton sought to connect his own "political vision" to that of the revolutionary author of the Declaration of Independence, Thomas Jefferson. Following his pilgrimage to Jefferson's home at Monticello and his journey to the District of Columbia along the very route traveled by the third president in 1801, Clinton's inaugural speech was laden with Jeffersonian references. I have in mind one remark in particular, his statement that "Thomas Jefferson believed that to preserve the very foundations of our nation, we would need dramatic change from time to time."

But, of course, as every child of the the sixties (such as Clinton) knows, that is not exactly what the Founding Father said. The words Jefferson himself proffered were: "I hold that a little *rebellion* now and then is a good thing, and as necessary in the political world as in the physical [emphasis added]."

How should we interpret Clinton's revision of the radical Jefferson? As an innocent act? Or, as I did (though hoping to be proven wrong), as an act in favor of the existing order by yet another representative of the governing class who, having campaigned in the name of "change," had no intention of actually rousing the historical memory and imagination of his fellow citizens for fear they might really pursue it?

Undeniably, the struggle for liberty, equality, and democracy is in retreat and we face a crisis of dramatic proportions, for Clinton's failures have actually intensified the sense of disappointment and betrayal felt by those very social groups traditionally supportive of a progressive politics. Not only right-wing columnists are composing the obituaries for radical-democratic politics in America. Similar pieces are appearing in the pages of the surviving periodicals of the left under headings like "The Death of Socialism" (*Nation*) and "Left for Dead" (*Village Voice*).

Nevertheless, we would do better to remember the words of the radical historian Howard Zinn. Explaining his "failure to quit," he says: "I can understand pessimism, but I don't believe in it. It's not simply a matter of faith, but of historical evidence. Not overwhelming evidence, just enough to give hope, because for hope we don't need certainty, only possibility. Despite all those confident statements that 'history shows...' 'and history proves,' hope is all the past can offer us...When I hear so often that there is little hope for change in the '90s, I think back to the despair that accompanied the onset of the '60s." And, if we think back still further, we would do well also to consider the state of the American Revolution in the winter of 1776.

To be sure, there are no guarantees. We have a long way to go, and, if we are to redeem the prophetic memory of America's promise and possibility and revive a truly progressive politics, we will need critical and radical voices, both veteran and original, capable both of articulating the diverse needs and aspirations of working people and the oppressed, and of cultivating visions and projects engaging of their consciousness and commitment.

The "pamphleteers" Greg Ruggiero and Stuart Sahulka have been laboring hard to realize those things. The present anthology offers a second outstanding selection of their efforts to publish, promote, and propagate a variety of voices and ideas of the American left in a timely and accessible manner. Significantly, the pages that follow are critical, but they deny cynicism and despair in favor of prospect and possibility. The Open Magazine Pamphlet Series may pose no immediate threat to the likes of televangelist Pat

Robertson and talkshow demagogue Rush Limbaugh. But who knows? Again, Howard Zinn may have put it best in his smartly titled *Declarations of Independence:*

> When we become depressed at the thought of the enormous power that governments, multinational corporations, armies and police have to control minds, crush dissents, and destroy rebellions, we should consider a phenomenon that I have always found interesting: Those who possess enormous power are surprisingly nervous about their ability to hold on to their power. They react almost hysterically to what seem to be puny and unthreatening signs of opposition... Is it possible that people in authority know something we don't know? Perhaps they know their ultimate weakness. Perhaps they understand that small movements can become big ones, that if an idea takes hold in the population, it may become indestructible.

I. The New American Crisis

HOPE FOR THE NINETIES

DAVID DELLINGER

A lot of people are discouraged because conditions are so bad for so many people and yet there is no mass movement demanding fundamental change in the economic and political system. But there is much more rebellion and experimentation with positive ways of relating to our fellow human beings than meets the casual eye or is made clear in the mass media. Although public discontent has not yet come to a dramatic head, there are more people today than at any time in my life who are seriously angry at the inhuman conditions under which they (or others) are forced to live—many more than in the Great Depression of the '30s, when I cut my political teeth.

Many of these angry, disillusioned people are either inactive or are active in ways not commonly seen as a movement for a new society. But we all live with contradictory impulses within us, and which become dominant at any particular time is influenced by external as well as internal factors. In the absence of a unified, contagious movement that offers hope for changing the way things are, most people suppress their better instincts (or express them in small ways) and live most of their lives in accord with established mores. While they do what they think they have to in order to live successfully, *even survive,* their better instincts endure, consciously or subconsciously, waiting for the time when they can come to life on a larger scale. And sooner or later, because the military-corporate elites and their two political parties are sitting on a whole series of unstable fault lines, a volcano of public discontent is bound to erupt.

SELF-SERVING POLITICIANS

Briefly, some people, discouraged by a lack of the mass demonstrations they have associated with an active movement, desperately placed their hopes in some "change" by electing a new administration. By now, however, it is clear that whatever good impulses Clinton (like everyone) has, he is above all a self-serving politician. Even during the period of widespread popular opposition to the Vietnam War, when he knew the war was a tragedy for its GI and Vietnamese victims, his dominating concern was "to maintain my political viability" within the existing system. He will never advocate, let alone fight for, anything fundamental that would repair the underlying problem. And the few "progressive" members of Congress are not significantly different. Like Clinton, their personal careers are more important to them than the fundamental changes that would bring justice and grassroots democracy. When Zoë Baird was nominated for Attorney General, newly elected multi-millionaire Dianne Feinstein lectured her for hiring an "illegal alien" rather than for taking over $500,000 annually from large corporations (first G.E., and then Aetna and Southern New England Telephone Company) to defend their oppression, pollution, and corruption, and in the case of G.E., its fraudulent charges of millions of dollars in arms sales. But the very status of aliens (most of whom are escaping U.S.-trained death squads and inhuman living conditions imposed by U.S. corporations and pro-U.S. dictators) is a denial of the welcome emblazoned on the Statue of Liberty.

Nor was the self-serving opportunism of Baird's replacement, Janet Reno, a subject for editorial comment. "Although she opposes the death penalty," AP reported, "Attorney General Janet Reno is supporting proposals that would reduce delays in executions and expand capital punishment to some 50 federal crimes." Having built her Florida reputation on the high profile but suspect prosecution of daycare owners charged with child abuse, Reno presided over illegal attacks on the cult at Waco, Texas, causing the execution of 86 people, dozens of them children. In defense of the final murders, she said that "after seven weeks of standoff, the [government's] team needed time off."

And how long will the public put up with such events as the bombing of Iraq because of an alleged plan by Saddam Hussein to assassinate ex-President Bush when he was in Kuwait? Even if Clinton was correct in his justification of that bombing, at least 20 countries would be similarly justified in bombing the United States because of U.S. attempts (sometimes successful) to assassinate leading members of their governments. No wonder the World Trade Center was bombed. And when U.S. forces in Somalia killed an estimated 100 Somalis (many of them civilians), President Clinton "strenuously argued against" an amendment to halt U.S. operations in Somalia within the next two months saying it "would weaken the presidency and would seem to be a sign of American weakness." He then initiated military action in which "[a]bout 300 Somalis are believed to have been...killed during the street fighting in Mogadishu on October 3, and the wounded included hundreds of women and children who were among the 700 treated in hospitals..." The *New York Times* faithfully reported the government's justification of the slaughter which asserted "the nature and degree of the force used by the U.S. and UN forces was...consistent with the right of self-defense under international law." In fact, the Somali attack against which the United States was "defending *itself*" was itself self-defense against a U.S.-led attack on an Aidid stronghold.

Such justification for illegitimate policies is not confined to foreign affairs. Those in power in the United States are desperate to legitimate not only their adventures abroad but also the cruelty with which they treat a majority of this country's residents. Rather than blaming a system which benefits only the few, they blame the failures on the victims—people of the wrong country, color, or view, the unemployed and underemployed, the homeless, people with AIDS, etc. Given the glut of scapegoating and the famine of justice, revolts of a more and more serious nature are inevitable. And sooner or later one of them will start a whole series of explosions, as the 1955 refusal of Rosa Parks to go to the back of a segregated bus led (unexpectedly) to the Montgomery Bus Boycott, sit-ins, and Freedom Rides in the tumultuous '60s.

MORE PROTESTS NOW THAN IN THE '60S

Until some new spark ignites the country, it is important to remember that the massive protests of the '60s set an artificial standard by which many people judge the present level of activity. Today, no single demand or issue dominates the movement or attracts public attention the way that the struggle for civil rights and then opposition to the Vietnam War did from 1956 to 1975. During the heyday years, even those who were working primarily on other issues went to the antiwar demonstrations, as they had gone to the August 1963 civil rights demonstration. This unity added to the public consciousness of massive unrest. By contrast, not everyone who is active today goes to the same city on the same weekend to shout the same slogans. Instead, the areas of activity have grown until, like Heinz, there are 57 different but related varieties and not one of them draws either the crowds or the media attention of its predecessors. But by my estimate, more people protested in Washington in 1992 than in any year of the '60s. The media, however, ignore the greater frequency of protests now and stress the smaller numbers at a particular event, thereby spreading the illusion that the days of social revolt are over. They intoned the same message all through the '70s when a revitalized women's movement was gaining energy, recruits, and momentum, and again in the '80s as a dynamic movement for the rights of lesbians and gays was getting under way.

It is not only the corporate media's sexism and homophobia that causes this distortion, but also their concern for preventing new volcanos from erupting. In the '60s, they learned how dangerous it is to elites when people believe in the power of a nonviolent resistance that goes beyond voting, lobbying, and writing letters to Congress. They also became increasingly sophisticated and effective in damping and coopting dissent.

This propaganda has not only affected the general public, but has led many activists to underestimate the importance of their work. When I went to North Dakota in the late '70s for an antinuclear demonstration at a missile site, I was met by Bob Lamb, a former antiwar stalwart and key activist around the 1969–70 Chicago Eight (later, Chicago Seven) conspiracy trial. "I hope you're not too disappointed in me," he said, "for having dropped out of the Movement." "Of course not," I answered. "You put in years of emergency living while fighting for social justice. Everyone who does that needs some kind of periodic breather to catch up with other aspects of their lives. By the way, what are you doing these days?" "Oh," he replied, "I'm working against strip mining in South Dakota." Since Chicago, Bob has worked with Physicians for Social Responsibility and has talked at high schools in opposition to the draft. These two basic, widespread activities, however, are not generally cited when people are gauging the extent of social revolt today.

There are also many people who sought out new sources of spiritual understanding and growth that would help them leave behind the shrillness, hostilities, and self-righteousness that were part of the most vocal (and media-emphasized) sections of the movement. Such people were labeled "drop-outs," not just by the media but also by some of their more one-dimensional former comrades. The search of younger people for a deeper dynamic in their lives has been similarly criticized. Instead of understanding the contributions such a quest could make to a more comprehensive and comprehending movement, Christopher Lasch castigated the "Me Generation," as more interested in looking at their navels than in being responsible members of society.

No path is ever faultless and many who took this one succumbed to temptations along the way—unhealthy subservience to a guru or New Age excesses. But on the whole it was a healthier period of exploration, discovery, and growth through personal trial and error than Lasch, the media, or even activists acknowledged. Because of it, many of today's activities are sounder than in the '60s. The spiritually based Liberation Theology movement, for example, is fighting the ravages of imperialism in Latin America, and the U.S. sanctuary movement here at home has helped many of the current victims of 500 years of genocide.

Activism in the '70s and '80s has also increased awareness that responsible politics requires more than demonstrating to ask Washington to change its ways. It calls for reworking relationships within our families, neighborhoods, workplaces, and regions. "The personal is the political." Or, as Charlie Parker once said, "Jazz comes from who you are, where you've been and what you've learned. If you don't live it, it won't come out of your horn." Many positive attempts to develop small-scale, grassroots institutions and activities are models for how everyone will act in a transformed and decent society—sharing burdens, rewards, and decision-making in an egalitarian manner. What is needed, I think, is for more of the individuals who are involved in these groups to extend their horizons beyond the immediate enterprise into the society as a whole.

Cornel West in *Race Matters* also uses the analogy of jazz, calling it

a mode of being in the world.... To be a jazz freedom fighter is to attempt to galvanize and energize a world-weary people into forms of organization with accountable leadership that promote [from a wider basis] critical exchange and broad reflection. The interplay of individuality and leadership is not one of uniformity and unanimity imposed from above, but rather of conflict among diverse groupings that reach a dynamic consensus subject to questioning and criticism. As with a soloist in a jazz quartet, quintet or band, individuality is promoted in order to sustain and increase the creative tension with the group—a tension that yields higher levels of performance to achieve the aim of the collective project.

That the movement for social change is beginning, if perhaps not quickly enough, to reflect these values is certainly a sign of hope. By contrast, too many groups in the past have reflected the competitiveness of society, as in "my issue is more important than your issue."

SOWING SEEDS

It is impossible to predict what spark will, like Rosa Parks's small rebellion, touch off a new and powerful movement. Many before her had defied the system. My first arrest in 1938 was with a group of whites who went upstairs to the "Negro" section of a Newark, New Jersey movie house. Our little action seemingly accomplished nothing, but it was important for us and for some of the black people we got to know and learn from. Thousands of similar seeds were sown during those seemingly unproductive years, seeds that broke through the surface after Rosa Parks acted.

Today millions are sowing diverse seeds without regard for tribe and boundary and with hardly a word from the mass media. A group of women traveled to Bosnia to work with rape victims and to set up therapy centers in this country for them to come to until they are ready to return to their native land. A series of nonviolent activists from Europe and the United States keep visiting the former Yugoslavia to help develop positive local strategies for resolving the conflicts. In the summer of 1993, some of my farmer neighbors in Vermont loaded tractor-trailers with hay to replace the crop which lay under Missouri flood waters. A local official noted: "It sort of renews your confidence in the system." But the farmers reject this system for a new one in which acts of human solidarity and sharing are not simply an emergency response but are part of everyday life. They want a system which values human relationships over striving for more money, power, and privilege than other people. The political expression of this system could include setting a maximum on private income and guaranteeing everyone the basic necessities of life.

And there is another factor at work fanning the many small sparks. The political system has broken down in a far more serious and permanent way than it did even during the Depression. Then, the New Deal and a series of seemingly drastic measures (drastic only in terms of the society's previous conceptions) appeased people's dissatisfactions a little. In fact, the system did not "recover" its class-based, racially limited "prosperity" until World War II and the arms race which followed it stimulated the economy and allowed military Keynesianism to kick in.

DEMOCRACY FOR THE FEW

Now the cold war is over and the power-elite is desperately seeking replacements such as the war on drugs (except those brought in regularly by the CIA) and a series of invasions—in Grenada, Panama, Iraq, and Somalia. But the economy is still failing and fewer and fewer people really believe the propaganda that "our system is triumphant" and should be established all over the world, with the United States as Superpower.

In actuality, the Soviet Union and the United States were different flawed experiments. In the Soviet Union, power was centralized in a one-party state, without the safeguards provided by political democracy and civil rights, so it failed even to achieve the economic democracy that had been the announced goal of the early revolutionists. Instead, a "New Class" of elites promoted their own privileges and power. By contrast, the U.S. experiment aspired to political democracy and rejected economic democracy. And now the results are dramatically clear. Who does not now know that our system, too, has failed by depriving millions of their basic human rights to food, housing, health care, and a safe and healthy environment? Who does not know that it fails to provide the meaningful work and self-esteem that would significantly reduce the number of people who turn to drugs—and the number of inner-city children who turn to drug-running—and the catastrophes that follow? Lacking economic democracy, we don't even have political democracy. The financial power of multi-billion-dollar corporations over electoral campaigns and over every branch of government has robbed citizens of meaningful control over the political (as well as economic) decisions that dominate their lives.

The lesson to be drawn from these two failures is that economic democracy and political democracy are inseparable; neither is possible without the other. And our society is filled with victims of our lack of both, some of whom are demeaned, castigated, and blamed for their desperate responses to the intolerable conditions. Our society is also layered with those whose response when the oppressed strike out is to declare self-righteously that "Violence is not the answer."

"But what, as a nation, did we really expect?" the *New Yorker* asked after the April 1992 Los Angeles riots. "The residents of our inner cities have for many years now been unable to lay claim to our sense of common humanity and simple decency. On what basis can we expect to suddenly lay claim to theirs?"

"Society," wrote Judge David Bazelon, "should be as alarmed by the silent misery of those who accept their plight as it is by the violence of those who do not."

THE POLARIZED SOCIETY

While the Soviet Union was falling apart, the number of billionaires in the United States tripled and the ranks of the homeless doubled. Shall we pretend that the children of billionaires and the children of the homeless are born equal since both groups will be able to vote at age 18 (if the children of the homeless live that long and don't end up in prison)? Some social workers estimate that more U.S. children die every month because of poverty than the number of U.S. combat deaths in the entire Vietnam War. And the rate of African-American incarceration in this "democracy" is six times that of whites. Shall we conclude that blacks have a proclivity for criminality in their genes or that the U.S. economy, culture, and system of "justice" are criminally racist? In Chicago, as one small example, upwards of 80 percent of the defendants in criminal court are black, but only .01 percent, or 27, of the 2,908 law partners are black. (There are also 15 Hispanic and nine Asian-American partners.) Putting a black Uncle Tom on the Supreme Court and a few others in well-paid positions in antisocial corporations does no more to promote justice than the practice, in the days of a more formal slavery, of having a few "house niggers."

I could continue with a carload of grim facts, but most people know the reality of oppression in one form or another: racism, sexism, classism, homophobia, etc. That constant oppression gives rise to anger and a desire for change is not disputable. The real question is *when* will this people's volcano erupt, as it did in the Soviet Union and swallow the elite clutching at its fault lines? And when it does explode, will we have a nonviolent movement that is active, disciplined, and imaginative enough to turn the revolt into positive, life-affirming channels that will have the power of a volcano without its mindless destructiveness?

If we want the explosion to unify the victims of various oppressions, it would help if the movement's more fortunate members learn to work hand-in-hand with those who lack basic human rights. White middle-class members will be more effective if they heed the sentiments of an African woman: "If you have come to help me, you are wasting your time. But if you have come because your liberation is bound up with mine, then let us work together."

FOR MLK: CAPITALISM, MILITARISM— AS EVIL AS RACISM

We need both small-and large-scale, grassroots and national initiatives that demonstrate the power of nonviolent force to achieve basic change in a way that riots and other forms of violence cannot. To become impatient and indulge in trashing, bombing, and preparing for armed struggle is the surest way to short-circuit the process and lose the prize, even if such a movement succeeds in "seizing power."

In the late '60s, some wonderful but impatient people said that "Martin Luther King was the most nonviolent man in the world and they killed him. Nonviolence doesn't work." But it was the fear of King's new, still developing opposition to *all* the violence of our system that caused some of society's masters to have him killed. They were terrified by the potential power of a movement that was based on King's belated acknowledgment: "The evils of capitalism and militarism are as great as the evils of racism." They also looked with great trepidation on his program "to bring the social change movements through from their early and now inadequate protest phase to a stage of massive, active, nonviolent resistance to the evils of…a system where some people live in superfluous, inordinate wealth while others live in abject, deadening poverty." As he said shortly before his assassination, "[f]or years I labored with the idea of reforming the existing institutions… a little change here, a little change there. Now I feel quite differently. I think you've got to have a reconstruction of the whole society."

For a struggle of this magnitude to succeed requires a well organized, broadly based and highly committed movement. To quote King again, "Until you're prepared to die, you can't begin to live." Soldiers risk death fighting for what they have been told is an honorable cause in the service of a community larger than themselves (the supposedly "democratic" country). In many ways, war was a high point of their lives, and the antiwar movement should begin to recognize this reality. But until a significant number of those of us who are fighting nonviolently for a genuinely democratic community, with justice for all, are willing to risk everything a soldier risks, we will not succeed in developing the only kind of movement that has a fighting chance of securing full human rights for everyone.

And let us not forget that such a movement should not be limited to concern for the most obvious victims of today's selfish competitions. The "winners" in those competitions suffer too. They lack the joys and fulfillments of living as sisters and brothers with their fellow human beings.

ROLLBACK

NOAM CHOMSKY

One of the great achievements of contemporary ideological warfare has been to debase the terms of political discourse so thoroughly that statements can be made that are not entirely false, if we keep to what has become conventional usage. As Orwell predicted, this achievement has undermined the possibility even of talking sensibly about what is happening in the world. Still, independent minds—including any authentic conservatives who might be located in the outer reaches of the political arena or intellectual world—can refuse to be swept up in the fashionable currents and use terms with their actual meanings to describe what is happening, and why.

For example, the elections of 1994 were described as a "political earthquake," a "triumph of conservatism" that reflects the continuing "drift to the right" on the part of the American population. The victorious Gingrich army of well-trained, well-funded "conservatives" called for a *Contract with America* that was to finally "get government off our backs" so that we can return to the happy days when the free market reigned. They set out to restore "family values," rid us of "the excesses of the welfare state" and the other residues of the failed "big government" policies of New Deal liberalism and Johnson's "Great Society." By dismantling the "nanny state" they hoped to succeed, where the Democrats had failed, to achieve the shared goal of all elite and leadership elements: to "create jobs for Americans" and win security and freedom for the "middle class." And they set out to take over and successfully lead the crusade to establish the American Dream of free market democracy, worldwide.

THE TRIUMPH OF CONSERVATISM

Most of this, we also heard just ten years ago, when Reagan was elected by a 2–1 vote, the second "conservative landslide" in four years. In his 1980 triumph, presidential historian William Leuchtenberg observed, "Reagan, far from having won in a landslide, got little more than a bare majority of the popular vote and only 28 percent of the potential electorate, and exit polls showed that the vote was not "for Reagan" but "against Carter," who had in fact initiated the policies that the Reaganites took up and implemented, with the general support of congressional Democrats: accelerating military spending (meaning, in particular, the state sector of the economy) while cutting back programs that aid the vast majority. Polls in 1980 revealed that 11 percent of Reagan voters chose him because "he's a real conservative"—whatever that term is supposed to mean.

In 1984, despite vast attempts to get out the vote, the totals increased by 1 percent. The percentage who chose Reagan because he was a "real conservative" dropped to 4 percent, while 70 percent of all voters with an opinion on the matter opposed Reaganite legislative programs, and public opinion studies showed a continuation of the steady drift toward a kind of New Deal–style welfare state liberalism on the part of the general population. Their concerns and desires were not articulated in the political system, however; one reason, surely, why voting was so sharply skewed toward privileged sectors.

The reasons why voting is so dramatically an elite affair in the United States are revealed by comparative studies. Analysis of thirty democracies showed "a significant correlation between high voter turnout and the presence of political parties representing clearly defined strata of society—that is, parties strongly tied to specific income classes, religious groupings, or language groups" (political commentator Thomas Edsall, 1984). In economic policy, Edsall added, the U.S. political system fails to represent "the interests of the bottom three-fifths of society." To use a phrase that is unspeakable in polite society without shock quotes, when the "class interests" of the privileged and powerful are the guiding commitment of all political parties, people who do not share these interests tend to stay home. The class pattern of abstention "seems inseparably linked to another crucial comparative peculiarity of the American political system," political scientist William Dean Burnham observed: "the total absence of a socialist or laborite party as an organized competitor in the electoral market." That absence relates to and is fortified by the effective dismantling of civil society: unions, political organizations, and so on.[1]

In the 1980s, the United States and Britain took the lead in the "triumph of conservatism," accelerating processes already underway. They therefore lead the developed world in impoverishment and degradation, inequality, homelessness, destruction of family values, hunger, and other values of contemporary "conservatism." A study by the British charitable organization Action for Children, founded in 1869 with the Queen as patron, concludes that "the gap between rich and poor is as wide today as it was in Victorian times," and in some ways worse. A million and a half families cannot afford to provide their children with "the diet fed to a similar child living in a Bethnal Green Workhouse in 1876," a "sad reflection on British society." Britain has proportionately more children living in poverty than any European country apart from Portugal and Ireland, and the proportion is rising faster than any country in Europe, though the United States still holds the lead.

Britain has also not yet matched the achievements of the doctrinal system crafted by our highly class-conscious business community, with the assistance of those whom the lively 19th-century working class press called "the bought priesthood" of respectable intellectuals. The fact that there is "class conflict" and that the rich and powerful mobilize state power to serve their interests, a truism to Adam Smith, remains within popular consciousness. The 1994 Gallup Political and Economic Index gives interesting information about popular attitudes on these matters (I put aside small numbers, 3–10 percent, expressing no opinion). The study reports that over four-fifths of the population think "there is a class struggle in this country" and that "too little" is being done "to level up the classes." Two-thirds "disagree strongly" with the statement "Britain is a classless society." Nine out of ten feel that the Government does "too little" for "the working class," four-fifths that it does "too much" for "the well-to-do," and over 90 percent that it does "too little" for "people living on small pensions/income." Half also think it does "too little" for "the middle classes." Three-fourths "think of Britain as divided into haves and have-nots," and a third describe themselves as among "the haves."[2]

Let's return to 1994, the next in the series of "conservative landslides," this time under the leadership of Newt Gingrich. "Republicans claimed about 52 percent of all votes cast for candidates in contested House seats, slightly better than a two-point improvement from 1992" (Richard Morin, director of polling for the *Washington Post*). One out of six voters described the outcome as "an affirmation of the Republican agenda"; 60 percent said it "was a repudiation of the Democrats." A "more conservative Congress" was considered to be an issue by a rousing 12 percent of the voters. An "overwhelming majority had never heard of" the Gingrich Contract with America, articulating the Republican agenda, though a majority opposed one of its central components: "defense increases," a code-word for public subsidies to advanced industry. The chief pollster of the *Los Angeles Times* pointed out that just before the election, 61 percent of those polled said "that spending for domestic programs should be increased."

All of this echoes the situation of a decade ago.

The opposition to Democrats is more nuanced. Clinton-style "New Democrats"—in effect, moderate Republicans—"lost their seats at twice the rate of their more liberal colleagues," Ken Silverstein and Alexander Cockburn report. The "more liberal" Democrats are those who tried to activate the old Democratic coalition of working people, women, the poor: the majority of the population who see themselves, correctly, as effectively disenfranchised.

To put these figures in further perspective, it must be recalled that voting was even more heavily skewed toward the wealthy and privileged than before. As compared with 1992, 7 percent more voters were wealthy, 7 percent fewer were working class, political scientist Peter Levine comments, noting also that Democrats were overwhelmingly preferred by voters who earn less than $30,000 a year and ran even with Republicans in the $30,000–$49,000 range. There was also a very large gender and color gap, white males voting mostly Republican, while women, Blacks and Hispanics voted for Democrats (overwhelmingly, in the Black-Hispanic category, where participation was low). Those with no more than high school education, along with those with postgraduate education, favored Democrats. Those who sensed a decline in their standard of living voted for Republicans by close to two to one—mostly white males with just high school degrees "whose economic futures are highly uncertain," Thomas Edsall observes; just those who would have been part of a left-populist coalition committed to equitable economic growth and political democracy, were such an option to intrude into our business-run political system.

The message, however, was just the opposite: Clinton must abandon the left-wing agenda that the voters had just overwhelmingly rejected and return to what he had promised to be in 1992: a "New Democrat." And he was quick to pick up the cues. In a satellite address to the National League of cities, "Clinton used some variation of the words 'work,' 'jobs' or 'working families' more than 40 times as he raised 'New Democrat' themes such as welfare reform, national service, lifelong job training, and the need to 'attack problems that feed dependency,'" the *Boston Globe* reported under the headline: "Clinton seen returning to 'New Democrat' stance." The report didn't say when he had left that stance for some different one, on any issue of importance to the rich and powerful. If he had, *Business Week* hadn't noticed. "Corporate America did fine riding in tandem with Clinton," the journal reports, though "it did equally well when they diverged."

Despite all his efforts to please, still business "basically hates the Clinton Administration," *Business Week* continues, and gives him "little credit" for advancing the corporate agenda. Why? The reasons they give, and cite from polls of executives, are hard to take seriously. But there is one very good reason. Leading sectors of wealth and privilege taste blood. They think, with some reason, that they have the world's population by the throat, and are in a position to roll back the hated welfare state for the general population and everything that goes with it: health and safety standards, labor rights and human rights generally. Given that awareness, it makes sense to "hate" anyone who may have a somewhat flawed commit-ment to the sole human value: "Gain Wealth, forgetting all but Self," "the New Spirit of the Age" denounced by the lively and vigorous working-class press 150 years ago, as working people fought to save human values from the rising tide of private tyranny.[3]

Yet another factor, scarcely noted here, has to be taken into account in evaluating the electoral results. Under the headline "Big money still garners the big vote," George Graham observed in the London *Financial Times* that money "spoke as loud as ever in the most expensive campaign on record." With a few notable exceptions, electoral victory tracked campaign financing closely—again, no departure from the norm and natural in a political system in which the less affluent majority does not participate and is scarcely represented.[4]

Voters selected "welfare reform" as their top priority, with health care reform second and crime also ranking high. These choices, which in part reflect a grasp of reality, also have to be understood against the background of recent propaganda offensives.

To begin with reality, for most of the population, conditions of life and work are grim and declining, something new in the history of industrial society. Median income declined even during the "Clinton recovery," falling to 7 percent below the 1989 level by late 1993, the Census Bureau reported. The decline was accompanied by—and in no small measure caused by—much-lauded improvements in "flexibility of labor markets." The latter is a technical term referring to elimination of job security and other such "market rigidities" that interfere with "economic health," another ideological construct. As designed for the purposes of population control, "economic health" is unrelated to the welfare of the population but crafted to measure what is valued by the rich: speculators, bond holders, investors, professionals who serve the state-corporate sector. Continuing the decline during the Reagan years, after a decade of stagnation, pay for private sector employees fell 4 percent from 1988 to 1994, with blue collar wages suffering most and white collar wages still below 1990 and well below 1988. Despite much misleading hype, the Bureau of Labor Statistics reports a continuing "shift to lower-wage industries and higher wage-occupations," executive and professional, while noting that the overwhelming majority of these are in lower-paid service industries (motel manager, and the like). That means sharply increased inequality, with the majority suffering reductions in absolute terms along with much worse work conditions.[5]

But some folks are doing just fine. "The percentage of corporate income devoted to payrolls is hovering near a record low," *Fortune* magazine reported in November 1994, having dropped sharply during the "conservative landslide" of the early 1980s, and again since 1992. With the "New Democrats" at the helm, "1993 was a bracingly upbeat year for the FORTUNE 500," the journal exulted in its April 1994 annual review of the state of the important people, who posted "dazzling" profits despite "virtually stagnant" sales growth. The ecstatic story was headed: "Hats Off! It Was a Heck of a Year"—at least, for those who matter.[6]

While in part realistic, the expressed concerns of voters reflect the great victories of the ideological warfare that has been conducted with relentless intensity since the early 1970s in the effort to overcome the perceived "crisis of democracy." Across the political spectrum, privileged sectors were naturally appalled by the attempts of the great majority of the population to escape from the apathy and marginalization that is their proper place and to enter the political arena, forgetting that in a democracy the role of the "ignorant and meddlesome outsiders" is to be mere "spectators," not "participants," as Walter Lippmann put it in his progressive essays on democracy 70 years ago, expressing the doctrines of "Wilsonian idealism." It therefore became necessary to renew with much greater intensity the constant campaign to tame and cage that "great *beast*," as Alexander Hamilton termed the "people" with horror and indignation as he was laying the foundations for state-guided industrial democracy. The beast may not yet be tamed, but it is being caged; sometimes quite literally, sometimes in chains of dogma and deceit, an important victory.

We may recall, in passing, that fear of democracy and freedom has always been one of the factors motivating the terror and sometimes outright aggression undertaken to eliminate "rotten apples" that might "spoil the barrel" and "viruses" that might "infect others," in the terminology favored by leading planners—the main concern, of course, being independence, whatever cast it takes. That helps explain the passion of Washington's terrorist wars in Central America in recent years, or to take a current example, Washington's not-so-tacit support for its trainees and associates in the Haitian military as they did their necessary work, and the restoration of the rule of their backers among the Haitian elite under the guise of "democracy," now that the work is done and the Generals can be sent off to the life of luxury, which, they understood correctly, would be their reward for services rendered. Behind the supercilious racist rhetoric about "civilizing Aristide" and teaching him "lessons in democracy" lies a real fear: that the democratic virus in Haiti might even infect these shores. People here might realize that we have a great deal to learn about democracy from the peasants and slum-dwellers of Haiti, who constructed a vibrant civil society that offered the "great beast" a chance to take some control over their lives. Their crime brings to mind the call for freedom for all people that was sounded for the first time in Haiti two centuries ago, outraging the civilized opinion of that day.

One consequence of the huge propaganda campaigns of the past several decades is the mood of "antipolitics" reported in feature stories. Concealed from public view is the fact that "politics is the shadow cast on society by big business," as John Dewey stated the truism familiar at least since Adam Smith, adding that as long as this is so, "the attenuation of the shadow will not change the substance." Reforms are of limited utility. Democracy requires that the source of the shadow be removed, not only because of its domination of the political arena, but because the very institutions of private power undermine democracy and freedom; again, an observation familiar back to the Founding Fathers.

But the source of the shadow has to be driven from the mind. Naturally, this is a leading theme of the literature of the ultraright foundations that are seeking to drive the educational system and media toward an even narrower fringe of the permissible spectrum. At the other extreme, Clinton campaign literature spoke movingly about workers and their firms and how government must help them; missing from the picture were bosses, profits, investors, and the like. There are "entrepreneurs," nice folk who appear now and then to help the workers and their firms. They then sink into the background along with the unmentionables, who are laboring for the common good, selflessly seeking to provide jobs and decent lives for ordinary people in the "civil society" in which all participate.[7]

The fanaticism of the effort to conceal the obvious has reached comic proportions. After the APEC summit in Jakarta in November 1994, front-page headlines announced that "Clinton Is Stern with Indonesia on Rights but Gleeful on Trade" (*New York Times*). The "sternness on rights" consisted of a few whimpers denounced by Indonesian human rights activists and labor leaders (those still out of jail), but the "Glee on Trade" was real enough. It reflects the successes of "the Administration's campaign of commercial diplomacy" that "will mean jobs for Americans," *Times* political correspondent Elaine Sciolino reported with admiration. Clinton firmed up $40 billion in joint projects in his campaign for "jobs for Americans"; at least $35 billion, possibly more, was an arrangement between Exxon and the Indonesian state oil company Pertamina to develop an off-shore natural gas field, which could "mean new jobs for U.S. businesses that help set up wells and off-shore platforms," the *Boston Globe* reported. Exxon's Indonesia affiliate and Pertamina are expected to sell the liquified gas almost exclusively in Asia. GE, Hughes, Fluor Daniel, and other major corporations won contracts as well for projects in Indonesia. Another Exxon-Pertamina project is a new plant to supply Indonesia's state-owned electricity company, the London *Financial Times* added, noting also that U.S. taxpayers are generously helping to fund the projects by credits from the U.S. Export-Import Bank, "part of new U.S. 'Tied-Aid' credit offers."

All of this is sure to provide a huge flow of jobs for Americans—at least lawyers, bankers, executives, and managers, maybe a handful of skilled workers for a short period. But profits for U.S. investors? Perish the thought! The good news for U.S. workers caused a sharp increase in Exxon's stock.[8]

Another victory for efficient propaganda is that people wildly overestimate the percentage of the federal budget that goes to foreign aid and welfare. In fact, over half of discretionary federal spending is devoted to the military, one reason why "the United States faces social and structural economic problems of a magnitude unknown to other economically advanced states," Benjamin Schwarz of the RAND corporation notes, including "higher rates of infant mortality, illiteracy, malnutrition, and poverty than any other advanced industrialized country." All getting worse, predictably, as the class war of the past decades intensifies in vigor and savagery. A study of the Bread for the World Institute reported a considerable decline in people suffering from hunger throughout the world in the 1980s, with only two exceptions: Africa, which registered an increase from 36 percent to 37 percent, and the United

States, where the numbers increased 50 percent from 1985 to 1990 as "conservative" reforms took hold, increasing since.

The problem is most severe among children, with effects that are permanent: it is well known that "development of the brain is strongly influenced by the quality of the nourishment and nurturance given to infants and children," among other effects of "adverse environments" early in life that can lead "to permanent defects in memory and learning" (medical researchers John Frank and Fraser Mustard). But hunger among the elderly is also "surging," the *Wall Street Journal* reports: "several million older Americans are going hungry—and their numbers are growing steadily," despite a federal law in force for 20 years "aimed at providing free meals to anyone over 60." Many are literally "starving to death" while some 5 million, about 16 percent of the population over 60, "are either hungry or malnourished to some degree"—again, phenomena unknown in other developed societies, which lag behind us in the crusade for freedom and justice. "The level of malnutrition and real hunger is only increasing," the assistant secretary for aging at the U.S. Department of Health reports.

To fully comprehend the meaning of such facts, one must bear in mind the unparalleled advantages of the United States. To select merely one indication, health and life expectancy levels of mid-18th-century Americans were not achieved by the *upper classes in Britain* until the early 20th century—not to speak of less privileged parts of the world. The social and economic catastrophe of American capitalism is quite an extraordinary phenomenon—for the "great beast," that is.[9]

Only 30 percent of the population are aware that military spending is the largest item on the Federal budget, and few of those know its scale or its purpose. Over a quarter think foreign aid is the biggest item. In fact, it is barely detectable. The United States has the most miserly record among the developed countries. The record is even worse if we exclude the parts intended to enhance U.S. control over Middle East energy reserves, "aid" to Israel, Egypt, and Turkey. By far the largest per capita component goes to a rich country, Israel—artificially rich, because of the completely unparalleled flow of foreign capital including not just "aid" but also tax-deductible contributions that are used to maintain the sharp divisions between first- and second-class citizens, and (despite disclaimers) for the joint U.S.-Israel project of incorporating the bulk of the occupied territories within the eventual state of Israel. Eliminate that, and U.S. aid virtually vanishes—putting aside its character and effects.

One-fifth of the population believe welfare to be the largest Federal expense. It is not too surprising, then, that the top priority for voters in 1994 was "welfare reform" (46 percent). The welfare system is "just out of control," voters felt, though it pays to look more closely at actual attitudes. Forty-four percent of respondents feel that we are spending "too much" on welfare and 23 percent "too little," economist Nancy Folbre notes, but when the phrase "assistance to the poor" is substituted for "welfare" in the same question, 13 percent say we are spending "too much" and 64 percent "too little." A reasonable speculation is that many people have absorbed Reaganite lies about "welfare Queens" (by insinuation, Blacks) driving Cadillacs, and believe that working people are supporting rich welfare recipients—as they are, but not in the sense they imagine; we return to that.[10]

As already noted, the second-ranking priority for voters was health care reform (37 percent), though the impressive ideological warfare of the past year has left people utterly confused about what the realistic options might be. Public debate was framed within narrow bounds, the Clinton plan being the "liberal option," with a few gestures to the "radical extremists" who thought the United States might consider joining the rest of the industrial world. The incomprehensible Clinton plan—basically, a giveaway to huge insurance companies—was rejected as just another "big government" proposal that would place people's fate in the hands of pointy-headed bureaucrats who steal our money by imposing a crushing tax burden; a publicly funded insurance program, to the extent it could even be considered, is still more odious in that respect.

The option preferred by the privileged is for the fate of everyone else to be in the hands of insurance company executives whose goal, as Milton Friedman can explain, is to ensure maximum profit and market share: meaning the worst possible health care; elimination of personal choice except for the rich; huge bureaucracies to micromanage physicians; public subsidy for advertising, profits, and multiple layers of high-paid managers and executives; and other massive inefficiencies that drive the United States off the spectrum in costs for heath care. The real meaning of the "conservative" option was illustrated right after the November 1994 election at the annual scientific convention of the American Heart Association, where leading specialists reported that insurers are increasingly unwilling to pay for preventive care that would reduce hospitalization rates by 75 percent (Dr. Lynne Stevenson of Boston's Brigham and Women's Hospital). In contrast, they are quite willing to pay for heart transplants—high-tech operations that enrich the right people and institutions.

One radical extremist thought that rarely reached threshold is that in a civilized society, the costs of health care should be borne by progressive taxation, on the basis of the principle that the poor should be exempted from taxation, which should "tax the higher portions of property in geometrical progression as they rise"—as observed by the noted Marxist Thomas Jefferson in a letter to his fellow-subversive James Madison. The United States is, again, off the spectrum on this aspect of human rights and needs, as measured by public share of health-care spending (which is as progressive as the tax system). The United States is far below any country that has achieved any form of development, even Greece and Portugal; it is barely above Turkey.[11]

"REALLY EXISTING CONSERVATISM"

The propaganda victories come into sharper focus when we compare popular perceptions with social and economic realities. Take welfare. It has sharply declined in real terms since 1970, Nancy Folbre observes, a downward spiral that is continuing, with more reductions in Aid to Families with Dependent Children (AFDC) in 1991 than in any year since 1981. From 1970, maximum AFDC benefits for a family of three with no other income fell over 40 percent, and the national average of AFDC benefits and food stamps combined is now at the level of AFDC alone in 1960 (before the food-stamp program was initiated).

A still more severe distortion is the unspoken premise that child care is not work: it comes free, like women's domestic labor generally—"the main reason why free-enterprise economies have worked relatively well over the decades," economist Sylvia Ann Hewlett comments. Child care therefore contrasts with Real Work: speculating in currency markets, devising tax shelters for the rich, arranging mergers and acquisitions that significantly reduce research and development and hence economic growth, and other contributions that rank high on the scale of social utility and merit according to standard dogma, which measures it by economic reward to the "worker." In particular, single women taking care of children are plainly not working, and therefore must be driven to the official workforce on grounds of "economic efficiency" (not to speak of justice), bipartisan doctrine holds. The assumptions are somewhere between nonsensical and insane, though reasonable enough within the general intellectual culture, with its tacit dedication to class warfare.

Even on the narrowest grounds, Folbre observes in the American Economic Association proceedings, "public policy literally transfers resources from parents to nonparents by providing social insurance based on participation in paid employment without explicitly valuing time, effort, or money devoted to children," who are, in the longer term, the crucial factor determining "economic health" even in the highly distorted ideological sense of the technical notion. When real incomes in the middle quintile (about $30,000 in 1992 dollars) are adjusted for child-care costs, they decline slightly through the 1970s, and then, quite sharply from 1980 to the present as "conservatism triumphed."[12]

Responding to the "public mood" that has been shaped by a propaganda offensive of unusual intensity and fervor, the highest priority for the new Gingrich conservatives is to dismantle the welfare system. They announced at once that they would repeal the Food Stamp Act of 1977, the Child Nutrition Act of 1966, the National School Lunch Act of 1946, the Emergency Food Assistance Act of 1983, and other federal laws intended to prevent hunger, particularly among children, which has not increased rapidly enough to satisfy the advocates of "family values" and "free market" verities. Furthermore, what programs remain are to be transferred to states, so as to bar any response to the typical sharp increase in need for food assistance when there is a recession, as in 1991–2, when food stamp rolls sometimes grew by 300,000 people a month. The plans will "lead to a dramatic increase in hunger," Senator Patrick Leahy observed realistically; but that's nothing that has ever troubled the more loyal servants of the rich. Also on the legislative agenda—with the support of the New Democrats—are work obligations for mothers (who do not "work," by ideological fiat) and reduction of AFDC, the main Federal Welfare program, which reaches 14.3 million people, over 9 million of them young children, who must "learn responsibility" and internalize our values: that there are no human rights, apart from what can be won in the labor market.

It would be unfair, however, to regard the leader, Newt Gingrich, as a heartless wretch. He proposes that the money saved from AFDC programs be used to build orphanages or "group homes" for children of families rendered destitute—the state being the proper provider for children, not their mothers, under the doctrine of "family values." Perhaps the proposal is intended as a special contribution to the 1994 International Year of the Family. Or perhaps it is simply another useful federal subsidy, providing benefits to the construction industry, lawyers, and other people of the right sort.[13]

The real meaning of "free market conservatism" is illustrated by a closer look at the most passionate enthusiasts for "getting the government off our backs" and letting the market reign undisturbed. Take Newt Gingrich, the leader of the victorious congressional army who are taking over under a "master plan" that relied on huge contributions for Gingrich's GOPAC committee from corporate donors and others whose identity is a carefully-guarded secret. The measures are of dubious legality; GOPAC is now being sued by the Federal Elections Commission on grounds that it "failed to register and report as a political committee." But legal questions aside, the power play was "a calculated political operation, unique on the contemporary American political scene" (Ellen Miller, director of the nonpartisan Center for Responsive Politics), yet another blow at the despised principles of democracy and the pretensions of the "great beast" to meddle where it doesn't belong.[14]

Gingrich represents Cobb County Georgia, which the *New York Times*—reasonably enough—selected in a front-page story to illustrate the rising tide of "conservatism" aimed at ridding us of the "nanny state." The headline reads "Conservatism Flowering Among the Malls," in this wealthy suburb of Atlanta, one of several that "offer—particularly to whites—a sense of prosperity and safety, conservative Southern values and a relaxed, friendly way of life." It's a "Norman Rockwell world with fiber optic computers and jet airplanes," Gingrich comments with pride. With its "history of inhospitality toward blacks," Cobb County is scrupulously insulated from any urban infection so that the inhabitants can enjoy the fruits of their "entrepreneurial values" and market enthusiasms in "the conservative heart of a conservative region," defended in Congress by the leader of the conservative triumph.

A small footnote: Cobb County receives more federal subsidies than any suburban county in the country, with two exceptions: Arlington Virginia, effectively part of the Federal Government, and Brevard County Florida, the home of the Kennedy Space Center. When we move out of the state system itself, Cobb County is the leading beneficiary of the "nanny state." Its largest employer is Lockheed Aeronautical Systems Company, which is designing the F-22 advanced tactical fighter and other military aircraft. Seventy-two-percent of the workforce are in white-collar jobs "in expanding areas of the economy like insurance, electronics and computers, and trade"—all carefully tended by "the nanny state." It's remarkably easy for conservative entrepreneurial values to flourish while one is feeding happily at the public trough.

Meanwhile praises to market miracles reach the heavens, notably where "conservatism is flowering among the malls."[15]

An interesting sidelight is the silence over this matter during the electoral campaign, when Gingrich propaganda was smashing the New Democrats. Notably absent is a simple rejoinder that would have stopped the juggernaut in its tracks: Gingrich is the country's leading advocate of the welfare state—for the rich. The reasons for the silence are not hard to discern: class interests prevail over narrow electoral ones. It's agreed across the board that the rich must be protected from market discipline by a powerful and interventionist welfare state.

Gingrich is the author of the "Contract with America," which calls for extending the double-edged "free market": state protection and public subsidy for the rich, market discipline for the poor. The Contract calls for "cuts in social spending," denying aid to children of "minor mothers" and those on welfare. Republican leaders add that they will support reductions proposed in the plan submitted by John Kasich, top Republican on the Budget Committee; its biggest cut is to be $50 billion from medicare and medicaid, the health programs for the elderly and the poor. But the Contract calls for an increase in welfare for the rich, by the classic means: regressive fiscal measures, and outright subsidy. These include increased tax exemptions for gifts and estates, capital gains cuts, reduced regulation for protection of health and safety standards, investment subsidies, more favorable rules for depreciation, and most important: "strengthening our national defense" so that we can better "maintain our credibility around the world"—so that anyone who gets funny ideas, like priests and nuns in Latin America, will understand that "What We Say Goes," as George Bush defined the New World Order while bombs and missiles were raining on Iraq.[16]

"National defense" is, of course, a sick joke, which would elicit ridicule outside of a commissar culture. The United States faces no threats, and already spends almost as much on "defense" as the rest of the world combined. As in the past, military spending is arguably increasing security threats, for example, by arms exports, which now provide 25 percent of revenue for "defense" contractors and dominate the international arms market, increasing sharply since the end of the Cold War. Clinton has just added an important innovation: for the first time, policy will "factor the health of U.S. weapons makers and the shape of the domestic economy into decisions on whether to approve foreign arms sales," the press reports; a natural step, now that the Soviet pretext has collapsed and it becomes necessary to face the facts more honestly.[17]

Unlike "defense" and "security," military expenditures are no joke. They ensure that we will be able to "behave, with others, multilaterally when we can and unilaterally as we must," the Clinton version of the traditional doctrine, delivered to the UN Security Council by Ambassador Madeleine Albright as it wavered over a resolution condemning Iraq. Albright instructed the Council that if need be, the United States would act alone because "We recognize this area as vital to U.S. national interests"—and we recognize no limits or constraints, surely nothing as ridiculous as international law, human rights, or the United Nations, as we pursue our role as self-appointed global enforcer.[18]

Apart from maintaining a particular form of "stability" in the interests of the world rulers, the Pentagon must continue to provide lavishly for Newt Gingrich and his rich constituents by means of a taxpayer subsidy to advanced industry. Nothing has changed in this regard since the early postwar period, when the business world recognized that the aircraft industry, established by public funds and wartime profiteering, "cannot satisfactorily exist in a pure, competitive, unsubsidized, 'free enterprise' economy" (*Fortune*) and that "the government is their only possible savior" (*Business Week*). For well-known reasons, the Pentagon system was revitalized as the "savior," sustaining and expanding the industry, now the leading "civilian" exporter, along with steel and metals generally, electronics, chemicals, machine tools, and other central components of the industrial economy. As long as the fable could be sustained, the cold war provided the pretext. The fraud was conscious, at least among those minimally astute. The first Secretary of the Air Force, Stuart Symington, put the matter plainly in January 1948: "The word to talk was not 'subsidy'; the word to talk was 'security,'" As industry representative in Washington, Symington regularly demanded enough procurement funds in the military budget to "meet the requirements of the aircraft industry," in his words. The story continues without essential change until today, in just about every functioning sector of the economy, and surely in Cobb County.

Furthermore, the story goes back to the origins of the Republic: economic historian Paul Bairoch describes the United States as the "mother country and bastion of modern protectionism," which was "born in the United States"—which may be unfair to our British predecessors, no laggards in the art. Protectionism is only one form of state intervention, and not the major one. As in the British case, there are intermittent deviations from the commit-ment to protect the rich from market discipline, related to the expectation of temporary gain under conditions of dominance. When need arises, "conserv-atives" are quick to call for increased state intervention, as in the Reagan years. Had market forces been allowed to function, there would be no U.S. steel or automobile industry today, not to speak of computer chips and elec-tronics generally. The Reaganites simply closed the market to Japanese com-petition while pouring in public funds.

Then-Secretary of the Treasury James Baker proudly proclaimed to a busi-ness audience that Reagan had "granted more import relief to U.S. industry than any of his predecessors in more than half a century." He was far too mod-est: it was actually more than all his predecessors combined, doubling import restrictions to 23 percent. One of the few authentic free trade advocates, inter-national economist Fred Bergsten, added that the Reagan Administration spe-cialized in the kind of "managed trade" that most "restricts trade and closes markets," voluntary export restraint agreements—which are "voluntary" in the sense that protection payments to the Mafia enforcer are "voluntary." This is "the most insidious form of protectionism," Bergsten pointed out, which "raises prices, reduces competition and reinforces cartel behavior." The 1994 Economic Report to Congress estimates that Reaganite protectionist measures reduced U.S. manufacturing imports by about one-fifth. Such measures have been expanded under Clinton, one example being the proposal to spend $1 billion to subsidize development and production of flat-panel computer display screens, subsidies barred by the GATT accords signed earlier.[19]

This is just the tip of the iceberg. The "bought priesthood" may spin tales about market discipline and its virtues, but business executives and the government that is their "shadow" will tolerate no such nonsense—for the rich, that is.

Gingrich's Contract is remarkably brazen. Thus the proposals for welfare for the rich appear under the heading "The Job Creation and Wage Enhancement Act." The section does include a provision for measures "to create jobs and raise worker wages"—with the word "unfunded" quietly added. But no matter. In contemporary Newspeak, the word "jobs" means "profits," so it is indeed a "job creation" proposal, which will continue to "enhance" wages downwards.

The pattern is virtually exceptionless. Former Senate Democratic leader George Mitchell was replaced in November 1994 by Olympia Snowe, a prominent conservative, whose campaign focused on protecting the Portsmouth Naval shipyard and Loring Air Force base—that is, making sure that federal largesse continues to flow, the benefits heavily skewed toward the wealthy, though the official mantra is "jobs." Even looking just at the narrow matter of welfare, we find much the same thing. The Center for Popular Economics (Amherst) estimates that when we consider direct benefits and tax breaks— masked welfare payments—an average household with income under $10,000 receives about 60 percent of the welfare provided to households with income over $100,000. Looking at details, total payments for food stamps in 1993 amounted to $25 billion, welfare and family support $16 billion, and supplemental security income (poor, elderly, disabled) $21 billion. These figures may be compared with the $49 billion in deductions for interest payments, mostly mortgage payments (80 percent to familes with incomes over $50,000, skewed more radically toward the higher reaches, for obvious reasons). Farm price supports, again skewed toward the wealthy, amounted to $16 billion. Total payments to the poor "add up to less than the three largest tax breaks that benefit the middle class and wealthy: deductions for retirement plans, the deduction for home mortgage interest and the exemption of health-insurance premiums that companies pay for their employees," Michael Wines reports in the *Times* in a rare window opened to the real world, noting further that "most tax breaks and payments to the well-situated are practically exempt from the debate over controlling expenditures."[20]

This, of course, is the merest fragment, not counting such matters as "business expenses" (dinners at elegant restaurants, prize seats at the opera and sporting events, club memberships, etc.), all small in comparison with the massive subsidies through the system of protection and subsidy by the "nanny state." Simply to indicate scale, in Canada, less extreme than the United States in its dedication to a nanny state for the rich, the National Council of Welfare estimates that day care facilities for the 750,000 children who need them would cost $1.5 billion, not a great deal more than the tax money lost by the business entertainment deduction.[21]

Reacting to the "Contract," Labor Secretary Robert Reich suggested that Congress end "corporate welfare as we know it," removing tax breaks for particular industries and agriculture that amount to tens of billions a year. He also noted that over a quarter of taxes go to pay interest on the national debt, most of it accumulated by the statist reactionaries of the 1980s, who played their spend-and-borrow games under the conservative disguise.

Reich's speech on economic and social policy was prominently reported—in the London *Financial Times,* though for accuracy, it did receive a few lines under "World-Wide Notes" in the *Wall Street Journal,* the same day.[22]

The principles are clear and explicit: free markets are fine for the Third World and its growing counterpart at home. Mothers with dependent children can be sternly lectured on the need for self-reliance, but not dependent executives and investors, please. For them, the welfare state must flourish.

Focusing on rich countries like ours is highly misleading, to put it mildly. The double-edged "free market ideology" has by far its most lethal effects in the traditional colonial domains, which, apart from the Japan-based area, are mostly an utter disaster, improving here and there only by ideologically-based economic measures that dispense with effects on people. While almost all industrial societies have become more protectionist in past years, the Reaganites generally led the pack. The effects on the South have been devastating, compounding the consequences of the IMF-World Bank structural adjustment programs, which have had a brutal impact on the poor majority while benefiting foreign investors and elite sectors linked to them.

Market distortions by the rich have been a major factor in doubling the already huge gap between the poorest and richest countries in the past generation. The 1992 UN Development Report estimates that various protectionist and financial measures taken by the rich countries have deprived the South of $.5 trillion a year, about 12 times total "aid"—most of it publicly subsidized export promotion. This behavior is "virtually criminal," the distinguished Irish diplomat and author Erskine Childers observed. He also notes that the West, under United States lead, blocked a 1991 resolution tabled at the General Assembly by the South against "economic measures as a means of political and economic coercion against developing countries," the favored technique, apart from terror, by which the United States has sought to destroy such independent upstarts as Cuba and Nicaragua—while never ceasing to sing odes to the free market. The fact is "very little known," Childers writes, "because of course such things do not get reported by the dominant Northern media." He hopes that some day this "wholesale moral abdication by Northern countries" will lead to "their utter shame before their own citizens," shame that will "start on the day when Northern academicians and NGOs" institute "a Blackmail Watch" to stand alongside the Human Rights Watches.[23]

Not tomorrow, we can be sure of that.

With hopelessly inadequate apologies to the victims, I'll put aside that terrible story of major crimes against humanity, for which we bear continuing responsibility.

The "hidden welfare state" for the rich, with its huge entitlements concealed by tax deductions and other devious means, scarcely enters the debate over welfare reform. But it is by no means unaffected. "Buried in the House Republicans' 'Contract with America' is a very sweet deal for the nation's big capital-intensive companies," the *Wall Street Journal* reported reviewing an array of tax breaks and other devices that will "provide a sizable subsidy" to corporations, possibly eliminating taxable income entirely for large firms, and increasing the deficit in accord with the Reaganite version of "fiscal conservatism." The program is carefully crafted so that its impact will not be felt until 1997—coincidentally, after the presidential election, something we are not supposed to notice. IRS officials predict a cost to the taxpayer of over $14 billion a year by the end of the decade.[24]

Notes

1. For references, see my *Turning the Tide* (South End, 1985), Chap. 5, Sec. 2.2.
2. See my *World Orders, Old and New* (Columbia, 1994); Gallup Political and Economic Index, Report 404, April 1994.
3. John Aloysius Farrell, *BG*, Dec. 3; *BW*, Oct. 10, 1994. See Norman Ware, *The Industrial Worker: 1840–1860* (Ivan Dee, 1990; reprint of 1924 edition).
4. Morin, *WP weekly*, Nov. 21–27; *LA Times*, Nov. 20, cited by Doug Henwood, *Nation*, Dec. 12; Silverstein-Cockburn, *Counterpunch*, Nov. 15; Gerald Seib, *WSJ*, Nov. 11; Levine, letter, *NYT*, Nov. 25; Richard Berke, *NYT*, Nov. 10; Edsall, *WP weekly*, Nov. 28–Dec. 4; George Graham, Nov. 10, 1994.
5. Aaron Bernstein, *Business Week*, Oct. 10, 1994. For more detail, see my *World Orders, Old and New* (Columbia, 1994); See Edward Herman, *Z Magazine*, Jan. 1995.
6. Fortune, Nov. 14, April 18, 1994.
7. See *World Orders*, for details and references.
8. Sciolino, Andrew Pollack, *NYT*; Susan Hightower, *AP*, Boston Globe; Manuela Saragosa, *FT*, Nov. 17, 1994.
9. Robin Toner, *NYT*, Nov. 16; Toner misinterprets the figures, failing to distinguish discretionary spending. Schwarz, "The Arcana of Empire and the Dilemma of American National Security," *Salmagundi*, Winter–Spring 1994; Theo Francis, *Chicago Tribune*, Oct. 14; Michael McCarthy, *WSJ*, Nov. 8, 1994. Frank and

Mustard, "The Determinants of Health from a Historical Perspective," *Daedalus: Health and Wealth,* Fall 1994.

10. Folbre, *Village Voice Literary Supplement,* Nov. 1992.
11. Robert Knox, BG, Nov. 16, 1994. Jefferson quoted by John Manley, "The American Dream," *Nature, Society, and Thought* vol. 1.4, 1988. Robert Evans, "Health Care as a Threat to Health," *Daedalus, op. cit.* Voter priorities, Seib, *op. cit.;* budget estimates, Toner, *op. cit.*
12. Hewlett, *Child Neglect in Rich Societies* (UNICEF, 1993). Folbre, *op. cit.;* "Children as Public Goods," AEA *Papers and Proceedings* 84.2, May 1994. Marc Breslow, *Dollars and Sense,* Nov./Dec. 1994.
13. Jason DeParle, NYT, Nov. 13; Robert Pear, NYT, Nov. 22, 1994.
14. Michael Kranish, BG, Nov. 20, 1994.
15. Peter Applebome, NYT, Aug. 1, 1994.
16. David Rosenbaum, NYT, Nov. 1, 1994.
17. BG-LA *Times,* Nov. 15, 1994.
18. Jules Kagian, *Middle East International,* Oct. 21, 1994.
19. See *World Orders.* Bairoch, *Economics and World History* (Chicago, 1993). Keith Bradsher, NYT, April 27, 1994.
20. John Milne, BG, Nov. 9, 1994; Nancy Folbre and the Center for Popular Economics, *The New Field Guide to the U.S. Economy* (New Press, 1995); Wines, NYT, Nov. 20, 1994.
21. Linda McQuaig, *The Wealthy Banker's Wife* (Penguin, 1993).
22. Jurek Martin, "Attack on business tax breaks," FT, Nov. 23, 1994. Pacifica Radio, Nov. 22; tapes distributed by David Barsamian.
23. Childers, "The Demand for Equity and Equality: The North-South Divide in the United Nations." Conference of the Jamahir Society, July 2, 1994, Geneva.
24. Alan Murray, WSJ, Dec. 5, 1994.

II. Globalization From Above: The New Corporate Order

AFTER THE SUMMIT

TOM ATHANASIOU

> The suicidial mentality of those in power is absolutely terrifying.
> —UN staffer, off the record

The Earth Summit—remember the Earth Summit?—may seem, at this late date, to be only another mega-media event from the far distant past. Nevertheless, it still rewards reflection, for at it all the plot lines that thread through the tangled textile of post–cold war environmental politics came together into one thick knot. There was no single Earth Summit, only that tangle of events and tendencies. The main event, of course, was the official United Nations Conference on Environment and Development—UNCED (pronounced "unsaid")—a politician's extravaganza and world-class media event (perhaps 8,000 reporters in all). But there were also the innumerable events of the Global Forum, located miles away along a freeway newly built to cut off the international masses from the hard knocks of Rio's slums. Even farther away was the Earth Parliament, a global summit of indigenous peoples.

The set was so varied that any named event must necessarily stand for many unnamed cousins. There were a number of indigenous-peoples' conferences and a huge variety of women's conferences, the largest gathering of Green parliamentarians to date, Ecotech (a very corporate eco-technology conference), youth conferences, and regional meetings by the score. And the summit was, in any case, only the climax of "the UNCED process," a series of international preparation conferences ("prepcoms" in UN lingo) that had been rising in tempo for over two years.

As the center of "alternative" activity, the Global Forum was inevitably disparaged as an "environmental Woodstock." This seems an odd honorific for an event that defined NGO (Non-Governmental Organization) broadly enough to include the World Bank, the Kuwaiti Ministry of Information, the International Chamber of Commerce, the Business Council for Sustainable Development, the American Nuclear Society, and even Petrobras, the Brazilian state oil company whose toxic dumping made it dangerous to swim at the very beaches that lay alongside the Global Forum.

The Earth Summit has attracted criticism of all kinds, most of it justified at one level or another. It has been called a fantastic waste of time and money, a gruesome anticlimax, a sprawling day-care center for environmental wannabes, the occasion for "the highest level international policy-centered mumbo-jumbo you can imagine."[1] All this is true, and yet, if only by dint of the volume of its hype and the scale of its circumstances, the summit marked the morning of Day Two in the story of environmentalism.

Is an overall judgment possible? One evaluative strategy is to focus on the summit's official products: the new UN Sustainable Development Commission (SDC), the defanged climate and biodiversity conventions, the hundreds of vague pages of *Agenda 21*, the summit's encyclopedic master treaty, the World Bank's "Global Environmental Facility" (with which it successfully purchased a new environmental legitimacy, and emerged from Rio as the fiscal agent for the brave green world of the twenty-first century). Such a focus on the official matters at least allows a judgment of failure—treaties, at least these treaties, will not make the difference.

But such a focus fails to capture the summit's larger significance. First, and despite the apologetic intention with which these words are usually pronounced, Rio was more a milestone than a final destination. The forces that made it necessary roil now as they did in mid-1992, and they are not likely to calm soon. As James MacNeil, the former Secretary General of the Brundtland Commission (famous for *Our Common Future*, the report that thrust "sustainable development" into our shared library of political cliches) put it at the start of the summit, "the days of Sunday School environmental politics are over. Now that we have brought development into the center of the environmental debate, we face a series of hard-fought battles."[2]

Just how hard can be inferred from the sweep of the emerging movement agenda. Wangari Maathai, the feminist, environmentalist, human-rights campaigner, and founder of the Kenyan Greenbelt Movement, sketched out its terms in her address to the official UNCED plenary. In identifying the following "issues vital to building environmentally sound and socially equitable societies," Maathai provided as good a semi-official statement of the task before the movement as we'll find for some time.

—eliminating poverty
—fair and environmentally sound trade
—reversal of the net flow of resources from South to North
—clear recognition of the responsibilities of business and industry

—changes in wasteful patterns of consumption

—internalization of the environmental and social costs of natural resource use

—equitable access to environmentally sound technology and its benefits

—redirection of military expenditures to environmental and social goals

—democratization of local, national, and international political institutions and decision-making structures.[3]

It is a daunting list, made all the more so by the chasm of content and spirit that separates it from the official treaties. This chasm is so wide that, even had the summit gone very well, it would not have narrowed much. Even if the Unites States had not insisted on cutting all CO_2 targets and timetables from the climate treaty, even if the biodiversity convention had been less polluted by corporate interests, even if the forestry convention had included northern as well as southern forests, even if the elites that control so much of the "developing world" were as interested in social justice as they profess to be, even if *Agenda 21* resembled the environmental Magna Carta it was so often hyped as being, even if all this had been true the gap between the official and activist agendas would have dwarfed the far-more-often reported gap between the Bush administration and the other industrial countries, between the hard and soft cops.

Greenpeace summed up the situation well. The day after George Bush's dismal address to the UNCED plenary, seven of its climbers defied Rio's lockdown security and, under cover of darkness, scaled its landmark Sugarloaf Mountain. Rappeling down its sheer face at the crack of dawn, they unfurled a 14,000 square-foot banner on which was pictured only a giant image of the home planet and a single word: *sold.*

A SEA OF LIES

A substantive response to the social-ecological crisis was not on the official agenda at Rio. For just this reason, and because the Bush administration—which was widely vilified for its (often successful) efforts to water-down the summit treaties—had lost power to a far greener crowd, it is instructive to review the role the United States played in Rio. What did it mean that the U.S. left weekly the *Guardian* could illustrate the cover of its Rio issue with with a Bushian snake "Strangling the Summit?"[4] What did it mean that the summit, as James Brooke put it in the *New York Times,* wound up "reviving anti-American sentiment rarely seen at international forums since the Vietnam war?"[5]

The surface answer is obvious, and Brooke gives it by quoting a Brazilian Social Democratic congressman, who stated that "U.S. intransigence is recreating the political atmosphere of the 1960s: all civil society and the press against the U.S."[6] But this answer only raises other questions. In truth, just about every major player in the world state system played its appointed role in the dark comedy of UNCED.[7] As Mark Valentine, then the issues director of the U.S. Citizen's Network on UNCED, put it after the fourth and final prepcom, "The U.S. was rarely alone in obstructing progress on *Agenda 21* and the Rio Declaration, and often was not even the principle malefactor."[8]

The details are grimly entertaining. For example, here is a description of a diplomatic minuet that occurred in the late stages of the discussion of the *Agenda 21* chapter on atmosphere. It comes from the *Earth Summit Times,* one of the three daily conference newspapers.

> The stickiest issue remaining is whether or not certain key phrases should be used repeatedly in the text. Saudi Arabia has objected to repeated references to "new and renewable" energy sources. On the other hand, the Saudis are insisting on multiple references to "environmentally safe and sound" technology. Some European countries with heavy investments in nuclear energy object to the worlds "safe and," suggesting that they approve of what is "sound" but not what is "safe and sound."[9]

Thus was the future adjudicated in Rio. The U.S. was the leader of the anti-environmental hoards, but it was rarely alone. The British led a long effort to dilute the European political will to impose carbon taxes, an effort later joined by poorer members of the European Community, and by OPEC. Taken as a bloc, the Europeans played a more complex role, and the Germans, in particular, came off as environmental good guys. German President Helmut Kohl, the first Northern leader to pledge to go to Rio, pushed the European Community, over the objections of the U.S., to support CO_2 reduction targets, and went beyond those targets to pledge a 25 to 30 percent reduction in Germany's CO_2 emissions by 2005. Germany was also the first European state to decide to sign the (very weak) biodiversity treaty, an act that persuaded Japan and even Britain to break with the United States and sign it as well.

The Japanese came off even better, and were widely reported to have emerged as "the first environmental superpower."[10] It is a status that Japan worked hard to acquire. As the *Financial Times* put it, "Japan approached Rio with a carefully planned diplomatic offensive backed by the largest offer of new environmental aid made at the Summit—some $500-million a year. Whatever Tokyo's motives—and sceptics were quick to hint that these were driven above all by self-interest—Japan added measurably to its international status in Rio. 'They're the owners of all the new issues—and they're getting it all so cheap,' said one senior Brazilian official with mixed admiration and regret."[11]

Of course, Japan is all but an environmental criminal state, especially with regard to logging, fishing, and the international plutonium trade. So reports like this should give us pause. As Walden Bello, the director of the San Francisco–based Institute for Food and Development Policy, put it, "Japan and Europe were really happy. They didn't even have to do anything to look good. They just had to have the good sense to shut up."[12]

The South's story is even more complex, and sordid in its own fashion. Malaysia, a leader in the South's opposition to the North's most hypocritical initiatives, is also a major force in the destruction of Southeast Asia's remaining tropical forests. China, which insisted on striking an entire paragraph from *Agenda 21* that detailed the environmental damage resulting from dam construction and water channelization, is pushing ahead with its fantastically destructive Three Gorges dam. In the climate negotiations, it must be said that in the end the developing countries joined with the U.S. to oppose even a vague commitment to "study ways their policies subsidize unnecessary waste and pollution."[13]

This is the context in which the Bush administration operated, and it should not be forgotten. The right–wing of the American political elite consists of ideologues, many of whom believe that "environment protection has replaced Communism as the great threat to capitalism."[14] We may justly celebrate their passing from power, but only if we learn to see what their obnoxious presence so obscured. As Mark Valentine put it, the Bush hard line provided "perfect air cover for everyone else to get away with anything they wanted. We were so good at being the ugly farting monster that no one else had any trouble looking great. Even Castro looked good. I mean, he gave a good speech, but jeez."[15]

BIODIVERSITY BLUES

That the real issues were only obscured by Bush-bashing can easily be demonstrated by a look back at the United States' refusal to sign the biodiversity convention. After all, it's not as if the convention, despite its lovely name, is a glorious milestone in the history of global environmental law. Peter Padbury of the Canadian Council for International Cooperation, a coalition of 130 Canadian NGOs, described it as "very complicated, very weak," and this may be charitable in the extreme.[16] The *Financial Times,* no hotbed of anticapitalism, quite agreed with the summit's green radicals when it commented that the biodiversity convention, "was originally proposed as a measure to preserve plant and animal life. But the real issue quickly became the exact opposite: how living organisms could be commercially exploited, and who should have the patent rights. The treaty that was finally agreed was more about commerce than about conservation."[17]

"Biodiversity" means different things to different people. While most governments and news media have focused public attention on the likely extinction of panda bears and seals, powerful northern nations have been primarily concerned with the far more economically significant area of agricultural crop seeds. And it is these seeds that best reveal the real significance of the biodiversity convention.

In recent decades the industrialized countries have stockpiled vast collections of economically significant seeds in "gene banks." These gene banks resemble huge refrigerators where wide varieties of seeds, and in particular, exhaustive collections of mainline agricultural families like grains, beans, and rices are stored against the anticipated loss of the ecosystems, most of them in the gene-rich South, from which they originated. This is seen as necessary because the diversity of these varieties—many of them developed by selective breeding over the last 15,000 years—have been "massively replaced by modern 'high yielding' variants, causing genetic erosion of unprecedented proportions." According to Spanish activist and researcher Henk Hobbelink, today's high-tech food crops, in other words, require continual "injections" of fresh genes from their parent ecosystems, and these genes are banked by organizations like the Consultative Group on International Agricultural Research (CGIAR), which is "conveniently located in the World Bank and effectively controlled by the North."[18]

At least half of all crop seeds collected in the third world are already in such northern gene banks, most of them in the United States and Europe. Hobbelink estimates the value of the annual genetic infusion into U.S. agriculture alone, in wheat, rice, and beans alone, as $680 million. Yet such "ex situ" collections were specifically excluded from the biodiversity convention. Due to both this exclusion and other recent changes in CGIAR rules, the contents of the CGIAR genebanks, despite the fact that they are nominally being held "in trust" for humanity, can now be patented. It is true that the United States led the effort to exclude ex situ gene banks from the convention, and to permit the patenting of the CGIAR gene bank; it is not true that only the United States benefits from these arrangements. Patent offices in the United States and Europe are now granting patents on genes with commercial promise, and under the terms of the biodiversity convention, the application of such "intellectual property rights" (IPRs) to lifeforms is quite explicitly allowed.[19]

Why then was the Bush administration so isolated in its refusal to sign the biodiversity convention? The key point appears to be that, while the convention allows existing northern genetic collections to be treated as the intellectual property of the North, it also grants the South such rights for in situ genetic materials—those that remain in field and forest. In so doing, it grants southern governments (not communities, an important point) IPRs for new genetic discoveries made in the South, discoveries which have become crucial to industrial agriculture and to the entire biotech revolution. The Bush administration balked, preferring to cede royalty rights to corporations "discovering" genetic strains, rather than to the countries in which they were found or the indigenous peoples that, in many cases, had developed them over millennia and, in many others, led corporate biologists to them.

A great deal of money is at stake. According to ethnobotanist Darrell Posey, $54 billion is already grossed each year, for drugs alone, as a result of what we might call "indigenous research," though less than 0.001 percent of that has ever been returned to the discovering communities.[20] Unlike most European nations, the Bush administration, anxious to nurture biotechnology (a major growth sector that U.S. firms still dominate), simply would not accept an increase and refused to sign. The important point is that this was only a businessman's disagreement, one that became a public-relations disaster for the Americans. In a final twist, the U.S. negotiators, bitter at the bad press they received for their refusal to sign, let it be known that they did not consider their industrial allies "sincere" in their intentions to abide by the convention. With the potential royalties being very high, they could well be right.

A word here about "trade." It was well known by the biodiversity convention negotiators that its IPR provisions eventually would need to conform to the market provisions of the General Agreement on Tariffs and Trade (GATT). What is most notable about the convention is that by U.S. insistence such harmonization has already occurred. In allowing the patenting of lifeforms, the biodiversity convention explicitly brings nature into the geo-economic fold. Indeed, the story of the biodiversity convention is significant not only for what it tells us about the conservation strategies that are to be taken in the next few years, but as well for what it says about the rising confrontation between the green and social justice movements and the economic globalizers massing under the banner of "free trade."[21] The biodiversity convention does have provisions that relate directly to protecting biodiversity. It has the real merit of sketching criteria by which national conservation plans should be considered adequate. These require the convention's signatories to establish protected areas, promote the preservation of endangered species and ecosystems, and act to conserve or even restore biological diversity. All these are laudable goals, though they must be seen in the larger context defined by the emerging IPR regime and by the globalization of economic models of life. It is, after all, hardly obvious that formal conservation measures will be as decisive as economic relationships.

THE PLANETARY CORPORATIONS

Given the rising prominence of environmental diplomacy it is often optimistically assumed that governments and the United Nations will soon act to save the earth. Unfortunately, there are reasons to doubt this conclusion, reasons that devolve not only to the limited authority that politicians hold over ruling social institutions—militarism, commodification, racism, advertising, and so on—but more specifically to the power of the transnational corporations (TNCs).

How best to summarize that power? Perhaps by noting that TNC activities involve a quarter of the world's productive assets, 70 percent of the assets in world trade, the majority of international financial transactions, and the lion's share of the world's advanced technology?[22] Even better, by noting that in the early 1980s, internal transfers within the 350 largest corporations already accounted for about 40 percent of total world trade, and that 70 percent of all trade was controlled by only 500 corporations?[23]

TNC activities account for half of all oil extraction and refining, and marketing of oil, gas, and coal—which make them responsible for a huge percentage of the global warming gases.[24] TNCs produce nearly all ozone-destroying chloroflurocarbons and related compounds.[25] TNCs dominate key minerals industries. For example, aluminum—an incredibly overused material which is quite fantastically energy-intensive to produce—has 63 percent of its mines and 66 percent of its refining controlled by only six companies.[26] TNCs control 80 percent of the land that globally is given to large-scale export agriculture, land that often has been taken over from local food production. Twenty TNCs account for over 90 percent of pesticide sales, and—in a terrifying development, given that many of these twenty are chemical companies—have also come to control a huge fraction of the world's seed stocks.[27]

In other words, TNCs are at once the architects and the building blocks of the global economy. That this is not obvious can perhaps be excused by the existence of a press that incessantly reports on the activities of governments and, increasingly, of the United Nations—but relegates discussion of the corporations to the business pages, where individual firms and economic sectors are minutely scrutinized but the overall economy treated in only the most discreetly abstract terms.

Given all this, and given the knowledge, common especially among activists from the South, of the roles that the TNCs play in the social-ecological crisis, many people were shocked to arrive in Rio and find not only the corporate greens of the Business Council for Sustainable Development (BCSD), but also the American Nuclear Society, Asbestos Institute of Canada, Australian Coal Association, Edison Electric Institute, Confederation of Brazilian Industry, International Council on Metals and the Envi-ronment, Global Climate Coalition, Japan Fisheries Association, and many others of similar ilk. Friends of the Earth International immediately compiled and distributed a list of corporate attendees, and plastering their Global Forum booths with Skull and Crossbones stickers announcing "Warning: Toxic Information."[28]

Historians will almost certainly look back on the Earth Summit as the point at where "greenwashing" finally and definitively crossed the thin line that separates green product advertising and single-corporation image ads (the sort of stuff immortalized in Chevron's "People Do" campaign) to large-scale, inter-corporate public relations consortia that, in both ambition and sophistication, go far beyond traditional green PR to sanitize the entire corporate enterprise.

Witness the BCSD's *Changing Course: A Global Business Perspective on Development and the Environment,* the executive summary that was *everywhere* in Rio during the Earth Summit, or at least everywhere impressionable gringos were likely to tread. As Stephan Schmidheiny, the Swiss billionaire who founded the BCSD puts it, "the title *Changing Course* was chosen with some care. While the basic goal of business must remain economic growth, as long as world population continues to grow rapidly and mass poverty remains widespread, we are recommending a different course toward that goal."[29]

This is not a book that can be properly understood without preparation. Schmidheiny, its putative author, is more an Al Gore than a Dan Quayle man, and apparently sincere in his fear of environmental crisis. The BCSD, for example, advocates "Full Cost Pricing," a move few other corporate NGOs have been willing to make. Full cost pricing means no subsidies, and, probably, virgin materials taxes, and is more commonly associated with alternative energy guru Amory Lovins and his ilk than the DuPont Chemical, Alcoa Aluminum, Shell Oil, and Nippon Steel corporados that populate the BCSD's ranks. Something funny is going on here, and while you will not find it spelled out in the pages of *Changing Course,* there are clues, like this quote:

> The fall of communism does not represent the total victory of capitalism. It is merely the end of a system that, as practiced in Eastern Europe and in the Soviet Union, reflected neither economic nor environmental truths. This should encourage those of us who believe in the efficacy of the marketplace to eliminate its failures and weaknesses and to build on its strengths. Market economies must now rise to the challenge and prove that they can adequately reflect environmental truth and incorporate the goals of sustainable development.[30]

This may be a bit triumphalist, but it is not a call for business as usual. Or is it? Greenpeace, which made a mission at Rio of attacking the BCSD, saw it as greenwash through and through. In its *Greenpeace Book of Greenwash,* issued in anticipation of the BCSD's public relations assault in Rio, this is quite clear: "While they proclaim that 'corporate environmentalism' is here, the TNCs are working to help create a new world order where international agreements and practices will give them unregulated, unparalleled power around the globe."[31]

This is the real nub of the issue. Were corporate environmentalists proposing to freely transfer new technologies to poor lands, democratize world markets, and support strict, uniform, and global environmental regulations, we might be compelled to admit that its partisans had undergone some weird and unexpected, but real, shift in perspective. Questions would remain, but it would be certain that something large had changed.

What is happening here is quite different. A small group of senior executives, many of them the heads of transnational corporations with criminal environmental and social records, have signed a public-relations manifesto that is most notable for its recognition of the need for technological and administrative changes in standard business practices. In this we may wish them luck, though it hardly seems that "business" has suddenly adapted itself to the ecological realities of this benighted planet.

Corporate environmentalism is, in fact, notable for the extent to which it appropriates the language and ideas of the traditional (northern) environmental movement. It favors technological solutions to narrowly defined ecological problems, seeks a form of "sustainable development" that somehow seems to imply no real social change, and generally avoids more troublesome political perspectives. To really understand it, one must shift from rhetoric to reality. The Earth Summit was not simply an opportunity for greenwashing, it was itself a greenwash, in which illusions of global change and democracy were used to draw attention from the real action.

A "COUP" AT THE UNITED NATIONS?

This became absolutely clear in New York, during the fourth UNCED prepcom, when rumors surfaced about a "coup" at the United Nations. As the details came to light, they told a strange and depressing tale about the reality of "international institution-building" after the cold war. Here they are, briefly:

In January of 1992, the U.S. favorite for the post of UN Secretary General, Boutros Boutros-Ghali of Egypt, took office. Promptly, and without consulting the General Assembly, he began a "reorganization" that included consolidating a number of the UN's largely autonomous economic and social groups into a centralized new Department of Economic and Social Development. In the process, he radically limited the independence of five organizations devoted to international development, including the UN Center on Transnational Corporations (UNCTC), which was renamed the Transnational Corporations Management Division and incorporated into the new department. The official, much-repeated reason for the reorganization was "efficiency," but despite the world-class bloat of the UN bureaucracy, many of those familiar with the reorganization find this explanation to be less than fully satisfying. They have reason to. Policy changes can be easily hidden in organizational restructurings, and, in this one, environmentalists, alternative development advocates, and the "developing countries" themselves were the clear losers.

Only a month later (the Bush administration was still in power) the right-wing Republican Richard Thornburg was appointed to the post of UN Administrative Under Secretary General. He arrived with a handpicked team that included at least two insiders from America's ultra-conservative Heritage Foundation (a significant point, given Heritage's long an vehement commitment to UN-bashing), and bent immediately to the task of continuing the restructuring. Just before Ghali's selection, Heritage had called for a new Secretary General willing and able to eradicate "the UN's hostility to market-based economic and legal arrangements that protect individual economic liberty" and to "take the dead hand of statist socialism off the rudder of the United Nations."[32] As Ghali and Thornburg arrived on the scene, though, its tone changed, and Burton Yale Pines of Heritage's UN Assessment Project was clear about the reason: "The Heritage Foundation hasn't changed its position on the UN. Absolutely not. There's been a change in the United Nations." That change had evidently gone so far that the United Nations was no longer "a forum for world Bolshevism and anti-Americanism."[33]

The "coup," as it was termed by an excited UN staffer who asked to remain anonymous, did not inspire confidence in the summit. However, it did offer an unusually clear look at the dynamics of post–cold war power, and in this regard the fate of the Center on Transnational Corporations is particularly revealing. The UNCTC has long been unpopular with the corporate class for its detailed research into the workings of the TNCs (most of the studies noted in the discussion of the transnationals, above, are by the UNCTC) and especially for its attempts to define and promulgate an international corporate Code of Conduct.

The last straw for the UNCTC was its *Transnational Corporations and Sustain-able Development: Recommendations for the Executive Director,* a report developed for the Earth Summit. *Recommendations,* as the report is known, was seen by the United States, Japan, and the TNCs themselves (which were intimately involved in the summit negotiations) as "an attempt at international regulation." And so they were. According to Harris Gleickman, a principal author of *Recommendations,* the document spells out "what would have to be done to have sustainably managed multinationals."[34] This seems a rather large statement, but it is certainly true that these regulations would make a difference if enforced, since they not only recommend "global corporate environmental management," as based on "the existing practices of environmentally leading businesses," but also "address other actors, particularly Governments and international organizations, since incentives and regulatory standards can allow markets to function more effectively."[35]

If *Recommendations* had found its way into the summit accords, the result could have been a precedent-setting advance toward official standards of global corporate conduct. But because the TNCs prefer "self regulation" and because of their great influence in summit negotiations, the recommendations were shelved in favor of a voluntary code of conduct drawn up by the BCSD.[36] In the end, the UNCTC's proposals were not even circulated to conference delegates, and *Agenda 21*—the Earth Summit's master treaty—contained only vague and unenforceable references to the multinationals.[37]

Chakravarthi Raghavan, the editor of *Third World Economics* and a long-time UN watcher, saw no mystery in any of this. During prepcom 4, he told an audience of NGO activists that "What we are seeing is a move to strengthen the hand of GATT, the IMF, and the World Bank. The power is being shifted from areas where there is some transparency, however limited, to areas in which the peoples of the world have no way of participating."[38] There is evidence enough for such an interpretation, though it is rarely noted in the mass media, where the "restructuring" of the United Nations is almost always taken to mean only a marginal expansion in the membership of the Security Council (that least democratic of the UN's bodies), and the establishment of a functional UN-based *military* force.

The real story, though, lies in the economic, social, and environmental institutions developing within the UN's economic and social departments (known, in UN lingo, as ECOSOC). In particular, the story lies in the fate of the UN's new Sustainable Development Commission (SDC), which—in one of the official Earth Summit's few successes—was established to monitor compliance with *Agenda 21* and the other UNCED treaties. Its establishment, according to Bill Pace of Washington's Center for the Development of International Law, should be seen as a victory of "NGOs and progressive governments" against a cabal of the large and powerful, "including India, China, the United Kingdom, Argentina, Japan, representing most of the North, as well as, Brazil, Austria, and Sweden, all of which opposed the creation of the SDC." Most of them "just wanted to get UNCED behind them," and "send in reports for a few years."[39]

The founding of the SDC, however, was only the beginning of a much longer battle. Maurice Strong wanted the SDC to have an independent secretariat, reporting only to the General Assembly. The United States and Japan disagreed, and the SDC was located within ECOSOC. It is easy to be cynical—or hopeful—about its fate. Peter Hanson, the former executive director of the UNCTC, would only say "that being placed into ECOSOC has led, in the past, to other worthwhile initiatives suffering death by bureaucratic suffocation." Bill Pace preferred to stress that, like the Human Rights Commission, the SDC can succeed only as an instrument of a larger movement, and that "what is really crucial is that the inter-governmental decision-making process be opened to NGOs, scientists, and civil society."

The politics here are Byzantine in the extreme, and it is impossible, at this time, to know if the SDC will have any real power. Clearly there is a "quiet" campaign underfoot in the United Nations to upgrade the status of the ECOSOC agencies, and clearly the establishment of the SDC has significantly abetted that process. The head of the SDC, Mr. Nitin Desai, is a former deputy to Maurice Strong, UNCED's Secretary General, and according to Harris Gleickman, has a strong "sustainable development background." The Clinton administration has gone on record as supporting continued "streamlining" in the United Nations. Richard Thornburg has been let go in favor of a new Clinton nominee. A new Department of Policy Coordination and Sustainable Development has been formed, and may host not only the SDC but a good deal of the staff of the former UNCTC as well. The battle, clearly, is not over.

Optimists, of course, cited the new Clinton administration, but one would be wise to cultivate a certain skepticism. The globalization of political and economic power is hardly good news, considering the undemocratic character of the global institutions to which this power is devolving. The United Nations, by far the most democratic of the lot, is itself a very mixed bag, and even at Rio it was clear that the summit actually marked a *reduction* in the United Nations' influence over environment and development. While the United Nations got the SDC, which is likely to emerge as a center of diplomatic politics and "soft law," the World Bank, which indulges only the barest pretense of democracy, emerged from Rio controlling the Global Environmental Facility, the planet's new environmental piggybank.

The pattern here hardly suggests a new era of global political and ecological cooperation, though it is all too consistent with the drift of events revealed in global trade agreements. NGOs are straining toward the democratization of global governance, but fundamental decisions seem always to be made by inaccessible bureaucratic institutions, while neither the basic logic of the global economy nor the overwhelming power of the planetary corporations ever quite comes to issue. The UNCED treaties prove the point. Then, when it may have made a difference, the desperate need to regulate large economic enterprises in general and the TNCs in particular was kept off the table. UNCTC's mandate for tracking the TNCs and the largest portion of its staff has been transferred to the UN Conference on Trade and Development. What little UN oversight of the TNCs that once existed has now effectively been purged. When it mattered, the TNCs were more than able to control the political agenda. Why should this not continue to be so? Brian Urquhart, who was Under Secretary General of the UN from 1974 to 1986, has gone so far as to suggest that "a second chamber of the General Assembly" be established to seat representatives of the "private sector."[40] Can we say that this will never come to pass?

STRAINED ENCOUNTERS

Northern environmentalists left Rio with a new sympathy for the southern point of view, in which environmental protection often seems less pressing, and more contingent on large-scale social change, than it does in the affluent North. For their part, southern activists tended to arrive in Rio in deeply skeptical moods. For example, Martin Khor of the Third World Network, who emerged during the UNCED process as a key NGO lobbyist, remarked that the Earth Summit was "no longer a forum on the environment, on greenhouse gas, or on scientific data, but rather a conference about commerce."[41] And Walden Bello, a Filipino, noting that it was the North that set the UNCED agenda, an agenda in which even "pure" environmental issues of great concern in the South—notably the widespread lack of access to fresh water, desertification, and the international toxics trade—did not rank prominent places, opined that UNCED "was a conference about environmental problems as they are seen in the North." It should have been called the "UN Conference on Environment as Seen by the North."[42]

What is interesting about this last remark is that only a few years back few northern environmentalists would have even understood it. In UNCED's wake, understanding is common. For tens of thousands of northern greens, it seems reasonable to hope, images of Brazilian poverty and doubts about environmental diplomacy will not quickly fade. Today, after UNCED, in a shrinking and unstable world where poverty and immigration are becoming major environmental issues, even the brief glimpses of the South that northern environmentalists had in Rio are likely to have continuing influence. Today, quite simply, planetary realities are becoming difficult to shut out.

These realities have recently been made clear by the UN Development Program, which demonstrated in its 1992 Report that the global polarization of wealth *doubled* between 1960 and 1989, by which time the richest fifth of the world's population received 82.7 percent of the world's total income while the poorest fifth received only 1.4 percent. In 1960, the top fifth of the world's population (a group that, significantly, includes most of the northern poor) made 30 times more than the bottom fifth; by 1989 the spread had increased to 60 times. Even these figures conceal the true scale of the injustice, for they are based on average per capita incomes within countries. If we instead compare the richest and poorest fifths of the world's people, the income differential rises to at least 150 to 1.[43]

Figures like this are hard to understand, especially for U.S. environmentalists, who inhabit a pinched and cloistered political tradition. Fortunately that tradition is weakening. Given the drift of planetary events, it is clear that "environmental justice" is the wave of the future. Even citizens of the United States have begun to understand that the rich are getting richer and the poor poorer, and it is no longer surprising to hear such understandings linked to others about the differential class and racial impacts of ecological degradation. If this trend remains in force, one might reasonably anticipate the emergence of an entirely new kind of northern environmental movement.

Still, an immense chasm divides northern environmentalism from even the most environmentally conscious development activism of the South. It is not merely that Northern environmentalism has so long stressed "population" (a real threat but a rather constipating analytic category) in its understanding of the ecological crisis, while southern activists are historically schooled in anti-colonial traditions that stress power relations and the "overconsumption" of the North. It is also that the ecological crisis comes altogether differently to the planet's poor than to those who know the more comfortable decline of the industrialized regions. We may live on the same planet as Brazilian or Malaysian greens, but we suffer different aspirations.

At issue here is "development," that strange second term of the Earth Summit equation. "Development" is a notion so cynical that it makes "progress," that ideological warhorse of the nineteenth century, look charming and naive in comparison. Without belaboring the point, it seems safe to insist on two basic matters. First, poor people, the majority of them, of course, living in the South, find their daily lives to be less tolerable than than do the people of the North. Consequently they are less susceptible to the odd and assiduously cultivated illusion that environmental protection is either possible or desirable without fundamental social changes. Second, that idea that humanity's great problem is "poverty," and that "development"—even more than "aid"—is its solution, has fallen into well-deserved ill-repute. It is a long time since 1949, when President Truman, in his inauguration speech, called for "a bold new program for making the benefits of our scientific advances and industrial progress available for the improvement and growth of under-developed areas."[44] It has become clear enough that, as German cultural theorist Wolfgang Sachs has put it, "The campaign to turn traditional man into modern man has failed," while "the old ways have been smashed, the new ways are not viable."[45]

These points are now so widely accepted that they almost define a planetary consensus of radical environmentalists and development activists. It is hardly a secret that urban-industrial and export-intensive models of modernization are leading to social decay and ecological degradation. Indeed, the green project, in both the North and the South is an attempt to define an alternative to this "development." That this project is an expansive one, that it unravels into a vast tangle of social and economic agendas, is now common knowledge.

It is no surprise that the details of this green alternative remain unclear, or that opinions differ over which matters are most crucial to its pursuit. What was a surprise at the Earth Summit was that despite the vast differences between northern and southern movements, the last few decades have seen the emergence of a rough global consensus about what must be done. Unlike the ancient days of the movement—say, 1970—ecology today is widely known as a science with strong and even inescapable political implications. Further, those implications are beginning to be widely understood.

On the other hand, the evolving movement is not alone on the planet. Indeed, "sustainable development," an increasingly official notion (see, for example, the World Bank's 1992 *World Development Report*), is not so much an attempt to develop a sustainable society as it is to save the notion of "development," to make it appear sustainable, and thus to bolster all the corporate, governmental, and bureaucratic interests that hide beneath its ideological umbrella. This is not the rhetoric of a social-ecological movement, but of the environmental profession, the "development set,"—and if the two are becoming difficult to distinguish, this at least tells us something about the complexity of the emerging situation.[46]

"Sustainable development" is, at best, contested terrain. Certainly the movement does *not* control it. Consider the World Bank as one of Earth Summit's obvious institutional winners. The bank emerged from Rio as the host to the "Global Environmental Facility"(GEF)—a combination green fund and greenwashing department that will almost certainly be more powerful than the UN's Sustainable Development Commission. Unfortunately, the bank—which is widely distrusted, not to say hated, throughout the South—has, to put it gently, its own agenda, one bound up not only with the ideological project of "development," but also with the more immediate, and all too real neo-liberal agenda of "free trade" and "structural adjustment."

This larger agenda was debated at the summit, but certainly to a lesser extent that it should have been. The publishers of the various summit newspapers were not particularly helpful. The *Earth Summit Times* (published by the green, U.S.-based, Island Press) for example, printed a few critical articles on the GEF and the World Bank, but a larger number of bland pieces that tended, like one by Jimmy Carter, to grant the GEF credit for a few unspecified "good projects," to call for reforms designed to democratize its management structure, and to conclude that "with these reforms, the GEF could become the vehicle through which funds are expended much more wisely than in the past."[47] Voices like that of Susan George, an associate director of the Transnational Institute who sees the bank as the most powerful and "avant garde institution of world capitalism" and calls the GEF "a very small tail wagging a very nasty dog," were rare, as were effective rebuttals to the bank's well-publicized claim that its recent "reforms" are both profound and consequential.[48] In actual fact, according to Juliet Majot, the editor of *Bankcheck Quarterly*, the GEF is a sign of the movement's failure. "That the green fund takes the form of a GEF based in the World Bank is an indictment of the World Bank reform movement. As a movement, we did not oppose the placement of the GEF soon enough or effectively enough, and some NGOs even supported its placement in the World Bank, seeing it as a sign of progress. They couldn't be more wrong."[49]

It is a chilling and frustrating situation. After years of hard organizing, as it becomes obvious even to politicians that the World Bank's policies cause immense suffering and catastrophe throughout the world, the bank not only launches GEF as a world-scale initiative in damage control, but the mainstream of at least the northern environmental movement, along with green-leaning politicians from around the world, embraces it as proof of a global environmental awakening. Al Gore is a fine example, as is his statement made during a Rio press conference that the U.S. "should be getting a lot more credit than it has for applying pressure to see that the GEF is more democratic, accountable, and transparent." When asked for evidence that this pressure—itself a mysterious and rarely accounted phenomena—was making progress against the bank's ingrained mega-engineering biases, he shot back that "World Bank President Lewis Preston says he's going to change that, and I believe him."[50]

Fortunately, not everyone is so easily confused, as soon became clear to the staffers of the bank's booth at the Global Forum. The booth was stuffed with slickly printed literature about the bank's environmentally friendly initiatives, including a poster heralding the coming of the GEF. Not long after the start of the summit, about 200 or so young activists, of no discernible group or nationality, approached the booth shaking rock-filled Cola-Cola cans in a Brazilian beat, and surrounded it chanting "No World Bank." They stripped it of its literature and "World Bank" signs (substituting a rough "People's Bank" banner), heaped it all into a giant wheelbarrow and set it alight. A few hours later the booth reopened, but bank officials declined to enter it again, abandoning it to their flacks.

FOLLOW THE MONEY

As for the southern governments, they chose to forget the radical demands of the past, and made "aid—usually known in Rio as "financing"—the centerpiece of their definitions of success and failure. This is the classic posture of poor southern governments, who rarely rock the international boat, and in any case feel themselves powerless in the face of a world system organized for the benefit of the North. Unfortunately, like all the other times when "realism" has demanded that social change be traded off for cash, the South's realism at Rio was of a failed and tragic variety. After extended negotiations, the world's assembled politicians settled on a funding strategy that relied almost entirely upon a reaffirmation of a long-ignored, twenty-year-old goal of aid commitments from the North of .7 percent of Gross National Product, "by the year 2000, or as soon as possible."[51] Only France agreed to meet the .7 percent target by 2000, while Japan, Britain, Germany, and several other large donors agreed to the target but not the deadline. The United States, which has never accepted the decades-old pledge to a .7 percent aid target, and commits only about .21 percent of its wealth in foreign aid, essentially ignored the whole discussion.[52]

By plying its hard line, the United States once again framed the debate in terms altogether unconvivial to fruitful new political departures. Aid is not the issue, for many reasons, the most obvious being that aid only returns to the South a fraction of what routinely is taken away. Susan George estimates that between 1982 and 1990 southern countries sent to the North, in debt service alone, an amount that exceeds all forms of aid by $418 billion, or about $50 billion a year. This equals about six Marshall Plans, in inflation-adjusted dollars paid by the poor to the rich.[53] And debt is just the tip of the iceberg. Visible though it may be, it is still far smaller than the larger masses lurking below the economic surface. These include the "unfair terms of trade" that pit undiversified, post-colonial, export-dependent economies the world over against each other, thus depressing the prices of primary commodities far below rational (or ecologically rational) levels, and all the other contrivances of global economy that systematically skews financial transactions to benefit the North. The annual cost to the South of these contrivances was often quoted at various UNCED NGO meetings as upward to $200 billion a year, and UNDP, adding "the lack of market opportunities," estimates them as "at least $500 billion a year."[54]

All this is obscured by the nation of "aid," which thus takes center stage whenever the geo-economic matters fundamental to North-South relations threaten to break into polite discussion. This was certainly the case at Rio, where the need for "sustainable development" was a rhetorical given, and the real debate revolved around its definition and implications. Of course, those implications are fairly momentous, and thus they remain far from the political agenda. Inevitably, with the United States leading the all-too-willing governments of the world in a short-sighted bout of denial and cosmetic greening, the official negotiations drifted far out into stagnant waters. It was clear that nothing real would change in Rio.

Martin Khor, in a pithy booklet published just before the final prepcom, argues that the environmental crisis has reached a point where "solutions cannot be attained through technological means alone, but will principally involve fundamental changes in economy, development models, lifestyles, distribution of resources and income, and international political relations."[55] Such dangerous truths easily lead to despair, but, here at least, Khor resists dark conclusions and argues that the crisis is an "opportunity to renew international cooperation," and to "focus the minds and wills of political and economic leaders as well as people and their organizations on broad cooperation strategies and mechanisms that will be mutually beneficial and ensure Earth's survival."[56]

Now, after Rio, the prospects for such a grand new age of international cooperation do not seem good. True, there has been a significant change in administrations here in the United States, but if Khor is right, if everything from lifestyles to the distribution of resources and income to international political relations must be transformed to avoid "greater and even more violent conflicts between nations in the near future," the new administration will make only the barest difference.[57]

Who is to blame for the condition of "the South?" Is it "the North," as was so often claimed by southern politicians at Rio? The two abstractions obviously leave something to be desired, though in the rich atmosphere of the UNCED process, where many northern greens first came into close contact with charismatic southern activists, it was difficult to avoid the charms of North-South rhetoric. The mouthings of the northern politicians, in constant contrast, were obviously in the service of rapine. Even Greenpeace, which should know better, told its members in a Rio follow-up that the South had "little choice but abandon any nobler planetary visions and demand a larger piece of the disintegrating global pie."[58]

This view excuses far too much. In lumping southern corporations, governments, and people together, it paints even vile actions as the inevitable consequences of northern domination, and verges on just the kind of third worldism that helped to destroy the new left. Malaysia illustrates the point all too well, for it was, if anything, the ideological leader of the South at Rio, and its ruling elites have made a mission of justifying both social repression and environmental destruction as the costs of "development." Malaysia is, for example, the home base of immensely rapacious logging companies that have gone beyond clear cutting on their native soil to compete with the Japanese and Thailanders for rights to destroy, say, Cambodia as well.[59] It was Malaysia that insisted that any forestry treaty would violate its "National Sovereignty," and that progress requires the destruction of the rainforest home of the indigenous Penan, who, according to Prime Minister Mahathir Mohamad, must decide if they want education and development or to "go to the jungle and live on monkeys."[60] Is this just a part of the fight for "a larger piece of the disintegrating global pie"?

Mahathir (who like Bush, first threatened to boycott the Earth Summit, but chose instead to attend and make it a platform for himself and his views) went on to argue that the North wants "a say in the management of our forests while we have no say on their carbon dioxide emissions. The day the North starts planting forests, and the day we have an industrial convention, we can have a forest convention." This is not an unreasonable position, and that is the problem. Today, for the record, the most extensive logging on the planet is not in "the South," but in Canada.

There are very difficult issues here, issues that devolve, ultimately, to the severity of the social-ecological crisis and, immediately, to an overlap of interests between southern activists and governments. This overlap confuses both northern and southern activists, though it is stickier in the South, where governments routinely seek legitimation as anti-imperialist champions. Long before Rio, Martin Khor, speaking to an audience of northern activists, sought to impress them with the environmental significance of the "unfair terms of trade" that southern producers suffer in the current world market. Unfortunately, his entirely reasonable screed against low commodity prices and high external debt seemed to pass, imperceptibly, into a defense of the clear cutting of the Malaysian rainforest. "If Malasia drops lumber exports by 80 percent, who will bear the burden? If it drops lumber exports by 80 percent, it must get four times as much per log."[61] This is true, as long as the Malaysian economy is dependent on the export of raw lumber. On the other hand, as we in the United States have learned from our own timber wars, exports of raw lumber are not really a very good way of maximizing export earnings.

That this is not obvious seems to be a sign of a strange sympathy with corporations and governments that routinely harass and arrest indigenous and environmental activists. The source of the sympathy is easily traced to weakness. The South has far less international leverage than it did during the cold war; in fact, the whole notion of "the South" as a cohesive geo-political force is in doubt. In what seems a sign of the times, the developing-country bloc—the so-called G-77—splintered during the climate negotiations into different factions, each pursuing its own economic interests. Meanwhile, the TNCs are immensely powerful, and making inroads into areas, like India, which had previously been able to maintain a degree of autonomy. Roberto Bissio of Uruguay's Third World Institute summed up the critical nationalism of many southern NGO activists, stating that "national capital still exists in Malaysia! The TNCs are subject to all sorts of controls. In such a context certain kinds of alliances with national capital make sense that would not make sense in Latin America, where there are only the TNCs. You have to understand that we are much weaker now than we were in the 1970s."[62]

This is not, however, the only way of viewing the situation. Here, for example, is the entirely unequivocal opinion of a well-known Brazilian NGO activist, who spoke frankly only on the condition of anonymity:

> In Brazil, even the elites—the contractors, miners, loggers, the remnants of the old military dictatorship—use the same arguments as the Third World Network. They rail against "green imperialism" as the "new colonialism" and so on, and speak for Brazil's right to ravage the Amazon, if that's what it takes to become a "developed" country. The Third World Network is totally sincere, but their arguments can very easily be misused. In Brazil, we made this mistake decades ago, siding with our local oligarchy against the international oligarchy. Now, parts of the Brazilian oligarchy are simply stealing the left's discourse of the fifties and sixties—using nationalist and "developmentalist" rhetoric as a cover for their real agendas. It's unbelievably crooked.

I quote X anonymously and at length, not to close the issue, but to suggest its complexity and sensitivity. These must both be recognized—especially because international NGOs networks are playing ever-increasing roles in global environmental politics. The terms by which those networks develop will make real and profound differences. Northern humility in the face of grim southern realities, and solidarity with the South, will be decisive, but true solidarity does not extend to the automatic acceptance of abstract and oversimplified formulas about North and South—formulas that altogether fail to capture the dilemmas and complexities of the international economy.

In this new international politics, little is what it first appears. The Biodiversity Treaty is as much about property as it is about life. The World Bank's GEF is largely an exercise in greenwashing. "Aid" is a cheap investment in a world system that benefits donors far more than recipients. "Development" is a big lie that is used to sell the most horrific of excesses, and if we are not careful, "sustainable development" could easily meet the same fate. Even solidarity, when cheapened to an easy, automatic sympathy, can curdle into a vile brew.

As one highly excited Latin American delegate put it at the pre-Rio "Roots of the Future" NGO conference—held in December of 1991 amidst the high-tech extravagance of Paris' huge new science and technology museum—it is past time "to stop talking about the 'North and the South' and the 'South and the North' and the 'North within the South' and the 'South within the North' and start talking about [I'm not quite sure about the translation here], 'the fuckers and the fuckees.'"

AFTER THE SUMMIT

New York Times correspondent William K. Stevens, in a summit wrap-up piece, argued that the very fact that "the world has grown more serious" about confronting ecological crisis helps to explain the confrontations and deadlock in Rio.[63] When, sometime in the last decade, it became widely understood that "economic development and reduction of poverty were essential to protecting the environment," it became simultaneously obvious that environmental devastation was no incidental side effect of an otherwise benign political-economic process. Thus was the stage set for issues far beyond the ambit of politics as usual.

Setting a stage, though, is only a small beginning. More important are the actors. In the end, the Earth Summit must be measured by its impact on the environmental movement, here and in the South. In this regard, the summit showed how far we have come and how far we have to go. UNCED brought activists together from around the planet, and though there was friction and disagreement, North-South confrontations never rose to dominate relations between activists. There were intense encounters by the thousand, but the main impact of these encounters was to create a shared sense of a common global effort. The environmental movement, now global, has yet to find a new internationalism, but the Earth Summit, for all its absurdities, was nevertheless a step in that direction.

Was the Earth Summit a failure? Yes. But it may be that in its failure it marked a process that may eventually succeed. Change did not come in Rio, but it did announce itself, even to the most conservative of the northern environmental groups. Barbara Bramble of the National Wildlife Federation (NWF), a "player" throughout the UNCED process, claimed at the Summit that her "organization has been incredibly affected. For the first time, I am now able to bring a full international agenda to our membership and let them see how U.S. policy affects so many other countries." Only a few months later, the NWF announced its support for Bush's draft of the NAFTA, which makes Bramble's Rio optimism seem a bit delusionary, but it may nevertheless have been justified. Even at NWF, the execs and the staff do not always see eye to eye.

At some hopelessly abstract level, there is only a single environment and development movement, as there is only one earth. Politically, though, it is past time to see that the future does not lie with the "already over-emphasized and over-funded national compromise branch of our movement," as it was called by the post-Rio grassroots U.S. Peoples' Alliance for the Earth Summit.[64] Ecology is now moving to the center of politics, as it must, and realists of all stripes must learn to see that—absent radical clarity and sometimes brutal truth—accommodation and rhetoric will crush us all.

The silences of the official UNCED treaties prove the point. There is, in them, scarce talk of poverty, trade, TNCs, democracy, population, consumption, immigration, militarism. Yet these are, quite simply, *the* decisive matters, the ones that will determine our fate. If there was a glimpse of hope at Rio, it was because these and other immensely difficult issues were the central concerns of an evolving global movement that actively seeks to face our real conditions of existence. One would be a fool to exaggerate the extent or power of that movement, or to claim for it any clear ascendance over environmentalism as usual, let alone adequacy in the face of the challenges of the emerging world order. Still, ideas have power, and in the "alternative treaties" hammered out in Rio by thousands of activists from around the world, in the conversations that fill the planet's NGOs and "environmental justice" groups, in the skepticism that troubles activities of even the mainstream movement, and most of all in the sense of a common project that is coming to citizens' groups throughout the world, there is at least the basis for hope.

The alternative treaties are themselves a milestone, though we may certainly be forgiven for being unfamiliar with them. The *New York Times,* in all its reams of Rio coverage, mentioned them not at all, while the *Los Angeles Times* favored them only with a snide story entitled "Strong Treaties Elude Even Activists at Earth Summit."[65]

In truth, the alternative treaties are not everything one might wish for. Still, there is more than a bit of *Schadenfreude* in the title of the *Los Angeles Times'* article, and at least a bit of inaccuracy. Is it weak to call, as does the *Alternative Treaty on Trade and Development,* for today's corporate-dominated trade agreements to be replaced by "an alternative International Trade Organization (ITO) designed with a participatory and democratic structure ensuring transparent, accountable and equitable decision making in accordance with the public interest instead of corporate interest"?[66] To insist, as does the *Citizens Commitment to Biodiversity,* that "the collections and the results of research deposited in national or international agricultural research centers, gene banks or otherwise, shall not be the object of restrictions, or in any way be considered as intellectual property"?[67]

These and the many other demands in the 37 alternative treaties may not seem reasonable in the near future, but judging by *Agenda 21* and the official treaties, saving the earth may also not be a reasonable goal. The alternative treaties at least offer a set of shared understandings, commitments, and some refreshing vision, on topics ranging from the "Big Environmental Issues" like biodiversity and climate change that defined the official summit, to trade, the regulation of the TNCs, consumption, militarism, racism, even cooperation between northern and southern NGOs. It is a deep, significant agenda, and it outlines the vision of a social change as fundamental as any dreamt of in the past. The difference, this time, lies in ever-louder ticking of the ecological clock.[68]

What is finally clear is that the fate of the earth will not be decided on the grounds of traditional environmental politics. As far as the future of the movement goes, the short-term goal must be a green politics that no longer brings to mind only the lawyers and lobbyists of the large Washington environmental groups. These groups will, of course, remain players, but with work and luck they too will evolve, and soon be only players in a larger drama that includes a great many others. It is not the green establishment that will lead us through the next 50 years, that will find means of using trade agreements to protect the ecosystem *and* to beat back the TNCs, that will democratize and strengthen the United Nations and the other global institutions, that will invent forms of global solidarity that avoid both northern arrogance and third-worldism, pioneer meaningful forms of democratic internationalism, lead the fight for land reform and sustainable agriculture, save the oceans and the forests, find a path to a solar-hydrogen transition, develop a coherent politics of consumption, and all the rest of it.

This is a crucial time, a time of "large history." The transition to "sustainability" is, quite visibly, about a "change of life," in just the expansive sense that the old Reds meant the term. Worldwatch president Lester Brown has taken to calling for an "environmental revolution," and then quickly backpedaling to stress that he intends only to invoke a sense of the massive technological and demographic shifts of the agricultural and industrial revolutions. These are, in some regards, apt and fair analogies, no doubt about it. But given the extent of the necessary changes, and the brief time remaining to make them, is it really wise to pretend that they capture the whole of it?

Notes

1. Dave Henson, "Introductory remarks"(presentation at the International People's Forum, held during prepcom 4, New York, NY).
2. James MacNeil, "Honesty, courage needed to save the Summit," *Earth Summit Times,* June 3, 1992, p. 1.
3. Wangari Maathai (presentation at UNCED Plenary, June 11, 1992).
4. "Strangling the Summit," *Guardian,* June 10, 1992.
5. James Brooke, "U.S. Has Starring Role At Rio Summit as Villain," *New York Times,* June 2, 1992, p. A5.
6. Ibid.
7. The single best overview of the UNCED negotiations, including the details of who nixed what, was written at the end of prepcom 4 by Angela Harkavy for CAPE '92, a coalition of large U.S. environmental groups. It is called *The Final Effort: A Progress Report on Preparatory Negotiations for the* UNCED. CAPE '92 was sponsored by National Wildlife Federation.
8. Mark Valentine, "PrepCom4: The Road to Rio is Paved with Good Intentions," *Earth Island Journal* (June 1992): p. 2.
9. Jack Freeman, "Atmosphere Debate Running out of Steam," *Earth Summit Times,* June 13, 1992.
10. Brooke.
11. David Lascelles and Christina Lamb, "A Game of Missed Opportunities," *Financial Times,* June 15, 1992.
12. Walden Bello, interview with author, July 1992.
13. *The Final Effort,* p. 15.
14. Lascelles and Lamb, p. 14.
15. Mark Valentine, interview with author, July 1992.
16. Peter Padbury, interview with author, July 1992.
17. Lascelles and Lamb, p. 14.
18. Henk Hobbelink, "Biodiversity at Rio: Conservations or Access?" *Capitalism, Nature, Socialism* 3. no. 4 (Dec. 1992): p. 120.
19. See *Cultural Survival Quarterly,* special issue entitled "Intellectual Property Rights: The Politics of Ownership" (Summer 1991).
20. Darrell Posey, "Protecting Biocultural Diversity," in *Beyond the Earth Summit: Conversations with Advocates of Sustainable Development,* ed. Steve Lerner (Bolinas, CA: Commonweal, 1992,) pp. 136–142. P.O. Box 316, Bolinas, CA 94924.
21. For a fine overview, see "GATT: The Environment and the Third World, An Overview," *Environmental News Network*. Address: 1442-A Walnut St., Suite 81, Berkeley, CA 94709. (510) 549-7768.
22. These statistics are from *Ongoing and Future Research: Transnational Corporations and Issues Relating to the Environment* (New York: United Nations Centre on Transnational Corporations, 1989), p. 6. Cited in *The Greenpeace Book*

of Greenwash (NY: Greenpeace, 1992). Available without charge from the Greenpeace HEIP Campaign, 1436 U St., NW, Washington DC 20009, (202) 462-1177.

23. "The Power of the Transnationals," *Ecologist* 22, no. 4 (July/Aug. 1992): p. 159.

24. Arjun Makhijani, A. van Buren, A. Bickel, S. Saleska, "Climate Change and Transnational Corporations, Analysis and Trends," UNCTC *Environment Series #2* (New York: United Nations, 1992), p. 47.

25. *Ongoing and Future Research,* p. 77.

26. Makhijani, et al., p. 77.

27. *Ongoing and Future Research.* See also Cary Fowler and Pat Mooney, *Shattering: Food, Politics, and the Loss of Genetic Diversity* (Tucson: University of Arizona, 1990), chapter 6.

28. "Friend of the Earth Hunts Wolves in Sheep's Clothing," undated press release distributed in Rio by Friends of the Earth International.

29. Stephan Schmidheiny *Changing Course: A Global Business Perspective on Development and the Environment* (Cambridge: MIT Press, 1992), p. xxii.

30. Ibid., p. 15.

31. *Greenpeace Book of Greenwash,* p. 1.

32. A number of university officials who I interviewed for my study of Asian American admissions made this point. "Help Wanted: A New Secretary General for the United Nations," *Heritage Backgrounder Update,* no. 157 (April 4, 1991). Address: 214 Massachusetts Avenue, N.E., Washington DC, 20002-4999.

33. Ian Williams, "Why the Right Loves the UN," *Nation,* April 13, 1992.

34. Harris Gleikman, interview with author, Jan. 14, 1993.

35. *Transnational Corporations and Sustainable Development: Recommendations for the Executive Director.* Unpublished report issued by the United Nations Centre on Transnational Corporations (UNCTC), December 16, 1991.

36. "Whose Common Future?" *Ecologist* 22, no. 4 (July–Aug. 1992): p. 163.

37. Martin Khor, "Regulating Transnational Corporations: The Biggest Gap in UNCED's Agenda," *Third World Economics* (April 16–30, 1992): p. 18.

38. Chakravarthi Raghavan's comment was made at "Trade, Environment and Development," a conference organized by the Institute for Agriculture and Trade Policy during prepcom 4 in New York.

39. Bill Pace, interview with author, Jan. 13, 1993.

40. James Ridgeway and Sabine Guez, "Triumph of the Will: The United Nations Joins the Trilateral Commission," *Village Voice,* May 19, 1992.

41. Marc Cooper, "Blame it on Rio," *Village Voice,* June 16, 1992.

42. Walden Bello, interview with author, July 1992.

43. *1992 Human Development Report,* p. 34.

44. Cited in Gustavo Esteva, "Development," in *The Development Dictionary: A Guide to Knowledge as Power,* Wolfgang Sachs, ed. (London: Zed Books, 1992), p. 6.

45. Maura Dolan, "Strong Treaties Elude Even Activists at Earth Summit," *Los Angeles Times,* June 11, 1992.

46. "The Development Set" is a wonderful poem by Ross Coggins, in Grahram Hancock, *Lords of Poverty: The Power, Prestige, and Corruption of the International Aid Business* (New York: Atlantic Monthly Press, 1989).
47. Jimmy Carter, "UNCED's challenge not impossible," *Earth Summit Times,* June 8, 1992.
48. Susan George, interview with author, Dec. 19, 1991.
49. Juliet Majot, interview with author, March 1992.
50. Juliet Majot, "For Your Eyes Only," *Bankcheck Quarterly* (July 1992): p. 5.
51. Juliet Majot, "No More than a Dream in Rio," *Bankcheck Quarterly* (July 1992): p. 1.
52. "Negotiators in Rio Agree to Increase Aid to Third World," *New York Times,* June 14, 1992.
53. Susan George, *The Debt Boomerang: How Third World Debt Harms Us All* (London: Pluto Press, 1992), pp. xv–xvi.
54. *1992 Human Development Report,* p. 48.
55. Martin Khor Kok-Peng, *The Future of North-South Relations: Conflict or Cooperation* (Penang, Malaysia: Third World Network, 1992), pp. 44–45. Address: Third World Network, 87 Cantonment Road, 10250 Penang, Malaysia.
56. Khor Kok-Peng.
57. Ibid.
58. "The Divide at the Summit," *Greenpeace* (July–Sept. 1992): p. 2.
59. Angela Gennino and Sara Colm, "The Killing Forests," *San Francisco Weekly,* June 24, 1992.
60. "Earth Summit: Mahathir Defends his Country's Logging Practices," Rio Press release from Inter Press Service, June 17, 1992.
61. Martin Khor, address to the World Affairs Council, San Francisco, October 1991.
62. Roberto Bissio, interview with author, Sept. 17, 1992.
63. William K. Stevens, "Earth Summit Finds The Years of Optimism Are a Fading Memory," *New York Times,* June 9, 1992.
64. "Draft proposal from People's Alliance for what to do with the post-Rio U.S. Citizen's Network on UNCED," written by some of the more grassroots-oriented members of the Citizen's Network Steering Committee, Aug. 5, 1992.
65. Maura Dolan, "Strong Treaties Elude Even Activists at Earth Summit," *Los Angeles Times,* June 11, 1992.
66. The alternative treaties are easy to get. Many are posted on the "UNCED.treaties conference" on *Econet.* The set is available for $10 from the U.S. Citizen's Network on UNCED (300 Broadway, #39, San Francisco, CA 94133). An annotated edition is under preparation and will be published by Commonweal.
67. *Econet.*
68. UNCED inspired a number of attempts to synthesize and state this agenda as a whole. Two notable examples, both of which will be worth reading for years to come, are Greenpeace's *Beyond* UNCED (available from local offices) and *Whose Common Future?*

NOTES ON NAFTA

NOAM CHOMSKY

Throughout history, Adam Smith observed, we find the workings of "the vile maxim of the masters of mankind: All for ourselves, and nothing for other people." He had few illusions about the consequences. The invisible hand, he wrote, will destroy the possibility of a decent human existence "unless government takes pains to prevent" this outcome, as must be assured in "every improved and civilized society." It will destroy community, the environment and human values generally—and even the masters themselves, which is why the business classes have regularly called for state intervention to protect them from market forces.

The masters of mankind in Smith's day were the "merchants and manufacturers," who were the "principal architects" of state policy, using their power to bring "dreadful misfortunes" to the vast realms they subjugated and to harm the people of England as well, though their own interests were "most peculiarly attended to." In our day the masters are, increasingly, the supranational corporations and financial institutions that dominate the world economy, including international trade—a dubious term for a system in which some 40 percent of U.S. trade takes place within companies, centrally managed by the same highly visible hands that control planning, production and investment.

The World Bank reports that protectionist measures of the industrialized countries reduce national income in the South by about twice the amount of official aid to the region—aid that is itself largely export promotion, most of it directed to richer sectors (less needy, but better consumers). In the past decade, most of the rich countries have increased protectionism, with the Reaganites often leading the way in the crusade against economic liberalism. These practices, along with the programs dictated by the International Monetary Fund (I.M.F.) and World Bank, have helped double the gap between rich and poor countries since 1960. Resource transfers from the poor to the rich amounted to more than $400 billion from 1982 to 1990, "the equivalent in today's dollars of some six Marshall Plans provided by the South to the North," observes Susan George of the Transnational Institute in Amsterdam; she notes also that commercial banks were protected by transfer of their bad debts to the public sector. As in the case of the S&Ls, and advanced industry generally, "free market capitalism" is to be risk free for the masters, as fully as can be achieved.

The international class war is reflected in the United States, where real wages have fallen to the level of the mid-1960s. Wage stagnation, extending to the college educated, changed to sharp decline in the mid-1980s, in part a consequence of the decline in "defense spending," our euphemism for the state industrial policy that allows "private enterprise" to feed at the public trough. More than 17 million workers were unemployed or underemployed by mid-1992, Economic Policy Institute economists Lawrence Mishel and Jared Bernstein report—a rise of 8 million during the Bush years. Some 75 percent of that is permanent loss of jobs. Of the limited gain in total wealth in the eighties, "70 percent accrued to the top 1 percent of income earners, while the bottom lost absolutely," according to M.I.T. economist Rudiger Dornbusch.

Structures of governance have tended to coalesce around economic power. The process continues. In the London *Financial Times,* James Morgan describes the "de facto world government" that is taking shape in the "new imperial age": the I.M.F., World Bank, Group of 7 industrialized nations, General Agreement on Tariffs and Trade (GATT) and other institutions designed to serve the interests of transnational corporations, banks and investment firms.

One valuable feature of these institutions is their immunity from popular influence. Elite hostility to democracy is deep-rooted, understandably, but there has been a spectrum of opinion. At the "progressive" end, Walter Lippmann argued that "the public must be put in its place," so that the "responsible men" may rule without interference from "ignorant and meddlesome outsiders" whose "function" is to be only "interested spectators of action," periodically selecting members of the leadership class in elections, then returning to their private concerns. The statist reactionaries called "conservatives" typically take a harsher line, rejecting even the spectator role. Hence the appeal to the Reaganites of clandestine operations, censorship and other measures to insure that a powerful and interventionist state will not be troubled by the rabble. The "new imperial age" marks a shift toward the reactionary end of the antidemocratic spectrum.

It is within this framework that the North American Free Trade Agreement (NAFTA) and GATT should be understood. Note first that such agreements have only a limited relation to free trade. One primary U.S. objective is increased protection for "intellectual property," including software, patents for seeds and drugs, and so on. The U.S. International Trade Commission estimates that

American companies stand to gain $61 billion a year from the Third World if U.S. protectionist demands are satisfied at GATT (as they are in NAFTA), at a cost to the South that will dwarf the current huge flow of debt service capital from South to North. Such measures are designed to insure that U.S.-based corporations control the technology of the future, including biotechnology, which, it is hoped, will allow protected private enterprise to control health, agriculture and the means of life generally, locking the poor majority into dependence and hopelessness. The same methods are being employed to undermine Canada's annoyingly efficient health services by imposing barriers to the use of generic drugs, thus sharply raising costs—and profits to state-subsidized U.S. corporations. NAFTA also includes intricate "rules of origin" requirements designed to keep foreign competitors out. Two hundred pages are devoted to rules to insure a high percentage of value added in North America (protectionist measures that should be increased, some U.S. opponents of NAFTA argue). Furthermore, the agreements go far beyond trade (itself not really trade but in large part intracompany transfers, as noted). A prime U.S. objective is liberalization of services, which would allow supranational banks to displace domestic competitors and thus eliminate any threat of national economic planning and independent development. The agreements impose a mixture of liberalization and protection, designed to keep wealth and power firmly in the hands of the masters of the "new imperial age."

NAFTA is an executive agreement, reached on August 12, 1992, just in time to become a major issue in the U.S. presidential campaign. It was mentioned, but barely. To give just one example of how debate was precluded, take the case of the Labor Advisory Committee (L.A.C.), established by the Trade Act of 1974 to advise the executive branch on any trade agreement. The L.A.C., which is based in the unions, was informed that its report on NAFTA was due on September 9. The text of this intricate treaty was provided to it one day before. In its report, the L.A.C. notes, "the Administration refused to permit any outside advice on the development of this document and refused to make a draft available for comment." The situation in Canada and Mexico was similar. The facts are not even reported. In such ways, we approach the long sought ideal: formal democratic procedures that are devoid of meaning, as citizens not only do not intrude into the public arena but scarcely have an idea of the policies that will shape their lives.

One can readily understand the need to keep the public "in its place." Though the scanty press coverage has been overwhelmingly favorable to

NAFTA in its present form, the public opposed it by nearly 2 to 1 (of the 60 percent who have an opinion). Apart from some meager rhetoric and a few interventions by Ross Perot, that fact was irrelevant to the presidential campaign, as were health reform and a host of other issues on which public opinion remains largely off the spectrum of options considered by the "responsible men."

The Labor Advisory Committee concluded that the executive treaty would be a bonanza for investors but would harm U.S. workers and probably Mexicans as well. One likely consequence is an acceleration of migration from rural to urban areas as Mexican corn producers are wiped out by U.S. agribusiness, depressing still further wages that have already dropped sharply in recent years and are likely to remain low, thanks to the harsh repression that is a crucial element of the highly touted Mexican "economic miracle." Labor's share of personal income in Mexico declined from 36 percent in the mid-1970s to 23 percent by 1992, reports economist David Barkin, while fewer than 8,000 accounts (including 1,500 owned by foreigners) control more than 94 percent of stock shares in public hands.

Property rights are well protected by NAFTA, the L.A.C. analysts and others note, while workers' rights are ignored. The treaty is also likely to have harmful environmental effects, encouraging a shift of production to regions where enforcement is lax. NAFTA "will have the effect of prohibiting democratically elected bodies at [all] levels of government from enacting measures deemed inconsistent with the provisions of the agreement," the L.A.C. report continues, including those on the environment, workers' rights, and health and safety, all open to challenge as "unfair restraint of trade."

Such developments are already under way in the framework of the United States-Canada "free trade" agreement. Included are efforts to require Canada to abandon measures to protect the Pacific salmon, to bring pesticide and emissions regulations in line with laxer U.S. standards, to end subsidies for replanting after logging and to bar a single payer auto insurance plan in Ontario that would cost U.S. insurance companies hundreds of millions of dollars in profits. Meanwhile Canada has charged the United States with violating "fair trade" by imposing E.P.A. standards on asbestos use and requiring recycled fiber in newsprint. Under both NAFTA and GATT, there are endless options for undermining popular efforts to protect conditions of life.

In general, the L.A.C. report concludes, "U.S. corporations, and the owners and managers of these corporations, stand to reap enormous profits. The United States as a whole, however, stands to lose and particular groups stand to lose an enormous amount." The report calls for renegotiation, offering a series of constructive proposals. That remains a possibility if the coalition of labor, environmental and other popular groups that has been calling for such changes gains sufficient popular support [see Amy Lowrey and David Corn, "Mexican Trade Bill: Fast Track to Unemployment," The *Nation,* June 3, 1991].

An October 1992 report from the Congressional Office of Technology Assessment reached similar conclusions. A "bare" NAFTA of the form now on the table would ratify "the mismanagement of economic integration" and could "lock the United States into a low-wage, low-productivity future." Radically altered to incorporate "domestic and continental social policy measures and parallel understandings with Mexico on environmental and labor issues," NAFTA could have beneficial consequences for the country. But the country is only of secondary concern to the masters, who are playing a different game. Its rules are revealed by what the *New York Times* called "Paradox of '92: Weak Economy, Strong Profits." As a geographical entity, "the country" may decline. But the interests of the "principal architects" of policy will be "most peculiarly attended to."

NAFTA, GATT, AND THE WORLD TRADE ORGANIZATION:

The New Rules for Corporate Conquest

KRISTIN DAWKINS

COUNTERING THE CORPORATE ORDER

It's called the World Trade Organization—a brand new institution designed to manage a world order based on corporate control of the planet's productive and reproductive rights. It is the crowning achievement of the Uruguay Round negotiations of the GATT, the General Agreement on Tariffs and Trade. Under the World Trade Organization each member country "shall ensure the conformity of its law, regulations and administrative procedures with its obligations as provided" in the new rules of the GATT. The World Trade Organization—or WTO—will have what they call "legal personality," as much authority in other words as the United Nations or the World Bank. One of its goals is "to achieve greater coherence in global economic policy-making" in tandem with the World Bank and the International Monetary Fund, says the founding document. However, the founding document makes no reference at all to the United Nations. The net result is that the nations of the world will have less and less of a voice in determining their economic futures.

Likewise, the North American Free Trade Agreement (NAFTA) establishes new international laws that can neutralize or override a given country's democratically enacted policies. Both the Uruguay Round of GATT and NAFTA arm transnational corporations with unprecedented political power. Both are the legacy of the Reagan-Bush agenda to "liberalize" trade and deregulate investment. Both were supported and finalized by President Clinton. Without the capacity to manage economic and financial flows, many countries, the United States included, will experience worsening deficits, sky-rocketing unemployment, and ecological catastrophe. Only by stopping the "free trade" agenda can we preserve the opportunity in countries all over the world to develop alternative models for rebuilding communities.

We came very close to stopping NAFTA in November 1993. Nationwide organizing among labor and environmentalists, consumers, farmers, and others produced the most powerful and popular coalition this country has seen in decades. Up until a few days before the final vote on NAFTA in the U.S. Congress, it looked like a majority of the House of Representatives would vote "no," thanks to grass-roots pressure nationwide. However, in a revealing display of the democratic process in America, the Clinton Administration persuaded a couple dozen legislators to switch their votes at the last minute by promising them billions of dollars worth of "pork," as it's called. Conservative columnist George Will wrote on November 11 that "votes are for sale and the President is buying."

Ralph Nader's office prepared a nice list showing that the pork included contracts for six C-17 military cargo planes for Texas representative Eddie Bernice Johnson, scaling back proposed cigarette taxes for North Carolina Representative Charlie Rose, allowing vegetables to continue being saturated with the cancer-causing, ozone-depleting pesticide methyl bromide for several Floridian congresspersons, delays in cleaning up the Boston Harbor, financing for the construction of new bridges and trade centers, aircraft carriers, and so on.

Although Congress voted 234-200 in favor of NAFTA, the coalition's efforts were not in vain. The American public saw how our democratic process really works and we learned which congresspeople cannot be relied upon under political pressure from the White House. We learned how trade negotiations affect jobs, health, and the environment and how our economy is linked with that of Mexico and other countries. Organized labor learned about environmental issues and environmentalists learned about labor rights. Members of consumer organizations learned how food safety is jeopardized by federal farm policy, and farmers found friends in the consumer movement. Activists from the United States formed alliances with activists from Mexico and Canada. Now we must build upon this experience to sustain a grass-roots national movement that can effectively collaborate with international partners to fight for a sensible economic development strategy—one that I characterize as community-based instead of corporate-based, even in the context of the global economy.

THE PRODUCTIVE AND REPRODUCTIVE SECTOR

Third World critics of free trade are very advanced in terms of devising alternatives to the corporate order. I'm not talking about utopian scenarios, but practical scenarios to ensure that community-based economic and political systems can continue to function. In the heart of the industrialized world, it sometimes is difficult to imagine what the alternative scenarios might look like. We stand to learn much from people in communities elsewhere in the world.

A community-based model for economic development is grounded in an understanding of the *productive* and *reproductive rights of the planet*. By productive rights, I mean productivity in the sense of the economy, labor force, plants, and technology that yield the gross domestic product. By reproductive rights I mean the ecology of the planet, the natural resources that exist, the biotic systems that enable life to continue, and the way in which humans interact with the environment. In both areas, the productive and reproductive sectors, the corporate agenda seeks to gain control over resources. We as a community movement, on the other hand, are trying to maintain or regain community control over those resources. Who but the communities which have lived with them for millennia, until the present Western model of development began to encroach, understand what the reproductive thresholds of a particular ecological system really are?

When you look at the famine in Somalia, or at any number of other communities that are in deep crisis, you can usually trace the reasons for that trouble back to the intervention of the Western mode of development. The Somalis were originally a nomadic people. What are called "warlords" in the media are actually tribal leaders of peoples who roamed throughout their territory. They had a particular lifestyle that existed in accord with the kinds of land and water resources that existed there. However, when the global economic system entered the picture, the indigenous social order was disrupted and quickly destroyed. Traditional agriculture systems in Somalia and elsewhere were displaced and eventually destroyed by corporate agribusiness which produces cash crops for exports, crops that the indigenous people in those communities cannot even eat. The cash crops, in turn, generate foreign exchange that is used to pay off debts to the World Bank, or to private banking institutions. In the end, virtually none of the profit derived from the natural resources of these countries goes back to the people. Their agriculture system becomes a cash crop, a variable in an equation controlled by the international banking industry.

To survive under corporate agribusiness control, the people then need to either purchase imported food or, in many cases, starvation ensues—in part because nomads and peasants lack cash to purchase foods and in part because cash crops are grown as monocultures based on single varieties of seed requiring extensive land use and chemicals, which destroy the soil and its biotic ecosystems. At that point people become unable to grow even subsistence levels of food for their own families. This is the cycle responsible for the desertification throughout Africa. It's also the cycle disrupting social systems that function in a very different context than what we think of as the Western social order. As a result, we have famine and war spreading throughout the planet.

HISTORY BEHIND GATT

In this century, GATT and the other Bretton Woods institutions—the World Bank and the International Monetary Fund—have been the main instigators of these kinds of patterns. They're called the Bretton Woods institutions because they were designed in a small New Hampshire town by that name. The world's financial elite convened there back in 1944. Their ostensible purpose was to help Europe and avoid a repetition of the conditions that led to World War II. The less ostensible but more valid interpretation of their interest in rebuilding Europe was that the United States still had a highly industrialized infrastructure producing products for which we did not have consumers. Rebuilding Europe was essentially part of a plan to increase markets for the U.S. productive sector.

Formalized in 1948, GATT is now an agreement among more than 100 countries, each of which, in theory, has equal power in negotiating the rules of global trade in resources and finished products. The seeming equality of participation of membership in GATT is actually an illusion. The power of decision making resides with those countries that have the largest market share for whichever product is being negotiated. U.S.-based transnational corporations control approximately 70 percent of grains worldwide. This means that when the United States starts negotiating food policy with other countries, if the other countries are importing and dependent upon us for their food supply, then they have no real political leverage with which to negotiate.

THE URUGUAY ROUND

Over the years, from 1948 to today, GATT has gone through a lot of negotiated changes. Negotiators for the Clinton Administration and Europe finally worked out a number of compromises to conclude the very controversial eighth round, called the Uruguay Round after the country in which it was started in 1986. With the creation of the World Trade Organization (WTO), if the signatory countries' congresses or parliaments endorse it, the very nature of trade policymaking will change. One likely change is that national decision-making processes to approve or disapprove new trade policies will disappear. Instead, the creation of international laws affecting trade-related economic, environmental, and other social policy will lie in the hands of unaccountable trade bureaucrats.

The Uruguay Round of GATT was encouraged by the chairman of American Express, James Robinson, III, who has since resigned. It was his and Ronald Reagan's initiative back in 1986 that got 108 countries to sit down together at the negotiating table. It is not therefore surprising that one of the proposals in the Uruguay Round was to add "services"—banking, insurance, and so on—to the GATT's authority. Gradually, nations would lose their right to base their economies on domestic banking, insurance, transportation, public utilities, and other critical service sectors. The impact would have been so grave that other countries have, so far, successfully fought off this proposal. Also in the Uruguay Round were proposals to deregulate agriculture in unprecedented ways. This text was drafted by Daniel Amstutz, a vice president of the Cargill Company, one of the biggest agribusiness firms in the world. It's not a coincidence that small farmers worldwide have been in the forefront of opposition to the deregulation of national agriculture polices. In this case, the opponents lost. The new World Trade Organization will enforce the new rules for agriculture which will create the conditions for a global race to the bottom in terms of food prices, food safety, and food quality, and spell the end of policies that promote national food security.

TRIPS, TRIMS, AND "TRADE BARRIERS"

The Uruguay Round of negotiations also opened a Pandora's box of non-tariff issues including two that are of special importance to developing countries: TRIPs and TRIMs. TRIPs are *trade-related intellectual property rights* and refer to the rules that would allow companies to strengthen their monopoly of patented intellectual property and new technology. Enforced by the new World Trade Organization, TRIPs inhibit economic development, slow the application of the best available, environment-friendly technologies, and hinder the development of non-resource-intensive industries in the Third World. Third World communities are opposed to the double standard in the way TRIPs will be applied. Third World proposals for TRIPs protecting their genetic resources and indigenous technologies were disregarded by the high-tech countries during the Uruguay Round negotiations and will not be recognized by the World Trade Organization.

Trade-related investment measures, called TRIMs, are now in place in many countries, so that when a major corporation comes into the country, the corporation is required to invest in certain areas of the local economy. One such TRIM requirement might be to buy a certain amount of the inputs for a product from the host country, so that there is some trickle down. Another requirement might be to employ a certain number of the country's people, ensuring a degree of job development. There are a wide variety of investment measures that countries impose upon foreign corporations when they come in. With the establishment of the World Trade Organization, however, those TRIMs will become illegal trade barriers. This is all part of the deregulatory regime of the Uruguay Round of GATT. The resulting drain of resources from a national economy to foreign investors will hinder the ability of many countries to promote local development and environmental protection.

From its beginning in the 1940s, GATT dealt mostly with tariffs, which are essentially taxes, on traded manufactured goods. In the intervening rounds it began to address what are called *non-tariff barriers,* the set of rules and regulations that countries impose upon trade. For example, a border inspection is considered a non-tariff barrier because the inspection is not reflected as a tariff on the traded goods. Under the Uruguay Round agreement, countries will be bound to a whole new set of rules that deregulate non-tariff barriers—rules that can override a country's own laws, including environmental regulations. For example, GATT dispute panels have obliged Indonesia to lift its ban on the export of raw logs and obliged Thailand to lift its ban on the import of tobacco—on grounds that these laws were "disguised barriers to trade." From a GATT-level, corporate perspective, another country's environmental regulations restricting the import of products that endanger health and safety or perhaps have been processed in an ecologically unsafe manner may be seen as unacceptable trade restrictions. The tuna-dolphin case probably explains this better than any other example.

THE TUNA-DOLPHIN CASE

My family boycotted tuna fish throughout my whole childhood. We participated in a long-term boycott campaign to require companies to use a new type
of fishing technique that didn't kill dolphins. After many years, we finally won,
and we all began to eat tuna fish again. But Mexico and some other countries
didn't have the resources with which to upgrade their fishing boats. They continued to fish with the old fashioned purse seine nets. In many cases, the fisher-
men lived in rural beach communities, yet when they brought their fish to
market they were able to sell into the global trade.

Mexico objected to our Marine Mammal Protection Act, and they used the
GATT to do so. They said that our ecological law protecting dolphins was a
barrier to their ability to trade in tuna fish. One key principle in the GATT
establishes that discrimination between "like products"—tuna fish from one
country vs. tuna fish from another country—is "illegal." A new precedent,
however, was set in the tuna-dolphin case. That precedent says that *you're not
allowed to discriminate on the basis of processes,* specifically. Essentially most
ecological measures—whether you're talking about smokestack scrubbers or
solar panels—involve alternative *production processes.* But, in this case, tuna
caught one way cannot be treated differently, said the GATT dispute-resolution
panel, than tuna caught another way.

If the tuna-dolphin case is a precedent, it means that in any number of areas
it would become illegal to restrict the import of products that were made with
ecologically unsound production methods. Now, if you're a poor, Third World
country, you might want to invest in environmental technologies, but you can't
afford to. This was one of the big issues at the Earth Summit: whether or not
technology transfer would be made possible through international policy. The
United States' position was, absolutely not: technology will be made available
at strictly commercial rates.

There is another important item to understand in the tuna-dolphin case. The
GATT panel ruling says that *no nation can pass a national law that affects territory beyond its national boundaries.* In the case of tuna fishing, national
boundaries are considered to extend for a 200 mile zone into the deep oceans.
Because our national law would apply to tuna caught beyond the 200 mile
zone, the GATT panel decided that our national law was unfair.

So, on the one hand, Mexico cannot afford to upgrade its fishing boats. On
the other hand, U.S. citizens are denied their right to pass laws banning

inhumane products. The solution to this conflict lies in the negotiation of international agreements that enable the transfer of technology and funds, through a variety of tariff and non-tariff mechanisms, to enable small- and medium-sized businesses throughout the Third World to invest in upgrading to meet ecological standards, so that a lack of environmental protection does not become a competitive advantage.

Now that the Uruguay Round negotiations are over, there is an effort among many environmentalists to counteract the tuna-dolphin precedent and allow countries to discriminate against goods that are not made with ecologically-sound "production-and-process-methods," a concept newly crowned with its own jargon and acronym—PPMs. The problem is that rules requiring ecologically sound PPMs could hurt a lot of Third World economies if they are not combined with rules ensuring affordable access to environmental technologies. To make matters worse, PPMs and other trade-related environmental policies are being planned by the 24 wealthiest industrialized countries through the Organization for Economic Cooperation and Development (OECD). While the OECD has invited some input from environmentalists in OECD countries, neither Third World governments nor Third World environmentalists are involved.

INTELLECTUAL PROPERTY AND THE BIODIVERSITY CONVENTION

The controversy in the tuna-dolphin case was exacerbated by the U.S. position in the Earth Summit negotiations where it was quite clear that our government had no interest whatsoever in making ecological upgrades possible for other countries. Nor was there even an interest in advancing ecological practices here in our own country. Two treaties indicate this quite clearly. The Biodiversity Convention, which ostensibly was intended to protect species, is not really about species. George Bush did not sign this treaty—alone among 156 signatories in Rio de Janeiro—because U.S. negotiators failed to draft a sufficiently strong TRIPs clause. Nevertheless, the treaty does permit biotechnology corporations to declare genes as their private property—a variation on the TRIPs rule of the new WTO.

Declaring genetic matter as corporate property prevents indigenous communities from participating in free trade and profiting from generations of unique cultivation. Transnational corporations introduce genetically engineered varieties of those plants into the global marketplace and reap all the profit.

Corporate scientists visit remote native communities, find out from the local people what plants have medicinal or food value, take samples back to the corporate lab for "engineering," and patent the resulting species as commercial products owned and controlled by the corporation. The community that developed the original material will not only receive zero benefits or royalties for having cultivated a unique species, but now they must actually *purchase* the seeds or derivative medicines to avoid violation of international patents and infringement of GATT laws.

Third World negotiators managed to achieve some rights under the Biodiversity Convention, including clauses that required some compensation be paid by patent-holders to the so-called country of origin for a given gene. President Clinton has now signed it, but his administration has made it clear that they will send it to Congress for ratification with an interpretive statement insisting "any access to or transfer of technology that occurs in this agreement recognizes and is consistent with the adequate and effective protection of intellectual property rights," thus strengthening the rights of the biotechnology industry while denying both the intellectual property rights of peasants, farmers, and indigenous cultivators of valuable genetic varieties and the financial difficulties of developing countries.

THE CLIMATE CHANGE CONVENTION AND OIL

The Climate Change negotiations had a somewhat different set of interests working. Here, oil companies stood to lose from strong regulations against global warming practices. You may remember that George Bush said he would not attend the Earth Summit in Rio—until the very last week prior to the conference. This was a tactic, a successful strategy which forced the world's industrialized countries to accept weaker treaty terms. Eventually, Bush went and the United States did sign it, but only after watering it down so that countries must merely *aim* to reduce their emissions—with no obligation to really do so under international law. To Bill Clinton's credit, during his first weeks as President he committed his administration to earlier, more stringent terms—a firm commitment to reduce carbon dioxide emissions to 1990 levels by the year 2000. When the Congress rejected his plan to tax energy consumption during partisan battles over his first budget, however, Clinton backed away from these goals.

Indeed, President Clinton's willingness to retreat from the oil-and-gas lobbyists during the first budget fight and his bombing of Iraq immediately upon taking office indicate it will be business-as-usual for the U.S. oil industry. Much of Clinton's foreign policy—especially his militarism—merely continues plans conceived during the Reagan-Bush years. The point is that too many of the foreign policy initiatives that have been promoted as socially, ecologically, or economically for the betterment of humanity are, in reality, just charades intended to increase the access of the largest corporations to other peoples' natural resources.

THE ROLE OF THE MILITARY

We need to question the role of the military in international affairs. If you look at what's happening in the United Nations right now, there are proposals for peacekeeping initiatives billed as humanitarian interventions in a dozen countries. The *Los Angeles Times* ran a report in 1992 showing that *two-thirds of Somalia's territory has been leased out to four oil companies.* Only a few other papers picked up that story, including the *International Herald Tribune* on January 19, 1993. Indeed, with massive budget cuts in the UN agencies for social and economic development and increases for "peacekeeping," the United Nations itself threatens to become a military instrument of corporate power.

The current Secretary General of the United Nations, Boutros Boutros-Ghali, comes from Egypt, the number two client state of the United States, second to Israel. Within two weeks of taking office as George Bush's favorite candidate for the top job at the United Nations, Boutros-Ghali eliminated the only agency in the world that was attempting to regulate transnational corporations, the United Nations Center on Transnational Corporations (UNCTC). Now, a much reduced staff relocated to Geneva is called the new Transnational Corporations and Management Division of the United Nations. However, the UNCTC's extensive data base and policy recommendations remain in the UN archives and are a valuable resource to keep in mind.

Boutros-Ghali and his secretariat have reorganized the entire UN system while shifting the budget of the UN General Assembly away from economic and social cooperation. So-called peacekeeping operations are controlled by the small group of 5 powerful countries with a veto in the UN Security Council. But let's be very careful about what UN peacekeeping really means. In Somalia, UN peacekeeping means fighting over natural resources that are of interest to the transnational corporations. When the "peacekeeping" forces employ Third World soldiers instead of our own sons and daughters, then the potential for a powerful resistance movement in this country is very much diminished.

We, as citizens of the United States, have a global responsibility to question and challenge the lethal use of our military in interventions throughout the world. We must challenge its use to access the natural resources of other countries. We also have a responsibility to monitor events at the United Nations and among the Bretton Woods institutions, where our government plays a leading role. We cannot accept free trade or any other international agreements that are designed to supply the corporate world with cheap resources and cheap labor.

NAFTA'S NEW WORLD ECONOMY

Allowing corporations to exploit land, labor, and natural resources is equally the agenda behind NAFTA as well as GATT. Both strategies weaken the nation-state by eroding regulatory barriers to trade. For now, NAFTA is between Canada, the United States, and Mexico. However, one of NAFTA's most important clauses goes unreported in the mass media—its *accession clause*. We will soon notice that most other Latin American countries, not to mention New Zealand and several Asian nations, begin negotiating for access to NAFTA.

The accession clause significantly alters the economy of NAFTA. If you think about it as a regional agreement between the United States, Canada, and Mexico, it's possible to anticipate some of the economic effects. With an active accession clause, NAFTA will have a much less predictable economic impact. Take the trade in sugar, for example. If NAFTA were limited to just Mexico, the United States, and Canada, we could anticipate the sugar trade to be displaced in the United States while Mexican farmers would experience the opportunity to develop that industry. With other countries signing on through the accession clause, however, sugar would be able to enter the North American market from almost anywhere in the world and compete with both the U.S. and Mexican sectors. Thus, the accession clause is the open door for corporations to locate anywhere in the world where costs will be lower and yet have easy access to the U.S. market.

It is difficult to estimate the impact the globalized economy will have on jobs—although economists try. Using a global model, an econometric forecasting associate at the University of Pennsylvania projects that 1,400,000 U.S. jobs are vulnerable under GATT. The University of Massachusetts and Skidmore College came out with a study that said that under NAFTA up to 450,000 jobs are vulnerable. Their results are based on the fact that Mexico and other poor countries have a comparative advantage in low wages and non-enforced environmental regulations making it desirable for companies to relocate from more expensive places like the United States.

The Bush Administration's cheeriest economic projection suggested that only 64,000 jobs would be created by NAFTA. Analysts from the Economic Policy Institute examined the Bush Administration study and found two assumptions built into the projection that make it laughable. The first laugh comes from their assumption of full employment in the United States. The second laugh comes from their assumption that the Mexicans will become wealthy through trickle-down policies and begin to purchase American products that continue to be made *in the United States* by companies that haven't run south to Mexico and elsewhere.

The jobs that we're going to lose first are entry-level labor positions. We're talking about jobs held by women and people of color primarily: jobs in the garment industry, the food processing industry, and, to some extent, the automobile industry. Many more family farms in the United States will also fail as price supports and other policies are declared "trade barriers" by both the World Trade Organization and NAFTA's new bureaucracies.

Still an agrarian society, Mexico stands to lose some 2 to 12 million jobs in agriculture. About a third of its people still live off the land. Many of them live in what we would consider poverty, but many of them are growing enough food to feed themselves and their families. Under the deregulation that NAFTA brings to the Mexican agricultural sector, price supports for the food they eat— corn and beans—will be considered a non-tariff trade barrier to U.S. agribusiness. The Mexican government will be obliged to eliminate price supports to Mexican farmers, and the people who grow corn in that country will no longer be able to afford to do so. Instead, they will have to buy corn from the United States. (The world price for corn is far cheaper than the price that the government pays to corn farmers in Mexico today.)

Treating labor as just another tradable commodity, NAFTA paves the road toward massive urbanization. Mexico City, already one of the largest and arguably the most polluted cities in the world, will be inundated with new immigrants. The number of new jobs that might be created in industry will not approximate those that will be lost in agriculture. Our borders will feel new pressure as more Mexicans trying to compete with us for fewer jobs attempt to enter the United States illegally, because there is no reform of immigration policy in NAFTA.

SETTLING DISPUTES: GATT VS. NAFTA

The NAFTA text explicitly states that its rules will be "consistent" with the GATT although there are various differences. The most significant, probably, is a reversal of the burden of proof in a dispute. Although, as Zen Makuch of the Canadian Environmental Law Foundation has pointed out, "the onus of proof only plays a determinative role in legal cases that are evenly balanced, and trade disputes have not, to date, demonstrated such a fine balancing of evidence and law." Under GATT, a nation is considered guilty unless proven innocent; that is, the defendant must prove that its trade practice does not discriminate or otherwise violate the rules. Under NAFTA, the complainant must prove its case.

Switching the burden of proof could give some protection to nations legislating environmental, health, and other social regulations that have trade effects—like those of Indonesia and Thailand which I mentioned earlier. For example, the GATT dispute-panel ruling against the Marine Mammal Protection Act might not have occurred under a NAFTA panel, where Mexico would have had to prove that this national law was not primarily a conservation measure.

However, because the United States, Mexico, and Canada are all members of GATT, most of their disputes would also be eligible for resolution under the new World Trade Organization. The NAFTA text affirms that, in such cases, the complainant may choose either set of rules; logic suggests that most complainants would choose the GATT rules, thus switching the burden of proof back to the accused. Then again, NAFTA says that the defendant can insist upon a NAFTA dispute-resolution panel if the case involves facts regarding certain environmental, health, and safety standards and certain international environmental agreements. But what are truly "facts"? Panels may be needed first to determine what is and is not factual—in aspects of policy that depend upon subjective judgments regarding risk, cause-and-effect, and so on.

Otherwise, a NAFTA dispute-settlement panel will consist of five members, not three as is traditional in the GATT. Also unlike GATT, a NAFTA panel "may" include experts specializing in fields other than trade; thus a nation may nominate environmentalists, lawyers, and "other" experts to the roster of potential panelists—although consulting this expertise is not obligatory. If both of the disputing parties agree, NAFTA will allow special scientific review boards to advise a panel on questions of fact. Separate provisions govern disputes over financial matters, intellectual property, agriculture, anti-dumping cases, and other cases brought to a NAFTA dispute proceeding. But just like GATT, NAFTA panels would be subject to strict confidentiality with no provision requiring public input.

In some ways, the NAFTA actually contradicts the GATT. For example, in NAFTA, Canadian farmers resisted negotiators' attempts to force them to discontinue managing the supply of dairy products, wheat, and other crops. Obviously, if you manage the supply you can avoid the kinds of gluts that cause prices to fall below sustainable levels and, at the same time, you can generally better manage food safety and farm income. But the new rules for agriculture in the Uruguay Round agreement will force Canada to end this very successful program.

The new World Trade Organization will also inhibit the setting of national food safety laws that are stronger than those established by an international body controlled by the food industry! "Codex Alimentarius," for example, is a standard-setting agency of the UN Food and Agriculture Organization, in which the Nestlés Corporation alone has more personnel representing different countries' governments than has any one government! The U.S. delegation at recent Codex meetings included advisors from General Mills, Kraft, Purina, Pepsi-Cola, Coca-Cola, etc. In the name of the U.S. government, these food industry representatives negotiated international standards governing pesticides, sanitation, and food additives that do less to protect people than our own national laws prescribe. Outside democratic checks and balances, corporations are gaining control of rules and regulations that compromise the quality of our lives and the well-being of the planet.

Under the Uruguay Round agreement, governments wishing to defend a national law that is stricter than what Codex has established must show that their domestic law is scientifically based and the least trade-restrictive way possible to achieve the stated goal. Innocent sounding enough, but can we believe the scientists employed by the R.J. Reynolds tobacco company when they claim that cigarette smoking does not cause cancer? Can we accept the notion that the less trade-restrictive policy of shipping beverages in recycled aluminum cans achieves the same environmental goal as the more trade-restrictive policy of returning and reusing bottles? I think these two examples show how these seemingly simple criteria—scientific justification and least trade restrictive—are subject to much judgment and political discretion. Yet, in the World Trade Organization, this judgment will be exercised by trade bureaucrats who view commercial activity as the end-all and be-all of international relations. Even the NAFTA, weak as it is, has a better approach to settling disputes than the Uruguay Round agreement of the GATT. Now we have to deal with both.

CLINTON'S "SIDE AGREEMENTS" LACK TEETH

In NAFTA, environmentalists and organized labor lobbied intensively for side agreements which would include citizens in the dispute-settlement process, provide adjustment for displaced workers, ensure the right to organize and strike, preserve higher standards, and clean up the toxic conditions in the unregulated industrial zones along the U.S.-Mexican border, called the *maquiladoras*. Lack of regulations in these zones has resulted in well-documented "free trade atrocities," as in the cases of babies being born without brains. In total disregard for human life, companies dump their wastes right into the streets—*with children playing in them!* The water supply that irrigates the agriculture belt along California and Texas is at risk, too, because it draws from the same untreated source. Clinton's side agreements, however, achieve none of these goals although they do set up bureaucratic systems where complaints can be formally lodged.

After a year of secret negotiations, the Clinton side agreements were finally made public. Critics found them weak. Some pointed out that they do not begin to fix major problems in the original text such as the emphasis on agricultural concentration or guarantees of undiminished energy exports. Others remembered the long list of Clinton's campaign promises—not the least of which was protection for national and state laws setting higher standards than those of the international bureaucracies. Of all the Clinton promises, however, the three new agreements address only the creation of trinational labor and environmental commissions and reiterate the original NAFTA terms regarding sudden gluts of imports, called "surges."

Some critics would have been satisfied with the supplemental agreements if they were ensured a dispute-settlement mechanism with "teeth." But the teeth are missing. Indeed, according to the *Journal of Commerce,* Mexico's chief NAFTA negotiator Jaime Serra Puche told the Mexican Senate not to worry about the threat of fines and trade sanctions resulting from the supplemental agreements. The trilateral commissions' powers are limited, he said on August 17, 1993, and the "exceedingly long" dispute-resolution process "makes it very improbable that the stage of sanctions could be reached." Furthermore, the maximum penalty would be a fine or suspension of benefits worth $20 million—peanuts to any of the three governments.

The text also carefully circumscribes which laws are subject to the jurisdiction of the trilateral commissions. Only those environmental laws affecting the production of tradable goods and services are at stake; laws whose "primary purpose" is natural resource management are explicitly excluded. Likewise, labor laws guaranteeing the right to freely associate and organize, to bargain collectively, and to strike are excluded; only "mutually recognized" laws and regulations addressing workplace health and safety, a minimum wage, and child labor are subject to dispute resolution. Neither commission may refer complaints—even those meeting all criteria—to a dispute-resolution panel unless two of the three countries' governments agree.

SCRAPS FOR THE PUBLIC

A careful reading shows that the three supplemental agreements altogether create ten new bureaucracies with responsibilities that are largely informational. Words like "consider," "consult," "report," "recommend," "promote," and "work toward" abound. And the entire side agreement on surges is, according to the three governments' official summary, merely an "Understanding" that "confirms the...effective use of Chapter Eight of the NAFTA" by establishing a Working Group on Emergency Action which "may make recommendations" to the governing bodies created by the NAFTA text itself.

On the other hand, an argument can be made that the side agreements enable a degree of accessibility. Working groups, advisory boards, and other channels of communication are established. Individual citizens may bring complaints to the environmental commission—although not to the labor commission where only national governments have standing. If a dispute panel is convened, panelists may have expertise in fields other than trade policy and a panel may, if all parties agree, summon environmental, labor, and other expertise.

In the context of accessibility, it is notable that the Clinton Administration chose to appeal and succeeded in overturning a federal judge's ruling that the National Environmental Policy Act requires an Environmental Impact Statement to be conducted on NAFTA. A Mexican coalition of labor, peasant, and environmental groups, also filed its own request for an evaluation of the environmental impact of NAFTA on Mexico, citing their Constitutional guarantees of "the right to health, the conservation of productive resources and the care of ecosystems and natural resources" and other national laws. It will require all the wit and resources of labor and environmental advocates to take advantage of the NAFTA commissions and test their usefulness as instruments of justice.

ORGANIZING & RESISTANCE

Armed peasants in Chiapas, a southern state of Mexico, denounced NAFTA as "a death sentence for the indigenous people." Chief among their demands are land reform and democracy, quite the opposite of NAFTA and its agriculture policy. In a letter published in Mexican newspapers, the Zapatista National Liberation Army explained that, a "handful of businesses, one of which is the state of Mexico, take all the wealth out of Chiapas leaving behind...ecological destruction, agricultural scraps, hyperinflation, alcoholism, prostitution, and poverty." In another letter addressed to President Clinton and the people of the United States, the Zapatistas implored us, "do not stain your hands with our blood by allowing yourselves to be the accomplices of the Mexican government."

In the spirit of alternative cooperative relations on our continent, Mexicans, Canadians, and U.S. activists organized numerous trinational meetings throughout the NAFTA negotiations. For example, the corn farmers from the three countries sat down and hammered out a policy on corn that would have satisfied all the farmers although it was ignored by government negotiators. Similarly, dairy farmers, timber workers, auto workers, environmental workers, and garment workers have had trilateral meetings of this sort.

A number of innovative proposals for using international agreements go beyond trade—which is essentially a commercial agreement—and bring in a comprehensive range of other issues. Cuauhtémoc Cárdenas, leader of the opposition party in Mexico, who many people believe won the election Salinas stole from him by fraud, has written an impressive and simple five-page paper outlining ten different items that would go into a fair *continental initiative* as he calls it—not a trade agreement, but a continental initiative.

Others are developing interesting ideas about technology and development. Herman Daly, an economist who just retired from the World Bank, has proposed a number of specific criteria for using technology to ensure sustainable development. Appropriate technology, Daly argues, would harvest renewable resources and create wastes at a rate no greater than the earth can replenish and assimilate them. The Green Forum (Philippines) argues that gross domestic product (GDP) only measures the wealth of corporations, whereas household income measures the welfare of the community. The Green Forum also incorporates ecological assets into its concept of "Community Networth." By substituting "ecological zones" for arbitrary political districts, it becomes easier to calculate the ecological costs of production that would be paid to a community by the corporations that exploit their natural resources.

Non-governmental groups at the Earth Summit in Rio de Janeiro negotiated among themselves about 40 "alternative treaties" (see the Econet conference, "unced.treaties") that cover a whole range of issues regarding international development and a fair world order. I worked on the one that addressed fair trade in very specific terms.

Unfortunately, implementing these and other proposals for fair international policies will be nearly impossible unless there is fundamental change in the structure of the Bretton Woods institutions to make them democratic, accessible, and accountable with economic opportunity and ecological economics balanced in a planetary approach to social development. The new World Trade Organization is a step in the wrong direction. So too are the shifts in the United Nations' budget from the General Assembly to the Security Council.

Global Village or Global Pillage?

Resistance to Top-Down Globalization

JEREMY BRECHER

For most of the world's people, the "New World Economy" is a disaster that has already happened. Those it hurts can't escape it. But neither can they afford to accept it. So many are now seeking ways to reshape it.

When I first started writing about the destructive effects of globalization some three years ago, the North American Free Trade Agreement was widely regarded as a done deal. The near defeat of NAFTA reveals pervasive popular doubt about the wisdom of an unregulated international market.

The struggle against NAFTA represented the first major effort by Americans who have been hurt by global economic integration to do something about it.

Like many mass movements, it included contradictory forces, such as the Mexico-bashing bigotry of Pat Buchanan, the populist grandstanding of Ross Perot, and the nationalistic protectionism of some in the labor movement. But other elements of the struggle against NAFTA prefigure a movement that could radically reshape the New World Economy. Out of their own experiences and observations, millions of Americans have constructed a new paradigm for understanding the global economy. Poor and working people in large numbers have recognized that NAFTA is not primarily about trade; it is about the ability of capital to move without regard to national borders. Capital mobility, not trade, is bringing about the "giant sucking sound" of jobs going South.

For the first time in many years, substantial numbers of people mobilized to act on broad class interests. I haven't seen a movement for years in which so many people at the grass roots took their own initiative. Typical was the unexpectedly large, predominantly blue-collar anti-NAFTA rally in New Haven, where a labor leader told me, "We didn't turn these people out."

NAFTA became a symbol for an accumulation of fears and angers regarding the place of working people in the New World Economy. The North American economic integration that NAFTA was intended to facilitate is only one aspect of a rapid and momentous historical transformation from a system of national economies toward an integrated global economy. New information, communication, transportation, and manufacturing technologies, combined with tariff reductions, have made it possible to coordinate production, commerce, and finance on a world scale. Since 1983, the rate of world foreign direct investment has grown four times as fast as world output.

This transformation has had devastating consequences. They may be summarized as the "seven danger signals" of cancerous, out-of-control globalization:

Race to the bottom. The recent quantum leap in the ability of transnational corporations to relocate their facilities around the world in effect makes all workers, communities, and countries competitors for these corporations' favor. The consequence is a "race to the bottom" in which wages and social and environmental conditions tend to fall to the level of the most desperate. This dynamic underlies U.S. deindustrialization, declining real wages, eradication of job security, and downward pressure on social spending and investment; it is also largely responsible for the migration of low-wage, environmentally destructive industries to poor countries like Mexico and China.

Global stagnation. As each workforce, community, or country seeks to become more competitive by reducing its wages and its social and environmental overheads, the result is a general downward spiral in incomes and social and material infrastructures. Lower wages and reduced public spending mean less buying power, leading to stagnation, recession, and unemployment. This dynamic is aggravated by the accumulation of debt; national economies in poor countries and even in the United States become geared to debt repayment at the expense of consumption, investment, and development. The downward fall is reflected in the slowing of global GNP growth from almost 5 percent per year in the period 1948–1973 to only half that in the period 1974—1989 and to a mere crawl since then.

Polarization of haves and have-nots. As a result of globalization, the gap between rich and poor is increasing both within and between countries around the world. Poor U.S. communities boast world-class unemployment and infant mortality. Meanwhile, tens of billions of dollars a year flow from poor to rich regions of the world, in the form of debt repayment and capital flight.

Loss of democratic control. National governments have lost much of their power to control their own economies. The ability of countries to apply socialist or even Keynesian techniques in pursuit of development, full employment, or other national economic goals has been undermined by the power of capital to pick up and leave. Governmental economic power has been further weakened throughout the world by neo-liberal political movements that have dismantled government institutions for regulating national economies. Globalization has reduced the power of individuals and communities to shape their destinies.

Walter Wriston, former chairman of Citicorp, recently boasted of how "200,000 monitors in trading rooms all over the world" now conduct "a kind of global plebiscite on the monetary and fiscal policies of the governments issuing currency... There is no way for a nation to opt out." Wriston recalls the election of "ardent socialist" Francois Mitterrand in 1981. "The market took one look at his policies and within six months the capital flight forced him to reverse course."

Unfettered transnational corporations. Transnationals have become the world's most powerful economic actors, yet there are no international equivalents to the national antitrust, consumer protection, and other laws that provide a degree of corporate accountability.

Unaccountable global institutions. The loss of national economic control has been accompanied by a growing concentration of unaccountable power in international institutions like the IMF, the World Bank, and GATT. For poor countries, foreign control has been formalized in the World Bank's "Structural Adjustment Plans," but IMF decisions and GATT rules affect the economic growth rates of all countries. The decisions of these institutions also have an enormous impact on the global ecology.

Global conflict. Economic globalization is producing chaotic and destructive rivalries. In a swirl of self-contradictory strategies, major powers and transnationals use global institutions like GATT to impose open markets on their rivals; they pursue trade wars against one other; and they try to construct competing regional blocs like the European Union and NAFTA. In past eras, such rivalries have ultimately led to world war.

In sum, the result of unregulated globalization has been the pillage of the planet and its peoples.

TRANSNATIONAL ECONOMIC PROGRAMS

What are the alternatives to destructive globalization? The right offers racism and nationalism. Conventional protectionism offers no solution. Globalization has also intellectually disarmed the left and rendered national left programs counterproductive. Jimmy Carter's sharp turn to the right in 1978; Francois Mitterrand's rapid abandonment of his radical program; the acceptance of deregulation, privatization, and trade liberalization by poor countries from India to Mexico; and even the decision of Eastern European elites to abandon Communism—all reflect in part the failure of national left policies.

But the beginnings of a new approach emerged from the anti-NAFTA movement itself. Rather than advocate protectionism—keeping foreign products out—many NAFTA opponents urged policies that would raise environmental, labor, and social standards in Mexico, so that those standards would not drag down those in the United States and Canada. This approach implied that people in different countries have common interests in raising the conditions of those at the bottom.

Indeed, the struggle against NAFTA generated new transnational networks based on such common interests. A North American Worker-to-Worker Network links grass-roots labor activists in Mexico, the United States, and Canada via conferences, tours, solidarity support, and a newsletter. Mujer a Mujer similarly links women's groups. The Highlander Center, Southerners for Economic Justice, the Tennessee Industrial Renewal Network, and a number of unions have organized meetings and tours to bring together Mexican and U.S. workers. There are similar networks in other parts of the world, such as the People's Plan 21 in the Asian-Pacific and Central American regions and the Third World Network in Malaysia.

These new networks are developing transnational programs to counter the effects of global economic restructuring. Representatives from environmental, labor, religious, consumer, and farm groups from Mexico, the United States, and Canada have drawn up "A Just and Sustainable Trade and Development Initiative for North America." A parallel synthesis, "From Global Pillage to Global Village," has been endorsed by more than sixty grass-roots organizations. Related proposals by the Third World Network have recently been published as "Toward a New North-South Economic Dialogue."

Differing in emphasis and details, these emerging alternative programs are important not only because of the solutions they propose, but also because those solutions have emerged from a dialogue rooted in such a diversity of groups and experiences. Some require implementation by national policy; some by international agreement; some can be implemented by transnational citizen action. Taken together, they provide what might be described as "seven prescriptions" for the seven danger signals of the unregulated global economy:

International rights and standards. To prevent competition from resulting in a "race to the bottom," several of these groups propose to establish minimum human, labor, and environmental rights and standards, as the European Union's "social charter" was designed to do. The International Metalworkers Federation recently proposed a ten-point "World Social Charter," which could be incorporated into GATT.

"A Just and Sustainable Trade and Development Initiative for North America" spells out in some detail an alternative to NAFTA that would protect human and worker rights, encourage workers' income to rise in step with productivity, and establish continental environmental rights, such as the right to a toxics-free workplace and community. Enforcement agencies would be accessible to citizens and could levy fines against parties guilty of violations. The Initiative especially emphasizes the rights of immigrants. Activists from non-governmental organizations in all three countries have proposed a citizen's commission to monitor human, labor, and environmental effects of trade and investment.

Upward spiral. In the past, government monetary and fiscal policy, combined with minimum wages, welfare state programs, collective bargaining, and other means of raising the purchasing power of have-nots, did much to counter recession and stagnation within national economies. Similar measures are now required at international levels to counter the tendency toward a downward spiral of inadequate demand in the global economy. The Third World Network calls on the IMF and World Bank to replace their ruinous structural adjustment plans with policies that "meet the broad goals of development...rather than the narrower goal of satisfying the needs of creditors." It also demands a reduction of developing countries' debt. "A Just and Sustainable Trade and Development Initiative" proposes that the remaining debt service be paid in local currency into a democratically administered development fund. Reversing the downward spiral also ultimately requires a "global Keynesianism" in which international institutions support, rather than discourage, national full-employment policies.

An upward spiral also requires rising income for those at the bottom—something that can be encouraged by international labor solidarity. Experiments in cross-border organizing by U.S. unions like the Amalgamated Clothing and Textile Workers and the United Electrical Workers, in cooperation with independent unions in Mexico, aim to defeat global corporations' whipsawing by improving the wages and conditions of Mexican workers.

Redistribution from haves to have-nots. "A Just and Sustainable Trade and Development Initiative" calls for "compensatory financing" to correct growing gaps between rich and poor. A model would be the European Union funds that promote development in its poorer members. The Third World Network calls for commodity agreements to correct the inequities in the South's terms of trade. It also stresses the need to continue preferential treatment for the South in GATT and in intellectual property protection rules.

Strengthened democracy. NAFTA, GATT, and similar agreements should not be used—as they now can be—to preempt the right of localities, states, provinces, and countries to establish labor, health, safety, and environmental standards that are higher than those set in international agreements. Above all, democratization requires a new opportunity for people at the bottom to participate in shaping their destiny.

Codes of Conduct for Transnational Corporations. Several transnational grass-roots groups call for codes of conduct that would, for example, require corporations to report investment intentions; disclose the hazardous materials they import; ban employment of children; forbid discharge of pollutants; require advance notification and severance pay when operations are terminated; and prohibit company interference with union organizing. United Nations discussions on such a code, long stymied by U.S. hostility, should be revived.

While the ultimate goal is to have such codes implemented by agreements among governments, global public pressure and cross-border organizing can begin to enforce them. The Coalition for Justice in the Maquiladoras, for example, a coalition of religious, environmental, labor, Latino, and women's organizations in Mexico and the United States, has issued a code of conduct for U.S. corporations in Mexico and has used "corporate campaign" techniques to pressure them to abide by its labor and environmental provisions.

Reform of international institutions. Citizens should call on the United Nations to convene a second Earth Summit focusing on democratizing the IMF and the World Bank, and consider formation of new institutions to promote equitable, sustainable, and participatory development. International citizen campaigns, perhaps modeled on the Nestlé boycott and the campaign against World Bank–funded destruction of the Amazon, could spotlight these institutions.

Multiple-level regulation. In place of rivalry among countries and regions, such programs imply a system of democratically controlled public institutions at every level, from global to local.

GLOBALIZATION FROM BELOW

These proposals provide no short-term panacea; they are objectives to organize around. The New World Economy is not going to vanish from the political agenda. Neither will the passions and political forces aroused by the NAFTA debate. Many of the same issues will resurface in connection with the Asia-Pacific Economic Cooperation and with GATT. As the fiftieth anniversaries of the IMF and World Bank approach, calls for their reform are being sounded all over the world.

The struggle against NAFTA has shown that those harmed by the New World Economy need not be passive victims. Many politicians were unprepared for the strength of the anti-NAFTA movement because it represented an eruption into the political arena of people who have long been demobilized. But to influence their economic destinies effectively, they need a movement that provides an alternative to the Ross Perots and Pat Buchanans. Such a movement must act on the understanding that the unregulated globalization of capital is really a worldwide attack of the haves on the have-nots. And it must bring that understanding to bear on every affected issue, from local layoffs to the world environment. "From Global Pillage to Global Village" suggests a vision to guide such a movement:

> The internationalization of capital, production and labor is now being followed by the internationalization of peoples' movements and organizations. Building peoples' international organizations and solidarity will be our revolution from within: a civil society without borders. This internationalism or "globalization from below" will be the foundation for turning the global pillage into a participatory and sustainable global village.

[The ideas put forth in this essay served as the basis for a South End Press book entitled, *Global Village or Global Pillage: Economic Reconstruction From the Bottom Up,* by Jeremy Brecher and Tim Costello. For ordering information, see the More Information section in the back of this book.]

POWER, HISTORY, & WARFARE

HOWARD ZINN

This essay is an edited transcript of a speech given
at the University of Wisconsin, Madison, March 21, 1991.

One does not make wars less likely by formulating rules of warfare.
War cannot be humanized. It can only be abolished.
—Albert Einstein

We historians always claim to talk about things in larger perspectives. Not like ordinary people. I would like to talk about the question of war, just and unjust war. I think there is a great danger of fighting a war that would make war acceptable once more. The Vietnam War gave war a bad name. The people who lead this country have been trying ever since to find a war that would give war a good name. It's important for us to sit back and think about the *problem of war*, of just and unjust wars.

I know there are people who don't like to talk in those terms, that is, the realists. I read an op-ed piece in the *Boston Globe* by Marvin Zonis. He teaches international political economy at the Graduate School of Business of the University of Chicago. Zonis writes:

President Bush conducted a war in the Persian Gulf at least partially to avoid the mistakes of Vietnam. He succeeded brilliantly in part of that challenge. He brought the war to a hasty conclusion without appreciable American casualties. It needs to be remembered that the U.S. fought this war for a different set of reasons than the war in Vietnam—Vietnam, a great strategic purpose. But here we fought the war to prevent Saddam Hussein and his brutal army

—I have to stop there. I thought: Show me a non-brutal army. He has a brutal army. We have a nice army—"from winning control over a significant proportion of world oil exports." That's what we fought for, he tells us. I thought we fought to free Kuwait. I thought we fought for noble purposes, but he's a specialist in international relations, and he's telling us like it is. He's a realist telling us, *Let's not talk about the morality of the war, let's not talk about freedom and democracy and liberation and so on. Let's talk about oil.* He's willing to talk about what Bush stopped talking about at a certain point in the game. At first Bush did talk about oil. Then he got the notion that, no, this is embarrassing. People will not die for oil. They will die for words: democracy, liberation, freedom, aggression, etc. So oil dropped out of the agenda, but of course it's there. It's always been there, very strongly.

We have political scientists who don't want to talk about rightness or wrongness, just or unjust. Machiavelli is their mentor. He's the great political scientist. He took the notion of politics away from the utopians and brought it down to earth. This is the way things are. Let's not talk about how things should be. I'm sorry for bringing the moral issue into this, but I thought it might be a thing to do. Erasmus, who was a contemporary of Machiavelli, saw war as totally evil. He said, "Whoever heard of animals slaughtering one another by the hundreds and thousands?" But this is what men do in war. Erasmus was a woolly headed—I don't really know what he looked like—soft, moralistic utopian who talked about how things *should* be. The political scientists, the realists, the people around the White House, the people who stock a lot of our political science and international relations departments, won't be found talking about things like that. There's a man who teaches courses on war somewhere in the United States named Michael Howard. He writes books about war. He talks about Erasmus and Machiavelli and shakes his head about Erasmus and says, "With all his genius, he was not a profound political analyst. Nor did he ever have to exercise the responsibilities of power." They say this a lot. *You don't know what it's like. You don't know how tough it is to be up there in the decision maker's seat. It's easy for you to come out for peace.*

Michael Howard says, "A realist understands that war is an institution which cannot be eliminated from the international system. All you can do about it is to codify its rationale and to civilize its means." So we've engaged in this process of civilizing the means of war. We've had all these conferences. All of you who were around at the beginning of the twentieth century remember the Hague Conferences and the Geneva Conferences of the 1930s limiting the techniques of war because you can't do away with war, all you can do is make war more moral. Einstein went to one of these conferences. I don't know how many of you know that. We like to bring up things that people don't know. What is scholarship, anyway? Einstein was horrified at World War I, as so many were, that great war for democracy, for freedom, to end all wars, etc. Ten million men died on the battlefield in World War I and nobody, at the end of it, understood why, or for what. World War I gave war a bad name...until World War II came along.

But Einstein was horrified by World War I. He devoted a lot of time to thinking and worrying about it. He went to this conference in Geneva. He thought they were discussing disarmament, to do away with the weapons of war and therefore to prevent war. Instead, he found these representatives of various countries discussing what kinds of weapons would be suitable and what kind of weapons needed to be prohibited. What were good weapons and bad weapons, just weapons and unjust weapons? Einstein then did something which nobody ever expected. He was a very private man, as those of you know who knew him like I did. He did something really uncharacteristic: He called a press conference. The whole international press came, because Einstein was...well, he was Einstein. They came, and he told this press conference how horrified he was by what he had heard at the international conference. He said, "One does not make wars less likely by formulating rules of warfare. War cannot be humanized. It can only be abolished."

We still have that problem of just and unjust wars, of unjust wars taking place and then another war takes place which looks better, has a better rationale, is easier to defend, and so now we're confronted with a "just" war and war is made palatable again. Now the attempt is to put Vietnam behind us, that unjust war, and now we have just wars. Or at least quick ones, real smashing victories.

I had a student a few years ago who was writing something about war. I don't know why a student of mine should write about war. But she said, "I guess wars are like wines. There are good years and bad years. But war is not like wine. War is like cyanide. One drop and you're dead." I thought that was good. What often is behind this business of *we can't do anything about war* and war's inevitability, be realistic, accept it, just try to fool around with the edges of it, is a very prevalent notion that you sometimes hear a lot when people begin discussing the war. Of course we see how successful they've been at humanizing the means of war with all these conferences. Fourteen minutes into any discussion of war someone says, *It's human nature.* Don't you hear that a lot? You just get a group of people together to discuss war and at some point somebody will say, *It's human nature.* What evidence is there? Genetic evidence? Biological evidence? There's no evidence that this is human nature. All we have is historical evidence. But Freud and Einstein—I like to drop Einstein's name twice in the course of an evening; I'll try to get Freud back in again—had a correspondence in 1932, which they allowed me to see, and Einstein asked Freud, "I'm puzzled. War, war. Isn't there something, you're a psychologist, isn't there something in human nature? If anyone knows about human nature it's you." Freud gives him a long response in which there's no evidence from psychology. Although Freud says, *oh, yes, it's human nature*, the only evidence he gives is history. He says, "This is the way it's been. People have fought wars and wars and wars. Therefore, I can only conclude..." We don't need Freud, a great psychologist, really a great thinker, to give us that argument, to tell us that. My brother-in-law can tell me that. And he does.

There's no biological evidence, no genetic evidence, no anthropological evidence. If the anthropologists look at these primitive tribes and what they do, *Ah, these tribes are fierce. Ah, these tribes are gentle.* It's just not clear at all. And what about history? There's a history of wars and also a history of kindness. But it's like the newspapers and the historians. They dwell on wars and cruelty and the bestial things that people do to one another and they don't dwell a lot on the magnificent things that people do for one another in everyday life again and again. It seems to me it only takes a little bit of thought to realize that if wars came out of human nature, out of some spontaneous urge to kill, then why is it that governments have to go to such tremendous lengths to mobilize populations to go to war? It seems too obvious, doesn't it? They really have to work at it. They have to dredge up an enormous number of reasons. They have to inundate the airwaves with these reasons. They have to bombard people with slogans and statements and then, in case people aren't really persuaded, they have to threaten them. If they haven't persuaded enough people to go into the armed forces, then they have to draft them into the armed forces. Of course the persuasion into the armed forces also includes a certain amount of economic persuasion. You make sure you have a very poor underclass in society so that you give people a choice between starving or going into the military. But if persuasion doesn't work and enticements don't work, then anybody who doesn't want to sign for the draft or who goes into the army and decides to leave is going to be courtmartialed and go to prison. They have to go to great lengths to get people to go to war. They work very hard at it.

What's interesting also is that they have to make moral appeals. That should say something about human nature, if there is something to be said about human nature. It must suggest that there must be some moral element in human nature. Granted that human beings are capable of all sorts of terrible things, human beings are capable of all sorts of wonderful things, but there must be something in human beings which makes them respond to moral appeals. Most humans don't respond to appeals to go to war on the basis of *Let's go and kill.*

No, *Let's go and free somebody. Let's go and establish democracy. Let's go and topple this tyrant. Let's do this so that wars will finally come to an end.* Most people are not like Theodore Roosevelt. Just before the Spanish-American War Theodore Roosevelt said to a friend, "In strict confidence"—you might ask then, how did I get hold of it; you read all these public letters that now appear, and they all start *in strict confidence*—"I should welcome almost any war, for I think this country needs one." Well. No moral appeal there. Just: "we need a war." You may know that George Bush, when he entered the White House, took the portrait that Reagan had put up there to inspire him, a portrait of Calvin Coolidge, because he knew that Calvin Coolidge was one of the most inspiring people in the history of this country. Coolidge had said: "The business of America is business." Bush took down the portrait of Calvin Coolidge and put up the portrait of Theodore Roosevelt. I don't want to make too much of this. But I will. What Theodore Roosevelt said, Bush might just as well have said. Bush wanted war.

Every step in the development of the Persian Gulf War indicated, from the moment that the invasion of Kuwait was announced, everything that Bush did fits in perfectly with the fact that Bush wanted war. He was determined to have war. He was determined not to prevent this war from taking place. You can just tell this from the very beginning: no negotiations, no compromise, no—what was that ugly word?—linkage. Bush made linkage the kind of word that made you tremble. I always thought that things were linked naturally. Everybody was linked, issues were linked, I thought that even the countries in the Middle East were somehow linked, and that the issues in the Middle East were somehow linked. No negotiations, no linkage, no compromise. He sent Baker on a long trip to Geneva, and people got excited. Baker met the Foreign Minister of Iraq, Tariq Aziz, in Geneva. What did they do? Bush says, no negotiations. Why are you going? Are you a frequent flyer? Amazing. No negotiations right up to the end. Who knows what might have come of any of those little overtures that Saddam Hussein made. I don't know how serious he was or what would have happened, but the fact is there were overtures that came, yes, even from Saddam Hussein, and they were absolutely and totally neglected. One came from a member of the Foreign Services of the United States who brought it personally from the Middle East and gave it to Scowcroft. No response, no response at all. Bush wanted war.

But fortunately, as I said, there aren't a lot of people like Theodore Roosevelt and Bush. Most people do not want war. Most people, if they are going to support a war, have to be given reasons that have to do with morality, with right and wrong, with justice and lack of justice, with tyranny and opposing tyranny. I think it's important to take a look at the process by which populations are, as this one was in a very short time, brought to support a war. This was a process which, on the eve of war, took a nation that was, according to surveys before January 15, divided half & half, 46 percent to 47 percent, on whether we should use force to solve this problem in the Middle East. Half and half. Of course, after the bombs started falling in Iraq, it suddenly became 75 percent and 80 percent. What is this process of persuasion? It seems to me we should take a look at the elements of that, because it's important to know that, to be able to deal with it and talk to people about it, especially since that 80 percent or 85 percent or now they report 89.3 percent, whatever, must be a very shallow percentage. It must be very thin, I think. It must be very temporary and can be made more temporary than it is. It must be shallow because half of those people before the bombs fell did not believe in the use of force. Public opinion is very volatile. So to look at the elements by which people are persuaded is to begin to think about how to talk to at least that 50 percent and maybe more that is willing to reconsider whether this war was really just and necessary and right, and whether any war in our time could be just and necessary and right.

I think one of the elements that goes into this process of persuasion is the starting point that the United States is a good society. Since we're a good society, our wars are good. If we're a good society, we're going to do good things. We do good things at home. We have a Bill of Rights and color television. There are lots of good things you can say if you leave out enough. It's like ancient Athens. Athens goes to war against Sparta. Athens must be on the right side because Athens is a better society than Sparta. Athens is more cultured. Sure, you have to overlook a few things about ancient Athens, like slavery. But still, it really is a better society, so the notion is that Athens fighting Sparta is probably a good war. But you have to overlook things, do a very selective job of analyzing your own society before you come to the conclusion that yours is so good a society that unadorned goodness must spill over into everything you do, including everything you do to other people abroad. What is required, it seems to me, in the case of the United States as the good society doing good things in the world, is simply to look at a bit of history. It's only if you were born yesterday and also if today you don't look around very sharply that you can come to the conclusion that we are so good a society that you can take the word of the government that any war we get into will be a right and a just war.

But it doesn't take too much looking into American history to see that we have a long history of aggression.

Let's talk about naked aggression—a long history of naked aggression. How did we get so big? We started out as a thin band of colonies along the East Coast and soon we were at the Pacific and expanding. It's not a biological thing, that you just expand. No. We expanded by force, conquest, aggression. Sure it says, "Florida Purchase" on those little maps that we used to have in elementary school, a map with colors on them: blue for Florida Purchase; orange Mexican Cession. A purchase. Just a business deal. Nothing about Andrew Jackson going into Florida and killing a number of people in order to persuade the Spaniards to sell Florida to us. No money actually passed hands, but we'll ignore that. Mexican Cession. Mexico "ceded" California and Colorado and New Mexico and Arizona. They ceded all of that to us. Why? Good neighbors? Latin American hospitality? They just ceded it to us? There was a war, a war which we provoked, which President Polk planned for in advance, as so many wars are planned for in advance. That's how the incident takes place and they say, *Oh, wow, an incident took place. We've got to go to war.* That was also a fairly short war and a decisive victory and soon we had 40 percent of Mexico. And it's all ours. California and all of that.

Why? Expansion. The Louisiana Purchase. I remember how proud I was way back when I first looked at that map and saw "Louisiana Purchase." It doubled the size of my country, and it was just by purchase. It was an empty space. We just bought it. I really didn't learn anything. They didn't tell me when they gave me that stuff in history class that there were Indians living in that territory. Indians had to be fought in battle after battle, war after war. They had to be killed, exterminated. The buffalo herds, their means of subsistence, had to be destroyed, they had to be driven out of that territory so that the Louisiana Purchase could be ours. It's a long history of expansion in the United States.

Then we began to go overseas. There was that brief period in American history, the period the textbooks call—that honest moment of a textbook—"The Age of Imperialism." 1898 to 1903. There, too, we went into Cuba to save the Cubans. We are always helping people. Saving people from somebody. So we went in and saved the Cubans from Spain and immediately planted our military bases and our corporations in Cuba. Then there was Puerto Rico. A few shells fired and Puerto Rico is ours. In the meantime Teddy Roosevelt is swimming out into the Pacific after the Philippines. Not contiguous to the United States? People didn't know. McKinley didn't know where the

Philippines were. And Senator Beveridge of Indiana said, "The Philippines not contiguous to the United States? Our Navy will make it contiguous." History of expansion, aggression, and continuing on.

We become a world power. Around 1905–1907, the first books began to appear about American history which used that phrase "America as a world power." That in fact was what we intended to do: to become a world power. It took World War I and then World War II. We kept moving up and the old imperial powers were being shoved out of the way, one by one. Now the Middle East comes in. In World War II Saudi Arabia becomes one of our friendly places. The English are being pushed more and more out of this oil territory. The Americans are going to come in. Of the "Seven Sisters," the seven great oil corporations, five of them will be American, maybe one will be British. In the years after World War II, of course, the Soviet Union was the other great power, but we are expanding and our influence is growing and our military bases are spreading all over the world. We are intervening wherever we can to make sure that things go our way. In 1940–41, at the beginning of World War II, Henry Luce, a very powerful man in America, the publisher of *Life* and *Time* and *Fortune* and the maker of presidents, wrote an article called "The American Century," anticipating that this coming century is going to be the American century. He said, "This is the time to accept wholeheartedly our duty and our opportunity as the most vital and powerful nation in the world and in consequence to exert upon the world the full impact of our influence. For such purposes as we see fit and by such means as we see fit." He was not a shy man. So we proceeded. While it was thought that rivalry with the Soviet Union, the other great superpower, was the central motive for the American foreign policy in the post-war period, I think it's more accurate to say that the problem was not communism, the problem was independence of American power. It didn't matter whether a country was turning communist or not, it mattered that a country was showing independence and not falling in line with what the United States conceived of as its responsibility as a world power. So in 1953 the government in Iran was overthrown and Mossadeq came into power. He was not a communist but a nationalist. He was a nationalist because he nationalized the oil.

Those things are intolerable, just as was the case with Arbenz in Guatemala the following year. He's not a communist...well, he's a little left of center, maybe a few socialist ideas, maybe he talks to communists. No, he's not a communist. But he nationalized United Fruit lands. That's intolerable. He offers to pay them. That proves that he's certainly not a real revolutionary. A real revolutionary wouldn't give a cent to United Fruit. I wouldn't. I've always considered myself a real revolutionary because I wouldn't pay a cent to anybody like United Fruit. He offered to pay them the price of their land, the price that they had declared for tax purposes. Sorry. That wouldn't do. So the CIA went to work and overthrew the Arbenz government, the Allende government in Chile also—not a communist government, a little marxist, a little socialist, quite a lot of civil liberties and freedom of the press, but independent—more independent of the United States than the other governments of Chile, a government that's not going to be friendly to Anaconda Copper and IT&T and other corporations of the United States that have always had their way in Latin America. That's the real problem.

That history of expansion, of intervention, not even to talk about Vietnam, Laos, Cambodia. Not to talk about all the tyrants that we kept in power, of all the aggressions not just that we committed but that we watched other countries commit as we stood silently by because we approved of those aggressions. Or when Indonesia invaded East Timor. Until Noam Chomsky brought up the name of East Timor into public discussion nobody had even heard of East Timor. The CIA had heard of East Timor. Anyway, Indonesia went into East Timor and killed huge numbers of people. The invasion, occupation, and brutalization that Saddam Hussein committed in Kuwait was small in comparison to the enormous bloodshed in East Timor, done by Indonesia, our friend, and with military hardware supplied by the United States. The record of the United States in dealing with naked aggression in the world, looking at a little bit of history, is so shocking, so abysmal, that nobody with any sense of history could possibly accept the argument that we sent troops into the Middle East because the U.S. government was morally outraged at the invasion of another country. That Bush's heart went out to the people of Kuwait, who suffered under Iraqi oppression. Bush's heart never went out to the people of El Salvador, suffering under the oppression of a government which we were supplying with arms again and again. Tens and tens and tens of thousands of people were being killed. His heart never went out to those people. Or the people in Guatemala, again whose government we were supplying with arms. It's a long list.

So you would have to be born yesterday to accept the argument that we were sending all these troops into the Middle East because we were morally offended by the aggression against Kuwait. But still, it is a moral appeal based on people's forgetting of history and on the ability of the mass media and the Administration to obliterate history, certainly not to bring it up. You talk about the responsibility of the press. Doesn't the press have any responsibility to teach some history to the people who read its newspaper columns? To remind people of what has happened five, ten, twenty, forty years ago? Was the press also born yesterday and has forgotten everything that has happened before last week? The press complained about military censorship. Of course, the big problem was not military censorship. The problem was self-censorship.

Another element in this process of persuasion is to create a manichean situation, good versus evil. I've just talked about the good, us. But you also have to present the other as total evil, as the only *evil*. Granted, Saddam Hussein is an evil guy. I say that softly. But he is. No question about it. Most heads of government are. But if you want to bring a nation to war against an evil person, it's not enough to say that this person is evil. You have to cordon him off from all the other tyrants of the world, all the other evil leaders of government in order to establish that this is the one tyrant of the world whom we have to get. He is responsible for the trouble in the world. If we could only get him, we will solve our problems, just as a few years ago if we could only get Noriega, we will solve the drug trade problem. We got Noriega, and *obviously* we've solved the drug trade problem. But the demonization is necessary, the creation of this one evil shutting out everything—Syria, Turkey, Egypt, Saudi Arabia—not letting people be aware of—and I didn't see the media paying any attention to this—to the reports of Amnesty International. If you read the 1990 report of Amnesty International, they have a few pages on each country. There are a lot of countries. A few pages on Iraq, Iran, Turkey, Syria, Saudi Arabia, Kuwait, Israel. You look through those pages and all those countries that I have just named show differences in degree but the same pattern of treatment of people who are dissenters, dissidents, troublemakers in their own country. In Israel, of course, it's the Palestinians. Israel has a more free atmosphere in the non-occupied territories, but in the occupied territories, Israel behaves the way Saudi Arabia behaves toward its own people and the way Syria and Turkey do. You see the same pattern in the Amnesty International reports, the same words appearing again and again. Imprisonment without trial. Detention without communication with the outside. Torture. Killing. For all of these countries. But if you want to make war on them, you single one out, blot out the others, even use them as allies and forget about their record. Then you go in. You persuade people that *we're against tyranny, aren't we? We're against brutality, aren't we?* This is the repository of all the evil that there is in the world. There are times when people talked that way. Why are we at war? *We've got to get him. We've got to get Saddam*

Hussein. What about the whole world? *Saddam Hussein. Got to get him.*

I would like to get him. I would like to get all of them. But I'm not willing to kill 100,000 or 500,000 or a million people to get rid of them. I think we have to find ways to get rid of tyrants that don't involve mass slaughter. That's our problem. It's very easy to talk about the brutality. Governments are brutal, and some governments are more brutal than others. Saddam Hussein is particularly brutal. Saddam Hussein uses chemical weapons and gas. That kept coming up. I remember Congressman Stephen Solarz, the great war hawk of the period: *Saddam Hussein used gas, used chemical warfare.* True, ugly and brutal. But what about us? We used napalm in Vietnam. We used Agent Orange, which is chemical warfare. I don't know how you characterize napalm. We used cluster bombs in Iraq. Cluster bombs are not designed to knock down military hardware. They are anti-personnel weapons which shoot out thousands of little pellets which embed themselves in people's bodies. When I was in North Vietnam during the Vietnam War I saw X rays of kids lying in hospital beds showing the pellets in the various organs of their bodies. That's what cluster bombs are. But gas? No. Chemical weapons? No. Napalm, yes. Cluster bombs, yes. White phosphorus, yes. Agent Orange, yes. They're going to kill people by gas. We're going to kill people by blowing them up. You can tell who is the cruel wager of war and who is the gentlemanly wager of war.

You can persuade people of that if you simply don't mention things or don't remind people. Once you remind people of these things they remember. If you remind people about napalm they remember. If you say, you know, the newspapers haven't told you about the cluster bombs, they say, *oh yes, that's true.* People aren't beastly and vicious. But when information is withheld from them.…The American population was bombarded the way the Iraqi population was bombarded. It was a war against us, a war of lies and disinformation and omission of history. That kind of war, overwhelming and devastating, waged here in the United States while the Gulf War was waged over there.

Another element in this process of persuasion is simply to take what seems like a just cause and turn it into a just war. Erwin Knoll used that terminology. I have used that terminology, and both of us, because we're so wise, seem to come to the same conclusions. That is, that there's this interesting jump that takes places between a just cause and a just war. A cause may be just: yes, it's wrong for Saddam Hussein to go into Kuwait, it's wrong for this and that to happen. The question is: does it then immediately follow that if the cause is just, if an injustice has been committed, that the proper response to that is war. It's that leap of logic that needs to be absolutely avoided. North Korea invades South Korea in 1950. It's unjust. It's wrong. It's a just cause. What do you do? You go to war. You wage war for three years. You kill a million Koreans. And at the end of the three years, where are you? Where you were before. North Korea is still a dictatorship. South Korea is still a dictatorship. Only *a million people* are dead. You can see this again and again, jumping from a just cause to an overwhelming use of violence to presumably rectify this just cause, which it never does.

What war does, even if it starts with an injustice, is *multiply the injustice*. If it starts on the basis of violence, *it multiplies the violence*. If it starts on the basis of defending yourself against brutality, then you end up becoming a brute. You see this in World War II, the best of wars. The war that gave wars such a good name that they've used it ever since as a metaphor to justify every war that's taken place since then. All you have to do in order to justify war is to mention World War II, mention Churchill, mention Munich. Use the word "appeasement." That's all you need—to take the glow of that good war and spread it over any ugly act that you are now committing in order to justify it. But World War II had a good cause, a just cause against fascism. I volunteered. I don't like to admit that I was in World War II, for various reasons. I like to say, "I was in a war." I suppose I admit that I was in World War II so that people won't think I mean the Spanish-American War. I volunteered for World War II. I went into the Air Force and became a bombardier and dropped bombs on Germany, France, Czechoslovakia, Hungary. I thought it was a just cause. Therefore you drop bombs. It wasn't until after the war that I thought about this and studied and went back to visit a little town in France that I and a lot of the Air Force had bombed, had in fact dropped napalm on, the first use of napalm that I know of was this mission that we flew a few weeks before the end of World War II. We had no idea what it was. They said it was a new type of thing we were carrying, the bomb. We went over and just bombed the hell out of a few thousand German soldiers who were hanging around a town in France waiting for the war to end. They weren't doing anything. So we obliterated them and the French town near Bordeaux on the Atlantic coast of France.

I thought about that, about Dresden, the deliberate bombing of civilian populations in Germany, in Tokyo. Eighty, ninety, a hundred thousand people died in that night of bombing. After our outrage, our absolute outrage at the beginning of World War II when Hitler bombed Coventry and Rotterdam and a thousand people were killed, how inhuman to bomb civilian populations. By the end of World War II we had become brutalized—Hiroshima, Nagasaki, and even after that. I have a friend in Japan who was a teenager when the war ended. He lived in Osaka. He distinctly remembers August 14. It was five days after the bomb dropped on Nagasaki (August 9), eight days after the bomb dropped on Hiroshima (August 6), and a day before the Japanese agreed to surrender (August 15). After Nagasaki it was very clear that they were about to surrender in a matter of days. But on August 14 a thousand planes flew over Japan and dropped bombs on Japanese cities. He remembers on August 14, when everybody thought the war was over, the bombers coming over his city of Osaka and dropping bombs. He remembers going through the streets strewn with corpses and finding leaflets also dropped along with the bombs saying: *"The war is over."*

Just causes can lead you to think that everything you then do is just. I suppose I've come to the conclusion that war, by its nature, being the indiscriminate and mass killing of large numbers of people, cannot be justified for any political cause, any ideological cause, any territorial boundary, any tyranny, any aggression. Tyrannies, aggressions, injustices, of course they have to be dealt with. No appeasement. They give us this multiple choice: appeasement or war. *Come on!* You mean to say between appeasement and war there aren't a thousand other possibilities? Is human ingenuity so defunct, is our intelligence so lacking that we cannot devise ways of dealing with tyranny and injustice without killing huge numbers of people? Can you imagine the police dealing with a speeding motorist by taking him out of his car and beating the hell out of him, fracturing his skull in ten different places? It's a sickness of our time. Somehow at the beginning of it is some notion of justice and rightness. But that process has to be examined, reconsidered. If people do think about it they have second thoughts about it.

One of the elements of this process of persuasion is simply to play on people's need for community, for national unity. What better way to get national unity than around a war? It's much easier, simpler, quicker. And of course it's better for the people who run the country to get national unity around a war than to get national unity around giving free medical care to everybody in the country. Surely we could build national unity. We could create a sense of national purpose. We could have people hanging out yellow ribbons for doing away with unemployment and homelessness. We could do what is done when any group of people decides and the word goes out and the air waves are used to unite people to help one another instead of to kill one another. It can be done. People do want to be part of a larger community. Warmakers take advantage of that very moral and decent need for community and unity and being part of a whole and use it for the most terrible of purposes. But it can be used the other way too.

The reason I've gone into what I see as this process of persuasion and the elements of persuasion is that I think that all of them are undoable. History can be learned. Facts can be brought in. People can be reminded of things that they already know. People do have common sense when they are taken away briefly from this hysteria which is created in the time of war. I can only describe the Persian Gulf War as a kind of national hysteria created by the government and collaborated in by the media. When you have an opportunity to lift the veil of that hysteria and take people out from under it and talk to people, then you see the possibilities. When you appeal to people's sense of proportion: What is more important? What is it that we have to do? People know that there are things that have to be done to make life better. People know that the planet is in danger, and that is far more serious than ever getting Saddam Hussein out of Kuwait. Far more serious. I think people also may be aware in some dim way—every once in a while I think of it, and I imagine other people must think of it, too—that we're coming to the end of the century. We should be able, by the end of this century, to eliminate war as a way of solving international disputes. We should have decided, people all over the world, that we're going to use our energy and our resources to create a new world order, but not the new world order of war, but a new world order in which people help one another, in which we divide the enormous wealth of the world in humane and rational ways. It's possible to do that. So I'm just suggesting that we think about that. I feel that there's something that needs to be done and something that can be done and that we can all participate in it.

REBUILDING AMERICA:

A New Economic Plan

SEYMOUR MELMAN

A new political/economic agenda for change in America is needed to replace the failed policies and institutions of the center coalition of Republicans/ Democrats and the conservative right. Political and economic decay in U.S. industries, infrastructure, community, and standard of living cannot be reversed by minor changes in public policies. The severity of unemployment and the abandonment of production and people by many managements require innovative solutions to hitherto neglected problems. These include: how to multiply jobs for rebuilding the country's damaged infrastructure and industry; how to carry out conversion from military to civilian economy; how to carry out a process of demilitarization; how to enlarge control over productive enterprises by working people to assure workplace democracy and competence in production; how to reverse the selective decay in American society. Changes of this quality are necessary for achieving significant advances with respect to issues such as racism, income distribution, gender discrimination, and elimination of military-political adventurism. No leader, candidate, or party has come forward with solutions to these problems.

A political/economic crisis of unprecedented quality is now visible in the United States, as the hallmarks of depression are all around us. Every large city has its shanty towns like the "Hoovervilles" of the 1930s. Full-time jobless rates probably exceed 15 percent, if we take into account the growing array of part-time, temporary workers, the uncounted "self-employed," and the millions who have lost hope of finding jobs, or who even entertained such hope. Millions are left without any income as jobless benefits are used up. Layoffs in the tens of thousands and factory closings in the hundreds are announced by industrial firms, brokers, and banks, including the blue chip enterprises. Pervasive racism and sexism mark minorities and women for victimization in employment, housing, and health care. Water mains burst in the centers of our cities, bridges and roads decay and become unsafe, libraries are closed, and the casualties in underfunded hospitals are a medical scandal. U.S. infant mortality rates, poverty rates, and illiteracy rates alike are among the world's worst for industrialized nations. By February 1992, one in ten Americans were receiving food stamps. We are all degraded by the presence of 5½ million children who know hunger as a normal state. Schools and universities are run-down and unable to properly equip their facilities or hire talented teachers, and are forced to turn away fine students for want of scholarship funds. All of these conditions mark a major product of the American economy: a growing under-trained, castoff population that is ignored and avoided. This crisis condition has two components: conventional features of business capitalist fluctuation; system decay that features a breakdown of competence for production.

Conventional malfunctions of our economic system include: overexpansion of consumer credit and speculative business investment, especially in commercial real estate; major inflation of security values—with prices that are unrelated to profitability; steadily growing inequality in income and opportunity between the haves and the have-nots. These features of business are accompanied by fluctuation in output and employment and have been present throughout the long history of industrial capitalism. But their presence does not explain the special qualities of the present political/economic crisis. For this it is necessary to take into account the particular features of system decay that have become acute.

During the last 40 years American managers have progressively abdicated the function of organizing work: production has been either consigned to overseas locations, or shut down entirely by firms. At the same time, major new investment is continued in military industry whose products are useless for consumption or further production. Abandonment of production is especially acute in the basic machinery producing industries of the United States (including: machine tools, construction machinery, electric generating machinery, textile machinery, mining machinery of all classes, etc. See Table 1). Dependency on imports for means of production is a hallmark of economic underdevelopment. Failure to invest in housing within reach of the lowest third of income receivers has helped generate homelessness on a large scale. Associated failures of productivity growth, high interest rates induced by massive federal borrowing for military expansion, and reduced government investment in infrastructure and conservation of natural resources have produced sustained economic decay and permanent unemployment. Meanwhile, wages to American industrial workers, until 1975 the highest in the world, now rank 16th among 30 major industrial countries. System decay is also reflected in the plague of air, water, and soil pollution that has been unleashed while federal regulators refuse enforcement of even modest measures to constrain further damage. In a word: the American industrial base is being reduced to a shambles.

Table 1

THE ROAD TO UNDERDEVELOPMENT
Production Worker Employment (in thousands) in Selected Machinery-Producing Industries of the U.S., from 1977 to 1987.

Industry	1977	1987	%Change
Machine Tools (Cutting)	37.2	18.6	-50.0
Machine Tools (forming)	16.1	8.9	-45.0
Machine Tool Accessories	39.9	34.5	-14.0
Power-driven Handtools	20.0	11.6	-42.0
Rolling Mill Machinery	5.4	2.2	-60.0
Carburetors, Pistons, Rings, Valves	26.0	17.3	-34.0
Turbines & Turbine Generator Sets	24.8	11.8	-43.0
Internal Combustion Engines	65.3	44.7	-32.0
Farm Machinery & Equipment	96.2	39.0	-60
Transformers (Except Electronic)	32.8	24.3	-26.0
Motors & Generators	74.1	56.4	-24.0
Electrical Industrial Apparatus, n.e.c.	12.2	9.1	-26
Calculators and Accounting Equipment	10.4	5.8	-45
Office Machines, n.e.c.	22.9	13.6	-41
Ball & Roller Bearings	41.3	29.3	-30
Air & Gas Compressors	19.1	12.3	-36
Blowers & Fans	18.6	15.9	-15
Speed Changers, Drives & Gears	17.6	11.7	-35
Construction Machinery	111.2	53.8	-42
Mining Machinery	20.3	8.2	-60
Oil & Gas Field Machinery	39.8	12.9	-68
Textile Machinery	18.3	10.5	-43

Source: U.S. Commerce Department, *Census of Manufactures,* 1987.
Notes: Numbers for these industries are for two years of complete, not sampled, census data. Next complete census in 1992. Drop in production workers is paralleled by drop in number of factories in each industry and by an increase in imports. For machine tools, imports supply 50 percent of U.S. sales. These data show U.S. move to Underdevelopment, the inability to produce the means of production and the dependency on imports for basic industrial equipments.

While competence in production was being undermined, a horde of talented men and women invented and operated an expanded "casino economy," featuring innovations like junk bonds and leveraged buyouts. Enormous profits and incomes were taken by lawyers, top managers, bankers, and their aides—even as productive organizations and facilities were dismantled for short-term profit. But all this money flow merely reallocated claims on available wealth while adding nothing to the store of consumer goods and services or means of production.

Since World War II, the largest identifiable block of capital utilization is accounted for by the military enterprise, which from 1947 to 1991 used up $8.7 trillion of resources representing fixed and working capital (1982 money values). This compares to the total money value of U.S. industry and infrastructure, (again for 1982) of $7.3 trillion. All this has been financed primarily out of tax revenue, plus federal borrowing that has resulted in a level of indebtedness that endangers the value of the currency. Severely damaged industry, infrastructure and populations are the unavoidable outcome of the permanent war economy. The war economy has also trained and installed a counter-productivity managerial class in 35,000 prime contracting establishments. Its normal functioning degrades the competence of the whole economy.

The U.S. war economy has produced extraordinary effects in the use of capital. A modern military budget is a capital fund; put to use it sets in motion the resources which in the ordinary industrial enterprise are termed fixed and working capital. In 1991, for every $100 of new civilian assets put in place in the U.S. the military separately was allotted $44. Compare this U.S. military-civilian ratio of 44:100 with that of Germany, 13:100, and Japan, 3:100. Civilian priority in these countries has yielded industrial modernity and rapid productivity growth.

This combination of conventional business crises and system decay has checkmated the ability of the federal government to conduct a strategy of military Keynesianism: using federal spending via the permanent war economy to regulate employment, income, and profitability. It is impossible, after 45 years of Cold War, to operate a national economy that can deliver both guns and butter—as during the brief four-year model of World War II.

The long period of cold war has transformed the mechanisms of government. The executive branch is dominated by the management of the military economy. The Congress has been functionally redefined, as a result of the activity of many members as virtual marketing managers on behalf of military contracts for industry, bases, and laboratories.

The end of the cold war has created a grave crisis for this government. The coalition of Republican and Democratic party officials in both the executive and legislative branches now confronts a professional crisis. The main political skills of many as intermediaries for bringing Pentagon money and jobs to local facilities, vital for the cold war period, have been rendered partially obsolete. The new reality leaves the center coalition of Democrats and Republicans unable to operate a traditional guns-and-butter policy. A sustained heavy demand for resources to operate the military economy checkmates the ability of lawmakers to make income or major public works concessions on behalf of the working people left stranded by the system decay.

Three policy responses to these problems are visible at this writing: the coalition center; the conservative right; and a new political/economic agenda.

THE CENTER COALITION OF REPUBLICANS AND DEMOCRATS

The center coalition represents, at its core, the top directorates of government, industry, business, and professional firms and institutions. It has proposed modest "peace dividends" and a gradual reduction of the military budget, in honor of the end of the cold war. Pentagon cutbacks are proposed in the range of $5–15 billion a year, and are associated with varying degrees of alternative use—emphasizing reduction of federal deficits and indebtedness. But these proposals from the Democratic-Republican center coalition hardly begin to meet the requirements for major repair of American industry and infrastructure—considering only the facilities and services that are generally acknowledged as government responsibility. A full response is on the order of $165 billion per year, so clearly the proposals from the coalition that dominated during the cold war fall far short.

Table 2

A PRODUCTIVE WAY TO SPEND $165 BILLION EACH YEAR

Comprehensive Housing Program	$30 Billion
Dept. of Education Extra Spending	$30 Billion
Repair of Roads, Bridges, Water & Sewer Systems	$26 Billion
Other Education Needs (Preschool, Facilities)	$23 Billion
Radioactive Waste Cleanup	$17.5Billion
Toxic Waste Cleanup	$16 Billion
Miscellaneous Health Costs	$12.5Billion
Electrification of U.S. Rail System	$10 Billion

Sources
Estimates by the National Commission for Economic Conversion and Disarmament based upon published reports of various expert studies identified in *NY Times*, 10/18/87, 3/23/88, 9/27/88, 10/13/88, 12/3/88, 1/6/89, 3/10/89, 3/29/89; cost estimate of electrification of U.S. rail system prepared by Professor John E. Ullmann (Hofstra); Michael Renner, "Enhancing Global Security," in *State of The World: 1989* (Norton,1989); U.S. Congress, Joint Economic Committee, *Hard Choices*, Feb. 25, 1984, Wash., DC, 1989; A. Bastian, N. Fruchter, C. Green, "Reconstructing Education," in M. Raskin, C. Hartman, eds., *Winning America* (Boston: South End Press, 1988), pp. 11, 197, 204; Center on Budget and Policy Priorities, "The Bush Budget," 2/17/89, p.10.

Considerations of a peace dividend are irrelevant to the managers of America's military state capitalism. The government and corporate managers of this economy are locked in—by occupational self-interest, by long professional habituation, and by ideology—to an industrial policy that accords priority to the armed forces as a primary instrument of both foreign and domestic policy. The same industrial policy selectively rejects investment in civilian research and development and new technologies, which would enable working people to be paid well while producing quality goods and services at low cost per unit. In 1993, German industry, paying 152 percent of U.S. wages, and Japan, paying 114 percent as much as the United States, are preeminent as world suppliers of machinery. A continuation of the center coalition's policies guarantees further economic, political, and human deterioration.

As both corporate and government managers abandon the organization of work, the consequences extend far beyond the realm of particular factories, unions, and communities. The whole economy is dragged down since the reduced creation of productive wealth translates into unemployment, poverty, homelessness, decaying facilities, and services of every sort. These conditions have led to two major political/economic groups in crisis. One is an embittered, deeply resentful, and hence politically dangerous population of formerly well-paid, blue- and white-collar workers comprising an economically castoff "middle class." In the absence of constructive resolution for their plight these people are susceptible to demagogic, extremist appeals (as the neo-fascists, skinheads, KKK, and the more "respectable" types like Pat Buchanan). A second development is the explosive growth of underemployed and undereducated populations located in the inner cities. Being mainly people of color, they are scapegoated by the extremist right. America's economically depressed "middle class" and inner city "third world" comprise a grouping hitherto unknown in this country, a *lumpenproletariat* (as in Germany in the 1930s): "dispossessed and uprooted individuals cut off from the social class with which they might normally be identified" (Webster's).

Corporate and government managers, preoccupied with short-term profitmaking and maintenance of military economy, have had little to offer to either section of the American *lumpenproletariat*. These managerial goals obstruct the major investments required for creating millions of jobs that would transform the present and prospective *lumpenproletariat* into parts of productive communities.

A partnership of corporate and government managers operated the U.S. political economy during the cold war. They have set in motion a class war against American working people by severely restricting their decision-making power and holding down their incomes. Corporate managers create stranded workers and communities by moving factories abroad to take short-term advantage of lower wages. Factories and stores are closed when profits are not high enough, destroying jobs and laying waste to entire communities. Top management has consistently opposed economic conversion planning and reinvestment of vast military resources in job-creating production of real wealth. This produces regional surpluses of once well-paid people made desperate for any new jobs, hence open to recruitment as "replacement workers." The ability of working people to organize and bargain through unions is abridged by legalizing the rights of employers to install "replacement workers" in place of strikers. President Reagan showed the way, as soon as he took office, by breaking the strike of the air traffic controllers and replacing them with military personnel.

Top managers of the military-industrial complex have extended their policy of class war abroad. By 1990 the United States had become the world's largest exporter of arms ($18.5 billion), and military and police training. The military budgets of third world countries (minus the oil-rich states) totaled $149 billion in 1988, three times the economic development aid received from the rich North. Military and police training sponsored by the U.S. government—notably in Latin America—has encouraged counter–trade union policies of repressive military dictatorships. In all this, the top government managers have been joined by their counterparts in the transnational corporations. The combination of economic collapse with strong-arm policies toward working people has produced desperate waves of immigration from third world countries, as from Mexico.

Racism, overt and covert, has been a principal instrument for disorienting, dividing, and weakening working people in their relation to management.

The center coalition of Republicans/Democrats conceals all this with shallow chatter about "values," family, and individual opportunity in the market.

THE CONSERVATIVE RIGHT

The response of the American extremist right—wearing a mask that they label "conservative"—affirms the character of economy and policy that has been practiced during the cold war and accordingly affirms a continuation of military state capitalism. At the same time, the rightist response features a rally-ing of nationalist sentiment in the United States—blaming Japan (and other foreigners) for diverse troubles of the American economy.

The rightist address to the well-being of the population also features overt and covert racist demagogy (anti-black, anti-immigrant, anti-Jewish, with links to classic propaganda on "international bankers" and "welfare queens"). By such means the American right has been mimicking the fascist "national" polit-ical pattern of other countries.

The right has been quick to respond to spreading disquiet and growing resentment engendered by massive job loss among white- and blue-collar work-ers. In the United States, as elsewhere, talented demagogues of the right have learned to play upon and amplify the deeply felt alienation of working people who are frightened by economic helplessness, their unexplained economic trou-bles, and their inability to improve their condition. This is a "socialist" aspect of the radical right appeal.

First David Duke and then Pat Buchanan have spearheaded an American campaign to marshall economically afflicted, unemployed, and otherwise disaf-fected workers around nationalist and/or racist slogans that are proclaimed as ways of addressing economic ills. They give voice to many of the readily per-ceived economic/political defects, failures, and inequities of American economy and government. American industrial decay is described as resulting from unfair Japanese competition, Japanese ultra-nationalist restrictions on U.S. imports, and the all-around activity of the Japanese government and business combines, making the latter unassailable. American conservatives typically discover scape-goats for U.S. industrial decline, rather than defining the actual causes of poor productivity or management-ordered plant closings in many U.S. industries.

Any post-1992 president and Congress will confront increasingly severe economic, political and social crises at home and abroad. At their core will be the limited capability of government and corporate top managers to organize work for the creation of acceptable jobs and living standards. They will be pressed to make specially forceful use of their powers, and without major institutional change a powerful totalitarian thrust is therefore unavoidable. The federal government is now dominated by the normally authoritarian mili-tary and secret war-making institutions of the Pentagon and CIA. (Note that $30–40 billion of recent Pentagon budgets have been "black"—secret from Congress and the public; the budgets of the CIA are not published at all.) *An intensification of authoritarian methods is reversible if, and only if, an admin-*

istration is committed to major institutional change that diminishes the centralization of power. This change will require a process of economic conversion in order to dismantle the centralized war economy, and significant measures of decentralization and local democracy. These prospects define the urgency of a new political/economic agenda for America.

A NEW POLITICAL/ECONOMIC AGENDA

The alternative to both a failing center and a radical right political campaign in the United States is a program of new political/economic reform that addresses the severe short- and long-term problems of American blue- and white-collar working people.

Economic conversion from a military to a civilian economy is a necessary key for enabling access to the vast resources allotted to the Pentagon: working people (especially skilled), the Pentagon's military machines whose value is about 50 percent of the worth of U.S. industry, and an annual budget that exceeds the sum of all U.S. corporate profits. The military now spends $49 billion annually for research and development; a transfer of $30 billion of that, for a start, to civilian research and development would be an important conversion element.

As many as 14 million new jobs in American industries are within reach. This requires restoring the means of production in American manufacturing industries, especially those that make capital goods, the means of production for all other industries. Such a perspective is beyond the bounds of present discussion in both the Democratic and Republican parties. But even half of this maximum—7 million new jobs—would erase the plague of major joblessness and transform the quality of debate on virtually every national issue.

By 1990 the captial goods industries accounted for 43 percent of all industrial employment but 60 percent of the jobs replaced in American industry by imports, the parallel closing of American factories and the movement abroad of finance capital.

In the accompanying table 3 I show for main manufacturing industries the portion of U.S. consumption that is met by imports, and the number of jobs foregone in their factories and offices owing to imports: 1,673,000 jobs in the Capital Goods industries alone and 2,780,000 in all of manufacturing. But restoration of several million new jobs requires new investments, especially of fixed capital representing land, buildings, and machinery.

Table 3

INVESTMENT TO RESTORE U.S. CAPITAL GOODS INDUSTRIES

Industry	Percent U.S. Consumption Met by Imports	Potential U.S. Jobs, Now Represented by Imports	Fixed Capital Required to Replace Imports With Domestic Production ($ billions)	Military Programs of Equal Cost ($ billions)
All Manufacturing	14.2%	2,780,000	$168.	Annual Cost of NATO to the U.S. ($160–$170)
All Capital Goods Industries	18.3%	1,673,000	$110.2	F-22 Fighter Program ($86.6) + SSN 68 attack sub program ($28.1)
Primary Metal Products	14.4%	110,000	$14.4	Navy Standard Missile Program ($12.3) + JTDIS comm. system ($2.0)
Fabricated Metal Products	7.8%	114,000	$5.2	M1A2 heavy tank program (upgrade of M-1)
Machinery (Except Electrical)	23.5%	444,000	$25.9	Trident II Missile Program
Electrical Equipment and Supplies	27.5%	448,000	$30.4	Titan Missile Program ($26.9) UTTMDS Upper Tier Theater Missile Defense System ($4.1)
Transportation Equipment	22.9%	428,000	$28.0	70% program cost of C-17 heavy cargoplane
Instruments and Related Products	13.8%	129,000	$6.3	RAH-66 Comanche helicopter program

From reports on the fixed capital used in U.S. industry we can readily calculate the average fixed capital investment per person now employed. The next column in the table shows the amount of fixed capital investment needed to replace imports with domestic production in each industry.

A notable feature of this perspective is that fresh investments would serve U.S. markets that already exist. Then the main problem for new investors is their ability to equal or exceed the product quality and price attractiveness of present imports.

The employment effect from this much fresh activity in U.S. manufacturing industries extends well beyond those directly engaged. For the new activity means a heightened demand for people to make materials and components for these expanded industries, and further employment to make the consumer products and services for the people newly employed. The employment effect would include 2.7 million newly employed in manufacturing, plus 11.3 million people in industries supplying materials, parts, and consumer goods and services to the expanded manufacturing labor force.

Where can the capital come from for the investments to achieve a substantial part of the implied program? In the right hand column of the accompanying table I show sets of military programs whose costs, in each instance, equals or exceeds the fixed capital needed for investment in the named industry.

A maximum new investment program in manufacturing as a whole would require $168 billion of new fixed capital. This magnitude is better appreciated when compared with the annual cost of NATO to the U.S. Treasury, $160–170 billion.

A major effort to restore production and employment in the Capital Goods industries—as listed in the table—would require a fixed capital investment of $110 billion. That sum is exceeded by the recently projected costs of the new Air Force F-22 Fighter program and the Navy SSN68 Attack Sub program.

The Transportation Equipment industries account for the direct loss of 428,000 jobs in the United States. The capital investment required to serve U.S. markets from new U.S.-based production is $28 billion, which corresponds to 70 percent of the program cost of the Air Force C-17 heavy cargo plane. The C-17 is supposed to replace the C-5 as a heavy freighter but has demonstrated both remarkable functional deficiencies and spectacular "cost growth."

How can such federal budget reductions be translated into investment capital? A part of the considerable sums so released could be tapped for the finance capital funds of new local economic development banks. The pool of money for financing the investment banks could also include money from individual investors, loan guarantees by city and state governments, and prudently invested parts of major pension funds.

From 1984 to 1992 trade unions, notably in the primary metals and clothing industries have undertaken to purchase majority ownership of their corporations through Employee Stock Ownership Plan buyouts. The total asset value of these purchases now exceed $1.5 billion. This method for new industrial financing has the special merit of enlisting ownership participation by the working people themselves, with the automatic effect of heightened responsibility and authority for improving the productivity of both labor and capital. Thereby they are better able to assure the security of their own incomes and employment through the operation of economically viable enterprises. Thus a number of machinists once employed by Boeing in Seattle have an active interest in a project for manufacturing high speed trains based on the Spanish Talgo 200 Pendular Train. That equipment has the stated merit of reliability, technical simplicity, unusual economy, and a solid track record of RR service.

The work of electrifying the main line railroads of the United States represents a set of long-term markets worth $180 billion. Hence, investment in new factories to make and maintain first rate equipment for this purpose has an assured U.S. market for at least the next 50 years.

Comprehensive conversion planning must be ordered by the President or Congress, it must be done in advance, and must be done locally in each defense factory, laboratory, and military base. The cornerstone of the comprehensive conversion law proposed in the Congress by Ted Weiss (D-NY) is this provision: "There shall be established at every defense facility employing at least 100 persons an Alternative Use Committee composed of not less than eight members with equal representation of the facility's management and labor." The composition of such committees insures that the members are committed and knowledgeable. This composition gives weight to people whose self-interest is tied to long-term production competence, as against short-term financial maneuvers that yield quick profit but degrade the production competence of an industry.

The professional judgment that planning must be done in advance is confirmed by ordinary experience. In industry this involves selecting new products, estimating their market, retraining employees, altering the organization of production, and redesigning plant facilities. Bases are convertible to industrial parks, schools, hospitals, airports, recreational facilities, etc. In military laboratories, the scientific staffs must match their knowledge with society's technological needs like renewable energy resources and preventing pollution. The first-hand knowledge possessed by defense establishment employees is essential for conversion. Thus, conversion must be done locally; no remote central office can possess the necessary knowledge of people, facilities and surroundings.

What can converted factories produce? Advanced designs of every sort of means of production and consumer goods: machine tools, electric locomotives, farm machinery, oil field equipment, and consumer electronics, etc. Modernizing infrastructure will require construction machinery and capital goods of many kinds. Electrification of U.S. railroads is a particularly desirable peace dividend project. This task, costing $180 billion, will require construction of entirely new industries for producing and maintaining equipment (from electric locomotives and rail cars to control equipment) that are not currently being designed, developed, or produced in the United States.

The Weiss conversion bill included a proposal that the Federal Council (cabinet level) named to oversee conversion shall "encourage the preparation of concrete plans for non-defense-related public projects addressing vital areas of national concern (such as transportation, housing, education, health care, environmental protection, and renewable energy resources) by the various civilian agencies of the government, as well as by state and local governments." Thereby a highly decentralized, nationwide process could be set in motion for the realistic planning of needed work, and for job and money requirements for cities, counties, and states. *To acquire the courage to break with their economic dependency on the Pentagon, employees, their communities, and Congressional representatives need blueprint-ready conversion plans that define an economic future for their factories, bases, and laboratories.* Conversion studies for factories, laboratories, and allied worker retraining are proper enterprise costs. Federal funding is needed for regional development planning for military base conversion; for converting the 90-odd major factories that are government-owned/company-operated; for a 1990s G.I. Bill of Rights; for retraining ex-Pentagon, CIA, NSA staffs; and for defense worker income support during actual conversion (as in the Weiss Bill). An annual levy of about 2 percent on Pentagon purchases can accumulate necessary federal conversion funding.

Economic conversion also prepares the way for negotiating international demilitarization—a course of policy for improving security that is anathema not only to the chiefs of the military industrial complex, but also to many of their working people who have known no sources of livelihood other than the manufacture of militarism. This extends from managers, engineers, and production workers to the shopkeepers and others whose cash flow has had its origin in the Pentagon and myriad intelligence, research, trade, propaganda, and university branches of the war-making institutions.

Managers in both private and state capitalism give top priority to maintaining and enlarging their decision power. Accordingly, government managers of military industry in the White House and the Pentagon as well as the top managers in the private firms can only be expected to resist economic conversion by all available means. For economic conversion necessarily entails a loss of their decision power. No civilian industry can deliver the same power and privilege as the military economy: profits are assured; goods are paid for before delivery; larger Pentagon contractors are virtually guaranteed against business failure; firms often receive what amounts to a "blank check" from the government that covers escalating costs. Managerially driven opposition to conversion planning also comes from the president of the United States and his secretary of defense who are, functionally, the chief executive officer and president of the military industry empire, operating through the Pentagon's central administrative office. With a staff of 500,000 controlling "acquisition," it is the largest such entity in the world.

Typically, the top managers of military industry have opposed any effort to convert to civilian work. They favor the Pentagon's policy called "adjustment." This means financial reorientation for the firm by new investments elsewhere— anywhere—and leaves responsibility for new jobs and skills to each individual through the mechanisms of the "free market." Like the managers of many civilian industrial firms, military enterprise top managers may be expected to abandon the function of organizing work and instead elect personal futures funded by ample "golden parachutes" and retirement benefits.

Job creation on a large scale requires particular institutional changes. Working people of all grades, including many "middle managers," must participate in competent production for the livelihood of themselves and their families. Top managerial abandonment of work organization has left many workers with no options besides jobs at a fraction of former pay or public welfare. That is why an increasing number of working people have sought out a new, extraordinary option—joint efforts by working people, unions, and communities to buy out and operate enterprises under their own control. Worker buyouts range from steel factories to supermarkets.

Worker buyouts can be an option for economic conversion, especially in the factories that are government owned and company operated. The land and facilities of military bases are typically turned over to local community ownership after they are declared "surplus" by the military. Why can't control of government owned military-industrial facilities also be transferred to their working people and community to the benefit of all concerned?

The creation of new institutions to facilitate worker ownership and control over production enterprises is a short-term response to the departure of corporate and government managers. But it is also a long-term investment—creating economic and allied institutions that carry the promise of workplace democracy and productive job creation as goals of enterprise.

These new institutions have the potential for replacing conventional characteristics of capitalism: occupational separation of decision-making from producing; hierarchy in decision-making; and the relentless pursuit of more decision power as a cardinal goal of management. While it is probably impossible to chart in advance the many-faceted development of workplace democracy, it is possible to define near-term effects. These include: joining decision-making with producing; deflating administrative hierarchy; productive job creation as a goal in place of profit/power maximizing.

Financing institutions are needed—a decentralized network, state by state and region by region—that serve both as sources of capital and as innovative designers and monitors of new and rebuilt enterprises. These can be banks, credit unions, loan guarantee agencies, coalitions of pension funds, with staffs that are competent to oversee both the planning of an enterprise and the monitoring of its continuous functioning. The same institutions can help to educate working people in the "mysteries" of enterprise administration, a further contribution toward workplace democracy.

In order to deploy public funds to jump-start and propel new productive investment, it is essential to confront the problem of public debt. The present $4 trillion federal debt, growing at $400 billion yearly, has been a primary result of military expansion combined with revenue reduction from a tax abatement for the super rich. But even with military budget cuts and a tax restoration for the super rich there will still be an annual deficit for some years. How should this deficit be understood? Debt in individual enterprise is justified if it finances new investment which generates at least enough income (return) to pay off that debt. Similarly, as federal funds are shifted to civilian/productive tasks, those expenditures can be seen as investments since new wealth is created: houses, hospitals, railroads, schools, clean water, factories, clean and renewable energy technologies, etc. All such goods are investments whose use enriches the community, making its people more productive and thereby yielding a rich return to the investing government in the form of tax revenues. But there are few such results from military products, which exit from the marketplace immediately upon being produced, consuming resources without giving consumption or further production use value. Thus, deficits to pay for productive investment are both bearable and desirable, while deficits on behalf of the military only weaken the economy.

A LESSON FOR AMERICANS: WEIMAR II?

The Weimar Republic of Germany was the site of a prolonged depression from the close of World War I until 1933, when the Nazis (National Socialist German Workers Party) took power by nomination from President Hindenburg. The Nazis lost no time in declaring the previous constitution and laws null and void and proceeded to install a totalitarian military form of state capitalism. The ascendancy of Hitler's party followed the unwillingness/inability of the governing Social Democratic party to make strong use of government to spur economy, employment, and income, and to form an alternative left-of-center grouping and policy. This failure of the Social Democrats opened the way for political mobilization from the right.

The Nazis appealed to the disaffected blue- and white-collar workers with a combination of "national" and "socialist" appeals. The nationalist appeal was based on ascribing a large part of Germany's economic troubles to the defeat in World War I and the penalties in territory and wealth applied by the Treaty of Versailles. The "socialist" part of the appeal included condemnation of the exploitation of German workers and emphasis on "Jewish international bankers" as a prime source of Germany's woes. Anti-Semitism was organized and pursued by violent methods as a way of fulfilling both the "national" and "socialist" aspects of Hitler's appeal.

But there was another side to the success of the Nazis in capturing popular attention. The vigorous campaign from the right in response to Germany's long and deep economic depression, strongly supported by German industrial managers, was bolstered by the failure of the socialist and communist parties to formulate and implement a radical program of reform necessary to address Germany's economic collapse. The Social Democratic party of Germany had over a million members, based upon a trade union membership of five million. At the same time the German Communist party at the end of 1932 had about 350,000 people enrolled. Both these political parties published scores of daily newspapers and other media, and operated large networks of trade union, community, and local government institutions. In the parliamentary elections prior to November 12, 1933, the combined Communist-Social Democratic vote exceeded that of the Nazis by nearly 1.5 million. But these parties of the German left-of-center were incapable of combining their considerable forces. This eased the way for Adolf Hitler's nomination to office by the president of Germany, General Hindenburg.

The failure of the German left grew out of two major conditions: first, the timidity of the Social Democratic party; second, the Communist party policy of "social fascism" which designated the Social Democrats, not the Nazis, as the main enemy. "Nach Hitler kommen wir" (after Hitler—our turn) was a Communist motto. The victory of the Nazis would hasten their ascendancy to power since the Nazis would "increase the misery" of the population who would then turn to the Communists. This remarkable formulation was controlled from Moscow and was a part of Stalin's policy of discouraging the political victory of a West European working class, whose economy would automatically overshadow the political economy of the Soviet Union.

I recount this outline of German events because their main lesson should not be lost on Americans. *The result of aggressive, well funded organization on the right, coupled with failure and catastrophic division in policy and organization on the left, opened a clear field for Hitler's party.*

POLITICS OF A NEW POLITICAL/ECONOMIC PROGRAM

A new political/economic agenda must address the full scope of damage done to industry, infrastructure, and quality of life by the long-enduring military state capitalism under federal government management. Accordingly, the major transitional components of this alternative policy must be grounded on demilitarization and economic conversion policies. These means alone have the potential for making available fresh resources on the scale required for creating millions of new jobs and repairing the major American human and physical decay. But a new political/economic agenda also requires a long-term policy to address the managerial system that has come to feature a growing inability and unwillingness to organize work.

For the longer term it is crucial to set in motion a sustained effort to encourage every sort of institution to create jobs and organize work based on non-managerial, cooperative, democratic forms of decision-making. Managers in private firms and in government have invented ways of continuing their money making and power extension, even as they curtail economically and socially useful work. Only the working people of all occupations require sustained conduct of *productive* work, because that activity is indispensable for their lives.

These political/economic characteristics form a framework of requirements for political organizing of every sort for the remainder of this century.

During the long cold war many Americans gave up hope for major change in the national politics of the United States. In place of concerted political effort, special purpose organizations were developed. These focused on particular issues: trade unions and working people; equal rights for women, African Americans, Native Americans, Hispanics; problems of the environment; health care; ethics in government; nuclear weapons; the condition of children; reproductive rights for women; education; care for the elderly, etc. From time to time temporary coalitions were formed, when particular issues seemed to dominate the national landscape and impelled unified action by combined groupings of the American left-of-center. However, these coalitions never gave sustained attention to the core characteristics of America's military state capitalism.

Following World War II, reform against racism and gender discriminations and toward greater equality in opportunity and income seemed feasible. That perspective has been markedly altered. As corporate and government managers have sponsored deindustrialization, job reduction, and a permanent war economy, the meaning of equal opportunity, for example, has been transformed. It has come to mean more equal sharing of less new wealth (such as housing), more equal sharing of decaying infrastructure, more equal sharing of a polluted environment, of less medical facilities, of less competent education, etc. When economic losses are suspected as the likely accompaniments of diminished racism and gender discrimination, then resistance to equalizing reforms is heightened. The holders of good jobs strive to reserve them for themselves and their kin, and resist claims for non-discriminatory entry. That is why it is necessary to address the underlying economic conditions that help engender racism and other inequalities.

Within a framework of demilitarization and ample funding for economic development, issues like racism can take on a new aspect. Improvement for disadvantaged African Americans and others in education, jobs, homes, etc., does not constitute or ensure an end to racism. The cultural, social-psychological, historical, and other components of racism are not like stains that may be quickly or easily erased. Racism is too multi-faceted, too ancient, too well regarded, and openly practiced by the most prestigious Americans (such as presidents) to be susceptible to wipe-out by either command or formal agreement. But serious economic improvement *would* make a major difference in the life circumstances, expectations, and achievements particularly of disadvantaged young minorities. Such improvement, especially as a part of economic development for all working people, contains both economic gain in its own right as well as a built-in counter-racist message. Occupation and earnings have powerful formative effects on most other aspects of life. It is thus reasonable to expect that economic improvement will yield improvement in race relations as well.

Growing incompetence in production and continued priority to the military-industrial complex checkmate prospects for serious improvement—issue by issue—in the range of reform subjects that have captured the commitment of many Americans during the last 45 years. If there is to be a competent new policy response to the political/economic crises of American society, then the participants in diverse reform movements will have to seek and identify their common ground and prepare to act in a *unified* manner. That is the importance of the transitional and long term policy recommendations for economic conversion, demilitarization, and worker control of productive enterprise. Success in these matters provides the means for—and is the necessary condition for—all the rest.

III. Popular Indigenous Struggles

STARTING FROM CHIAPAS

The Zapatistas Fire the Shot
Heard Around the World

MARC COOPER

This essay was written six months prior to the Mexican Presidential election in 1994. We have preserved the references of the original in order to allow a window into the moment. Since its original publication several new political earthquakes shook Mexico. PRI candidate Colosio was shot dead in March 1994 in mysterious circumstances. His replacement, Ernesto Zedillo, benefited from fears of uncertainty and won the presidential elections. The Cardenista opposition claimed fraud. The EZLN says its voice remains unheard.

SAN CRISTÓBAL DE LAS CASAS, MEXICO*—When some 800 mostly Mayan Tzetal soldiers of the Zapatista Army of National Liberation (EZLN) occupied the local city hall last January 1st, declaring war against the Mexican government on behalf of the "miserable and dispossessed," they scored a victory heretofore unattainable by any other hemispheric insurgent movement. They took over and held a First World city.

I say city, because this is no banana backwater—almost 100,000 people live here (the Salvadoran guerrillas at their height never controlled a town of more than a few thousand). And I say *First World* because San Cristóbal's narrow streets are not only clogged with too many cars and belching busses, but also because they are lined with shops selling most—if not all—the imported paraphernalia of modernity: BMX bikes, Nintendo and Sega video games, dish antennas, Mont Blanc and Pelikan pens, cappuccino, organic and vegetarian lunches, and even study seminars in Karma and Reincarnation hawked by some ex-pat Gringos and aimed at those very First World, hairy-legged ecotourists who feel so much better about themselves for coming here to gawk at Indians instead of ogling the bikinis and buns in Acapulco.

Not that this place, 700 miles southeast of Mexico City, is a metropolis either. Indeed, compared to any First World capital, this colonial outpost with its graceful porticos, balconies and shaded plazas, is no more than postcard quaint. But nevertheless, as waves of crass Yankee consumerism washed ever southward over the years, it seems that the global marketplace reached its highwater mark right here. Step out of town either to the east or south and you are unremittingly marooned in the Third World (in fact, so quickly does the consumerist tide end that just a few miles away in a place called San Juan Chamula, some entrepreneurs have figured out a way to make Pepsi so exotic that local Indians have been persuaded to purchase the soda for their daily religious rituals).

So when the 800 Zapatistas poured into the municipal offices here, opened the police and property archives and set them on fire, and when another thousand—maybe two thousand—of their comrades simultaneously seized five other nearby towns, opening the food warehouses to the poor, chasing out and in some cases killing the local police, dismantling another town hall stone by stone with sledgehammers, yet another with axes and saws, and then fought the Mexican Army to a standstill for more than a week, they were not acting out some pathetic revolutionary *retablo* left over from the Central American cataclysms of the Eighties. No. Precisely because the EZLN chose San Cristóbal as its major theater of operations, because the timing of the uprising coincided with the implementation of NAFTA, and certainly because of the complex nature of the EZLN and what it is fighting for, this Chiapas rebellion is much more than an Indian Uprising, far more significant than a recycled Marxist guerrilla movement. The shots fired in Chiapas on January 1 signal the End of the End of History. Rather than the final rattle on the snake of revolution, Chiapas is the first armed battle *against* the Global Market and simultaneously—in a way Americans cannot grasp—*for* Democracy.

The 12-year-old project of the current and previous Mexican administration to bring this country into the First World—in the words of Carlos Fuentes—as instantly as brewing a cup of Nescafé, has crashed on the hard beach of political reality. Hundreds of millions of foreign investment dollars, a red hot stock market, the dismemberment of the social welfare state, the nurturing of a new class of Mexican yuppies—yuppies hell, a new class of Mexican *Billionaires,* and all crowned by NAFTA, as much as went up in smoke along with the San Cristóbal town records. "Just when we're telling the world and ourselves that we were looking like the U.S., we turn out to be Guatemala," says one Mexican friend, a writer.

And not surprisingly, adds veteran opposition politician Herberto Castillo. "Those who applauded our growing economy, what they ignored, what they olympically ignored," he says, "is that while the rich got richer, the nation got ever poorer."

Mexican President Carlos Salinas de Gortari, a Harvard-educated technocrat, attempted to modernize the country that his "Institutional Revolutionary Party"—PRI—had ruled in one-party fashion for more than six decades using the reverse formula employed by Gorbachev. "It was the Chinese way," says long time political activist Luis Hernandez. "Economic modernization without real democracy. Perestroika, without glasnost. Now that plan is in pieces. And without there ever being even any real perestroika."

NAFTA, which many Mexicans argue was mostly intended as a U.S.-provided political prop for Salinas and the PRI, might now ironically turn out to be the detonator that blows him and his party out of power. Just when it seemed the PRI would easily ride the Trade Agreement to sure victory in Presidential elections the most unthinkable of all Mexican taboos, the unseating of PRI, is now on the lips and minds of millions of Mexicans—all thanks to the powerful political shockwaves unleashed by the Zapatistas in Chiapas.

To say that the timing of the EZLN attack was dazzling is an understatement. If the Zapatistas had struck before the signing of NAFTA, "it would have made passage very problematic in congress," as one U.S. Embassy official says. But the way would have been clear for the Mexican state to retaliate massively, frying the EZLN and probably tens of thousands of civilians in a scorched earth campaign. But by waiting until January and the kicking in of NAFTA to launch its offensive, the EZLN put the Mexican establishment in a political pickle. With Big Trading Brother's eyes cast southward, the Mexican Army would have to restrain itself.

But more brilliant than EZLN timing is its political strategy. Mostly unreported in the American press is that the EZLN has nothing in common with the guerrilla vanguards of the last 30 years. The Zapatistas' mortal threat to Salinas, PRI, and NAFTA is that instead of proposing what they could never achieve and what would turn all of Mexico against them—seizure of power and the installation of a revolutionary dictatorship—the Zapatistas call for the two things most Mexicans support which are, not coincidentally, the only two things the PRI is unwilling and unable to provide: truly free elections and real democratization of Mexico.

Election fraud is a long-time PRI tradition in a country where no real opposition was allowed to prosper. But when the PRI was faced for the first time with a viable opponent, Salinas won the Presidential sash in 1988, with barely

50.7 percent of the vote. PRI officials vehemently claimed that any vote fixing was a thing of the past, that Salinas had won fair and square. But millions of Mexicans loudly protested that Salinas had stolen the election from center-left opposition leader Cauhtemoc Cardenas (who still refuses to accept Salinas as the "duly-elected" president) and the country teetered in uncertainty for months. Again in 1991, opposition partisans occupied dozens of rural city halls, and criss-crossed the nation with militant marches, once again claiming PRI fraud in state elections. In these last five years, almost 300 Cardenista supporters have been killed in political violence, and each national election seems prelude to full scale confrontation. NAFTA, in many ways, was designed to provide the PRI with the cloak of legitimacy and stability necessary to deflate the opposition and its protests.

But now the eruption of the Zapatistas on to the political stage has turned Mexican politics upside down. With presidential elections only six months away, the PRI's time for maneuver is in critical countdown. Overnight the national political debate has shifted from a focus on markets and monetarism to one of aiding the poor and the indigenous, of increased reform and more social spending. All and all a golden opportunity once again for opposition candidate Cauhtemoc Cardenas whose very name and chiseled facial features invokes an image of indefatigable Indian resistance to conquest, and whose father Lazaro is remembered by the poor as the boldest of Mexican reformist presidents.

In short, the PRI has less than 200 days to figure out a way not to lose the elections. Or it could try to jimmy them. But this time around, fraud, even the suggestion of fraud, could be suicidal. Mix in the resulting widespread protests with an already simmering Zapatista insurgency and you have the recipe for full-scale civil war and insurrection.

Certainly, the Mexican government's initial response to the uprising revealed anything but the sort of democratic vocation that George Bush and Bill Clinton swore to be the ethos of a new, reformed PRI. Foreigners and "catechists" blamed as "professional manipulators" of the poor were singled out as the cause of the tumult. Government spokespersons refused to let the words EZLN or Zapatista sully their discourse, referring to the rebels in an Orwellian way as only "transgressors of the law." During that first week, as bombs and rockets rained down on hillside villages, tanks rolled into town squares, Mexican army troops began door to door searches for subversives.

But as mounting reports of journalists being rocketed, and cadavers showing up with their hands tied behind their backs brought in caravans of national and foreign human rights workers, as the world's newspapers dedicated whole pages to the "forgotten" poor of Chiapas and the heart-rending indigenous face of the "other Mexico," as hundreds of public declarations from unions, universities, and neighborhood groups across Mexico poured forth condemning the violent tactics of the EZLN but nevertheless endorsing the rebels' call for reform, a cold panic set in at President Salinas's official Los Pinos residence.

Mexican policy toward the outside world has always been a game of images, and the image now roaring out of Chiapas on the wings of Air Force bombers was the wrong one. With an opposition call for a truce and negotiations building like a political snowball, President Salinas moved to pre-empt and co-opt. For the first time in modern Mexican history a local political event—the Chiapas rebellion—had near immediate repercussions in the Presidential cabinet. On the eleventh day of the conflict, Salinas fired a number of hard-line and key ministers and replaced them with a group of respected, and fairly independent liberals.

The former Mayor of Mexico City, and then Foreign Minister, Manuel Camacho Solis, a PRIista with a rep for being open to talking to the opposition, was named as a special, non-governmental, nonsalaried, Peace Commissioner and handed the mandate to hammer out an agreement with the EZLN. In rapid-fire succession, Camacho Solis as much as recognized the EZLN, asked a leading Bishop—who only days before had been accused of leading the EZLN —to be his chief aide, called on the Zapatistas to begin a no conditions dialogue with him, and arranged for Salinas to institute a unilateral cease-fire with and general amnesty for the rebels. "No less than a full 180 degree turn-around overnight," says Mexican novelist Paco Ignacio Taibo II. "The Zapatistas had won more in 11 days than the Salvadoran guerrillas got in 11 years. No PRI government had ever been forced to make so many spectacular capitulations." So dramatic had been Salinas's turnaround that some political commentators argued that, in effect, Salinas had met the EZLN demand for a "transitional government" to take Mexico into the August elections.

I catch a full blast of the new national political line as I sit in a Chiapas hotel room and, along with a reporter from the McNeil-Lehrer News Hour, interview "Peace Commissioner" Camacho's top adviser Juan Enriquez. Like his boss Camacho, like the President, the 35-year-old, fair-skinned Enriquez is a product of Harvard Business School, and even here on the outskirts of the Southern Mexico jungle he wears his tasseled loafers, beige chinos, and a Brooks Brothers chambray blue shirt under his navy lambswool pullover. But in truly flawless English, Enriquez tonight sounds more like an anthropology professor than an MBA. Faintly ridiculous, fairly unnerving is it to watch this very model of Mexican elitism sit here and spin like a top about "poverty," "government mistakes," "indigenous rights," "solving the root causes of the conflict," and the "need for more education, more health, more jobs, more balanced rural development."

I mean, who does he think's been running this country for the last 65 years? Wasn't it just three days ago that he was Chief of Staff to the Foreign Minister when Camacho held that post? "We're now going to have to be a lot more careful in modernizing Mexico," Enriquez says, now that the News Hour cameras have been turned off. "Until now there's been a lot of arrogance in that process. That will have to change."

And soon, he agrees. And then even he admits that Great Unthinkable Thought. "The government has to be seen making real changes before the August elections," he says. "Either that, or none of this thing is going to work."

Two compelling sets of circumstances lead one to believe that "this thing"— a negotiated return to Mexican business as usual—is, indeed, not going to work: the military strength and strategy of the Zapatistas, on the one hand; the lack of real political will for reform by the government, on the other.

The Mexican government may be in a hurry to settle this dispute, but not the Zapatistas. "The Zapatistas operate on the time schedule of the Gods," says one organizer who knows them well. "Their tactic now will be to flirt with Camacho and maybe even sit down at the table with him. But, in the end, they will stick to their demand for a transitional government and free elections. Either the government gives in to that, which is hard to imagine, or on the eve of elections, the Zapatistas walk and then strike again if the PRI wins. Only this time God knows how many peasants from Michoacan and Oaxaca will join them."

In the meantime, the EZLN conserves its military strength. In none of the six towns it held earlier this month was the rebel army dislodged, it simply withdrew. "The army will never find them in their home bases," says one activist who spent years organizing peasant unions in Chiapas. "The jungle is so thick that the sun doesn't hit the ground. You can make sure that the Zapatistas didn't organize for 10 years to fight for only 10 days and then disappear."

Ten years is actually an understatement. Though the Mexican government claims the EZLN presence as a surprise, its organizing roots go back at least to a celebrated Indian Congress in Chiapas in 1974. A plethora of radical and revolutionary organizing projects were spawned and dozens of peasant and Indian unions co-mingled with veteran leftist activists of the generation of 1968.

"The presence of radical groups in the jungle was something we and everyone else knew about for years," says the union activist. "The state incubated them, the collusion between landlords and the police, fomenting conflicts between peasant groups. By whatever name we knew of the Zapatistas as they worked for years in our area. First they were very discreet, working within already existing institutions, at least until 2 years ago. Then it became clear they had their own agenda and strategy, and I have to say they have grown very quickly."

By May 1993 several Mexican press reports told of increasing guerrilla activity in the Chiapas region. Outside analysts report that a wave of kidnappings has netted the Zapatistas as much as $10 million in ransom, though the EZLN deny kidnapping as a fundraising tactic. Several sources confirm that this past September a number of Indian and rural communities voted to not plant the fields thereby consciously deciding to go to war. That same month, say Mexican government sources, military intelligence had compiled detailed videos on the Zapatista presence. But, apparently, a political decision was made by the Mexican government to not imperil a then-pending NAFTA approval by launching a noisy counter-insurgent campaign. The Zapatistas, it argued, could be contained with social welfare programs.

But that decision backfired. In part because of a gross under-estimation of Zapatista strength. Mexican political scientist Jorge Castaneda, an expert on the Latin American Left, says that unlike the Salvadoran or Guatemalan guerrillas that set themselves up as a vanguard in search of a social base, the Zapatistas carefully built up their mass support for years and only *then* drew an army from their ranks. "This is a guerrilla movement destined only to grow as long as it doesn't commit mistakes—which till now it hasn't, and as long as it has money and logistical networks—who knows, but it seems probable, as long as it doesn't lose its ranks—and the number of casualties it suffered or the prisoners it gave up indicate the contrary, as long as it does not alienate its supporters—and the gains won so far constitute the best argument in many years in favor of armed struggle in all of Latin America. Under these circumstances, time works in favor of the Zapatistas. They certainly can't be in any hurry to negotiate in a serious way."

Nor is it clear there's much to negotiate. To travel from San Cristóbal into the highland heart of Chiapas is to marvel not only at the rocky pine forests and the bursts of banana trees, eucalyptus and yellow and orchid-colored vines and wildflowers exploding alongside the rutted highway, but also to descend into a world of base-level impoverishment which seems to have changed hardly at all since the collapse of the Mayan empire a thousand years ago. Fractured into more than 20 different language groups, and still wearing magenta, and aquamarine and hot pink and orange and crimson costumes, and still walking down jagged hills on bare feet in search of water, the Mayan Tzetales, Tzotziles, Choles, Tojolobals, Zoques, and Mames make up about a third of Chiapas's 3 million inhabitants.

Three-fourths of the indigenous people are illiterate. Twenty percent of Chiapan adults have no employment. Sixty percent make no more than the minimum wage of four dollars a day. Fifty-five percent of the country's hydro-electric power is produced here, yet thirty percent of the homes have no electricity, twice as many have only dirt floors.

The most productive land is held by large *caciques*—all powerful landowners with the police and private militias at their beck and call—turning Chiapas into one of the worst consistent violators of human rights in all of Mexico. Reduced to scratching out subsistence crops of corn and beans from tiny and exhausted parcels of land, the average impoverished farmer fights a daily battle with hunger. Whatever product is left over he sells on the national market. At least until now. Under NAFTA there is legitimate fear that cheap food imports from the United States will wipe out whatever small margin currently exists for the small producers. Bad news for the ninety percent of Chiapas communities already classified as economically "marginal."

And yet, it is here in Chiapas where the Mexican government has spent the most amount of its so-called Solidarity money, it social welfare program. This underlines a central truth: the problem in Chiapas isn't just economic. Rather it's the archaic, mummified and authoritarian political structure, a *menage à trois* of the PRI, the landlords and the security forces that cements in place such brutal exploitation. And to ask the PRI to solve this problem, to negotiate it away, is to ask the PRI to sever its own decades-old political base. Hence, the simple brilliance of the Zapatistas demanding political reform, not revolution.

Pulling into the town of Ocosingo—"gateway to the Lancondan jungle"—a two hour ride east from San Cristóbal through a series of Army checkpoints, the intact political monopoly of the PRI is immediately evident. The night before, in Juan Enriquez's hotel room, cultured talk of a new peace movement sounded soothing. Here in Ocosingo, one of the six towns the Zapatistas held for a few days, there is a more aggressive interpretation. Though the army has declared a truce, hundreds of its troops occupy the town. Townswomen navigate long lines in search of government food relief only to find that at the last moment soldiers deny them food unless they can prove who and where their husbands are, lest they be Zapatistas. At last count, soldiers took away 139 locals accused of being subversives.

The PRI Mayor, in the meantime, has lined up some 200 peasants in a "peace" march and leads them on a parade around the town square, chanting for the Army to please stay on. As the parade passes by the Catholic parish, the mayors' men shout insults at Padre Pablo, who they imply is a guerrilla supporter. Later on inside Pablo's courtyard, a number of demonstrators stand around taking shade and sipping water. They tell me they participated only because the Mayor was keeping an eye on them. They laugh at the thought that Padre Pablo is a guerrilla. But even they admit to a certain sympathy for the Zapatistas. "When they came into town one of them started talking to me," says a 60-year-old subsistence farmer. "They came from the jungle," he said. And then he said, "Why are some men rich when some are so poor? Why do we have to pay for water when God made the water for all of us? Why do some men have so much land and others don't when God made the earth for all of us? We are all Mexican *campesinos*," he said. "We both need to eat the same." I agreed with him.

On the outskirts of town, at the local cemetery, a gravedigger shows me the mass grave the army asked him to make earlier in the month. Eleven people are buried in an unmarked plot, in a corner of the graveyard, next to a three-foot square hole in the concrete wall facing the street. Eight of the bodies are supposedly Zapatistas killed in fighting. Three others, says the gravedigger, are civilians killed by soldiers for violating curfew. The bodies had been piled up outside the cemetery wall, 25 yards from the main gate. "Instead of carrying the bodies through the gate," says the gravedigger, "they opened up that hole in the wall, dragged the bodies a few feet into the cemetery and buried them right there. They didn't want to bother to bring them through the front gate."

Halfway back to San Cristóbal sits the dusty village of Oxchuc, another Zapatista target, one more town that would make even Sergio Leone squirm. If God ever made one little acre to encapsulate every ill that besets Mexico it is

Oxchuc. At it's market, shoppers jostle to pick up the half-pound gutted rats for sale as stew stock—75 cents each. Vendors warn me that the town is "divided" and that I shouldn't ask too many questions.

Within a few minutes the political fault lines emerge. In the town square, the PRI Mayor has gathered up his loyal men for another blood rally like the one in Ocosingo. But here there's no lip service to peace. The PRI claim that a local opposition group, the 2000 member Civic Association, is really the Zapatistas. "When the subversives came to town, I saw the guys from the Civic Association join them and start tearing down all the municipal buildings," says one of the Mayor's followers.

No one can explain to me how it is possible with so many Zapatistas living in town for the PRI to get not 90 percent, not 99 percent, but exactly 100 percent of the 11,300 votes cast here in the 1991 election. One possible answer emerges from searching through the rubble of local PRI office trashed by the guerrillas. There scattered over the floor are boxes of official election ballots— from the 1985 vote—ballots that should be only in possession of election officials not party workers.

A half mile from the Mayor's rally, the Civic Association has called together an emergency meeting of its own. As 200 delegates stand in a school room for one hour to hear their leader's report, I can understand nothing. The meeting is in Tzetal and only a dozen or so words come out in Spanish: "bombardment...arrests...human rights...individual rights...they told us to fuck off..."

As the meeting broke up, organizer Francisco Gomez tells me in Spanish that his group is worried that today the mayor will have the homes of the leadership of the Civic Association bulldozed. In the past six militants have met such a fate. Three others have been killed in political shootings. For the last 5 years, Gomez says, the Mayor's office has refused the Association members birth records, draft certificates and other vital papers. "They hate us, they hate what we stand for, but we are peaceful."

What about the rumors that the Association is part of the EZLN, I ask.

"The Zapatistas did pass through here," Gomez answers. "And some people went off with them. Some because they were forced to, and others because after five years of frustration they see no other way out. I find that what the Zapatistas ask for is just. We don't have land and there are people here who eat once every three days."

The next day as many as 1000 army troops arrive in two dozen trucks and Armored Personnel Carriers, supported by Air Force combat aircraft. The mayor climbs into a jeep with two army officers and begins patrolling this fiefdom, pointing out alleged subversives. Within a few hours at least 16 people have been detained. The leadership of the Civic Association, with whom I spoke the day before, has gone underground. Things are back to normal in Oxchuc.

Perhaps only temporarily. All of Mexico is in frenetic ferment. An atmosphere like that of the Prague Spring has prevailed since the first of the year. In Chiapas, 140 peasant and Indian organizations, after an unprecedented day-long unity meeting, have issued a call for total social and political reform. Similar rumblings are heard from the states of Tabasco, Hidalgo, Oaxaca, and Guerrero.

In the capital of Mexico City some 80,000 police have heightened security in the wake of a half dozen bombings. But even in the bourgeois capital there's much more a mood of giddy, upbeat expectancy of real change than there is of fear. By 10:00 A.M. every morning the opposition daily *La Jornada*—which has committed as much as 25 pages a day to the political crisis sparked by the Chiapas rebels—is sold out while stacks of pro-government papers linger into the evening.

The PRI's official presidential candidate—Luis Colosio—has become the Invisible Man, overshadowed by Peace Commissioner Camacho. And in a land where PRI candidates expect and unfailingly, until now, receive about as much attention as say an Egyptian Pharaoh, this unprecedented fact alone brings glee to millions of Mexicans. The best measure of President Salinas and the PRI's predicament is to understand that Camacho is the arch-rival of Candidate Colosio. And Camacho was the odds-on favorite to be named as Salinas's successor until the President opted for the more loyal and docile Colosio.

When Salinas had to turn to Camacho as peace negotiator it was an astounding recognition of weakness. Camacho was, in effect, the last living, ranking PRIista with enough public integrity to pull off his mission. And therein lies the government's conundrum. If Camacho fails to negotiate a lasting peace, PRI goes into the election with a guerrilla war at its back. On the other hand, to the degree that Camacho is successful, the PRI candidate, Colosio is diminished. Worse for the PRI is that Camacho might bolt the PRI and join up with Cardenas. Not too far-fetched a scenario, given that Cardenas himself was once a PRI governor before founding his opposition Revolutionary Democratic Party.

Facing the August 21, 1994 elections, says Mexico's top political columnist Carlos Ramirez, the PRI may have run out of options. "The EZLN can extend the armed conflict at low intensity until August and then sign a peace agreement if the elections are clean or launch a big offensive in different parts of the Republic to protest fraud," says Ramirez. "Perhaps [President] Salinas fears the defeat of Colosio and wishes to repeat the electoral unpleasantness of 1988. In that case the only real guarantor of the elections will be not the Federal Electoral Institute, but the Zapatista Army."

Whatever the outcome of the elections, so many Mexicans are not waiting around for change. Before Salinas declared a government cease-fire, opposition leader Cardenas called for a massive night-time Mexico City street demonstration calling for a truce. In classic PRI style, Salinas chose the morning of the planned march to announce his unilateral cease-fire. As I prepared to go to the march with a group of friends, many speculated it would be a small affair, rendered redundant by Salinas's maneuver.

But as we got to the downtown Monument to the Revolution at 5 P.M. a sea of humans roiled before us. Contingents of university students, health workers, Indian groups, the homeless, smartly-dressed bureaucrats and office employees, architects, writers and journalists, neighborhood organizers and professional political agitators converged in the most joyous, euphoric, and infectiously optimistic march I can remember since the sixties. I joined the contingent led by the masked wrestler Superbarrio, who in his red and gold lamé outfit has become a folk hero symbol of resistance to greedy landlords and repressive authorities.

As high as our spirits were, they soared further as we saw the crowds multiply geometrically as we thundered along the city's main boulevards toward the colonial era National Palace, the Zocalo. Who could not be moved by the thousands of carefully hand-lettered cardboard signs that blossomed along the route expressing the heartfelt thoughts of so many ordinary good, people who didn't have to be told what to yell or shout or think and could still understand how their own personal destiny was linked to that of others. "We want solutions for our brothers in Chiapas" read one sign. "Enough hunger and misery. We want respect" read so many others.

Moving through the cement and glass gullies of the most populous city in the world, our ranks continuing to swell, vendors did brisk business with stenciled T-shirts proclaiming "I am a Zapatista!" And "All of Mexico is Chiapas!"

No one said it so bluntly, but what fueled our cheer was the knowledge that the hypnotic, one-way-only trance-mantra of the last fifteen years of Global This and Global That had been beautifully snapped. That the eerie light provided by the muzzle flashes of two thousand Tzetal fighters had captured in a freeze frame—for the whole world to see and recognize—the total absurdity of opening Price Clubs and Domino Pizzas and Taco Bells in Mexico and calling that progress, the imbecility of grown men with advanced degrees quoting the economic theorems of an orange-haired and narcoleptic Ronald Reagan, the inanity of starting to believe that less really is more especially if it is for the more needy. With this notion in their hearts, 150,000—maybe 250,000 Mexicans—in any case more people than anyone can remember in any demonstration since 1968—streamed for two-and-a-half hours into the nation's town square, intent on stretching this into something lasting, committed to rolling back those who have rolled over them and thought they would continue doing so forever, and facing toward, what I think was the North, shouted and laughed, "First World! Ha! Ha! Ha!"

ORIGINAL DECLARATION OF WAR FROM THE LACANDON JUNGLE BY THE ZAPATISTAS TO THE PEOPLE OF MEXICO

MEXICAN BROTHERS AND SISTERS:

WE ARE A PRODUCT OF 500 YEARS OF STRUGGLE: first against slavery, then during the War of Independence against Spain led by insurgents, then to avoid being absorbed by North American imperialism, then to promulgate our constitution and expel the French empire from our soil, and later the dictatorship of Porfirio Diaz denied us the just application of the Reform laws and the people rebelled and leaders like Villa and Zapata emerged, poor men just like us. We have been denied the most basic social services so they can use us as cannon fodder and pillage the wealth of our country. They don't care that we have nothing, absolutely nothing, not even a roof over our heads, no land, no work, no health care, no food nor education. Nor are we able to freely and democratically elect our political representatives, nor is there independence from foreigners, nor is there peace nor justice for ourselves and our children.

But today, we say ENOUGH IS ENOUGH. We are the heirs of the true builders of our nation. The dispossessed, we are millions and we thereby call upon our brothers and sisters to join this struggle as the only path, so that we will not die of hunger due to the insatiable ambition of a 70-year dictatorship led by a clique of traitors that represent the most conservative and sell-out groups. They are the same ones that opposed Hidalgo and Morelos, the same ones that betrayed Vicente Guerrero, the same ones that sold half our country to the foreign invader, the same ones that imported a European prince to rule our country, the same ones that formed the "scientific" Porfirista dictatorship, the same ones that opposed the Petroleum Expropriation, the same ones that massacred the railroad workers in 1958 and the students in 1968, the same ones that today take everything from us, absolutely everything.

To prevent the continuation of the above and as our last hope, after having tried to utilize all legal means based on our Constitution, we go to our Constitution, to apply Article 39 which says:

"National Sovereignty essentially and originally resides in the people. All political power emanates from the people and its purpose is to help the people. The people have, at all times, the inalienable right to alter or modify their form of government."

Therefore, according to our constitution, we declare the following to the Mexican federal army, the pillar of the Mexican dictatorship that we suffer from, monopolized by a one-party system and led by Carlos Salinas de Gortari, the maximum and illegitimate federal executive that today holds power.

According to this Declaration of War, we ask that other powers of the nation advocate to restore the legitimacy and the stability of the nation by overthrowing the dictator.

We also ask that international organizations and the International Red Cross watch over and regulate our battles, so that our efforts are carried out while still protecting our civilian population. We declare now and always that we are subject to the Geneva Accord, forming the EZLN as our fighting arm of our liberation struggle. We have the Mexican people on our side, we have the beloved tri-colored flag highly respected by our insurgent fighters. We use black and red in our uniform as our symbol of our working people on strike. Our flag carries the following letters, "EZLN," Zapatista Army of National Liberation, and we always carry our flag into combat.

Beforehand, we refuse any effort to disgrace our just cause by accusing us of being drug traffickers, drug guerrillas, thieves, or other names that might by used by our enemies. Our struggle follows the constitution which is held high by its call for justice and equality.

Therefore, according to this declaration of war, we give our military forces, the EZLN, the following orders:

FIRST: Advance to the capital of the country, overcoming the Mexican federal army, protecting in our advance the civilian population and permitting the people in the liberated area the right to freely and democratically elect their own administrative authorities.

SECOND: Respect the lives of our prisoners and turn over all wounded to the International Red Cross.

THIRD: Initiate summary judgments against all soldiers of the Mexican federal army, who we accuse of being traitors to our country, and the political police that have received training or have been paid by foreigners and against all those who have repressed and treated badly the civil population and robbed or stolen from or attempted crimes against the good of the people.

FOURTH: Form new troops with all those Mexicans that show their interest in joining our struggle, including those that, being enemy soldiers, turn themselves in without having fought against us, and promise to take orders from the General Command of the Zapatista Army of National Liberation.

FIFTH: We ask for the unconditional surrender of the enemy's headquarters before we begin any combat to avoid any loss of lives.

SIXTH: Suspend the robbery of our natural resources in the areas controlled by the EZLN.

To the People of Mexico: We, the men and women, full and free, are conscious that the war that we have declared is our last resort, but also a just one. The dictators are applying an undeclared genocidal war against our people for many years. Therefore we ask for your participation, your decision to support this plan that struggles for work, land, housing, food, health care, education, independence, freedom, democracy, justice and peace. We declare that we will not stop fighting until the basic demands of our people have been met by forming a government of our country that is free and democratic.

JOIN THE INSURGENT FORCES OF THE ZAPATISTAS.

—General Command of the EZLN, 1993

Zapatista Communique

The following statements were delivered to three Mexican newspapers for publication. In them, the Zapatistas (EZLN) reiterate the motives which led them to take up arms on January 1, and proposes different paths to bring peace to the state of Chiapas. Statement of January 6, 1994.

"Here we are, the dead of all times, dying once again,
but now with the objective of living."

TO THE MEXICAN PEOPLE:
TO THE PEOPLE AND GOVERNMENTS OF THE WORLD:
BROTHERS & SISTERS:

Beginning on January 1 of this year, Zapatista troops initiated a series of political-military actions whose primary objective is to make the miserable conditions in which millions of Mexicans live—especially we the indigenous people, known to the Mexican people and the rest of the world. With these actions we also want to make known our decision to fight for our basic rights through the only means that government authorities leave us: armed struggle.

The extreme conditions of poverty in which our fellow countrypeople live have a common cause: the lack of liberty and democracy. We believe that authentic respect for liberty and the people's democratic will are indispensable requirements for improving the economic and social conditions in which Mexico's dispossessed live. For this reason we raise the flag for the improvement of the Mexican people's living conditions and demand free and democratic policies. With this goal we ask for the renunciation of Carlos Salinas de Gortari's illegitimate government and the formation of a transitional democratic government which will guarantee clean elections throughout the country on all levels of government. We reiterate the validity of our political and economic demands and through them we try to unite the Mexican people and their independent organizations so that, through all forms of struggle, a national revolutionary movement is formed which allows the existence of honest and patriotic social organizations for the improvement of Mexico.

From the beginning of our fight for freedom we have not only been attacked by repressive government bodies and the federal army but also slandered by the federal and state governments and the media that try to spoil our struggle by telling the Mexican public that our struggle is promoted by foreigners, professional terrorists with shady interests, and anti-patriotic people seeking personal benefits. In view of these slanders and lies, the EZLN feels obliged to clarify the following:

FIRST—Our EZLN has no foreigners in its ranks or command nor has it received any support or assistance from foreign governments or revolutionary movements in other countries. The news reports saying that Guatemalans serve in our army and that they were trained in our neighboring country are stories invented by the federal government to undermine our cause. We have not had nor have any connection with the El Salvadoran FMLN or with the URGN in Guatemala nor with any other armed movement in Latin America, North America, Europe, Africa, or Asia. The military tactics we use were not learned from Central American insurgents, but from Mexican military history—that of Hidalgo, Guerrero, Mina, the resistance to yankee invasion in 1846–1847, the popular resistance to French intervention, the heroic gestures of Villa and Zapata, and the indigenous resistance throughout the history of our country.

SECOND: Our EZLN has no connection to Catholic religious authorities nor any other creed. We have not received orientation, direction, or support from any ecclesiastical structure nor any of the dioceses of the state of Chiapas, the apostolic nuncio, the Vatican, or anyone. Our ranks are composed primarily of Catholics but there are also some from other religions and creeds.

THIRD: The majority of the EZLN troops are indigenous people from the state of Chiapas, this being the case because we indigenous represent the most humiliated and dispossessed sector in Mexico, but also, as you can see, the most dignified. We are thousands of armed indigenous people and behind us are thousands of our relatives. So we are dozens of thousands of indigenous people in struggle. The government says that this is not an indigenous uprising, but we think that if thousands of indigenous people rise up in protest, then it is indeed an indigenous uprising. Also participating in our movement are Mexicans from other social origins and distinct Mexican states. They agree with our cause and have joined us because they oppose the exploitation we suffer. Just as these non-indigenous Mexicans have joined us so will others because our struggle is national and it will not be limited only to the state of Chiapas. At the present time, the political leadership of our struggle is totally indigenous. 100 percent of the Indigenous Revolutionary Clandestine Committee (CCRI) in the combat zone belong to the Tzotzil, Tzeltal, Chol, Tojolabal, and other ethnicities. As of right now, not all the indigenous people of Chiapas are with us because many brothers and sisters are still subject to the government's ideas and lies. But we are many thousand and they will have to pay attention to us. The use of masks and other means to hide our faces is a basic security measure and a type of vaccine against local leaders.

FOURTH: The arms and equipment used by our people are varied and, understandably, have not been shown publicly in their totality to the press nor the civil population in the municipalities that we occupied on January 1 and 2, 1994. These arms and equipment were collected little by little and prepared through 10 years of silent accumulation of forces. The "sophisticated" means of communication that we have can be found in any store that sells imported articles. To obtain the arms we never resorted to robbing, kidnapping, or extortion. Furthermore we maintained ourselves with the resources provided by honest and humble people throughout Mexico. It is due to the fact that we never resorted to banditry to obtain resources that the State's repressive apparatus never detected our actions during ten years of serious and careful preparations.

FIFTH: Some have asked us why we decided to begin now if we have been prepared for some time. The answer is that before we tried all pacific and legal means without results. During these 10 years more than 150 thousand of our indigenous brothers have died from curable diseases. The federal, state, and municipal governments' economic and social plans do not contemplate any real solutions to our problems and they are limited to giving us charity every time elections come around. But the charity only lasts a few moments and then death returns to our homes. For this reason we think that we have had enough of dying useless deaths and that we must fight for changes. If we die now it will not be with embarrassment but with dignity, as was the case for our ancestors. We are prepared to die, another 150 thousand if this is necessary, to awake the people from the dream of deception in which the government keeps them.

SIXTH: The conditions for "reconciliation" that the government is trying to impose on us are unacceptable to our organization. We will not put down arms until the government has fulfilled the demands that we set out at the beginning of our struggle. We propose the following conditions to begin dialogue:

A) The recognition of the EZLN as a belligerent force.
B) A cease-fire on both sides in the combat zones.
C) The withdrawal of federal troops from the communities with full respect for the rural population's human rights and the return of federal troops to their respective bases in distinct parts of the country.
D) The ceasing of indiscriminate bombardments of rural populations.
E) With a base in the three anterior conditions, the formation of a national mediation commission.

Our troops promise to respect these conditions if the federal government does the same. In the opposite case, our troops will continue their advance towards the capital of the country.

Our EZLN reiterates that it will follow the laws of war approved in the Geneva convention, respecting the civil population, the Red Cross, the press, the wounded, and enemy troops who hand themselves over to our forces without fighting.

WE MAKE A SPECIAL PLEA TO THE NORTH AMERICAN PEOPLE AND GOVERNMENT:

To the former so that they initiate acts of solidarity and support for our compatriots, and to the latter so that they suspend all economic and military support to the Mexican federal government for being a dictatorial government that doesn't respect human rights and because the said help will be used to massacre the Mexican people.

TO MEXICANS:

The military balance of the struggle as of January 5 brings the following results:

1. LOSSES SUFFERED BY ZAPATISTA: 9 dead and 20 seriously wounded who are being cared for in our campaign hospitals. An undetermined number of slightly wounded who will return to their posts for combat and 12 lost in action. We have not included in these numbers our wounded soldiers who were executed in cold blood by federal army officials. The number of these companions has not been determined as our troops are still fighting in Ocosingo.

2. LOSSES SUFFERED BY THE ENEMY FORCES (INCLUDING POLICE AND FEDERAL SOLDIERS): 27 dead, 40 wounded, and 180 prisoners who surrendered to our forces and were later freed with no harm done to their physical beings. There are at least 30 more dead that have not been confirmed. These losses in addition to an undetermined number of wounded, occurred on January 4 in the mountains south of San Cristóbal de las Casas when bombs dropped by Mexican Air Force planes fell on army soldier trucks which are operating in the zone.

3. DESTROYED OR DAMAGED ENEMY WAR MATERIALS: 3 helicopters (one in Ocosingo and two in San Cristóbal de las Casas-SCLS) and three artillery planes (all three in San Cristóbal de las Casas), 15 radios, 15 transport vehicles, 4 state judicial police torture centers.

4. FREED PRISONERS: 230 in the four jails which were attacked and freed by EZLN forces (2 in SCLC, 1 in Ocosingo, and 1 in Las Margaritas).

5. RECUPERATED WAR SUPPLIES: Approximately 207 arms of different calibers (M-16, G-3, M-2, pistols, fine lances, and shotguns) and an undetermined number of depots. 1,266 kilograms of dynamite and 10,000 TNT detonators. More than 20 transport vehicles. An undetermined number of radio communication apparati used by the police, the army, and the air force.

TO THE NATIONAL AND INTERNATIONAL PRESS:

We call to the attention of the honest national and international press the genocide that the federal military forces are carrying out in the municipalities of San Cristóbal de las Casas, Ocosingo, Altamirano, and Las Margaritas as well as in neighboring towns where they are indiscriminately assassinating civilians whom they later present as fallen members of the EZLN. Some of the dead Zapatistas that the federal army claims, are presently enjoying adequate health. The federal troops' attitude differs from our own which is one of always protecting the lives of innocent people to which civilians in these cities will attest. The majority of damage done to public and private buildings which have been appropriated by the Zapatista troops was done by the federal troops when they entered into the four municipalities.

TO THE FEDERAL ARMY:

The present conflict unmasks once again the true nature of the federal army and presents it in its true essence: indiscriminate repression, the violation of human rights, and the total lack of military ethics and honor. The federal army's assassinations of women and children in the region demonstrates that the federal army is one with no control. We make a call to federal army officials and troops to disobey orders to exterminate civilians and summarily excecute wounded soldiers and prisoners of war and remain within the margins of military ethic and honor. We reiterate our invitation to government soldiers to leave the evil government's ranks to join the just cause of our people who want only to live with justice or die with dignity. We have respected the lives of the soldiers and the police who have surrendered themselves to our forces while you summarily execute the Zapatistas that you find wounded and unable to fight and those who surrender to you. If you begin to attack our families and refuse to respect the lives of wounded troops and prisoners then we will begin to do the same.

TO THE MEXICAN PEOPLE:

Lastly, we make a call to workers, poor peasants, teachers, students, progressive and honest intellectuals, housewives and professionals, and to all politically and economically independent organizations to join our struggle within their milieus and in all possible forms until we achieve the justice and liberty that all Mexicans long for.

WE WILL NOT PUT DOWN OUR ARMS!

WE WANT JUSTICE, NOT PARDON OR CHARITY!

From the mountains in southwestern Mexico. CCRI-CG of the EZLN. Mexico, January 1994.

—*Insurgent Sub-Commander Marcos's Signature*

Excerpt from a Zapatista Communique

In our dreams we have seen another world. An honest world, a world decidedly more fair than the one in which we live now. We saw that in this world there was no need for armies and peace, justice and liberty were so common that no one talked about them as far-off concepts, but instead as things such as bread, birds, air, water, as one says book and voice. This is how the good things were named in this world. And in this world there was reason and goodwill in the government, and the leaders were clear-thinking people; they ruled obeying. This world was not a dream from the past, it was not something that came to us from our ancestors. It came from ahead, from the next step we were going to take. And so it was that we started to move forward to attain this dream and make it come and sit down at our tables, light our homes, grow in our cornfields, fill the hearts of our children, clean our sweat, heal our history. And it was for all. This is what we want.

Nothing more, nothing less.

Now we follow our path towards our true heart to ask it what we must do. We will return to our mountains to speak in our own tongue and our own time.

Thank you to the brothers who looked after us all these days. That your footsteps follow our path. Goodbye.

Liberty! Justice! Democracy!

Respectfully, Subcomandante Marcos.
From the southeast of Mexico.

WHO IS MARCOS?

Responding to a press report that EZLN Subcomandante Marcos is homosexual, the Zapatistas wrote:

> Marcos is gay in San Francisco, black in South Africa, Asian in Europe, a Chicano in San Ysidro, an anarchist in Spain, a Palestinian in Israel, a Mayan Indian in the streets of San Cristóbal, a gang member in Neza [a huge Mexican slum], a rocker in the National University [a folk music citadel], a Jew in Germany, an ombudsman in the Defense Ministry, a communist in the post–Cold War era, an artist without gallery or portfolio...

> A pacifist in Bosnia, a housewife alone on Saturday night in any neighborhood in any city in Mexico, a striker in the CTM [the docile pro-government union federation], a reporter writing filler stories for the back pages, a single woman on the metro at 10 p.m., a peasant without land, an unemployed worker... an unhappy student, a dissident amid free-market economies, a writer without books or readers, and of course, a Zapatista in the mountains of southeast Mexico.

> So Marcos is a human being, any human being, in this world. Marcos is all the exploited, marginalized, and oppressed minorities, resisting and saying, "Enough."

LEARNING FROM NATIVE PEOPLES

WINONA LADUKE

I want to address some of the things that are important to the Anishanbeg and to the wider community of native peoples. I'd like to talk about *Kieweydon,* which means "going home" in our language. It refers to the process of going home and finding home. I think that is essentially what we need to be talking about. It is a challenge that people of this society face in belonging to a settler culture. They have been raised in this land, but they do not know its ceremony, its song, or its naming. Early settlers re-used names from other places, calling their settlements "New England," "New Haven," and "New York." But at the same time there are all these indigenous names that coexist with them. I think naming, and knowing why names *are,* is very important in restoring your relationship with the earth and finding your place. Restoring this relationship is our challenge.

To introduce myself, I'll tell you a little bit about my work and about where I come from. I'm basically a community organizer. I returned to the White Earth reservation about ten years ago after being raised off-reservation, which is a common circumstance for our people. I then began to work on the land issue, trying to win back or buy back our reservation lands. In our community, I am identified as Muckwuck clan, Bear clan, Mississippi band, Anishanbeg. That's my place in the universe. The headwaters of the Mississippi are on our reservation; that's where the river starts and that's where we are in the world.

"Anishanbeg" is our name for ourselves in our own language; it means "people." We are called Ojibways in Canada and Chippewas in the United States. Our aboriginal territory, and where we live today, is in the northern part of five American states and the southern part of four Canadian provinces; it's in the center of the continent and is called the Wild Rice Bowl or the Great Lakes region. Today we are probably the single largest native population in North America. There are at least 250,000 Anishanbeg, and in Quebec there are Anishanbeg as well as Cree and Inuit, who are our cousins. So we are a very large native population in North America, but we're on both sides of the border, and most people don't know who we are or know much about us. That ignorance also stems from the way Americans are taught about native people.

There are about seven hundred different native communities in North America. Roughly one hundred are Ojibway or Anishanbeg communities, but we're different bands. In Alaska, there are two hundred native communities; in California, there are eighty. In Washington state, there are fourteen different kinds of Indian people living on the Yakima reservation alone. All different kinds of indigenous people live in North America: all culturally and historically diverse. The same situation is found on a larger scale when you look at the entire continent, the Western Hemisphere, and the world. I want you to rethink the geography of North America in terms of cultural geography, in terms of land occupancy.

Now, if you look at the United States, about four percent of the land is held by Indian people. That is the extent of today's Indian reservations. The Southwest has the largest native population, and there's a significant population on the Great Plains. In northern Minnesota, there are seven big reservations, all Ojibway or Anishanbeg. But if you go to Canada, about eighty-five percent of the population north of the fiftieth parallel is native. So if you look at it in terms of land occupancy and geography, in about two-thirds of Canada the majority of the population is native. I'm not even including Nunevat, which is an Inuit-controlled area the size of India in what used to be called the Northwest Territories.

If you look at the whole of North America, you find that the majority of the population is native in about a third of the continent. Within this larger area, indigenous people maintain their ways of living and their cultural practices. This is our view of the continent, and it is different from the view of most other North Americans. When we look at the United States and Canada, we see our reservations and reserves as islands in the continent. When Indian people talk about their travels, they often mention reservations rather than cities: "I went to Rosebud, then I went over to North Cheyenne." This is the indigenous view of North America.

Going beyond North America, I want to talk about the Western Hemisphere and the world from an indigenous perspective. My intent is to present you with an indigenous worldview and our perception of the world. There are a number of countries in the Western Hemisphere in which native peoples are the majority of the population: in Guatemala, Ecuador, Peru, and Bolivia. In some South American countries we control as much as twenty-two to forty percent of the land. Overall, the Western Hemisphere is not predominantly white. Indigenous people continue their ways of living based on generations and generations of knowledge and practice on the land.

On a worldwide scale, according to Jason Clay, there are about five thousand nations and a hundred and seventy states. Nations are groups of indigenous peoples who share common language, culture, history, territory, and government institutions. That is how international law defines a nation. And that is who we are: nations of people who have existed for thousands of years. There are about a hundred and seventy—maybe more now, about a hundred and eighty-five—states that are recognized by the United Nations. For the most part, these states are the result of colonial empires or colonial demarcations. And whereas indigenous nations have existed for thousands of years, many of the states which exist in the world today have been around only since World War II. That is a big difference. Yet the dominant worldview of industrial society is determined by these young states, not by the five thousand ancient nations.

The estimated number of indigenous people in the world depends on how you define indigenous people. It is said that there are currently about five hundred million of us in the world today, including such peoples as the Tibetans and the Mongolians. I define indigenous peoples as those who have continued their way of living for thousands of years according to their original instructions.

That is a quick background on indigenous people. It should help you understand that my perspective, the perspective of indigenous peoples, is entirely different from that of this society.

Indigenous peoples believe fundamentally in natural law and a state of balance. We believe that all societies and cultural practices must exist in accordance with natural law in order to be sustainable. We also believe that cultural diversity is as essential as biological diversity to maintaining sustainable societies. Indigenous peoples have lived on earth sustainably for thousands of years, and I suggest to you that indigenous ways of living are the *only* sustainable ways of living. Because of that, I believe there is something to be learned from indigenous thinking and indigenous ways. I don't think many of you would argue that industrial society is sustainable. I think that in two or three hundred years this society will be extinct because a society based on conquest cannot survive when there's nothing left to conquer.

Indigenous people have taken great care to fashion their societies in accordance with natural law, which is the highest law. It is superior to the laws made by nations, states, and municipalities. It is the law to which we are all accountable. There are no Twelve Commandments of natural law, but there are some things which I believe are true about natural law. And this is my experience from listening to a lot of our older people. What I am telling you is not really my opinion, it's based on what has happened in our community, on what I've heard people say and about their knowledge. We have noticed that most things which are natural are cyclical: the moons, the tides, the seasons, our bodies. Time itself, in most indigenous worldviews, is cyclical. We also have experienced and believe that it is our essential nature and our need always to keep a balance in nature. Most indigenous ceremonies, if you look to their essence, are about the restoration of balance. That is our intent: to restore, and then to retain, balance. Nature itself continually tries to balance, to equalize.

According to our way of living and our way of looking at the world, most of the world is animate. This is reflected in our language, Anishanbeg Mohem, in which most nouns are animate. *Mandamin,* the word for corn, is animate; *matik* the word for tree, is animate. So is the word for rice, *menomin,* and the word for rock or stone, *asid.* Looking at the world and seeing that most things are alive, we have come to believe, based on this perception, that they have spirit. They have standing on their own. Therefore, when I harvest wild rice on our reservation up north, I always offer *sema,* tobacco, because when you take something, you must always give thanks to its spirit for giving itself to you, for it has a choice whether to give itself to you or not. In our cultural practice, for instance, it is not because of skill that a hunter can harvest a deer or a caribou; it is because he or she has been honorable and has given *sema.* That is how you are able to harvest, not because you are a good hunter but because the animal gives itself to you. That is our perception.

And so we are always very careful when we harvest. Anthropologists call this reciprocity, which means something anthropological, I guess. But from our perspective it means that when you take, you always give. This is about balance and equality. We also say that when you take, you must take only what you need and leave the rest. Because if you take more than you need, that means you are greedy. You have brought about imbalance, you have been selfish. To do these things in our community is a very big disgrace. It is a violation of natural law, and it leaves you with no guarantee that you will be able to continue harvesting.

We have a word in our language which describes the practice of living in harmony with natural law: *minobematesewin.* This word describes how you live your life according to natural law, how you behave as an individual in relationship to other individuals and in relationship to the land and all the things which are animate on the land. *Minobematesewin is* our cultural practice; it is what you strive toward as an individual as well as collectively as a society.

We have tried to retain this way of living and this way of thinking in spite of all that has happened to us over the centuries. I believe that we do retain most of these practices to a great extent in many of our societies. In our community they are overshadowed at times by industrialism, but they still exist.

I would like to contrast what I've told you about indigenous thinking with what I call "industrial thinking." I think that the Lakota have the best term to describe this way of thinking. It is actually a term about white people, although industrial thinking is not done only by whites. Indigenous peoples have interesting terms for white people: they are usually not just words, they are descriptions encapsulated in a word. I will tell you about one: the Lakota word for a white person is *washishu*. It is derived from the first time the Lakota ever saw a white person. There was a white man out on the prairie in the Black Hills, and he was starving. He came into a Lakota camp in the middle of the night, and the Lakota of course were astonished to see him. So they began to watch him to see what he was doing. He went over to the food, took something, and ran away. A little while later, the Lakota looked to see what he had taken: he had stolen some fat. So the Lakota word for a white person, *washishu,* means "he who steals the fat." Now, that is a description which doesn't necessarily have to do with white people but has to do with industrial society. He who steals the fat. That's what I'm talking about when I refer to the industrial worldview.

Industrial thinking is characterized by several ideas which run counter to indigenous ideas. First, instead of believing that natural law is preeminent, industrial society believes that humans are entitled to full dominion over nature. It believes that man—and it is usually man of course—has some God-given right to all that is around him, that he has been created superior to the rest.

Second, instead of modeling itself on the cyclical structure of nature, this society is patterned on linear thinking. I went all the way through its school systems, and I remember how time, for example, is taught in this society. It's taught on a timeline, usually one that begins around 1492. It has some dates on it that were important to someone, although I could never figure out to whom. The timeline is a clear representation of this society's linear way of thinking. And certain values permeate this way of thinking, such as the concept of progress. Industrial society wants to keep making progress as it moves down the timeline, progress defined by things like technological advancement and economic growth. This value accompanies linear thinking.

Third, there is the attitude toward what is wild as opposed to what is culti- vated or "tame." This society believes it must tame the wilderness. It also believes in the superiority of civilized over primitive peoples, a belief which also follows a linear model: that somehow over time, people will become more civilized. Also related of course is the idea behind colonialism: that some people have the right to civilize other people. My experience is that peo- ple who are viewed as "primitive" are generally people of color, and people who are viewed as "civilized" are those of European descent. This prejudice still permeates industrial society and in fact even permeates "progresive" thinking. It holds that somehow people of European descent are smarter, have some better knowledge of the world than the rest of us. I suggest that this is perhaps a racist worldview, that it has racist implications. That is, in fact, our experience.

Fourth, industrial society speaks a language of inanimate nouns. Even words for the land are becoming inanimate. Jerry Mander and other people discuss this idea when they talk about the "commodification of the sacred." Industrial language has changed things from being animate, alive, and having spirit to being inanimate, mere objects and commodities of society. And when things are inanimate, "man" can view them as his God-given right. He can take them, commodify them, and manipulate them in society. This behavior is also related to the linear way of thinking.

Fifth, the last aspect of industrial thinking that I'm going to talk about (although it's always unpopular to question it in America), is the idea of capi- talism itself. In this country we are taught that capitalism is a system which combines labor, capital, and resources for the purpose of accumulation. The capitalist goal is to use the least labor, capital, and resources to accumulate the most profit. The intent of capitalism is accumulation. So the capitalist's method is always to take more than is needed. Therefore, from an indigenous point of view, capitalism is inherently out of order with natural law.

Based on this goal of accumulation, industrial society practices conspicuous consumption. Indigenous societies, on the other hand, practice what I would call "conspicuous distribution." We focus on the potlatch, the giveaway, an event which carries much more honor than accumulation does. In fact, the more you give away, the greater your honor. We make a great deal of these giveaways, and industrial society has something to learn from them.

Now, over the past five hundred years the indigenous experience has been one of conflict between the indigenous and the industrial worldviews. This conflict has manifested itself as holocaust. That is our experience. Indigenous people understand clearly that this society, which has caused the extinction of more species in the past hundred-and-fifty years than the total species extinction from the Ice Age to the mid-nineteenth century, is the same society that has caused the extinction of about two thousand different indigenous peoples in the Western Hemisphere alone. We understand intimately the relationship between extinction of species and extinction of peoples, because we experience both. And the extinction con-tinues. Just last year the Bureau of Indian Affairs, which has legal responsibility for people like myself—legally, I'm a ward of the federal gov-ernment—declared nineteen different indigenous nations in North America extinct. The rate of extinction in the Amazon rainforest, for example, has been one indigenous people per year since 1900. And if you look at world maps showing cultural and biological distribution, you find that where there is the most cultural diversity, there is also the most biological diversity. A direct rela-tionship exists between the two. That is why we argue that cultural diversity is as important to a sustainable global society as biological diversity.

Our greatest problem with all of this in America is that there has been no recognition of this cultural extinction, no owning up to it, no atonement for what happened, no education about it. When I ask people how many different kinds of Indians they can identify, they can scarcely name any. The mythology of America is based on the denial of natives. Nobody admits that the holocaust took place. This is because the white settlers believed they had a God-given right to the continent, and anyone with this right wouldn't recognize what hap-pened as holocaust. Yet it was a holocaust of unparalleled proportions: Bartholomew de las Casas and other contemporaries of Columbus estimated that fifty million indigenous people in the Western Hemisphere perished in a sixty-year period. In terms of millions of people, this was probably the largest holocaust in world history.

Now, it is not appropriate for me to say that my holocaust was worse than someone else's holocaust. But it is absolutely correct for me to demand that my holocaust be recognized. And that has not happened in America. Instead, nobody knows anything about the native people, not even people as educated as yourselves. Why? Because this system is based on a denial of our existence. We are erased from the public consciousness because if you have no victim, you have no crime. As I said, most Americans can hardly name a single Indian nation. Those who can are only able to name those which have been featured in TV Westerns: Comanche, Cheyenne, Navajo, Sioux, Crow. So the only image of a native which is widely recognized in this society is the one shown in Westerns, which is a caricature. It is a portrayal created in Hollywood or in cartoons or more recently to a minimal degree in "New Age" paraphernalia. We do not exist as full human beings in this society, with full human rights, with the same rights to self-determination, to dignity, and to land—to territorial integrity—that other peoples have.

The challenge that people of conscience in this country face is to undo and debunk the mythology, to come clean, become honest, recognize our demands, and understand the validity of our demands. People must see the interlocking interests between their own ability to survive and indigenous peoples' continuing cultural sustainability. Indigenous peoples have lived sustainably in this land for thousands of years. I am absolutely sure that our societies could live without yours, but I'm not so sure that your society can continue to live without ours. This is why indigenous people need to be recognized now and included in the discussion of the issues affecting this country's future.

I'd like to tell you now about indigenous peoples' efforts to protect our land and restore our communities. All across this continent there are native peoples in small communities with populations of one hundred, five hundred, even five thousand who are trying to regain control of their community and their territory. I could tell you many stories of these different struggles, but I'll use my own community as an example. Here is our story.

The White Earth Reservation, located at the headwaters of the Mississippi, is thirty-six by thirty-six miles square, about 837,000 acres. It is very good land. A treaty reserved it for our people in 1867 in return for relinquishing a much larger area of northern Minnesota. Of all our territory, we chose this land for its richness and diversity. There are forty-seven lakes on the reservation. There's maple sugar, there are hardwoods, and there are all the different medicine plants my people use: our reservation is called "the medicine chest of the Ojibways." We have wild rice, we have deer, we have beaver, we have fish—every food we need. On the eastern part of the reservation there are white pine stands. On the part furthest west, there used to be buffalo, but this area is now farmland, situated in the Red River Valley farmland. That is our area, the land reserved to us under treaty.

Our traditional forms of land use and ownership are similar to those of a community land trust. The land is owned collectively, and we have individual or, more often, family-based usufruct rights: each family has traditional areas in which it fishes and hunts. In our language, the words *Anishanbeg aking* describe the concept of land ownership. They translate as "the land of the people," which doesn't infer that we own our land but that we belong on it. This definition doesn't stand up well in court, unfortunately, since this country's legal system upholds the concept of private property.

Our community enforces its traditional practices by adhering to *minobemateisewin*. Historically, this involved punishing people who transgressed these rules. For instance, in our community the worst punishment historically—we didn't have jails—was banishment. That still exists in our community to a certain extent. Just imagine if the worst punishment in industrial society was banishment! With us, each person wants to be part of the community.

We have also maintained our practices with careful management and observation. For example, we have "hunting bosses" and "rice chiefs," who make sure that resources are used sustainably in each region. Hunting bosses oversee trap-line rotation, a system by which people trap in an area for two years and then move to a different area to let the land rest. Rice chiefs coordinate wild rice harvesting. The rice on each lake is unique: each has its own taste and ripens at its own time. We also have a "tally man," who makes sure there are enough animals for each family in a given area. If a family can't sustain itself, the tally man moves them to a new place where animals are more plentiful. These practices are sustainable.

My children's grandfather, who is a trapper, lives on wild animals in the wintertime. When he intends to trap beavers, he reaches his hand into a beaver house and counts how many beavers are in there. (Beavers are not carnivorous, they won't bite.) By counting, he knows how many beavers he can take. Of course, he has to count only if he hasn't already been observing that beaver house for a long time. This is a very sustainable way to trap, one based on a kind of thorough observation which can come only with residency. Further, I suggest that this man knows more about his ecosystem than any Ph.D. scholar who studies it from the university.

As I have described, the White Earth Reservation is a rich place. And it is our experience that industrial society is not content to leave other peoples' riches alone. Wealth attracts colonialism: the more a native people has, the more colonizers are apt to covet that wealth and take it away, whether it is gold or, as in our case, pine stands and Red River Valley farmland. A Latin American scholar named Eduardo Galliano has written about colonialism in communities like mine. He says: "In the colonial to neocolonial alchemy, gold changes to scrap metal and food to poison. We have become painfully aware of the mortality of wealth, which nature bestows and imperialism appropriates." For us, our wealth was the source of our poverty: industrial society could not leave us be.

Our reservation was created by treaty in 1867; by 1889 the Quakers had begun to take our land away. The General Allotment Act was passed at the national level, and the Quakers decided to use it to teach Indians the concept of private property. They divided our reservation into eighty-acre parcels of land and allotted each parcel to an individual Indian. The Quakers hoped that through this change we would somehow become yeoman farmers, adopt the notion of progress, and become civilized. But the allotment system had no relationship to our traditional land tenure patterns. In our society, a person harvested rice in one place, trapped in another place, got medicines in a third place, and picked berries in a fourth. These locations depended on the ecosystem; they were not necessarily contiguous. But the Quakers said to each Indian, "Here are your eighty acres; this is where you'll live." Then, after each Indian had received an allotment, they declared the rest of the land "surplus" and gave it to white people to homestead. On our reservation, thirty-two of our thirty-six townships were allotted, and four townships with the best pinelands were annexed by the state of Minnesota and sold to timber companies. What happened to my reservation happened to reservations all across the country.

The federal government was legally responsible for this; they turned our land into individual eighty-acre parcels, and then they looked the other way and let the state of Minnesota take some of our land and tax what was left. When the Indians couldn't pay the taxes, the state confiscated the land. How could these people pay taxes? In 1900 or 1910 they could not read or write English.

I'll tell you a story about how my great-grandma was cheated by a loan shark. She lived on Many-Point Lake, where her allotment was. She had a bill at the local store, the Fairbanks grocery store, and she had run it up because she was waiting until fall when she could get some money from trapping or from a treaty annuity. So she went to a land speculator named Lucky Waller, and she said, "I need to pay this bill." She asked to borrow fifty bucks from him until treaty payment time, and he said, "Okay, you can do that. Just sign here and I'll loan you that fifty bucks." So she signed with her thumbprint and went back to her house on Many-Point Lake. About three months later she came in to repay him the fifty bucks, and the loan shark said, "No, you keep that money; I bought land from you instead." He had purchased her eighty acres on Many-Point Lake for fifty bucks. Today that location is a Boy Scout camp.

This story could be retold again and again in our communities. It is a story of land speculation, greed, and unconscionable contracts. It exemplifies the process by which native peoples were dispossessed of their land. The White Earth reservation lost 250,000 acres to the state of Minnesota because of unpaid taxes. And this was done to native peoples across the country: on a national average, reservations lost a full two-thirds of their land this way.

By 1920, ninety-nine percent of original White Earth Reservation lands was in non-Indian hands. By 1930, many of our people had died from TB and other diseases, and half of our remaining population lived off-reservation. Three generations of our people were forced into poverty, were forced off our land and made refugees in this society. Now a lot of our people live in Minneapolis. Of twenty thousand tribal members, only four or five thousand live on reservation—five thousand out of twenty thousand. That's because we're refugees, not unlike other people in this society.

Our struggle is to get our land back. That's what we've been trying to do for a hundred years. By 1980, ninety-three percent of our reservation was still held by non-Indians. That's the circumstance we are in today. We have exhausted all legal recourse for getting back our land. If you look at the legal system in this country, you will find that it is based on the idea that Christians have a God-given right to dispossess heathens of their land. This attitude goes back to a papal bull of the fifteenth or sixteenth century declaring that Christians have a superior right to land over heathens. The implication for native people is that we have no legal right to our land in the United States or in Canada. The only legal recourse we have in the United States is the Indian Claims Commission, which pays you for land; it doesn't return land to you. It compensates you at the 1910 market value for land that was seized. The Black Hills Settlement is one example; it's lauded as a big settlement, with all this money going to the Indians, but its only a hundred and six million dollars for five states. That's the full legal recourse for Indian people.

In the case of our own reservation, we had exactly the same problem. The Supreme Court ruled that to regain their land Indian people had to have filed a lawsuit within seven years of the original time of taking. Now, legally we are all people who are wards of the federal government. I have a federal enrollment number. Anything to do with an Indian state is subject to the approval of the Secretary of the Interior. So the federal government, which is legally responsible for our land, watched its mismanagement and did not file any lawsuits on our behalf. The Courts are now declaring that the statute of limitations has expired for the Indian people who, when their land was taken, could not read or write English, had no money or access to attorneys to file suit, and were the legal wards of the state. We have therefore, the courts claim, exhausted our legal recourse and have no legal standing in the court system. That is what has happened in this country with Indian land issues.

We have fought federal legislation for a decade without success. Yet we look at the situation on our reservation and realize that we must get our land back. We do not really have any other place to go. That's why we started the White Earth Land Recovery Project.

The federal, state, and county governments are the largest landholders on the reservation. It is good land still, rich in many things. Yet at the same time, when you do not control your land, you do not control your destiny. That's our experience. What has happened is that two-thirds of the deer that are taken on our reservation are taken by non-Indians, mostly by sports hunters from Minneapolis. In the Tamarack National Wildlife Refuge, nine times as many deer are taken by non-Indians as by Indians, because that's where sports hunters from Minneapolis come to hunt. Ninety percent of the fish taken on our reservation are taken by white people, and most of them are taken by people from Minneapolis who come to their summer cabins and fish on our reservation. Each year in our region, about ten thousand acres are being clear-cut for paper and pulp in one county alone, mostly by Potlatch Timber Company. We are watching the destruction of our ecosystem and the theft of our resources; in not controlling our land, we are unable to control what is happening to our ecosystem. So we are struggling to regain control through the White Earth Land Recovery Project.

Our project is like several other projects in Indian communities. We are not trying to displace people who have settled there. A third of our land is held by the federal, state, and county governments. That land should just be returned to us. It certainly would not displace anyone. And then we have to ask the question about absentee land ownership. It is an ethical question which *should be* asked in this country. A third of the privately held land on our reservation is held by absentee landholders, who do not see that land, do not know it, do not even know where it is. We ask these people how they feel about owning land on a reservation with the hope that they will be persuaded to return it.

Mahatma Gandhi did something like this sixty years ago in India in the Gramdan movement. Some million acres were placed in village trust as a result of Gandhi's moral persuasion. The whole issue of absentee land ownership needs to be addressed, particularly in America where the idea of private property is so sacred, where somehow it is ethical to hold land that you never see.

Our project also acquires land. It owns about nine hundred acres of land right now. We bought some land as a site for a ceremonial roundhouse, a building that holds one of our drums for ceremonies. We bought back our burial grounds, which were on private land, because we believe that we should hold the land our ancestors lived on. These are all small parcels of land. We also just bought a farm, a fifty-eight-acre organic raspberry farm. In a couple of years we hope to get past the "You Pick" stage and into jam production. It is a very slow process, but our strategy is based on this recovery of the land and also on the recovery of our cultural and economic practices.

We are a poor community; people look at our reservation and comment on the eighty-five percent unemployment. They do not realize what we do with our time. They have no way to value our cultural practices. For instance, eighty-five percent of our people hunt, taking at least one or two deer annually, probably in violation of federal game laws. Seventy-five percent of our people hunt for small game and geese. Fifty percent of our people fish by net. Fifty percent of our people sugarbush and garden on our reservation. About the same percentage harvest wild rice, not just for themselves; they harvest it to sell. About half of our people produce handcrafts. There is no way to quantify this in America. It is called the "invisible economy" or the "domestic economy." Society views us as unemployed Indians who need wage jobs. That is not how we view ourselves. Our work is about strengthening and restoring our traditional economy. I have seen our people trained and retrained for off-reservation jobs that do not exist. I don't know how many Indians have gone through three or four carpenter and plumber training programs? It doesn't do any good if after the third or fourth time you still don't have a job.

Our strategy is to strengthen our own traditional economy (thereby strengthening our traditional culture as well) so that we produce fifty percent or more of our own food, which we then don't need to buy elsewhere, and eventually produce enough surplus to sell. In our case, most of our surplus is in wild rice. We are rich in terms of wild rice. The Creator, Gichimanitu, gave us wild rice—said we should eat it, said we should share it; we have traded it for thousands of years. A lot of our political struggle is, I am absolutely sure, due to the fact that Gichimanitu did not give wild rice to Uncle Ben to grow in California. Commercial wild rice is totally different from the rice we harvest, and it decreases the value of our rice when marketed as authentic wild rice.

We've been working for several years to increase the price paid to us for the rice we gather from fifty cents per pound to a dollar per pound, green. We are trying to market our rice ourselves. We try to capture the "value added" in our community by marketing it ourselves. We went from about five thousand pounds of production to about fifty thousand pounds last year that we sold off our reservation. This is our strategy for economic recovery.

Other parts of our strategy include language immersion programs to restore our language, drum ceremonies, and our cultural practices. These are part of an integrated restoration process that is focused on the full human being.

In a larger picture, in northern Wisconsin and northern Minnesota our community is working hard to exercise extra-territorial treaty rights. Under the 1847 treaty we have reserved-use rights to a much larger area than just our reservations. These are called extra-territorial treaty rights. We didn't say we were going to live there, we just said we wanted to keep the right to use that land in our usual and accustomed ways. This has led us to a larger political strategy, for although our harvesting practices are sustainable, they require an almost pristine ecosystem in order to take as much fish and rice as we need. To achieve this in northern Wisconsin and Minnesota, the tribes are entering into a co-management agreement to prevent further environmental degradation as a first step toward preserving an extra-territorial area in accordance with treaty rights.

There are many similar stories all across North America. A lot can be learned from these stories, and we can share a great deal in terms of your strategies and what you're trying to do in your own communities. I see this as a relationship among people who share common issues, common ground, and common agendas. It is absolutely crucial, however, that our struggle for territorial integrity and economic and political control of our lands not be regarded as a threat by this society. Deep set in settler minds, there's fear of the Indian having control. I've seen it on my own reservation: white people who live on the reservation are deathly afraid of our gaining control over half our land base, which is all we're trying to do. I'm sure they are afraid that we will treat them as badly as they treated us.

So I ask you to shake off your fear. There's something valuable to be learned from our experiences, from the Shoshone sisters in Nevada fighting the missile siting or from the James Bay project. Our stories are stories of people with a great deal of tenacity and courage, people who have been resisting for centuries. We know that if we do not resist we will not survive. Our resistance will guarantee our children a future. In our society we think ahead to the seventh generation; however, we are sure that the ability of the seventh generation to sustain itself will be dependent on our ability to resist now.

Another important consideration is that traditional ecological knowledge is unheard knowledge in this country's institutions. Nor is it something that an anthropologist can extract by mere research. Traditional ecological knowledge is passed from generation to generation. We who live by this knowledge have the intellectual property rights to it, and we have the right to tell our stories ourselves. Traditional ecological knowledge is not an appropriate subject for a Ph.D. dissertation. There is a lot to be learned from our knowledge, but you need us in order to learn it, whether it is the story of my children's grandfather reaching his hand into that beaver house or of the Hyda up on the Northwest coast who make totem poles and plank houses. The Hyda say they can take a plank off a tree and still leave the tree standing. If Weyerhaeuser could do that, I might listen to them, but they cannot.

Traditional ecological knowledge is absolutely essential for the future. Crafting a relationship between us is absolutely essential. Native people are not quite at the table in the environmental movement—for example, in the management of the Great Plains. Environmental groups and state governors sat down and talked about how to manage the Great Plains, and nobody asked the Indians to come to the table. Nobody really even noticed that there are about fifty million acres of Indian land out there in the middle of the Great Plains that according to history and law has never yet had a drink of water. Reservations have been denied water over all these years because of water diversion projects. When water allocations are being discussed, someone needs to talk about how the tribes need a drink.

One proposal for the Great Plains is a Buffalo Commons: the Buffalo Commons would include one hundred and ten prairie counties that are now financially bankrupt and are continuing to lose people. The intent is to restore these lands ecologically, bringing back the buffalo and bringing back the perennial crops and indigenous prairie grasses that some are experimenting with. I think we need to broaden the idea, though, because I don't think it should be just a Buffalo Commons; I think it should be an indigenous commons. If you look at the present population in the area, the majority are indigenous peoples who already hold at least fifty million acres of the land. We know this land of our ancestors and should rightly be part of a sustainable future for it.

I think the last thing to talk about is the necessity of shifting our perception. There is no such thing as sustainable development. Community is the only thing in my experience that is sustainable. We all need to be involved in building sustainable communities. We can each do that in our own way—whether it is European-American communities or Denay communities or Anishanbeg communities—returning and restoring the way of life which is based on the land. To achieve this restoration, we need to reintegrate with cultural traditions informed by the land. That is something I don't know how to tell you to do, but it is something you're going to need to do. Garrett Hardin and others are saying that the only way you can manage the Commons is if you share enough cultural experiences and cultural values that you can keep your practices in order and in check: *minobematesewin*. The reason we have remained sustainable for all these centuries is that we are cohesive communities. The only way to be sustainable is to be enough alike in your community that you can live together on that land.

Finally, I believe the issues deep in this society that need to be addressed are structural issues. This is a society which continues to consume too much of the world's resources. You know, when you consume this much in resources, it means a constant intervention into other peoples' land and other peoples' countries, whether it is mine or whether it is the Crees' up in James Bay or whether it is someone else's. It's meaningless to talk about human rights unless you talk about consumption. And that's the structural change we all need to address. It is clear that in order for us to live, you have to change society because if this society continues in the direction it is going, the consequences will be felt on our reservations and our way of life. This society has to be changed! We have to be able to put aside its cultural baggage, which is industrial baggage. Do not be afraid of discarding that baggage. It's not sustainable. The only way we're going to make peace between the settler and the native is to leave behind that cultural baggage.

I'm going to end on the following page with this poem I've always liked by Louise Erdrich, who is one of my people. It's called "Jacklight."

We have come to the edge of the woods, out of brown grass where we slept
   unseen.
Out of knotted twigs, out of leaves creaked shut, out of hiding.
At first the light wavered, glanced over us, then it clenched into a fist of light
   that pointed, searched out, divided us.
Each took the beams like direct blows the heart answers.
Each of us moved forward alone.
We have come to the edge of the woods, drawn out of ourselves by this
   night sun,
This battery of polarized acids that outshines the moon.
We smell them behind it, but they are faceless, invisible.
We smell the raw steel of their gun barrels, milk oil on leather, their tongues
   of sour barley,
We smell their mothers buried shin deep in wet dirt.
We smell their fathers with scoured knuckles, teeth cracked from hot
   marrow.
We smell their sisters with crushed dogwood, bruised apples, fractured cups,
   and concussion of burnt hooks.
We smell their breath, steaming lightly behind the jacklight.
We smell the itch underneath the caked guts on their clothes.
We smell their minds like silver hammers, cocked back, held in readiness,
   for the first of us to step into the open.
We have come to the edge of the woods, out of brown grass where we slept
   unseen,
Out of leaves creaked shut, out of our hiding.
We have come here too long.
It is their turn now, their turn to follow us.
Listen! They have put down their equipment. It is useless in the tall brush.
And now they take the first steps, not knowing how deep the woods are,
   and lightless.
How deep the woods are.

IV. Our Right to Know: Freedom of Information

THE INFORMATION SUPERHIGHWAY:

500 Ways to Pave Over the Public

HERBERT I. SCHILLER

OPEN: Professor Schiller, we'd like to ask you questions about the changes occurring in America's information landscape and how those changes are altering the public sector.

Right now the major media are promoting, advertising, and exciting people with talk of an "information superhighway." The corporate-owned media are doing their best to dazzle us with all the new consumer opportunities we'll have in an interactive 500 channel future which will enable us to shop from our bedrooms. You, on the other hand, are among a small group of scholars who scathingly criticize this portrait of things. Instead of a "global village" you foresee a global mall owned and controlled by corporations who are largely unaccountable to the nation-states in which they operate. Will you elaborate on this for us?

SCHILLER: I would have no objection to a genuine expansion of communication channels in this country or globally, if I had even the slightest reason to believe that those channels would be used in a social direction, and address the staggering amount of unmet needs that people have in the United States and around the world. There are untold educational needs, there are untold health needs, and there are untold general cultural needs of a very wide variety. There are untold recreational needs of a very different character than what we are receiving. So, I don't have any problem with the introduction of more channels for communication. But I get very uneasy as I follow the discussions of control and the beginnings of the implementation of policy in what is called the electronic superhighway.

Nothing of what I am going to say is any secret. Most information about this is available to the public. Not *everything* is available of course, but a great amount of what's going on you can lookup and read about. There's a great deal of boastful commentary and promotional hype, and a lot of it clearly reveals what the underlying plans and intentions are for this highway. In fact, the best source of information is not even in the promotional materials of the big companies; the best source of information is in the point of view expressed by the American government itself, in the documents expressing Clinton and Gore's views called the *National Information Infrastructure (NII) Agenda For Action.*

Behind all the hype the interests shaping the electronic highway are corporate interests. Huge companies are doing the most natural thing in the world to them; following their own corporate interest. They're following their *balance-sheet requirements.* They want to find new markets. They want to find markets that will give them very lucrative rates of return. This is how the corporate economy operates. They take their own set of aims, doctor them up, and present them as the aims of the entire society. But if we think about it, our interests are very different from these corporate interests. As the NII policy is being formed and implemented, the interests of the general public are being marginalized. It is not for the public's sake, but for the interest of this much smaller group of influential companies that all of this discussion, all of these programs, and all of this policy-making are moving ahead.

OPEN: Your article in the *Nation* (July 12, 1993) suggests that commercial expansion is resulting in the extinction of the public sphere. Can you comment more on this?

SCHILLER: Yes—A clear example of this can be seen in the case of public libraries. The public library has been one of the most democratic institutions in American history. When you read the biographical accounts of this country's most distinguished writers and you come across what influenced them to become a writer, many times you'll find them describing what a tremendous debt, or what gratitude they owe to public libraries. It was a place they entered without any real barriers, picked a up a book, and sat down and read. The public library has been one of the most progressive institutions in America. Yes, it's got deficiencies. No one's saying it's a *perfect* institution. But, by and large, in comparison, it's been a much more democratic institution than others. And one of the cardinal principles of the public library system is that information is to be available for everyone, and it's to be available without cost. Free. Funding comes from the community. Therefore, the principle of unlimited and free public access has been the cornerstone of this democratic institution. And what's happening now? As with so many other things in this society, information is being turned into a good for sale. A good that you buy. A good that's made available on the basis of payment—a commodity. Commercialization is spreading in many different ways—and not through one single coordinated measure.

Of course information has always been, in part, a commodity. Books and newspapers were always sold. But a really massive change has been under way due to the technologies that can transfer and reorganize bits of data and information, and now an area that never had the attention of private enterprise is being regarded as source of massive profit.

An information industry has been developing since 1968. Companies involved in the industry will all say that they are doing very valuable things. It's true that they are creating certain information services that were never available before. One wouldn't argue with that. But they're doing it on a commercial basis which means that information which once was, if available, free, now is sold. If you have any experience accessing databases, for example, you know that you have to pay.

OPEN: As With Lexis or the Internet...

SCHILLER: The Internet isn't costly compared with Lexis which is a very expensive service. High-powered corporate law firms have so much money that these services represent no large expense. If you're in such a firm you can connect with the information at no personal cost, but if you're outside the firm, as an ordinary individual, and you want to access the material in Lexis or Nexis, you will pay a very heavy charge. This is what I mean by the commercialization of information.

The amounts and kinds of information available are increasingly refined and sophisticated. For example, a person can search out how judges voted on a given court case, and how many cases represent a particular point of view. All of this information is available "on line," but it's available commercially, and the costs can be substantial.

Almost everywhere you go in our society you can see commercialization coming in and taking over. Information is just one area where you see this happening, and of course the information-area commercializing the fastest is government, which has previously made its information available for free. To a certain extent, government data is still accessible and free, but more and more of the government's data is being funneled into private, commercial vendors who repackage it and then sell it for profit. Information, at that point, is no longer freely available to the public, but to whoever can pay for it at the prices that are commercially established. Putting basic items or basic kinds of goods into a commercial format, you almost automatically create divisions in your society, because not everybody has the same ability to pay. And this is what's going on. The entire education system is experiencing this trend, from the public schools to the universities.

A typical representative of the commercial trend is Channel One, the company which Chris Whittle founded—but which he no longer controls. Channel One broadcasts into approximately 15,000 high schools, and delivers the commercial message right into the classroom. It's the ultimate example of what I'm talking about, where a public arena gets transformed into a commercial pit. And what Channel One is doing in the classroom is being done to people in every sector of society. Anywhere you go your senses are invaded and intruded upon. Whether you are at home, at work, commuting, or out shopping, nearly every crevice of our social space is disfigured by corporate influence and commercial control. We are targets. We are all living, walking, sitting targets, all day, all night, all the time. And in a very short time there may no longer be any truly public space left.

The complete commercialization of space and information is proceeding rapidly. A fundamental quality of American life is being changed, and being changed under our noses. Ironically, each one of these changes is being hailed as a marvelous benefit to the population. It's an an unbelievable trick that's being performed. Things that are fundamentally changing for the worse—the limiting of access to information and the commercialization of public space— are being presented as wonderful benefits in the offing. It's a sickening con-game, when you cut out the hype and really think about it.

OPEN: In a scenario where large blocks of information are owned by corporations entire classes of people will be excluded. The emerging information superhighway will further alienate society insofar as there won't be free access for all people anymore, it'll be a pay-only access if you can pay for it.

SCHILLER: It's a very uneven "if," because not everybody is operating with the same budget. And then, of course, almost all of these things that are being discussed, described, and presented are done so in glowing and benign terms. For example, part of the Clinton Administration's job in the building of an information superhighway involves auctioning off long-term leases to frequencies on the radio spectrum.

This is a tremendous change. And it is happening almost without comment or debate. What does this mean? It means, in this particular case, a portion of public property, the radio spectrum, justifiably considered a natural resource, just like a timber stand, or a waterfall, or any of the wonderful things that exist in nature, is being appropriated by private interests.

OPEN: That's like Exxon taking a national park away from the public.

SCHILLER: Exactly. All of these things are public property, *national* resources. Radio was originally intended as a people's resource, and as such it has been very badly abused and mismanaged, there's no question about it. The people who have received licenses to broadcast have failed in their commitment to the public mandate. Radio broadcasters have screwed the public and used the radio spectrum for their own personal profit while they were under mandate to serve the public's interest.

OPEN: The 1934 Federal Communications Act required that broadcast stations operate "in the public interest, convenience, and necessity."

SCHILLER: This Act protected the use of public property—the radio spectrum. Up until the present time, public property was considered, in a sense, inviolate. Now, the government is under enormous pressure from a massive onslaught of corporate users, who are no longer satisfied with getting short-term leases. ABC, CBS, and all the other big networks have huge sections of the spectrum *licensed* to them, *not given* to them. They have their lease automatically renewed without having to conform to "the public interest, convenience, and necessity" in any substantive way. Now the government is actually auctioning off licenses to the highest bidder. How do they present this to the people? They say, this is a wonderful opportunity to raise billions of dollars and bring an end to mismanagement of the spectrum. They tell the general public that ten billion dollars will be raised. Most people are impressed. The Administration sells off something that most of us have little knowledge of. Where is it? What is it? It's very intangible. The public loses access to a natural resource, and the government gets ten billion dollars while saying that everybody will be benefitting. That's the kind of baloney that's being passed on to people these days.

OPEN: An article in the *New York Times* (Sept. 24, 1993) pitched the auctioning of the radiowaves as pro-consumer insofar as Jane and Joe Consumer will be able to use cellular phone services at a fraction of the present cost. That's how we're sucked into it, thinking that we'll "gain" lower charges for something like cel-lular phone usage while actually losing a piece of a Yosemite or Yellowstone, a national resource.

SCHILLER: I believe it's something that is irretrievable. Our laws ultimately cater to the private property owners, not public interest. As soon as we turn public property into private property, it becomes a permanent and irretrievable loss for public use. The ten billion dollars that the U.S. government is claiming it will raise *is nothing* for a resource that goes on and on and on. So they hold out this picayune bribe, as if we're all going to be enriched from this.

I think this is the most costly single example of conversion of public resources into private resources, one which we will have to pay for endlessly. The money the public will have to pay to access the radio spectrum after it's leased off will far exceed the money the government garners from selling the leases. If it were otherwise, these companies wouldn't purchase the leases to begin with. More importantly, we will no longer be able to decide for ourselves—not as individuals, but as a community, a national public—how this resource should be used. Maybe we don't want to give the radio spectrum out to the cellular phone industry. We have to ask, who's going to use these services? And for what purposes? Once you hand this over to corporate control you alienate it from the public arena, you lose your democratic rights over its disposition and how it will be used. It's a profound decision we're accepting. What's so upsetting is that it occasions no discussion.

OPEN: Why the sudden imperative to auction these long-term leases as you mentioned?

SCHILLER: The argument of those who are happy with this new policy is that the spectrum, up to this point, has not been used efficiently.

What if, as a society, we had a very different set of criteria of what is and isn't efficient and what is and isn't profitable? What if we were about to lease out the airwaves to a whole range of public-interest users and there was no concern asking, how many billions can we make from this? We have to always ask, is the community benefiting? Is the community utilizing this in a way that's valuable? How could you ever calculate the value of utilizing the spectrum for the community's benefit? It's priceless.

A vast chunk of the channels are *still* held by the military, the Department of Defense. They use it for all kinds of purposes: navigational, satellites, spying, etc. I think the military still controls half of the spectrum. If you want to look where the spectrum is not being handled efficiently, take a look there.

OPEN: And it's the non-military spectrum that's going up for grabs?

SCHILLER: Yes, without a doubt. So there you have the picture. They're just dishing out the public end, claiming endless benefits, saying we're all going to be getting a return, and basically changing the way our lives will be in the long-term future. Unless, of course, there are some kinds of resistance that challenge these developments.

OPEN: So, the portrait that you're painting is of the "Mall" replacing the town forum.

SCHILLER: Definitely.

OPEN: You have written that you see the tangible ownership of this new social network—in communications, corporate mergers, and the development of the "information highway"—as ushering in the death of the public sector.

SCHILLER: Yes, unless one chooses to build the information highway on the existing model of the Internet. The Internet was started with military funds from the Department of Defense, but those were *public funds*. And the military, obviously, had its own interest in establishing an electronic network, and clearly a lot of our research in the last fifty years has been militarily funded and militarily targeted. Then the National Science Foundation (NSF) got into the act, and they put up some funding. The amounts of money provided by the NSF were not very great, but it was enough to start an experimental network used primarily by university researchers. People in academia began hooking into networks all around the country, and exchanged research, findings, questions, and data. As time went on, the network attracted more and more users. If you were in a university, either as a faculty member, or as a student, you could hop on and use the system without cost—so it functioned more or less as a truly democratic system, more like a library than a mall. You can communicate with whomever you want by way of electronic mail, E-Mail. But now the Internet is in the process of being converted into a more commercial system.

OPEN: How is the process of privatizing the Internet taking place?

SCHILLER: I can't give you all the specifics, but, for example, as of 1994, the NSF withdrew the twelve million dollars that it annually grants to the Internet. The money has to come from somewhere. That's where the corporations rush in and the commercialization begins. Quite likely, Internet's going to meet the same fate that radio broadcasting met back in the '20s and '30s—

OPEN: To play devil's advocate for a moment, corporations like Channel One and Dun & Bradstreet might ask why corporate and public interests cannot exist side by side? They would argue that they are, in fact, providing substantially new information services. What do you see as the contradiction there?

SCHILLER: It's a Faustian bargain. You sell your soul for a temporary benefit. Consider Channel One's infiltration of the public school system. What are the implications? Channel One gets into the school, puts on its program, and provides news which is ridiculous, because the news they're force-feeding the kids is just a watered-down version of the trivia they give to the adults. What they give to the adults is abysmal, so you can imagine what the kids get.

Channel One's formula is to package ten minutes of news with two minutes of commercials. Kids in a Channel One school are exposed to this everyday, five days a week. What are the implications of this? What are the consequences? First of all, you get a false notion that the kids are really benefiting from the news. There's no reason to believe this whatsoever. What are kids getting out of this? At the very best, they get a superficial familiarity with a couple of names and places. It's just a mish-mash, which is bad enough, but what's worse is that the children become the commercial targets for the corporations that have the money to advertise on Channel One. Salesmanship and selling enters the classroom. And it attempts to legitimize itself as being just as educational as the basic fundamentals. It's an entirely one-directional benefit—with the commercial advertisers and Channel One, not the students, reaping all the benefits. I don't see the kids getting anything whatsoever. Channel One provides some of the most grotesque examples of present-day commercialism.

In addition, Channel One brings in so-called educational posters and educational bulletin boards, and puts them in the classes or the corridors of the schools. The section of the poster that's an advertisement is placed at the kids' eye-level, and the so-called informational component is above the kids heads—they get a stiff neck. It's obviously crude stuff, but it's a good example of what they're thinking about, where their interests are, and how their presence injures the educational environment.

OPEN: Channel One has a pattern to each show. There are only two "issues" covered in each program, and four commercials. But all things considered, they did have a critical slant on the presence of U.S. troops in Somalia, that is, without bringing in too much of the background. What do you make of this?

SCHILLER: Well, is it something that you think is characteristic of all their programs? I would like to see, let's say, a dozen tapes, and see what the trends in perspective are. Almost any subject that is discussed on commercial TV is trivialized. And it's because advertising is the dominant factor. There are probably a lot of opponents to U.S. activity in Somalia, which does not necessarily mean that these are far-seeing, socially minded people. Channel One's "coverage" could be coming from a number of perspectives, including a racist one. The same thing could be true of Haiti. So its difficult for me to say what was particularly *critical* in Channel One's presentation.

OPEN: Well, not that they developed a comprehensive perspective, but that they even questioned our presence in Somalia itself raises an eyebrow. I do not mean a full-scale critique, but an unsupportive perspective was implicit.

Perhaps this is a tactic used to appear as a critical, independent voice.

SCHILLER: I don't know. But they are very aware that they're being looked at. They are probably far more deliberate about what they're doing and attempt to give what would look like an even-handed or certainly not just a normal, corporate perspective. That's my guess. I would really want to see more of Channel One's program before we can regard Channel One of being capable of having a clear perspective on anything other than acne cream and candy bars.

OPEN: Professor Schiller, another *broad* area to discuss is public resistance to all of this, resistance to the penetration of public space by corporations like Channel One and the Star Broadcasting Network, another place-based media, as Whittle calls it. Where are you seeing resistance to this? What kinds of venues do you think are best for people to explore and defend against, let's say, the selling off of the public airwaves or the "mallification" of our social fabric, and the development of a information highway that's not like a library, but like a department store. What kinds of activist strategies do you recommend in the months and years ahead?

SCHILLER: Some of the possibilities for resistance will come out of the contradictory situations that these developments produce. They will produce certain kinds of discordances, certain kinds of problems for one or another groups or sectors in the society. Such developments then lead to certain types of questioning. For example, I was in Connecticut a couple of weeks ago, and nearby in Greenfield, Massachusetts a couple of local communities had organized to keep out Walmart, the giant chain store. Now, ordinarily an outfit like Walmart is able to convince people that when it comes to town everybody will benefit, people will get lower prices and a larger variety.

This is far from being a massive national movement, but the Massachusetts community won, and Walmart was forced out. The basis for the organizing was the protection of local interests, and the protection of local autonomy. Community resistance *can* prevent corporate giants from dominating everyone's space.

Right now there's a lot of opposition to violence on TV, and some of the big boys have to agree. Congress says there's too much violence but they're not really worried about this. The point is that there is a large constituency out there. It's like a seed-bed for those who can come and give a *reasonable* interpretation—a different, a *genuinely different,* alternative. What's happening is that Congress uses violence on TV as a scapegoat, a distraction from the deeper issues.

OPEN: There actually was a case where someone was set on fire, and the cartoon *Beavis and Butthead* was blamed.

SCHILLER: These things are, of course, possible, but they do not express the common conditions we see and live with. The real conditions are homelessness, massive poverty, and fantastic racism in the cities. Look at the "discussions," "debates," and media-reporting that go on around any election. The real issues are routinely ignored—racism, unemployment, poverty, hunger, inadequate facilities, daycare centers, medical facilities. These are the primary social questions. It's too easy to say that so-and-so kid went wrong and shot somebody because he saw a program on TV. Violent TV programs might trigger outbursts, but I don't think it's the underlying cause. The underlying cause is our *social conditions*. And it's these underlying social conditions that have to be explained and worked on. The whole media question needs to be understood in terms of these conditions. Once you begin talking to people about this aspect of our national experience, you will not have the support of the large-scale media.

OPEN: Professor Schiller, if the corporate media trivialize everything that they report, and their only business is to buy and sell public attention to corporate advertisers, how can we ever engage in the public dialogue necessary for policy changes? How can we counter this in real and meaningful ways other than through the change of ownership. It seems like it comes to this. We always feel a frustration with media watchdog groups—noble as their efforts are to correct media biases in race and gender and class—the underlying problem of corporate ownership is never really engaged. Commercial ownership of the media is the source of our problem; it's what we have to challenge, and it's a monolith that few groups are willing to engage.

SCHILLER: You're right on target with that. I don't think you can tackle the media head-on. We need to go *around* them. The central question is the structure of media ownership. You're not going to get a discussion of this from the very institutions that are organized in this way. In other words, you won't see CBS, ABC, or NBC actually exploring issues of hegemony and domination.

OPEN: Bagdikian, and Parenti, and Chomsky have all published reams about this.

SCHILLER: Issues of media ownership and control are no secret, they're well known.

OPEN: But at the same time we're so paralyzed at exactly this point. To go around the media monoliths is to leave unchallenged the issue of commercial ownership, and then the only real alternative is for us to challenge with independent media networks.

SCHILLER: It's an unequal battle. Strengthening an independent media system is something that needs to be pursued, because you know you're not going to get access into the corporate media system. I just don't see it happening, not at least at this particular stage.

We need to recognize that the whole system is riding very high right at this particular time. Washington doesn't have to look over its shoulder at whether or not there is a significant socialist model to contend with; the cold war destroyed whatever there was out there. Just look at the unrelenting pressure put on the ten million people of Cuba. Washington doesn't want the slightest possibility of a social alternative to exist. So, when I say they're riding high, I mean that they no longer feel any serious challenge to their expansion. They can always use what happened in Eastern Europe and the former Soviet Union as their ideological ploy against socialism. And for the moment the ploy works—*for the moment*. I don't think it's going to work forever, because the problems here are becoming so great that people fast forget what was happening on the other side of the world, and they demand changes in the structure here. Eventually things are going to change and then your voice is going to be heard.

The question is, what can we do in the meantime? I can't see being able to get a fair shake in the media. However, it is at least imaginable that political pressure could make our sclerotic, representative government pay a little attention to the needs of people who are being ignored. When people are running for office, a crucial political question to ask now is: What are your views on the media? In what ways do you plan to open up the media? Are you going to press for the cable company in our community to make ten channels available for public use? What are they going to say? No? Why not? You can do that. Now as I say, it's obvious it will be hard sledding, but it's within the range of a reasonable dialogue.

One of the biggest problems is that the entertainment and information media want massive audiences, and they don't want to run into any problems with any social questions. How many movies did they make about the labor movement? After all, America is made up of people who work. Where is the history of these people? Where's the day-in-and-day-out history of the African-American population? Where's the day-in-and-day-out history of *women*? You know, not just *one* program, or one woman made into a biography. Where's the whole history of the people? Where's the whole history of protest movements in America? Can you imagine the kind of dramatic material that could come from American protest movements? The entertainment people are always saying that they don't have enough dramatic material. Who are they kidding?

There are lots of things that can be done. We're not asking for censorship. We're not asking for curtailment. We're asking for the corporations to open up opportunities for people who have something to say, people who have talent, people who have ability who are shut out because of monopolistic structures. This is a positive approach for us to take.

What can we do? We can begin by alerting the population on a national level as to what is happening and begin stimulating debate. What are the needs of this country? How will they be met? How are they going to be met with the means proposed? These are the questions we need to ask before society is rewired by a corporate-run information superhighway.

STAKING A CLAIM IN CYBERSPACE

Ensuring a Public Place on the Info Highway

NANCY C. KRANICH

Where can you find a place that entertains, educates, provokes, challenges, and informs people, no matter what their age, religion, disability, sexual orientation, social and political views, national origin, economic status, or literacy level?...a place that allows people to think freely and explore ideas from all over the world?...a place that protects public privacy?...a place that respects the rights of intellectual property holders while ensuring fair use by information users?...a place that provides public access to print, video, electronic, and audio information resources no matter where they reside?...a place that encourages equitable access to a diversity of information resources?...a place that supports the easy and effective exchange of information? This is a place envisioned in cyberspace. This is a place that resembles our nation's libraries. Will such a public space have a place in cyberspace? Or will the nation's information superhighway dead end at a shopping mall where all transactions and pleasures are negotiated in the marketplace?

Local and long-distance telephone, cable television, computer, and even electric companies are racing to dominate the market for tomorrow's information services. No longer limited to plain old telephone or television services, these new information conglomerates are rushing to position themselves as *the* electronic, multi-media interactive information, entertainment, and shopping services of tomorrow. With the convergence of new technologies and several recent decisions blurring the more traditional lines between information carriers and providers, various private interests are realizing that their future promises a highly profitable marketplace where they can control both the transmission and content of information.

Until recently, communications providers reached consumers by such routes as telephone wires, coaxial cables, electric lines, and home delivery. With the development of fiber optics and the convergence of telecommunications technologies, a single cable can now provide all these services. No longer constrained by legal barriers, telephone and cable companies are prepared to offer information and video dialtone services, setting the stage for a communications revolution and a major realignment of the information marketplace. Every day, headlines announce yet another unlikely alliance between telephone, cable, newspaper, and wireless communications companies. This partnership frenzy will have a major impact on the shape and texture of the information world of tomorrow. Freed from technological and regulatory constraints, private interests such as phone, cable, and newspaper companies are pressing Wall Street, the Congress, the Courts, legislatures, governors, regulatory bodies, and the Administration for a position of dominance over the technological fantasy world of the future—a position that is likely to be controlled by massive transnational corporations rather than the governing bodies that regulated these companies in the past.

This evolving National Information Infrastructure (NII) has almost limitless potential for social empowerment, democratic diversification, and creative education. The NII will transform the creation and flow of information, which is to say that it will transform the raw material of our individual and collective consciousness. The NII has the potential to increase access to government, and facilitate democratic participation and initiatives by all segments of our society. No doubt, everybody could benefit—but only if the NII is designed and regulated in accordance with democratic principles, and not just the imperatives of competition and the market.

The telecommunications marketplace is likely to promote and stimulate the competition, innovation, and profitability necessary for companies to invest in upgrading our nation's information infrastructure. But how can policy makers ensure that the private sector will offer these upgrades at an affordable monthly rate to customers? How will public broadcasting and educational channels be financed and allocated bandwidth on the superhighway? And how will the public's right to know and right to privacy be ensured? How will our civil liberties and constitutional powers be excercised in the emerging electronic environments? How will everyone be guaranteed access when competitive services rather than franchises are urged to bid for consumer's business in a deregulated competitive environment?

THE BREAKUP OF THE BELL SYSTEM

In 1984, the settlement of an antitrust suit brought by the U.S. Department of Justice against AT&T caused the breakup of the Bell telephone system. That decision, known as the Modified Final Judgment (MFJ), prohibited the seven newly created Regional Bell Operating Companies (RBOCs) from entering unregulated businesses such as electronic information services and telephone equipment manufacturing. Separate legislation passed that year prohibited the RBOCs from entering the cable television business as well. In 1988, presiding Judge Harold Greene, of the U.S. District Court for the District of Columbia, modified those restrictions, allowing the RBOCs to provide information gateways and limited electronic information services. In 1991, the precedent set by other court decisions prompted Judge Greene to lift restrictions even further, thereby allowing the (RBOCs) to enter the highly lucrative information services industry. That same year, the Federal Communications Commission proposed that phone companies be permitted to provide "video dialtone" services, as long as they did not own the television programming. More recently, several of the RBOCs have separately sought and received approval to offer cable television services.

While the RBOCs were extending their boundaries into the information services and cable television arenas, the Congress passed the High Performance Computing Act which established the National Research and Education Network (NREN) through an upgrading of the Internet. This emerging high capacity computer network, originally developed to link research and educational institutions, libraries, government and industry, will run on fiber optic cables laid by the telephone and cable television industries—cables capable of transmitting high speed, high bandwidth data, voice and video signals. Various switching and compression technologies will soon allow hundreds of interactive, two-way transmissions to flow through the same cable simultaneously. Hence, both the legal and technical barriers to developing the NII are gone. All that is needed to facilitate this convergence is a conducive political, corporate, and financial environment.

As the Clinton Administration, Congress, the FCC, the Courts, the corporate sector, public interest groups, librarians and others contemplate these issues, the threshold of a new era in telecommunications/media/information infrastructure unfolds. The horizontal integration of computer and communications technologies, the vertical integration of industries, the convergence of media formats, are all transforming the way we work, learn, play, and participate in our democracy.

NII INITIATIVE

For at least fifteen years, Vice President Albert Gore, Jr., has contemplated the electronic future of information. From his earliest days in the House of Representatives, Gore envisioned the power of a marriage of technology and democracy. While in Congress, Gore sponsored the High Performance Computing Act of 1991 which called for the development of the National Research and Educational Network (NREN) and the Gateway to Government bill (which eventually passed as the Government Printing Office Electronic Information Access Enhancement Act). In 1992, Gore brought his vision of the information superhighway to the Presidential campaign and later to the Clinton Administration's National Information Infrastruc-ture (NII) Initiative. In order to ensure support from the private sector, particularly those corporate executives who rallied behind Clinton in the Presidential race, Gore abandoned many of his initial recommendations for government involvement with the NII in order to accommodate the interests of media conglomerates eager for commercial development of the technological and programming components of the NII.

On September 15, 1993, the Clinton Administration outlined an *Agenda For Action* for the National Information Infrastructure and issued an Executive Order calling for the establishment of a U.S. Advisory Council to assist Secretary of Commerce Ron Brown with developing national strategies for the NII. The President defined the NII as "the integration of hardware, software and skills that will make it easy and affordable to connect people with each other, with computers, and with a vast array of services and information resources." A few months later, Vice President Gore detailed the Administration's intentions for the development of the NII during speeches at the National Press Club on December 21, 1993, and at the Academy of Television Arts and Sciences in Los Angeles on January 11, 1994. Gore presented goals for a legislative and administrative agenda that would be based on five underlying fundamental principles:

- Encouragement of commercial investment;
- Provision and protection of competition;
- Provision of open access to the network;
- Take action to avoid creating a society of information "haves" and "have nots";
- Encouragement of flexible and responsive government action.

The Vice President's remarks focused primarily upon the marketplace, promising to chart a new course toward deregulation of the communications industry by removing legal and regulatory barriers that prevent telephone, cable, and long distance companies from entering each others' businesses.

Gore reached beyond the marketplace, however, when he challenged corporations to provide free links from the information superhighway to every classroom, library, hospital, and clinic in the United States to the NII by the Year 2000. This challenge needs close monitoring, given Chris Whittle's precedent of free links to schools when the give-away is profit-driven. Gore, furthermore, called for open universal access to the network and expressed concern about avoiding a society of information "haves" and "have nots." Of course, he did not elaborate upon these concerns or indicate how companies would be expected to carry out these goals if they were deregulated. Nor did he clarify the vagueness of his promise to *"Take action to avoid creating a society of information 'haves' and 'have nots.'"* Nevertheless, the Clinton Administration has followed Gore's speeches with legislative initiatives that complement the efforts already underway by several members of Congress—efforts that specifically encourage corporate deregulation without elaborating specifically how certain public interest goals will be met.

In order to coordinate the Administration's efforts to implement information infrastructure policy, the President established an inter-agency Information Infrastructure Task Force (IITF) under the direction of Secretary Brown. The IITF includes three committees: Telecommunications Policy, Information Policy, and Applications. These task forces have set up various working groups which are holding numerous public hearings around the country on such topics as intellectual property, universal service, and privacy protection. In January 1994, Secretary Brown named most of the members of the NII Advisory Council, who will comment on the recommendations of the task forces. The Council includes several representatives from state and local governments, libraries, labor unions, and even a few community groups. The membership, however, is heavily weighted toward private sector industries certain to benefit from NII developments. Public interest groups were disappointed that so few appointees represented their concerns, and business groups had hoped that business users would be included. Nevertheless, the Council includes a broader spectrum of interests than originally proposed.

Given the economic thrust of the NII initiative, the pro-corporate make-up of the Advisory Council, and the extensive outreach that Vice President Gore and Secretary Brown are extending toward the telecommunications business, there remains little doubt that the economic potential of the information superhighway underlies efforts behind the NII developments. But an information infrastructure geared to mass markets may not be amenable to providing the full range of services that democracy needs and the public desires. An unregulated marketplace may stimulate innovation, and maximize the profitability of infrastructure-related companies, but won't necessarily further access and availibility, and may even widen the gap between information haves and haves-nots.

The marketplace has a natural tendency, however, to exclude certain societal public interest goals. As communications and media industry giants stake their claims in cyberspace, the public interest must not be overlooked. The new national infrastructure must ensure "public spaces" that are filled by educational and research institutions, libraries, non-profits, and governmental organizations charged with promoting and fulfilling public policy goals. These public spaces must encompass a public sphere of free speech and open intellectual discourse, unhampered by market forces and disconnected from political forces. These spaces must facilitate public interest and non-profit needs if democracy is to exist in the new electronic landscapes.

The challenge is how to ensure public interest goals and democratic powers in a system that is privately owned and market-driven. In a competitive market, corporations are not likely to provide universal service without the captive revenue base of a dominated local market. Monopolistic control, the corporations argue, would allow them to subsidize certain users or services in return for an ensured return on their investments. In a competitive market, providers will still need to subsidize those left out for a variety of reasons. Furthermore, if huge sums of money are needed to upgrade infrastructure universally, providers are not likely to be small businesses or even multiple mega-firms, but monolithic, transnational corporations.

If dominant firms merge to assemble the necessary capital and market shares, the Justice Department will need to take action in order to limit single company control over national communications and news, particularly when traditional boundaries between conduit and content providers are crossed. The government will also need to intervene to ensure the availability and equity of balanced perspectives through reinvigorated equal time, fairness doctrine, and common carrier provisions formerly imposed on broadcast, cable, and telephone companies. The government will also need to guarantee protections for the independent and alternative media who could be easily locked out from the new resources.

Infrastructure building in the United States has a long and honorable history of publicly supported functions coexisting with the private sector. Public transportation, public libraries, public schools, public parks, and public broadcasting are among the precedents. The public character of the national information infrastructure will atrophy if left solely to the whim of profit driven corporate programmers. The NII must incorporate social values such as freedom of expression, equitable access, and public spaces—values that preserve democracy and intellectual freedom in American society.

ENSURING PUBLIC SPACE WITHIN CYBERSPACE

No doubt the National Information Infrastructure will be owned, controlled, and dominated by unregulated media giants that are "driven" by profit, not the hope for cultural understanding, greater democracy, the decrease of poverty, or educational enhancement. How, then, will "public spaces" in the NII be created and maintained? How can cultural and public interest communities inhabit the NII and establish the necessary bridges for a functional democracy? If the public's right to know is to be protected within an deregulated NII economy, we must all stand up and speak out for our rights, along with those most concerned with ensuring the free flow of information in our society—librarians and educators. We must work together to advocate the right to public space in this newly unregulated information arena. We must speak with one voice, as the Public, if our concerns are to be heard and heeded. We must propose workable solutions that achieve many of the goals for the NII but also achieve the needed balance between private-sector interests and public goals. We must counter the heavy influence of commercial corporations by harnessing the voting strength of the general public whose right to know on equal, ready, and equitable terms must be protected.

We who believe in freedom of information must insist that the precedent set by the Communications Act of 1934 (granting airwave rights to broadcasters in return for public service) be recast and diligently enforced on the NII. We must also require that private-sector firms building this new infrastructure return some of their gains to support public interest initiatives. These initiatives might include:

1) The establishment of a Corporation for Public Networking;
2) The evolution of the Internet into a more widely accessible National Research and Education Network;

3) The development of C-Span-type programming at the state and local levels; and

4) The expansion of the nation's extensive library programs and networks.

A CORPORATION FOR PUBLIC NETWORKING

A Corporation for Public Networking could develop and foster public spaces or "electronic commons" on the network for use by educational institutions, libraries, researchers, museums, health care facilities, governments, and non-profit organizations. If telecommunications carriers are allowed to operate in a deregulated market, citizens must not only insist upon appropriate safeguards, but mandatory investments which would contribute to a public interest Network pool and infrastructure modernization. Funds contributed to this pool would be used to develop and foster public spaces on the network for purposes such as cultural expression, education, information sharing, research, community organizing, public health, access to government, advocacy and activism, and electronic "town halls."

As conceived by representatives of the American Library Association, such a national institution would coordinate and support the development of public interest networks through

- Contracting and managing the collective purchase of commercial telecommunications services for public interest user communities. Such a national institution (and its grantees or subcontractors) would be entitled to procure telecom services at the most favorable rates and conditions. Preferential rates would be necessary.
- Encouraging and assisting the development of local and regional community network services that serve the interests of community institutions and state agencies. Developing new public service applications in areas such as education, health, and public information. Articulating user input into the development of high level interconnection and interface protocols and standards.
- Assisting public interest users through education, training, technical assistance, and consulting programs.

This model provides one means for telecommunications service providers to discharge their public service obligations. A considerable portion of the funds contributed to the pool would come back to the companies through the purchase of services. The model would enable schools, libraries, and others to articulate their technological, policy, and pricing needs; aggregate their purchasing power of private-sector telecommunications services; provide supplemental services as needed, which the market may not support; and provide education and training in the use of the technology.

Such a model would foster public-interest goals at affordable and predictable rates. It would create public spaces, electronic parks, and free zones on the network to balance all the incentives given for the development of a commercial information superhighway. We clearly need to provide a public place in cyberspace, and establishing a Corporation for Public Networking is one democratic approach for doing so.

THE INTERNET MODEL

Over the last decade, a massive, non-commercial computer network called the Internet has evolved connecting millions of individuals, organizations, and newsgroups around the world. The Internet represents a new phase in human communications. It enables people to exchange computer files of text, sound, image, video, and multimedia information, to communicate through electronic mail messages, and experiment with role playing, debates, and discussions that involve many people all at the same time. The Internet includes such offerings as "freenets" serving local communities, special interest citizen-operated bulletin boards, library networks and education services, state government networks, regional and national cooperative networks serving educational and research users, and electronic mail services.

The Internet offers subscribers broad access to diverse resources. Users can generate and distribute their own work to individuals or groups, as well as review and receive materials from thousands of sources. They can readily forward, capture and print, as well as revise most of the electronic data available. While the Internet has limited user-friendly software, the recent availability of such indexing and access tools as Gophers, WAIS, Archie, Veronica, and the World Wide Web permit simple random navigation to many important resources around the world.

Use of the Internet requires no more than a computer and a modem. Many guides are available to interpret applications and direct users to appropriate tools and resources. For those without accounts or equipment, libraries in every community are becoming well equipped to teach users the basics, provide them access and even temporary accounts, and ensure them use of the resources most important to their needs. The democratic, egalitarian nature of the Internet provides people with an electronic community conducive to camaraderie and the sharing of information and ideas. Many use the Internet through flat-fee accounts. Uninhibited by pay-per-view charges, users are sparked by a pioneering spirit to explore far away places at will. As the Internet evolves into the higher-capacity, higher-speed National Research and Education Network (NREN) and becomes more universally available, it will provide the backbone for the development of an electronic community.

THE C-SPAN APPROACH

Brian Lamb, Chief Executive Officer of C-Span, founded the Cable-Satellite Public Affairs Network to provide gavel-to-gavel coverage of Congress. At its first televised session of the House of Representatives on March 19, 1979, Representative Albert Gore stepped up to a microphone on the House floor and proclaimed the marriage of television and open debate. Today, C-Span covers both the House and Senate on two public affairs channels which serve as a model for comprehensive coverage of government deliberations at all levels. C-Span was formed as a non-profit cooperative of the cable industry, with funding from cable television subscribers of a few cents per month.

Coverage on C-Span serves as an unedited chronicle of the nation's public life. When Congress is not in session, the network covers public policy conferences and think-tank panels, broadcasting conventions of both the major and minor political parties, and follows candidates all over the country side. C-Span shows life as it happens, without commentary, spin, or editing. Personal positions about the stories and events covered are not revealed. This in-depth coverage of the American political system allows the public to examine the deliberations of politics closely and make personal judgments about the positions of their representatives. In addition, it offers an opportunity for public involvement by opening the telephone lines for viewer call-in many times each day. While most stations plague their audiences with sales pitches and soap operas, C-Span airs real-time speeches, quorum calls, and free-form debates. C-Span brings to the public a true opportunity to understand how our democracy works. Its popularity and impact proves that the American public can make up their own minds about political events and policies and it demonstrates that it can be done at low cost without frills and commentary.

According to a C-Span poll, 74 percent of its viewers voted in the 1990 mid-term elections compared with the national turnout of 36 percent, an indication that exposure to the political system encourages active participation.

The programming aired on C-Span is an invaluable and powerful learning and research tool. It transports us directly to the halls of Congress and the White House, allows for journalistic-style coverage of Congressional hearings and press conferences, offers excellent real-life examples of the art of persuasion, and provides a comparative record of Congressional floor debates on tape with printed versions of the Congressional Record for evaluating how policies really emerged. C-Span's Classroom Program specifically promotes educational use of this powerful teaching tool. As a member, educators interested in the free resources provided by C-Span can dial an 800-number hotline about daily broadcasts, subscribe to a monthly newsletter, and attend a C-Span sponsored seminar to learn to incorporate C-Span's numerous resources for enhancing classroom teaching. Among the many worthwhile sessions taught at the seminar are visual literacy, techniques and models for using video in the classroom, and advice on obtaining tapes from the Public Affairs Video Archives at Purdue. Due to C-Span's liberal copyright policy, teachers are also encouraged to tape broadcasts for classroom use or assign them for viewing in the Library.

C-Span's neutral stance and comprehensive coverage of governmental deliberations is an ideal model to replicate on state and local electronic superhighways. The network's promotion of educational use and non-commercial copyright policies ensure an ideal environment for critical thinking. Programming costs are low and require only limited broadcast facilities. The network also offers an interactive capability, enlisting viewer participation in its numerous call-in programs. Unfortunately, the network is not universally available since its broadcast venue is cable television, and all local providers do not offer both channels 24 hours each day. Furthermore, the nature of the broadcasts may not suit everyone's taste. As the funder, the cable television industry is not supposed to interfere with programming selection or impart a particular point of view. But if programming aired did not support the industry's viewpoints, would continuous support and influence by the industry be ensured? As a model, C-Span actively demonstrates the power of electronic democracy and needs to expand its reach far beyond the Capitol beltway.

LIBRARIES

Thomas Jefferson saw libraries as the building blocks of democracy. Since his time, libraries have flourished, providing free unrestricted access to the world's knowledge for all citizens in every community. The nation's 115,000 school, public, academic, and special libraries enable millions of Americans to learn, access, and explore. Libraries have long worked cooperatively to share resources and extend access to their collections no matter where users reside. Through inter-library loan and other programs, they connect residents of the smallest towns with materials from the great libraries in our cities and universities and from institutions abroad.

Libraries began adopting computing technologies thirty years ago, first to streamline operations and then to share cataloging through a standardized record format and through data exchange over telecommunications networks. By the early 1980s, many libraries provided users direct computer access to the contents of their collections and to commercial indexing and abstracting services. These linked systems permitted libraries to coordinate their efforts and to share resources effectively. In the last decade of the century, libraries are extending their boundaries onto the electronic frontier, loading extensive files onto the Internet for all the world to search.

Today, libraries are heavily automated and now serve as both producers of and gateways to electronic resources such as community information and referral files, full text databases and reference services, e-mail and list servers, digitized images, and gopher and freenet services. Many are involved in a wide array of other virtual library activities, and play a leading role in the evolution of new information services. Librarians surf through remote files to locate resources for their users and teach the public information literacy skills. They use networks to locate materials held in libraries around the world. They respond to questions asked by users from their home keyboards. They offer talking speech synthesizers that permit the visually impaired to read and communicate electronically. They serve as community access cable television stations and produce local programming. And they teach their communities to utilize computer and video tools for effective action. In sum, libraries use the new media to educate, involve, and empower their diverse communities.

Librarians already have staked their claim in the developing national information infrastructure. After all, they are the information professionals who represent the more than 100 million people who use the nation's 115,000 libraries. More than half of the country's adults as well as three-quarters of its children use public libraries. Together, America's libraries form the central nervous system for public information, and Americans are looking to libraries to ensure them a place in cyberspace.

Librarians excel at identifying, acquiring, organizing, housing, preserving, archiving and assisting in the use of information. They have extensive experience working with community groups in providing essential local information and promoting the public's right to know. Furthermore, local libraries serve as the community's historic, cultural, political and social record and are identified as a center for reflection and stimulation by area residents. And the information contained in libraries tops consumers' wish lists for services on the information superhighway according to an MCI Multi-Media Survey released the same day as Vice President Gore's NII speech in Los Angeles.

What the library community brings to the information infrastructure issue is the perspective of cooperative, not competitive, information professionals serving the public interest. Politically neutral institutions, libraries are charged with facilitating public access to information in all its forms. The library mission includes providing such access regardless of a person's economic status or education level. In an electronic age, this mission requires equal, ready, and equitable access to the nation's telecommunications infrastructure, access that will be even more crucial in the future. Without technologically sophisticated libraries available in every community, the evolving NII can only intensify the gulf between the information rich and the information poor.

Librarians have voiced concern over theses issues ever since Judge Greene issued his Modified Final Judgment and broke up the Bell telephone system in 1982. They have protested high "post-divestiture tariffs" on private lines used by library networks. They have also played a key role in promoting the development of the National Research and Education Network (NREN).

Another arena in which librarians have played a major role is in protecting the public's access to computerized government information. The Reagan Admin-istration increased the privatization of the government's computerized databases, resulting in more expensive and less available access to government information. Over the last decade, librarians took numerous steps to stop this erosion of access to government information. Since 1981, the American Library Association has produced the semi-annual, award-winning "Less Access to Less Information By and About the U.S. Government." The Association also testified before Congress, contested many legislative and administrative actions, drafted and got passed alternative legislation ensuring public access and worked closely with other groups to protect the public's right to know by forming the Coalition on Government Information—a coalition consisting of fifty public interest groups and professional associations dedicated to ensuring, protecting, and promoting public access.

Thanks to the efforts of librarians and their Coalition partners, the public has gained free access to electronic copies of the Congressional Record and Federal Register. These groups were also successful in forcing the release of the White House electronic mail files which revealed secret actions to arm Nicaraguan Contras in what became the Iran-Contra affair. Many of them worked together to develop low-cost public access over the Internet to the Securities and Exchange Commission's EDGAR database which includes reports from public companies. They blocked the Education Department's attempt to copyright the ERIC database, thereby limiting use of that important information. And they fought hard to stop the Federal Maritime Commission from charging re-use fees for public tariff data.

These earlier forays helped assure an affordable, dedicated channel for the free flow of ideas. But more recent struggles are immensely complicated by the difficulty of separating the traditional domains of conduit and content, of telecommunications policy and information policy. This overlap raises the stakes for libraries and their users well beyond the more customary concerns of equal and equitable access and fair prices. It forces us all to return to the roots of our democracy's principles and contemplate how to extend them into the emerging information infrastructure—an infrastructure that is prompting the alliance of strange bedfellows between formerly competing profit-seekers.

PRINCIPLES FOR PUBLIC ACCESS

How will the public interest be served by an information infrastructure that is built, owned, and operated by profit-driven commercial interests? Can American democracy survive in the Information Age if the NII is operated like a privately owned shopping mall rather than like a consitutionally protected town square? Will the electronic NII provide access to only a limited few? What prices will we pay and will they be too high for students, the unemployed, the elderly and others who are not equipped to pay? How will the public school system teach electronic literacy? How will public awareness of current events be insured for those who cannot pay for online time or for those who simply never learned how to use the new technology? Where will Americans find alternative voices and a balance of information from a diverse cross-section of society?

Over the past few years, the American Library Association (ALA) has assessed how the emerging electronic superhighway will affect public access to information. A forum featuring major industry stakeholders and public interest groups was held at the 1992 Annual Conference. With funding from the Council on Library Resources and the National Science Foundation, ALA later brought together representatives from fifteen library associations at a September 1993 Policy Forum to draft principles for evaluating NII proposals. Many of these library groups are also working with other education, research, and public interest organizations, most notably the Telecommunications Policy Roundtable which has drafted its own set of "Public Interest Principles" in order to renew the commitment to a public interest telecommunications policy.

As the library community formulates its own positions on the numerous developments affecting the national information infrastructure, it is relying on its underlying values and longstanding principles to guide proposals under consideration around the country. Among these are the principles developed at the September 1993 Policy Forum, which were later endorsed by many of the participating library organizations:

FIRST AMENDMENT RIGHTS AND INTELLECTUAL FREEDOM: Access to the NII should be available to all regardless of age, religion, disability, sexual orientation, social and political views, national origin, economic status, location, information literacy, etc. The NII service providers must guarantee the free flow of information protected by the First Amendment. Individuals should have the right to choose what information to receive through the NII. An open, fair, and competitive marketplace must encourage a diversity of providers, including small and independent programmers in order to foster a healthy marketplace of ideas, viewpoints, and robust debate.

PRIVACY: Privacy must be carefully protected and extended. Comprehensive policies should be developed to ensure that the privacy of all people is protected. Personal data collected to provide specific services should be limited to the minimum necessary. Sharing data collected from individuals should only be permitted with their informed consent. Individuals should have the right to inspect and correct data files about themselves. Transaction data should remain confidential.

INTELLECTUAL PROPERTY: Intellectual property rights and protections are independent of the form of publication or distribution. The intellectual property system should ensure a fair and equitable balance between rights of creators and other copyright owners and the needs of users. Fair use and other exceptions to owners' rights in the copyright law should continue in the electronic environment. Compensation systems must provide a fair and reasonable return to copyright owners.

UBIQUITY: Libraries should preserve and enhance their traditional roles in providing public access to information regardless of format. Network access costs for libraries, educational organizations, government entities, and non-profit groups should be stable, predictable, and location insensitive. Resources must be allocated to provide basic public access in fostering the development of the information infrastructure.

EQUITABLE ACCESS: The NII should support and encourage a diversity of information providers in order to guarantee an open, fair, and competitive marketplace, with a full range of viewpoints. Diversity of access should be protected through use on non-proprietary protocols. Access to basic network services should be affordable and available to all. Basic network access should be made available independent of geographic location. The NII should ensure private, government, and non-profit participation in governance of the network. Electronic information should be appropriately documented, organized, and archived through the cooperative endeavors of information service providers and libraries.

INTEROPERABILITY: The design of the NII should facilitate two-way, audio, video, and data communication from anyone to anyone easily and effectively.

Librarians are also concerned with ease of use. The underlying technology should be invisible to the user, both to lower user barriers and to encourage provision of private and public sector services. At the same time, both novice and sophisticated users should be accommodated. While locator systems and user interfaces through network and service design can help, they are not suited for directing all users to all needed services. Librarians can help users navigate through information overload and complex protocols, but they cannot substitute for faulty structural design.

The Telecommunications Roundtable, seeking to insure that the national data highway is not strictly a profit driven construct, brought together more than 60 nonprofit, library, consumer, labor, and civil rights groups to announce its principles on October 26, 1993, through a document entitled "Renewing the Commitment to a Public Interest Telecommunications Policy." The Roundtable's statements, many of which complement those proposed by the library groups, include:

1. UNIVERSAL ACCESS—All people should have affordable access to the information infrastructure. Fundamental to life, liberty, and the pursuit of happiness in the Information Age is access to video, audio, and data networks that provide a broad range of news, public affairs, education, health, and government information and services. Such should be provided in a user-friendly format, widely available to everyone, including persons with disabilities. Information that is essential in order to fully participate in a democratic society should be provided free.

2. FREEDOM TO COMMUNICATE—The information infrastructure should enable all people to effectively exercise their fundamental right to communicate. Freedom of speech should be protected and fostered by the new information infrastructure, guaranteeing the right of every person to communicate easily, affordably, and effectively. The design of the infrastructure should facilitate two-way audio and video communication from anyone to any individual, group, or network. The rights of creators must be protected, while accommodating the needs of users and libraries. Telecommunication carriers should not be permitted to constrain the free flow of information protected by the First Amendment.

3. VITAL PUBLIC SECTOR—The information infrastructure must have a vital civic sector at its core. For our democracy to flourish in the twenty first century, there must be a civic sector which enables the meaningful participation of all segments of our pluralistic society. Just as we have established public libraries and public schools, we must create free zones and "electronic commons" in the new media landscapes. This will require the active involvement of a broad range of non-profit institutions—schools, universities, libraries, community groups, and governmental organizations. It will also require vibrant public telecommunications networks at the national, regional, and state level.

4. DIVERSE AND COMPETITIVE MARKETPLACE—The information infrastructure should ensure competition among ideas and information providers. The information infrastructure must be designed to foster a healthy marketplace of ideas, where a full range of viewpoints is expressed and robust debate is stimulated. Individuals, non-profits, and for-profit information providers need ready access to this marketplace if it is to thrive. To ensure competition among information providers, policies should be developed to lower barriers to entry (particularly for small and independent services); telecommunications carriers should not be permitted to control programming; and antitrust policies should be vigorously enforced to prevent market dominance by vertically-integrated media monopolies.

5. EQUITABLE WORKPLACE—New technologies should be used to enhance the quality of work and to promote equity in the workplace. Because the information infrastructure will transform the content and conduct of work, policies should be developed to ensure that electronic technologies are utilized to improve the work environment rather than dehumanize it. Workers should share the benefits of the increased productivity that these technologies make possible. The rights and protections that workers now enjoy should be preserved and enhanced. To encourage nondiscriminatory practices throughout the information marketplace, public policy should promote greater representation of women, people of color, and persons with disabilities at all levels of management.

6. PRIVACY—Privacy should be carefully protected and extended. A comprehensive set of policies should be developed to ensure that the privacy of all people is adequately protected. The collection of personal data should be strictly limited to the minimum necessary to provide specific services. Sharing data collected from individuals should only be permitted with their informed consent, freely given without coercion. Individuals should have the right to inspect and correct data files about them. Innovative billing practices should be developed that increase individual privacy.

7. DEMOCRATIC POLICY MAKING—The public should be fully involved in policy making for the information infrastructure. The public must be fully involved in all stages of the development and ongoing regulation of the information infrastructure. The issues are not narrow technical matters which will only affect us as consumers; they are fundamental questions that will have profound

effects on us as citizens and reshape our democracy. Extensive efforts should be made to fully inform the public about what is at stake, and to broaden discussion and debate. The policy process should be conducted in an open manner with full press scrutiny. Effective mechanisms should be established to ensure continued public participation in telecommunications policy making.

THE STAKES

What is at stake in this skirmish to dominate the nation's evolving information infrastructure is the flourishing of media conglomerates at the expense of public access, the transformation of conduit suppliers into content programmers, the ascendence of super stations and super stores where local information services and merchants once flourished, and the emergence of push button consumerism rather than interactive education. If not controlled, cyberspace will encompass 500 channels of highly profitable, entertaining vaporware inadequate to serve the full spectrum of society's cultural, democratic, and educational needs. This trend is already unfolding.

While national, state, and local governments are promoting investment in infrastructure, they are seeking to privatize the dissemination of government information and to slash expenditures for this purpose. While the Clinton Administration is calling for the development of the National Information Infrastructure which can reach into every community, it is recommending elimination of several important local library programs that can assist community residents onto the NII. As Vice President Gore is challenging telecommunications companies to connect libraries and schools by the year 2000, local governments are cutting library and school budgets, resulting in less hours and quality services to their constituents. While specialized television channels are proliferating on cable networks, the Corporation for Public Broadcasting, National Public Radio, and community access stations are taking several weeks of air time to raise funds in order to compensate for diminishing government support. While local broadcast stations are charging cable companies for retransmission of their programs, cable companies are replacing local channels with super stations and placing community access channels at the top end of the spectrum, far away from the channel surfer's serendipitous review of the evening's offerings. While most evening newspapers have ceased publication and many local morning papers are endangered, nationals like *USA Today* which offer virtually no local news are becoming the dominant publication in many markets. While radio stations are no longer required to broadcast news and public-interest programming to obtain operating licenses, local stations are forgoing the production of their own news, lessening diversity and eliminating the only access to local news for many. While Barnes and Noble superstores are replacing neighborhood bookstores, high-volume marketing techniques are favoring the major publishing conglomerates over small and alternative presses. The trend is toward the homogenizing, the commercial, and the monolithic.

The workforce is faring no better in the telecommunications industry than local libraries, bookstores, and broadcast networks. While over-leveraged media conglomerates like Time-Warner make headlines seeking alliances with cable, computer, and telephone companies, one-third of Time's library staff is being laid off. While Viacom is taking over Paramount Communications, the Company's publishing division, largest in the United States and second largest in the world, has joined other publishing conglomerates in pruning titles from their lists, dismissing long-time editors and laying off technical and support staff, and shutting down imprints deemed unprofitable. And while telephone companies are proposing mergers with other major telecommunications firms, they are announcing substantial payroll cuts, with Nynex and GTE leading the way with 17,000 projected cuts, followed by 10,000 at Pacific Telesis, and 9,000 at US West.

Clearly, the benefits of the emerging information infrastructure are yet to impact positively on the local workforce or community information network. Every day, decisions about the future of national, state, and local information policies are being made almost exclusively by industry representatives. Librarians, educators, public interest groups, and consumers are not being represented and protected as this major transformation takes place in each community. Without their input, our new information infrastructure will be a dominated, democratically dystopic space that shuts out those without the cash to pay.

AN ACTION AGENDA

Librarians and public interest groups have pleaded with Congressional committees, Administration officials, and state and local representatives to pay attention to their special needs and potential contributions in the development of the

NII. Too often, this development is considered the sole domain of the industries building the network. The public interest community simply cannot afford to sit back and let the information infrastructure debate be framed by special interests whose profits depend on the proliferation of entertainment and home shopping.

We the American public must stake our democratic claim in cyberspace. We must:

- stay informed, and immerse ourselves in the issues and debates;
- join non-profit and educational groups that advocate public spaces and access within the infrastructure;
- urge that public interest representatives be named to various task forces and advisory councils on telecommunications issues at the federal, state, regional, and local levels;
- get local libraries, schools, and other non-profit groups connected and make their valuable resources available over the network;
- let users know that libraries and schools serve as their local gateways to the national information infrastructure;
- demonstrate the social benefits and cultural empowerment that these new communications technologies can give;
- write articles for local newspapers;
- urge people to speak out to politicians;
- involve technical experts with policy issues and seek their advice in proposing alternatives to the infrastructure models sought by industry officials;
- encourage local library and public interest groups to discuss and adopt NII principles similar to those issued by the American Library Association, the Telecommunications Policy Roundtable, and other non-profit groups;
- sponsor programs, speakers, and events about the NII featuring all the stakeholders and invite the press and local officials;
- establish local freenets and other communication vehicles to share community concerns, information, events, and opportunities over the network;
- encourage government agencies and non-profit groups to convert their information resources to electronic formats and disseminate them widely over the networks at no cost to users; and

• support efforts of libraries, schools, arts, and media organizations to utilize multi-media facilities to share their rich resources with the community and to train residents to do the same.

Technology and corporate profit alone should not determine how the public will receive and distribute information. Concerned citizens must force technology and public policy to respond to social and intellectual needs. We must recognize what is at stake. We must realize that democratic access to information is not going to be available without organizing and mobilizing. We must understand and articulate the public's demand for information power. And we must demand that our government actually represent our public interest in determining the rules of the road on the information superhighway.

The persistent and consistent voice of the public can compete and win the battle over control of the NII. We must stand up and voice our legitimate concerns. We must use our differences as our focal strength and learn from the alliances we form with other groups and people. We must publicize our success stories and capture the public's imagination. We must resist the homogenization of culture and the privatization of democracy that unregulated commercialization creates. Public spaces should be commercial free, based not on profit and competition for it, but culture, learning, and the cooperative spirit. We must convince other stakeholders that they stand to gain from involving a vibrant civic sector in the new information marketplace. And finally, we must revise the terms of the discourse. We must rekindle the concept of the informed citizenry. If we do not, no one will design that place in cyberspace that ensures public space for our democratic society to thrive and flourish.

A CALL TO ACTION

LAURA POWERS

In the foregoing pages, Nancy Kranich makes a persuasive case for public participation in planning for a national information infrastructure. The NII will be pervasive and society-shaping—a central nervous system for education and information as well as for commerce—and it is far too important to be governed solely by the market. "Technology and corporate profit alone," says Kranich, "should not determine how the public will receive and distribute information. Concerned citizens must force technology and public policy to respond to social and intellectual needs."

The challenge now is to determine how the citizens who have such a stake in the shape of the NII can achieve power and make their concerns heard. This will be most effective if we can make it happen locally—if we commit ourselves to envisioning and advocating community information infrastructures that serve the public interest.

In the midst of grand visions of the electronic future, it is easy to forget that access to cyberspace will mean very little if there is not public information access in the communitites where we live and work. Public libraries, public arts programs, and non-commercial video and media across the country are struggling for survival. It is sobering to see the Clinton Administration propose billions to develop applications for high-tech computing and then cut library programs from the federal budget, as it did for fiscal year 1995.

To ensure a democratic information infrastructure in the next century, we must first tackle the information-access issues that affect our communities right now: funding for libraries, community media centers, and public access television. The effort to bring about technology that responds to the public will begin locally because this is where the absence of information access is first most strongly felt. In New York City in 1992 and in Chicago in 1993, communities organized successfully to win back slashed hours and services. From Glens Falls, New York to Pasadena, California, citizens have recently passed ballot measures that guarantee libraries' long-term financial security. In these communities, the sense of outrage that came from arriving at the library (for a literacy class, for a book they needed for school, for health or financial information) and finding the doors locked moved people to action.

But as the media landscape transforms, new kinds of organizing will be needed. As a convergence of technology occurs at the corporate level, it is incumbent on us—library advocates, proponents of the Internet and civic networking, people who work in public access television, community and alternative media activists, and advocates of public schools—to converge also, at a local level. This will increase our power: if state and local governments try to make technology and information policy solely in terms of an "economic development" agenda that serves private companies, we will be ready to demand that there also be a clear education and public information agenda; that policies for ensuring equitable access are firmly in place; that public space both online and in the physical world be valued and supported; and that citizens are able to produce programming and use technologies to engage in civic discourse. We can make certain that the information infrastructure supported by our taxes and consumer dollars will serve wide social interests as well as narrow market ones.

Vice President Gore maintains that new communications technologies will "allow us to build a society that is healthier, more prosperous, and better educated...allow us to strengthen the bonds of community." But experience tells us that the mere existence of technology will allow us nothing. It is through activism, through support for public information and media institutions at the grassroots, that we can make of the NII the powerful democratic and educational tool we need it to be.

V. Defining the Struggle: Lessons from the Front Lines

ON MALCOLM X

His Message and Meaning

MANNING MARABLE

MALCOLM X RISING

The militant figure of Malcolm X is being rediscovered in the United States. Signs of this rediscovery and renaissance of interest in Malcolm X are everywhere. The leading black nationalist and political radical of the 1960s, Malcolm's image and words are continually popularized in films, music videos, posters, poetry, and political literature. In 1989, Spike Lee's film, *Do The Right Thing,* depicted the state of inner-city race relations, ending with a quotation from Malcolm X. Look around: in cities and university campuses people are wearing caps and T-shirts of Malcolm X and his uncompromising slogan: *By Any Means Necessary.*

Taking more than 10 months and $33 million to produce, Spike Lee's film, *Malcolm X,* has amplified America's interest in Malcolm and is thrusting his message and meaning into the very center of mass culture. In a year to be remembered for both the L.A. riots and the election of the first black woman to the U.S. Senate, Lee's film has brought Malcolm to the cover of dozens of mainstream magazines from *Newsweek* to *Esquire.* Lee himself described the film as a "spiritual journey"—a journey Lee is not alone in taking: more than 25 Malcolm X books were released around the time of the film. In March 1993, Lee's film was joined by a second Malcolm X film produced by PBS.

For many African-American communities and college campuses, there are now hundreds of public forums and cultural events on May 19 that commemorate Malcolm X's birthday. In Washington, D.C. for the last two decades, a Malcolm X Day celebration has been held in mid-May. For the last 7 or 8 years, a group of "Sisters Who Remember Malcolm" has organized an observance for Brother Malcolm X in Philadelphia. In Harlem, African-American nationalist Preston Wilcox has created the Malcolm X "lovers network." In Cleveland, Ohio, Omar Alibay and others have held a major series of events on Malcolm X's birthday. Black nationalist scholars and others now explore the life and legacy of Malcolm in a critical manner.

CONTENT AND IMAGE

"Never accept images that have been created for you by some one else. It is always better to form the habit of learning how to see things for yourself; then you are in a better position to judge for yourself." —December 12, 1964

Why the rising interest in Malcolm X? Ron Daniels, former director of Jesse Jackson's national Rainbow Coalition and organizer for the multicultural "New Party," explains the interest in Malcolm this way: "Malcolm X was an excruciating critic of America's system of virulent racism, oppression, domination and class exploitation of Africa and the Third World. His voice is claiming renewed expression in a new generation that finds the continuing reality of racism, poverty, violence, and oppression for African people in America intolerable. Especially among young African Americans, there is an increased militancy to *'fight the power.'*" Malcolm's living symbol, his fighting spirit, has become symbolic of a new degree of militancy, commitment, and empowerment within the African-American community.

And yet much of the attention around the figure of Malcolm X assumes an uncritical cultural character. There is a tendency to drain the radical message of a dynamic, living activist into an abstract icon, to replace radical content with pure image. Both African-American communities and progressive movements are challenging this tendency toward Malcolm X, a problem that has long gripped the legacy of Martin Luther King, Jr., and to a much greater degree. It freezes King's ideological and political development on the steps of the Lincoln Memorial on that hot August afternoon in 1963 during the march on Washington.

Half forgotten and deliberately obscured are the final radical years of King's public life, his commitment to the struggle against the Vietnam war, his embrace of social democratic economic positions, and his mobilization of a poor people's march on Washington in 1968.

Similarly, the prophetic and charismatic figure of Malcolm X has experienced a series of misinterpretations and partial distortions during the twenty-five years since his assassination, which have undermined his actual political significance within black history. With the exception of Martin, Malcolm X certainly ranks as the most influential African-American political figure of the mid-twentieth century. In the general public mind, and in most textbooks, there is a regrettable pattern of juxtaposing King and Malcolm, which emphasizes King's philosophy of non-violence and commitment to racial integration against X's verbal militancy and demands for "the ballot or the bullet." Martin's peaceful methods are praised, while Malcolm is still frequently attacked as a racial demagogue or danger-ous nihilist.

But the actual historical record points toward an increased ideological affinity between these two central political figures. Both men were profoundly religious activists whose critique of institutional racism and, subsequently, American capitalism, were rooted in an ethical and moral opposition to *all* forms of human domination. Both Malcolm and Martin became gradually disillusioned with their earlier ideologies—conservative black nationalism and reformist, petty bourgeois integrationism—and moved decisively to the left in their final two years. Long before King uttered any public criticisms against the Johnson administration's escalation of American military involvement in southeast Asia, for example, Malcolm had denounced the war in anti-imperialist terms. Before King assumed leadership in the domestic peace movement, calling for a greater international perspective among African Americans, Malcolm had already charted the way by advocating that African-American formations make direct contacts with African revolutionaries, and seek to obtain official status within the United Nations. Malcolm comprehended that American capitalism and the state could not be opposed effectively without building solidarity and support among other progressive forces throughout the world. These common political insights and the realization that the domestic struggle for democratic rights and self-determination by African Americans were directly linked with the larger international struggle of exploited classes and colonized nations and were ultimately the central factors which made both men dangerous to the American government. Both Martin and Malcolm had become powerful and threatening centers of resistance which could have culminated in more radical and unpredictable movements.

How often are we reminded that Martin Luther King, Jr. was one of the most trenchant critics against the Johnson administration's pursuit of the war in Vietnam? How many people recall that when Martin died he was organizing black sanitation workers in Memphis, Tennessee? How many people recall that when Martin Luther King, Jr. died he was charting a program that was a precursor to Jesse Jackson's vision of the Rainbow Coalition? Forgetting reinforces the tendency to turn our movement leaders into icons that omit the full message of their personal and political biography. Let us not allow this tendency to drain the message and meaning of Malcolm X.

Part of the difficulty in refocusing the actual political contributions, legacy and evolution of Malcolm X and relating them to contemporary struggles is the confusion generated by much of the literature written about him since 1965. While there is a massive and very eclectic body of contemporary and historical writing about Martin Luther King, Jr., there is far from an equal amount of historical writing about Malcolm X. For example, progressive historian Clayborn Carson, author of the excellent study of the Student Nonviolent Coordinating Committee, is currently in the process of organizing Martin Luther King, Jr.'s personal archives at Stanford University. There is much for Carson to draw from because King frequently contributed to periodicals and authored several books before his death. By contrast, the great bulk of primary literature on Malcolm X is extremely fragmented. Only a portion of the thousands of speeches, interviews, and public statements he gave in his life have been transcribed and published. Researching his life and work is difficult because there still is no consolidated Malcolm X archive. We find historians receiving federal support for projects that focus on Franklin Delano Roosevelt, Woodrow Wilson, and even Booker T. Washington. However, how many progressive people of color have had their life-work researched and archived under funding granted by the National Endowment for the Humani-ties? There seems to be a plethora of funds available for the reconstruction of mainstream figures, or even an African-American leader whose development can be persevered in a way that censors out the more radical aspects of his or her life-work.

Martin Luther King, Jr.'s life is presented in this way. He's acceptable up until the time that he gives the "I have a dream" speech, and the work that follows is selectively forgotten. To understand Malcolm, none of his development can be omitted.

FBI SURVEILLANCE

It's ironic that the most comprehensive source of material on Malcolm X is the FBI file collected through intensive covert surveillance. There are over 2,200 pages of illegally-acquired documents in the file. Without a court order or warrant, Malcolm's letters were summarily intercepted, copied, and filed. We now have dozens of unpublished speeches that the FBI secretly recorded and transcribed. We've checked out their transcripts with those speeches that were re-corded by the activists who were with Malcolm. The FBI's are better! They had better equipment. The irony is that it was all paid for by the American public.

Going through the FBI material allows us to see some of the damage done by efforts to minimize the outreach of Malcolm X. Some authors who popularize Malcolm X freeze his work at one stage and argue that his ideology doesn't advance beyond his relationship with Elijah Muhammad and the Nation of Islam. This interpretation ignores the fact that black nationalism is not a monolithic political ideology but a spectrum of cultural, economic, and political positions which are grounded in the dynamics of black resistance to race and class domination in the United States and indeed throughout the African diaspora. The basis of African-American nationalism is the national identity, collective consciousness, and experience of people of African descent in the United States, a consciousness of nationality which is at odds with the mainstream culture, ideology, and political values held by this system. The roots of this alternative national consciousness were established during slavery, when African Americans constructed a world view, sense of family, culture, and their own rituals of dignity and pride in who they were as human beings.

BLACK NATIONALISM

Black nationalism is a political and social tradition that includes certain characteristics. First, black nationalism advocates black cultural pride and the integrity of the group, which implicitly rejects racial integration. Second, it identifies with the cultures of Africa and advocates either immigrating there or maintaining extensive contacts with Africans. (Of course, black nationalists also advocate interaction between African Americans, African Caribbeans, and Africans on the continent of Africa itself.) Third, black nationalism works toward the construction of all-black social institutions such as self-help agencies, schools, and religious organizations and support for group economic advancement, such as black cooperatives, "Buy Black" campaigns, and efforts to promote capital formation within the African-American community. Finally, black nationalism advances political independence from the white-dominated political system and supports the development of all-black political organizations and protest formations.

Despite the rich tradition and strong presence of black nationalists in the black freedom struggle, black nationalism goes virtually unrecognized by mainstream historians of the African-American experience. If one opens a book on the history of black people in the United States, we find a great deal of information about integrationism, about the traditions of the NAACP, the Urban League, and civil rights organizations. But taking that wealth of information by itself misses the truth about the black experience. The truth about the black experience is, as Du Bois once put it, that people of African descent in this country are indeed Americans in the sense that we were born here, in the sense that we fight for full democracy and civil rights here, and in the sense that we fight against any barrier that defines us as second-class human beings. In that sense, yes, we are indeed involved in a fight for civil rights and social justice. But we are *also* people of African descent. We are *also* people who have a cultural, aesthetic, social, and political connection with the broader African world. The point is this: Malcolm's work advanced black nationalism, and anyone who interprets Malcolm and says that he repudiated that tradition, or claims that he turned his back on black nationalism toward the end of his life, is incorrect, wrong, and unsupported by the evidence. Malcolm X was first, last, and *always* a black nationalist.

It is crucial to note that there has always been an internal ideological split and tension within this black nationalist tradition. Since the mid-nineteenth century, there have always been conservative black nationalists who emphasize certain political positions, such as strict racial separatism and a distrust of dialogue or alliances with progressive white formations. The conservatives emphasize African cultural values and frequently support private economic market mechanisms for group advancement. In other words, they advocate a kind of black capitalism. On the other side of the ideological split is the radical black nationalist tradition. Revolutionary black nationalists are critical of capitalism and advance that capitalism, as an economic system coming out of Europe, ensconced in the United States, and perpetuated through corporations across the world, strangle the possibility of black liberation and black development. They tend to be intolerant of capitalism.

Secondly, revolutionary black nationalists tend to advocate a more radical version of Pan-Africanism. They say, yes, we are an African people and we can unite culturally with our sisters and brothers abroad, but we should unite politically in overthrowing imperialism, and overthrowing Western colonialism. Therefore, they advance black nationalism in a more militant way. Both are parts of black nationalism, but they constitute two traditions within one overall movement.

Finally, radical black nationalists recognize that institutional racism evolves in direct conjunction with the development and maturation of capitalism in the Western hemisphere, and that over the last four centuries, it provides the ideological and cultural justification for the continued exploitation and oppression of black people, wherever we are. It is for this reason that revolutionary nationalists say that it is not enough to only fight against racism. Liberation, from this perspective, comes with overcoming capitalism as well.

The second major political tradition in black America, intergrationism, also has its historical roots in the pre–Civil War period. Leaders such as Frederick Douglass, Roy Wilkins, Thurgood Marshall, Whitney Young, and James Farmer, and civil rights organizations such as the NAACP and National Urban League, have advocated the complete assimilation of black Americans into the cultural, social, economic, and political mainstream of white America. For integrationists, any form of racially identifiable institutions retarded the realization of a color-blind social order. The integrationist strategy generally did not question the systemic relationship between institutional racism and capitalism, nor was it ever as popular as a cultural ideology among the black working class and poor as it was within the upper levels of the negro petty bourgeoisie.

Consequently, negro integrationists were usually opposed to all forms of black nationalism as forms of "racial chauvinism," whether conservative or radical versions. Malcolm X was perceived as a nihilistic, black "racist" whose verbal abilities and charisma threatened the goals of the civil rights movement. They attempted to undermine his popularity among the masses of urban, working-class blacks. For example, only days after Malcolm's assassination, Bayard Rustin offered this smug prediction: "White America, not the negro people, will determine Malcolm X's role in history." NAACP journalist Henry Lee Moon was even more determined to obliterate the "dangerous" legacy of the black nationalist. "Malcolm was an anachronism," Moon wrote in the April, 1965 issue of *Ebony* magazine, "vivid and articulate but, nevertheless, divorced from the mainstream of negro American thought."

George Breitman's *Last Year of Malcolm X* goes too far in the opposite direction, attempting to project the entire political trajectory of Malcolm into the political prism of Trotskyism. Malcolm was certainly sympathetic to socialism and could be termed a *left*, black nationalist by February 1965—a nationalist who also was a Pan-Africanist, internationalist, and supportive of a class analysis to an extent. But there is certainly no evidence that he was on the verge of becoming a Marxist in terms of either Trotskyism or international Communism. Malcolm was moving rapidly toward what might be termed a "race/class" analysis, a black nationalist who recognized the centrality of class divisions within American society, and who also understood that the concentration of wealth and power in the hands of the capitalist ruling class helped to perpetuate racial exploitation.

Another problem in reconstructing Malcolm's image was created, ironically, by Alex Haley, the editor of the *Autobiography of Malcolm X,* and the author of the historical novel *Roots.* Most Americans, black and white, who have encountered Malcolm have only read the *Autobiography,* a very moving but also misleading work. Haley insisted that Malcolm agree that any tape-recorded statements given and approved would be used in the final text, and that Malcolm not be permitted to revise or edit his words in any manner. Malcolm agreed to these terms in the early 1960s. By 1965, as he was reviewing the final drafts, Malcolm "winced" repeatedly, in Haley's words, at many of the passages which reflected his earlier ideas. Haley himself was a journalist, not a student of black nationalism; politically, he was profoundly integrationist, and inclined toward supporting Republicans. Consequently, the *Autobiography* doesn't convey the actual ideological growth and political maturity of the later Malcolm.

Understanding these different political orientations is essential for understanding the message and meaning of Malcolm X. Malcolm's trajectory is only clear within this context, and for Malcolm, that began with the Nation of Islam.

THE NATION OF ISLAM

The Nation of Islam was *the* dominant, black nationalist formation from the Garvey black nationalist movement of the 1920s through the black power insurgence of the 1960s. The Nation of Islam's creator, the honorable D.W. Fard, was born in Detroit's African-American neighborhoods during the Great Depression, and was at first an obscure salesman. After four years of preaching an ideology which mixed Sunni Islam with black nationalism, D.W. Fard succeeded in recruiting to his cause about 8,000 converts by the middle of the 1930s. He established the Fruit of Islam, a paramilitary organization, the Muslim Girls Training Class, a school specifically for women members of the nation, and the University of Islam. After Fard's disappearance (or death), his chief lieutenant, Elijah Muhammad, became the leader of this burgeoning religious black nationalist movement. During the 1930s, a number of people in the Detroit-based movement fought for leadership with the Honorable Elijah Muhammad. It is for this reason that Elijah Muhammad moved his organization from Detroit to Chicago in the early 1940s.

At this point, an event took place that greatly accelerated the development of the Nation of Islam. Muhammad was unjustly convicted and imprisoned during World War II for resisting the draft. While in a federal prison, Elijah Muhammad realized that African-American churches, the NAACP, the Urban League, the other civil rights organizations, made no effort to help the most oppressed and victimized of all African-American people: the black prisoners. It was Elijah Muhammad's genius to form programs to work with and transform the most depressed of his race, those who were addicted to narcotics, pimps, convicts, young delinquents, prostitutes, the permanently unemployed, and the under-educated. Thus, during the postwar period, the Nation of Islam began to recruit from these groups with astonishing success. By 1960, the group's membership was between 65,000 to 100,000 nationwide. Under Elijah Muhammad's tight discipline and pro-black nationalist creed, thousands of people addicted to drugs joined the Nation of Islam and quit their dependence on narcotics. People who had been depressed, people outside of jobs, people outside of hope found a sense of humanity and human dignity by joining the Nation of Islam. By 1960, over three-fourths of the Nation's members were young African Americans between the ages of 18 to 35. Members donated a significant portion of their personal income, as much as one-third of their annual income, to the Nation, which directed the funds into the construction of Islamic schools, temples, and businesses. By 1960, the Nation of Islam owned one-half-million dollars worth of real estate in Chicago alone. The Nation's expansion during this period was largely attributable to Elijah Muhammad's recruitment of a gifted and charismatic spokesperson named Malcolm Little.

THE EMERGENCE OF MALCOLM X

Malcolm Little was converted to the Nation of Islam while he was in prison. He had been a petty hustler, a criminal in Boston and New York's ghettos. Leaving prison in 1952, Malcolm Little was renamed Malcolm X, the X symbolically repudiating the white man's name which he had carried. Elijah Muhammad carefully nurtured Malcolm X's career within the Nation of

Islam's hierarchy. By 1955, Malcolm had become the minister of Harlem's Temple No. 7, and in the late 1950s, he began to travel extensively throughout the country delivering talks on the liberation of his people. Political leaders began to relate to the Nation of Islam, recognizing that Elijah Muhammad's absolute control over so many thousands of potential voters represented an important political power block. Adam Clayton Powell, Jr., the most prominent black elected official during this period, attended a leadership conference organized by Malcolm X in Harlem in 1960. Fidel Castro met with Malcolm for private political discussions the same year.

The FBI had been planting agents in the Nation of Islam since the 1940s, and as Malcolm evolved as a leader and the Nation of Islam grew, the FBI intensified its infiltration and surveillance of the organization. The Nation of Islam's temples were illegally wire-tapped, members were watched, and tax records were combed and scrutinized. As of 1955, Malcolm's letters were illegally opened, transcribed, and re-mailed by the Feds. By 1960, the surveillance on Malcolm escalated to the point whereby a group of agents were specifically assigned to trail and document his activities and statements.

As the Nation of Islam prospered, white liberals and black integrationists became fearful of the movement's stunning success in attracting working-class African Americans and low-income people. Scholars studied the Nation and drew parallels between the Nation of Islam and the rise of fascism in Europe. One white sociologist described the nation as "the hate that hate produced," a racial cult similar to "Hitler and the white citizens' councils of the South." Black sociologist and writer, C. Eric Lincoln, in *Black Muslims in America,* expressed the concern that "the black Muslims virulent attacks on the white man might threaten the security of the white majority and lead those in power to tighten the barriers which already divide America." Civil rights leaders actually began to speak out against the Nation of Islam. In August 1959, Roy Wilkins, then the head of the NAACP, declared that the Nation of Islam had a "white hate doctrine which was as dangerous as any group of white racists." The Nation of Islam clearly "furnishes ammunition for the use of white supremacists." James Farmer of CORE denounced the Nation as "utter-ly impractical and dangerous." Farmer argued, "after the black culture was taken from us during slavery, we had to adopt to the culture here." So, Farmer rea-soned, by rejecting integration, the Muslims were aiding and abetting the dynamic of racial segregation.

With his sure grasp of African-American history, Malcolm X responded to

Farmer this way: "We who are Muslims, followers of Elijah Muhammad, do not think that an integrated cup of coffee is sufficient payment for 310 years of slave labor in America." Malcolm understood that there was something fundamentally flawed with the philosophy of liberal integrationism if its vision ended with joining the mainstream. If the mainstream is oppressively and inherently racist, sexist, and exploitational, why would those who are most oppressed by it want to join? This was Malcolm's argument. He argued that it is not a case of dark mankind wanting either integration or separation. It is a case of wanting freedom, justice and equality. It is not integration that most blacks in America want, it is human dignity. This emphasis accounts for Malcolm X's meteoric rise in popularity among millions of African-American people, most of whom were neither members of the Nation of Islam, nor heard him preach in the temples of the Nation, but heard him in other venues outside of the dynamics of his religious organization.

Malcolm X's style of speaking was almost hypnotic among black audiences. As the key spokesman for the Nation of Islam, Malcolm advanced a militant message that challenged and changed the lives of millions of poor and oppressed African-American people. In the typical sermon, Malcolm spoke words like these:

> My beautiful black brothers and sisters, look at your skins. We're all black to the white man, but we're a thousand and one different colors. Turn around. Look at each other. During slavery it was rare if one of our black grandmothers escaped the white rapist slavemaster. That rapist slavemaster who emasculated the black man with threats, with fear until even today the black lives with fear of the white man in his heart. Think of it! Think of the black slave man filled with fear and dread hearing the screams of his wife, his mother, his daughter being taken in the barn, in the kitchen, in the bushes, and you were too filled with fear of the rapist to do anything about it.

He would speak for hours on end, working with people, talking with groups, individuals, families, and children. He said he would sometimes become so choked up after the hours of work every day that "sometimes I would walk in the streets until late into the night. I would speak to no one for hours, thinking to myself about what terrible things had been done to our people here in the United States."

Malcolm's evolution quickens in 1962 and 1963 for several reasons. First, by 1962, his personal prominence begins to create tensions and organizational rivalries within the Nation of Islam. Second, he began to speak out less on religious issues and more on contemporary political issues. The Islamic newspaper he had founded, *Muhammad Speaks,* was ordered to print less and less both by and about him. In 1962, there are almost no articles published on Malcolm X. By 1963, nothing. He is the main spokesperson of this organization, and the Nation of Islam's newspaper features nothing about his work. Muhammad's tight authoritarianism prohibited Malcolm and other more activist-oriented ministers from becoming more involved in African-American political struggles.

Finally, two events forced Malcolm to make a fundamental decision about his relationship with the Nation of Islam. On July 3, 1963, two former secretaries of the Nation filed paternity suits against Elijah Muhammad, claiming that the sixty-seven-year-old patriarch had fathered their four children. Any other Muslim member of the Nation of Islam would have been promptly expelled for the crime of adultery. Yet Muhammad maintained his high post even after personally admitting to Malcolm and other leaders in the Nation that the charges were actually true. After Malcolm interviewed the two women he learned that Muhammad had privately described him as "a dangerous threat to his own position." Hearing this cut Malcolm in the heart like a knife.

BY ANY MEANS NECESSARY

When President Kennedy was assassinated in 1963, Malcolm commented to the press that Kennedy's murder was a case of "the chickens coming home to roost, that the hate in white men had not stopped with the killing of defenseless black people, but that hate, allowed to spread unchecked, had finally struck down this country's Chief of State." If one takes the whole quote in context, it makes a great deal of sense. The chickens *had* come home to roost. That's what Oliver Stone would say, and that's what Malcolm X had said. Yet the Nation of Islam and Elijah Muhammad used this statement, which was only common sense, as a pretext for neutralizing Malcolm X. Malcolm was ordered into silence for ninety days, forbidden to teach in his own mosque and forbidden to speak with the media. Returning to New York after his meeting with Elijah Muhammad in Chicago, Malcolm X was shattered to discover that the word had been given to several Muslims on the street to assassinate him.

After Malcolm's ninety days of silence it became clear that the Nation of Islam had no intention of reinstating him. Realizing this, Malcolm made the decision to leave the organization, and on March 8, 1964 he announced the creation of a new organization, Muslim Mosque, Incorporated. Malcolm informed the press that he was now prepared to concentrate on local civil rights actions in the South and elsewhere and "shall do so because every campaign for specific objectives can only heighten the political consciousness of the negroes and intensify their identification against white society."

Malcolm X had less than one year to live, but during those twelve months he lived at least twelve years. It was at this point that we find him building a revolutionary organization rooted in the tradition of black nationalism, an organization based primarily in New York City. During this period, Malcolm revisioned many of his older ideas into a clear and uncompromising program that was both anti-racist and anti-capitalist. Like W. E. B. Du Bois before him, Malcolm X and the OAAU planned to submit to the United Nations a list of human rights violations and acts of genocide committed by the United States. Both asserted that fighting racism through the American court system was impossible because the court system, like the FBI, was part of the system that perpetuated racist policies. As Malcolm put it, "you take the criminal to court," not the American court, but the World Court: You use the United Nations as the forum to raise questions of human rights inside the United States. Malcolm broke with the logic of political reformism. He criticized African Americans for endorsing Lyndon Johnson's 1964 presidential candidacy. He predicted with grim accuracy that the Johnson administration would stop far short of providing a meaningful economic and social program which would benefit the masses of African-American people. Malcolm X criticized the negro middle class's commitment to private enterprise. During his trip to Africa, Malcolm learned that black revolutionaries abroad had ended their tolerance of capitalism by defining economic liberation in terms of socialism.

Malcolm said: "You can't have racism without capitalism. If you find anti-racists, usually they're socialists or their political philosophy is that of socialism." The OAAU began developing a program that would build a resistance movement in the United States, promote the election of black candidates to public office, organize voter registration drives, promote rent strikes to create better housing conditions for African Americans, build all-black community schools, create cultural centers, and initiate black committees for community and neighborhood self-defense against racist attacks.

By early 1965, Malcolm began to realize that his older messianic vision of an inevitable race war was also incorrect. "America is the first country that may actually have a bloodless revolution," he said. Bloodless revolution depended on the ability of African-American people to develop a strategy of fundamental economic, political, and social change and to act in concert with other elements of the oppressed in this country. Malcolm began to see that the connections between racial oppression and class exploitation were fundamental and systemic in American society. He began attracting supporters from all levels of the civil rights movement, people in the Student Nonviolent Coordinating Committee, the Congress of Racial Equality, and even from inside the NAACP. He traveled south to Selma, Alabama to work with the members of SNCC. He spoke at Tuskegee Institute. He was fast becoming a voice for the most progressive African Americans involved in the freedom struggle.

Now, thirty years after his assassination, we see the same mistakes made around Martin Luther King, Jr. being made around the life-work of Malcolm X: frozen image replacing the message and meaning. Understanding Malcolm X means understanding his evolution *over time* and seeing how his perspectives into the problem of racial inequality in America became far more specific, clear, and analytical by the end of his life. The best way that we can document this development is through a speech he gave in Selma, Alabama, only weeks before he was killed.

In what may be his greatest address, his "I am a field negro speech" delivers his most effective presentation of the class contradictions within the African-American community and the necessity for uncompromising radical struggle. He reminded his listeners that,

> there were in black history two kinds of negroes. There was the old house negro and the old field negro. The house negro always looked out for his master. When the field negroes got too much out of line, he held them back in check. He put them back on the plantation. If the master got hurt, he'd say, 'What's the matter, boss? We sick?' However, there were the field negroes who lived in the huts, who had nothing to lose. They wore the worst kind of clothes. They ate the worst food. They caught hell. They felt the sting of the lash. And they hated this land...

After a historical analysis of slavery and the class divisions within the African-American community, Malcolm observed that there were two positions working toward black liberation. There was a conservative tradition that said, don't get involved in political struggle, for Elijah Muhammad said that if there is police brutality we should not mobilize against it publicly. Malcolm said there is another alternative, one that says, yes, we are indeed black nationalists, and we must struggle to empower our people by any means necessary. So Malcolm said,

I am a field negro. If I can't live in the house as a human being, I'm praying for that house to blow down, I'm praying for a strong wind to come along...If the master don't treat me right and he's sick, I'll tell the doctor to go the other way. But if we are all of us going to live as human beings, then I am for a society in which human beings can practice brother and sisterhood.

If one analyzes the late Malcolm X, you see the deepening of his radical and revolutionary vision. He moves away from the blatant sexism of Islam. He recognizes from his experiences in Africa that all progressive nationalist movements embraced the fundamental equality of women. December 1964: "It's noticeable that in the Third World societies, where they have put women in the closet and discouraged her from getting sufficient education and don't give her the incentive by allowing her maximum participation in whatever area of the society in which she's qualified, they kill her incentive and kill her spirits." By the end of his life, Malcolm X realized that the struggle for liberation was not just a struggle against racism and corporate capitalism. He began addressing other forms of domination that must be fought by people who truly believe in full democracy and equality, and that meant struggling against women's oppression.

Following Malcolm's death and the publication of *Autobiography,* the Black Power revolt erupted across the country. Community-based activists rejected the reformist politics of the NAACP and embraced the militancy and uncompromising language and style of Malcolm. Yet here again, there was ambiguity, as people engaged in this political mimicry. As Julius Lester noted in late 1966, the renaissance of contemporary black nationalism represented "the angry children of Malcolm X," activists who had rejected integration, black-white alliances, participation in electoral politics, and the belief in the reformation of the system. But out of nearly every tendency of the nationalist spectrum selected from Malcolm's rich tapestry, only those threads which coincided with their immediate interests were adopted.

Many black nationalist separatists tried to "freeze" Malcolm within the framework of a "race-first" analysis, reducing their mentor's statements during his final year to irrelevancy. The Black Panther party also attempted to appropriate the image of Malcolm X, but focused on the seemingly insurrectionist elements of Malcolm's discourse. Panther co-founder Huey Newton frequently described his formation as the genuine "heirs of Malcolm X." For Panther Minister of Information Eldridge Cleaver, Malcolm X symbolized an irreconcilable alternative to King and "the whole passel of so-called negro leaders and spokesmen who trifle and compromise with the truth in order to curry favor with the white power structure." But this version exaggerated the actual differences between the late Malcolm and the more progressive phase of King's political life. Indeed, only three weeks before his death, Andrew Young invited Malcolm to come to Selma, Alabama, during a major desegregation campaign. When Malcolm X arrived on February 3, 1965, King had just been arrested. Over 1300 demonstrators had also been imprisoned protesting Jim Crow. Malcolm X confided to Coretta Scott King that he wanted "Dr. King to know that I really didn't come to make his job more difficult. I really did come thinking that I could make it easier. If the white people realize what the alternative is, perhaps they will be more willing to hear Dr. King."

CONTINUING THE STRUGGLE

Today, Malcolm X represents courage, the search for truth, freedom, and dignity for African-American women and men. Malcolm was courageous enough to say, yes, I made mistakes. Yes, I was wrong at certain times. And yes, I have learned that the search for truth means many false paths. But the courage of leadership and the price of vision is in admitting and overcoming those weaknesses. Malcolm's greatness will never be found as a frozen icon on a mantelpiece. His greatness is found in realizing a simple, basic truth: that the greatness in Malcolm is the greatness in ourselves. When young people see Malcolm on a mantelpiece, iconized and frozen, his message and meaning are lost. Bringing Malcolm X down to the people honors him, and by keeping his message and meaning alive we honor ourselves, our capacity for struggle, and our search for truth and human dignity. Not that Malcolm was right in everything. If Malcolm were here, he'd say, "Don't freeze me and turn me into a statue! Understand me as a person who struggled for dignity, who fought for freedom, and who died trying to live in a way that could bring honor to ourselves." We need to understand that Malcolm's greatness is best observed by continuing his work, by challenging the power, by fighting for freedom, by linking up with oppressed people, no matter where they may be, by fighting all systems of domination and exploitation, whatever form they may take. In this way, we not only honor the life and legacy of Malcolm X, we honor the drive for democracy and liberation in ourselves.

BREAKING BREAD:

A Dialogue Among Communities in Search of Common Ground

CORNEL WEST AND BELL HOOKS

This dialogue is an edited version of the talk given at the High School of Fashion Industries in New York City on June 21, 1994.

MODERATOR: The Breaking Bread project was initiated by the African-American Commission of the Democratic Socialists of America. Our initial goal is to start a dialogue of healing among the diverse communities of New York City. Fundamental to the project, however, is a belief that our communities cannot be truly healed until there is a greater level of economic and social justice. We recognize that any effort at either healing or justice must be as broad-based and diverse as possible.

The project takes its name from a book in a series of dialogues by Dr. Cornel West and Dr. bell hooks, two of our foremost scholars and social critics. As developed by West and hooks, Breaking Bread is an olive branch extended by African Americans in an effort to bring people together on the basis of shared interests. New York City Breaking Bread has adopted their model, which employs a positive vision and language, links racism, sexism, homophobia and economic injustice, and confronts these common oppressions in order to change the way we talk with and about each other.

Here, Cornel West and bell hooks share a dialogue about what divides us, what unites us and how we can come together around a common agenda to develop a plan for action to obtain economic and social justice.

BELL HOOKS: Cornel and I are concerned about the question of hope. Earlier in the day I asked Cornel, "Don't you feel, as we go around talking and so many people come out, that far from feeling that our will to struggle is dead, it feels as though people are hungry for change?" I kept thinking about Howard Thurmond's book *Deep is the Hunger*. I feel like we're in the midst of a tremendous hunger for change, and it's that hunger and that yearning that brings us into the struggle. I was thinking about Cornel. Cornel has been going through so many difficult times lately. I wrote a note, reminding him of that bit of scripture that says, "Count it all joy when you meet various trials." Because we've been thinking a lot over the years as we've worked together about joy in struggle. It's that joy that we want to evoke at the beginning of the dialogue. He and I were talking earlier about how the white-dominated mass media have bombarded us with images in the last two years conveying a sense of black men and women not being able to speak together, not being able to dialogue or cross our differences, across the multitude of issues that might separate us, and how important it is for us to be able to stand as an example of the reality that all over the United States black men and women are engaging in joyous struggle and dialogue together.

CORNEL WEST: I deeply appreciate those who've been pulling for me, because it's true that it's been a rough time. My dad is gone. I miss him so much and I loved him so much. And yet I am reminded that I come from a tradition that refuses to give misery and grief and sorrow the last word. I must say, though, just standing here with bell hooks and being in dialogue with my friend and comrade and colleague, I can't help but be fired up on a certain level. That level has to do with joy in struggle, with the recognition that there are some networks that can support one, that there are some communal bonds upon which one can fall and be projected into a new sense of possibility. That's what we're here to talk about. We're talking about vision, we're talking about hope, and what we are up against. If we don't come together, fuse together, then we ultimately hang separately. We slide down a slippery slope that we see around us wherever we look. And not only in this city, but in chocolate cities all across this nation.

BELL HOOKS: The left has great difficulty dealing with the place of love in political struggle. What happens at those moments when we do feel weary, when we do feel that the rug is being pulled out from under us. It's at those times when we're not only bombarded by those forces from outside, but struggling from within our own ranks, that we need real solidarities. This raises the question about the place of dissent within solidarity. I don't always agree with Cornel. He doesn't always agree with me. And yet we can come together across our differences and yet understand that what binds us is deeper, more meaningful, constant to us. It's our will to love in radical political struggle that binds us, that inspires us to come to the table with one another and to be able to deal with disagreement and dissent. One of the things that we wanted to start off with was that sense of the importance of dissent to struggle, and that rather than getting depressed or demoralized when we don't agree, we have to see that dissent is essential to political practice.

CORNEL WEST: I think in part that means to cultivate a sense of critique without it degenerating into castigation. That's so very important. We must be able to bring critique to bear without people feeling that somehow one is pulling the rug from under them. We have to associate critique with empowerment rather than disempowerment. That's so very important at a time in which the crisis is raging now in this country, when death and destruction and disease are ravaging so many communities. We must come up with ways of encouraging and empowering one another but acknowledging that critique and dissent are integral elements of that struggle. I think to talk about love, of course, is so very important. You recall James Baldwin talked about love as something that is daring and difficult and dangerous. He talked about love as a going out and a growing up. He talked about love as one of those forms of affection and critical affirmation, and that's the kind of talk about love that must be integral to struggle. I was just thinking the day before yesterday about the O. J. Simpson situation. I must say, given the sadness of those now gone and the sadness of brother O. J. right now, sitting in the cell, that we must not forget about the deep love of brother Cowlings calling for O. J. He was willing to go down for his friend. Why? Because he recognized that service and sacrifice that O. J. had engaged in for him had made a difference in his life. And that when we think of struggle and joy in struggle we should also think about sacrifice, sacrifice based on principles and vision. It's that kind of gut bucket, visceral, long solidarity friendship that must be an integral element of any serious talk about struggle. What we need here in New York City and in this nation is to generate the kinds of bonds of trust so we can not just go down together, but we can rise together against the powers that be.

BELL HOOKS: Situations like this, Cornel, when seen as a feminist, are particularly troubling. I'm sure people are not rushing up to Cornel, as people have said to me, and saying, "I don't care about O. J. I'm thinking about that woman." Part of growing to political maturity is recognizing that we can never afford *not* to think about any party in our efforts to grow, because we are engaged in protracted struggle. We have to look more deeply as a culture into the psychology of domestic violence, into men who batter, into compelling men to think about patriarchy. I think that one of the most difficult things about really growing in love in political struggle is trying to make that space where you allow anyone to come back into a progressive politics. You open that door and allow people to come in from whatever space they've been at. If we close the doors, we end up being that political left that has no mass-based constituency. The right isn't closing its doors. The religious right has programs of diversity that are drawing people of color in. If you look at all the religious cults you've seen on television, if you read what those black people said who didn't die in Texas, but who said that in that space, they found more of an end to racism than in this culture as a whole. There's a tremendous challenge that has to be brought to the left right now that has to do with a politics of compassion and love. If we are to address one another in the same way that the right addresses people across so many boundaries of class and sexual preference, etc., we have to talk about what it would mean to not have an arrogant politics on the left, a politics that seeks to close people out because they haven't read the right books, because they're not quoting Althusser. A mass-based politics is concerned about things like love and ethics and family values. A tremendous challenge that I feel constantly as a black woman on the left is how to articulate a framework of struggle, a progressive struggle, that meets people where they are, that is able to say to people, "I can engage you right where you are." Progressives should be willing to go to people where they are and to talk about what kinds of resources, what kinds of knowledge, what kinds of concrete struggle we can engage in collectively that will allow us to promote a transformative, liberatory politics.

CORNEL WEST: When we reflect on what divides us, we have to first recognize that we are in an economic situation in which a small number of people have a disproportionate amount of wealth, power and privilege. This does not demonize anybody or any group. But when you have a situation where one percent of the population owns forty-eight percent of the total net financial wealth and ten percent own eighty-six percent of the wealth, and the bottom forty-five percent own two percent of the wealth, you're going to see some scrambling over crumbs. So much of the struggle that goes on among groups that belong together is that they reach the conclusion that somehow they can gain access to the mainstream by getting a bigger crumb than the other group. The issues of race and ethnicity and gender have their own logic, yes, but their logics are inseparable from the fact that the corporate elite, a bank elite and often political elites who are beholden to those elites, resemble kings and queens in the period of monarchs, and have a disproportionate amount of power. If it is the truth indeed that one percent of the population actually deserve forty-eight percent of the wealth, let's see the argument. Where is it? We've got twenty percent of our children of all colors living in poverty and forty-two percent of young brown brothers and sisters living in poverty and fifty-one percent of black brothers and sisters living in poverty in the richest nation in the history of the world. What's going on? Let's have a public debate about it. And this economic situation is inseparable from the cultural and spiritual impoverishment that sister bell is talking about. In this situation, everybody wants to get over, which means that market moralities and mentalities become predominant and not humane values like struggle, like love, care, concern, service to others, even the personal ones like tenderness and kindness and sweetness. You all remember Otis Redding? *Try a little tenderness?* So the non-market values are pushed to the margins. We are living in a culture that's more and more revolving around cold-heartedness and mean-spiritedness. It reinforces the racial polarization. It reinforces gender polarization. It brings hostility and animosity to the surface. We have to tell the truth about how we got into this mess and we have to preserve the best of the moral visions to provide a way out. Progressives have an obligation to do that even in the most difficult of times. Not getting down-hearted and falling into the self-fulfilling prophecy of fatalism and cynicism and pessimism and feeling better about yourself that you're so right about your skepticism and pessimism and fatalism. No. We're talking about cutting against the grain.

BELL HOOKS: It just shocks me when I go around the country and young people tell me, "The civil rights movement didn't do anything. The sixties were a failure." I say, "Wait a minute. We wouldn't be sitting in this room if the civil rights movement was a failure. We wouldn't be able to fellowship." Look around you. I always think that at moments like these you just need to take a moment and look around you at the multiculturalism, the diversity that's present. We know that most of us are not fellowshipping across the lines of class, culture, ethnicity, etc. "How did we lose the powerful momentum?" That's the question we should be asking. We shouldn't be sending out a message that the political movements failed. We should be talking about how we failed to keep alive the momentum that those movements created. I have this new book called *Killing Rage: Ending Racism.* I've been writing about the fact that the whole idea of black is beautiful did not fail. That revolutionized many of our lives. A lot of black people that were steeped in self-hate about their body, about who they were, were changed utterly during that historical moment. Now we may ask, why are some of those people walking around dripping with the Jerry

Carol juices and what have you today? It's not that the moment was a failure. What prevented that moment from being sustained? Let's talk deeply about the question of white supremacy. Those of you who know my work know that I prefer the term "white supremacy" to "racism" because I go again and again out to groups of people who say, "But racism doesn't exist any more." People associate racism with overt discrimination, whether or not black people are hanging from trees. Think about it. Think about the masses of people in this country who looked at the Rodney King video and did not see racism. These issues are what divides us. One of the major things that divides us is our failure to understand how white supremacy works in our lives, how the kind of judgments people make affect the quality of our lives.

I just moved to New York. I'm going to be a regular professor at City College in the fall. I have the honor, and I say this not to be immodest, but because it is an honor, to be the first black woman Distinguished Professor at 137th Street. As a Southerner—and we've always heard that the South is the place of certain forms of exclusion—I have to tell you that I'm not naive about racism, and I'm not naive about white supremacy. But I have never encountered the kind of racism looking for housing that I encountered in this city anywhere else in the United States. After I had given my cancelled checks, after I had shown my tax returns, after I had done every little thing that you could possibly do, I still encountered racism. The racism shifted from, "Well, you're OK, but we're concerned about the type of people you might bring to the building." One of the most important coalitions is the Coalition for the Homeless. One of the major issues in our lives is around the question of housing—housing for everyone. Think about all the places in the world where people could be living but there's a class of people that say, "We don't want those groups of people in our neighborhood." Think about what that means in our lives when we talk about what are going to be the sites in the future for progressive change, one of those arenas is going to be the question of housing. Where are our feminist cooperative housing projects? One of the issues we have about women and violence is that many of us feel that we cannot leave the shelter we live in to go somewhere else. Every city in the United States right now should have an example of feminist cooperative housing, of what it means for women with children to be able to own a small space, to have some control over their lives, to be able to leave situations of abuse because they have somewhere to go. I know what it means to have somewhere to go when you're hurt. When you've been a woman that's been abused in this society and you go out your door it's easy to identify other women in a similar predicament.

The whole arena of patriarchy and housing has not been something feminism has focused on in this society precisely because of the way class values have determined feminism. If you're already living in a nice house, if you already feel like you've got certain things, you may think abortion is the central issue. One of the reasons we can't always come together is we disagree about what types of issues should take priority in our lives. So part of envisioning a different future for the left is envisioning what it might mean to listen to other people's needs. It's total nonsense to stand up and try to act like patriarchal pornography doesn't encourage violence and objectification of women. It does. But the fact is, that is not why patriarchy exists. And if we want women to have more control over our lives within this structure, then let's focus on the kinds of things—jobs, literacy, housing, within a radicalized feminist movement—that would in fact make those things central to the agenda.

CORNEL WEST: I think bell's talk about the 1960s is very important, and especially so for young brothers and sisters of all colors. There are two basic myths in my view about the sixties. One is that there was no progress, given the time and energy and lives spent in the struggle. It's been thirty years since those three brothers were shot in Mississippi. *There was a war going on in the 1960s.* Black people were leading it, but they had a broad enough vision to invite all those who had the courage and vision to join. Within nine years, fifty percent of all poor people were lifted out of poverty. That is a relative victory. When brother Michael Harrington wrote his classic of 1962 and Dwight McDonald wrote a review in the *New Yorker,* over sixty percent of black people were living in poverty. It is still too many, but now it's thirty-three percent—a relative victory, but still a depth of social misery and socially induced form of suffering. But the point is, we've got to get beyond this American mentality that says, when there's a problem, you push a button and it's over. No such thing. We're talking about 244 years of inheritable slavery. We're talking about over 80 years of Jim Crow and lynching. You don't overcome a deep problem like that in nine years of social engineering. But we have to have a sense of history when we talk about the sixties. It was relative victory and setback. COINTELPRO and so forth and so on. Political prisoners are still lingering in America's jails. But the second myth is the notion that somehow, and this is especially for young folk, everybody was in on the struggle. You meet older people these days who'll say: "I was there with Martin. I was there with Malcolm. I marched in Mississippi." They're lying, they're lying, don't believe the hype! And that's especially for young people. Why? Because young people think when they call a meeting and only nine progressives show up, they have no possibility. Don't forget that in 1961 just twelve people were showing up. In 1957 it was three people who were showing up. It was one sister in December of 1955 who refused to move to the back of the bus. It's always a critical minority. We're not talking about some movement in which everybody's in on the struggle. Martin Luther King, Jr. was unpopular in America, no matter what corporate America does every time they trot out their tarnished image of Martin Luther King. Malcolm X, in the black community and outside, had to cut against the grain. Even my mother had questions about Malcolm. But the point is they had to cut against the grain and they went with the people that they had. They just wanted to ensure that the people had character and integrity and were willing to go down and go the long distance, the long haul, as it were. That's what you have to keep in mind when you're in this kind of struggle for freedom and justice. Setbacks, yes. But never completely down where you cannot get up and get moving again, even if only for the moment you turn to a little culture to soothe you and heal you. Turn on a little Otis Redding to help you get through. Listen to John Coltrane. Not just so you can be psychologically sensitive to people of color, but because it nourishes the soul. That's the only way we make it through sometimes!

BELL HOOKS: Cornel talks a lot about the conversion process. The left has difficulty in dealing with those of us who are religious. People want to deal with Cornel West because he's so brilliant, so they can forgive him for being religious. They say he may talk about God a little bit as long as he goes on and talks about Heidegger. But what does it mean for us to be able to think of having a left? Some are discomfited by being in the presence of people who have deep, institutionalized religious beliefs. People have been troubled by Cornel and I using the word "conversion" in relationship to radical politics. But how do you avoid a "conversion" to the left when you grow up in this culture? How many of us have had the luxury? We know about middle-class, white people who have had the luxury of being born into the radical, book-writing left. But many of us have not had such luxury, and we come to our radical politics through an experience of conversion, through people showing us.

The parents of a lot of our friends have died. I see my own father getting ill. I hear about Cornel's father. I think about the meaning of being able to hold on to those individuals who have led you in that conversion process. I think about Walter Rodney, about Paulo Freire, about how much *Pedagogy of the Oppressed* turned my head around. I think about Malcolm X. For those of us for whom Malcolm X is a political mentor, we think about him not as an icon, but in relationship to what he taught us about the meaning of struggle and sacrifice. One of the most tremendous lessons that I've learned from Malcolm X was, when you're going down a path and you are exposed to something on that path that tells you must shift your thinking, you shift it! What I talk about all the time in my work is shifting your paradigm. What does it mean to have both the courage and the humility to critique yourself? To be vigilant in that critique? How often do we get to hear about Malcolm X having the humility to be able to stand up with millions of people and say, "This is where I had blind spots. This is where nationalism was leading me not to value the politics of solidarity." There comes a time when nationalism has to be critiqued, when black people have to talk about the ways we can identify with solidarity, with blackness, with the struggle to end white supremacy, that are not nationalistic. I'm here to tell you as a feminist that whenever people talk about nation-building they are talking about controlling women's bodies. They are talking about patriarchy. It's OK that there are those of you who might disagree with me. The point of dialogues like this is to listen to one another. I get bored when people say they've never heard it before but they're disagreeing right way. Think about it. Go to the literature about building nations and you will see forms of racial supremacy, ethnic supremacy. You will see notions of parity. Read Shahrazad Ali's new book *Are You Still a Slave?* We can not just throw these literatures away because they are going out into our communities and into the minds of black people all over America. They tell us that we are not safe with people who are not like ourselves; that we have to judge each other and say, *"Are you black enough?"* This is not about a politics of solidarity. A politics of solidarity says that every black person is black enough to stand up in the struggle to end white supremacy. That's a gesture of loving blackness.

CORNEL WEST: We need strategies for de-gangsterizing society. There are a number of different levels other than talk about eliminating guns. We need to de-gangsterize our minds, our souls, as well as our bodies. We need to talk about policy, in terms of big money on ammunition, gun control, reaching out to those who are armed and organized and trying to create certain kinds of troops, such as what is going on right now across the nation in terms of various gang troops, trying to deal with the drug culture, the market forces that are a material base for so much of the gun culture and so much of the shooting that goes on. We need debates about the legalization of drugs. We need debates about ensuring black folk have employment, decent-paying permanent jobs rather than low-paying temporary jobs as an alternative. There's a number of different registers and levels here. But it's about countering the increasing gangsterization of American society. What are the countervailing forces? Of course, those non-market values that I alluded to will be integral to the organizing and mobilizing around a number of particular issues. That has to do with bonds of trust. That has to do with what it means to be able to work together across race and gender, based on the permanent government, the powers that be, the most powerful institutions in our society, which are transnational corporations, of course.

BELL HOOKS: The question of education is central. I'm disturbed by the increased separation of youth, as though there are the issues that youth have to deal with and there are the issues that adults have to deal with. When did such a separation begin? As a young black woman I learned how to be a revolutionary in the black church; my religious upbringing was a place where I learned the liberatory struggle. One of the things we learned in those places was that no matter how young you were, your commitment to the struggle could be as profound, as deep, as powerful as the oldest person in that space. So that I think we have to dismiss the notion that there has to be some kind of separate youth struggle. Powerful, brilliant youth should be leading our struggle, period. It's a profound challenge to grownups who are into hierarchy to believe that there may be something you have to learn from an eighteen-year-old who has a more enlightened level of consciousness. That to me is a form of humility in praxis as well. To think about not keeping the sense of separate groups. What does it mean to start thinking about learning from groups of people that you had previously felt had nothing to teach you? I think that is an important shift.

CORNEL WEST: Just a quick word about young brothers and sisters. In the past, young people have always played a disproportionate role. They've played a role far beyond their numbers, partly because of their idealism, partly because of their activism, partly because of their sense of sacrifice. But one can never play a fundamental role in struggle unless one is willing to courageously cut against the grain of one's peers. That's fundamental. When I was coming along, we had a genius named Sly Stone who was writing songs like "Thank You for Letting Me Be Myself." We knew that people will never be free until we are all free to be ourselves. You can't free your mind and your body and your soul if you're locked into peer pressure and trying to wear a mask and pose and posture like you were a star. Sly also said, "Everybody is a star." Don't put up with the star system that's been imposed on you by a market culture. All of us are everyday people. We have a role to play. When significant numbers of young people reach the conclusion that they are fundamentally going to be themselves in the sense that they're going to cut against the grain, be open to criticism from elders but also know that some of what the older folk are putting forward is played out, but still building on the best of what the young folks have created, then elites begin to tremble in their boots. I already see it in the hip-hop culture and rap music. When I hear KRS1, I know that there's some serious critique going on. I'm not trying to idealize. I know that they are part and parcel of an attempt to deal with the market culture and therefore market the very rage that they're alluding to, but they also know that ultimately they have to organize and mobilize on the ground. Already significant numbers of young folk are doing that, so we don't want to think that somehow all young people have been seduced by the market culture. All of us are deeply affected by the market culture, no doubt. But for me it has to do with this issue of trying to be oneself so one can strip the various roles and masks that are played: their white supremacist mask and role, their patriarchal ones, the ones that think that to be cool is in fact to reproduce your own oppression. It's a strategy for ruling elites to define what it is to be cool as contributing to your own oppression! What a game being played!

We need to be able to reach out in as many ways as possible. We've still got to have the kind of scope that Sly Stone had, or Arrested Development has, or KRS1 has, and we must also work with cultural artists to get our message across. This is very, very important.

BELL HOOKS: Where is our agenda for the nineties for young people? If I had to name a single force in my life as a young person that propelled me to be that person who could stand up to my parents when I needed to, who could stand up to my father's domestic violence when I needed to, when I think about that force, I would have to say that that force was critical literacy. I grew up in a black church that was concerned with literacy. When we went away to school, we got little rewards. Education was being affirmed. A critical agenda for the nineties for young people has to be a critical literacy. Don't just wear your Malcolm X hat; really study Malcolm X. Wouldn't it be incredible if instead of quoting "I have a dream," which we all know by now, people could quote from "A Testament of Hope," when Martin Luther King talks about why we must be anti-militaristic, why we as black people, in solidarity with people of the world, cannot afford to support imperialism and militarism? Why can't we all quote those passages from Martin Luther King? Critical literacy seems to me to be a powerful agenda for youth in the nineties. That means that we can come together in communities and study and talk together and listen to music and deal with that music in a critical context.

I told Madame Star that I had talked to Ice Cube and she asked me, How was it? I said, "It was good to talk to the brother. He's a thoughtful brother." It's good to cross the boundaries of location. It's good for so-called stars to cross those boundaries with one another and talk to one another. I wish the whole world could have been listening to me and Ice Cube when the brother was trying to throw some lame shit at me about, "All we need is a father in the home." I kept pushing the brother and saying, "You mean to tell me that if we have unloving, dominating, cruel black fathers in the home, we're going to have this new generation of black revolutionaries?" If you were present in that dialogue you would have seen us pushing against one another with the kind of critical affirmation that Cornel exemplifies and talks about. Finally Ice Cube had to admit, "You're right about that. It's not enough to have a father in the home. You've got to have a *conscious* father and a *conscious* mother in the home."

Now I'd like to ask Cornel a difficult question about armed struggle and the place of love. Do you think there's ever a need for violence in liberatory struggle?

CORNEL WEST: I'm not a pacifist, but I do have deep admiration for pacifists. I don't agree with them, but I believe that they are motivated by the right values. I believe that one must exhaust all options and possibilities for non-violent struggle. One does that precisely because one never, ever wants to either lead people or be lead into a dead end or a cul-de-sac. People are already suffering. You don't want to increase their suffering. And two, because any time one takes the life of another human being it is in some sense tragic, even when those human beings are on the other side of the barricades. But I do in fact believe that there are extreme circumstances under which the only option left is to go down violently. I say that with a heavy heart. But it's real.

I fundamentally believe that Nelson Mandela and others had attempted to use every non-violent option available, and yet they had still been crushed. Therefore they had to go underground. I can see myself fighting in World War II even given apartheid America, because fascism is that vicious, and working people's movements around the world were being crushed by fascist movements that had monopolized instrumentalities of violence and were extending world domination. Those are extreme circumstances. At the moment I think that one of the things that progressives must always resist is to engage in rhetorics of violence at a symbolic and cathartic level, when one is not prepared, organized, mobilized. I've seen this with young people all the time, anybody in America who is serious about violence is not talking about it. I don't think that one can envision a violent option for progressives at this moment that would be advantageous for the very people that are struggling to win. But at the same time, I also recognize that history is unpredictable. Therefore one acknowledges that a variety of different options must always be entertained. I say this as a Christian.

Love ye one another. Jesus drove out the merchants from the temple. That's why they put him on the cross. He had to kick behind in the temple because the money changers were thoroughly corrupt in the space that he took seriously, almost as if the marketeers were becoming hegemonic in the space that he considered to be consecrated and sacred, and he felt that at that moment dialogue would not be the appropriate response. That's a very extreme circumstance, but he did engage. For those coming out of different traditions, there's a variety of different examples. But I say that as someone who tries to take this more robust conception of love seriously, not the namby-pamby, sentimental, nostalgic kind of love that we see in Hollywood. I'm talking about the kind of love in which you push to the edge of life's abyss and you fall back on people who can rely on you. If you end up in a wheelchair they can still be there for you. That's the kind of love I'm talking about. That's real. That's powerful. That's concrete. For people who say, I don't understand this notion of conversion, on a personal level you can say, *Fall in love,* and you know what I'm talking about. On another level you can say, *Join a movement,* and you know what I'm talking about. I once looked at the world this way. Now I have a different set of lenses through which I can see the world. I once looked at myself this way, but I explored the inner wilderness of myself and discovered things that I had not wanted to confront and someone allows me to do that. That's what I'm talking about in terms of conversion or transformation or the turning of the soul or any language you want to get people to go another way to struggle for justice.

BELL HOOKS: As a feminist, particularly in terms of critiquing male violence against women and children, I don't feel that I am as clear about this question as Cornel is. I brought that up because I think that part of what we hope for in our future movements is that space where we can have someone who is exceptionally clear and we can listen and ponder what they say. Where we can also give testimony to our lack of clarity. I have a lack of clarity on this issue. It's something that I'm struggling with. I'm involved with engaged Buddhism. I think a lot about the question of violence. I don't call myself a Buddhist because I don't feel that I have let go of my violent impulses. These are the kinds of questions that we don't often have a public forum about, so I just want to thank Cornel for the beauty of that answer.

Whenever we speak about ending white supremacy, any group of people who are both victimized by white supremacy or who are allied with that struggle should feel included. One of the dilemmas we're all facing now is, Why should all of our names have to be called in order for us to feel included? It's important to be as inclusive verbally as we can be. We need the kind of critique that doesn't end up taking us right back to these competing hierarchies of oppression. A lot of black people feel, Why is it Asian Americans don't identify more with black people? I think that this is a critical issue. The Asian Americans I know do feel identified with black people, so they don't necessarily feel that they are being excluded if something specifically black is being talked about. That doesn't mean to say that we as black Americans do not have a political responsibility to learn as much as we can about diverse Asian ethnicities and to engage in particular struggles in solidarity and to name those struggles directly and concretely. But every moment that we don't name those struggles directly and concretely is not a moment of exclusion. I think it's important to point that out. I'm concerned that if I'm encouraging people to struggle together to end white supremacy, I am talking about ending that white supremacy that allows us to take pleasure in a movie like *Menace to Society*, that allows us to support the oppression of Asian groups all over the society. I think we have to be careful because a lot of times groups that see themselves as somehow sandwiched between other groups often don't feel that white supremacy is their issue. And yet, one of the neglected issues is the way the notions of white supremacy that permeate different Asian cultures keep us apart. I feel that too often we're made to feel that it's the responsibility of black people to address that particular white supremacy and not our collective responsibility.

One of the things that we've learned a lot about is how difficult it is to bring together large groups of people with a different kind of strategy. What kind of settings can we create where there can be more dialogue, where there can be respectful kinds of dialogue? We have to constantly think about new strategies for how we come together to dialogue.

People too often confuse solidarity with nationalism. People do not need nationalism to come together in solidarity. We do not need nationalism as African Americans. African Americans can be engaged in movements of solidarity in the interests of ending white supremacy, not in the interests of creating a nation. This is a tremendous lesson we have to learn from recognizing that diverse African peoples came here. They did not all speak the same language. They did not all have the same heritage and legacy. The issue is not how we're building a nation, it is how we will build a politics of solidarity that will allow us to create a society that is free from all forms of racism.

CORNEL WEST: The most important thing for me is that we're at a crossroads in this country, just as many of us are at a crossroads in our lives. We have to ask fundamental questions such as, What kind of people do we really want to be in a civilization that is in such profound decline and decay? Who do we see when we look in the mirror each morning? These seem to be personal questions, but they have much to do with the moral character of our struggle, with the kinds of visions that we end up putting forth. Even when we jump in to allow the larger structural analysis and historical analysis and so forth and so on, we're at a point now where the issues of integrity and character and solidarity and trust become basic. Why? Because so many people have reached the conclusion that everybody's out to manipulate everybody else. This is the market culture that I'm talking about. If we're unable to provide credible—not perfect—examples to cut against that grain, then the most sophisticated analyses and the grandest of visions become sounding brass and tinkling cymbal because nobody believes that people are serious about what they are doing. And we have reached that point. One of the reasons why it's so very important for progressives to come together is that we've got to preserve that kind of spirit in a very, very difficult time. So when we come together we talk at these different levels because the crisis cuts so deep and precisely because we're at such a crossroads. It always encourages me and inspires me to see that there's enough folk around who can be leaven in a loaf, who reach the conclusion that we're just here for a short time, let's treat one another in ways such that we want to see it passed on long after we are gone, politically, morally, structurally, socially, in terms of justice at the highest level and in terms of kindness at the most intimate level.

Copies of this dialogue are available on video or audio tape from the Learning Alliance—see the "More Information" section.

VI. Progressive Struggles in the Age of Gingrich

THIS IS WAR!

TOM FRANK AND DAVE MULCAHEY

> You know what we are to them? Literally, we're the same as the corn and
> the beans that grow around here. We're a renewable resource.
> —Dave Frasier, a striking rubber worker, Decatur, Illinois

There's a war in Decatur, a war that to outside observers must seem strangely
noiseless and inscrutable. Virtually a third of the city's industrial work force is
either on strike or locked out by its employers. The unions that represent
these workers at the three affected plants—1,800 at Caterpillar, 1,250 at
Bridgestone, and 760 at A.E. Staley—have joined forces, assisting each other
in the day-to-day business of battle, sharing experiences and resources, and
uniting in a rare instance of pan-union solidarity. To people who live in
Decatur, the battle lines in this wrenching contest between labor and management are clearly drawn. Everyone knows which side they're on and how they
got there.

And yet from the outside the Decatur troubles are mysterious, baffling, and
nonsensical. The news media are willing to admit that what's going on in
Decatur is important, maybe even historically significant. But no one seems to
know why. Even as the Associated Press places the Decatur struggle among the
ten most important news issues in Illinois (number four, to be exact), newspapers and TV cannot present the economic agonies of central Illinois as anything
but a tragedy—unplanned, unintended, and just plain sad. What's happening
does not fit easily into the narratives of progress, consumption, and corporate
benevolence that make up the official version of what's happening in the late
20th century.

According to the ecstatic voices of the nation's responsible opinion leaders,
the 1990s are supposed to be a golden age of entrepreneurism, the dawning of a
glorious new order called the "global economy." As information technology
conquers space and time to an extent previously unimaginable, the final steps in
capitalism's century-long process of "modernization" are finally being taken.
Production everywhere is now in the hands of gigantic international mega-cor-
porations. Capital can zip around the globe in minutes, crossing boundaries at
whim, pooling wherever benefits and wages can be driven the lowest. Flexibility

and impermanence have become the key aspects of all stages of production, and the certainties of the past—including job security and a living wage—must be abandoned in the interests of "competitiveness."

As business has taken virtual command of the world economy, so its principles have begun to enjoy an unprecedented hegemony over the American mind. No previous period in American industrial history—not even the "conformist" 1950s—has seen such intellectual and cultural unanimity about the unassailable centrality—indeed, the desirability—of the profit motive as the organizing principle of social life. Both parties now compete for the patronage of the same affluent corporations; both scramble to enact legislation favorable to business and business only. Theorists like Francis Fukuyama trumpet the demise of dissent, and politicians like Newt Gingrich do Calvin Coolidge one better: not only is the business of America business, but the culture and learning of America is business also. The efficacy of the "free market" is now recognized to be a fact of nature: immutable, inevitable, and inexorable.

But just watch for a few minutes more, and you'll witness a curious, inexplicable, and horrifying sight. June 25, 1994, for reasons known only to themselves, the Decatur police used pepper gas to attack a group of locked-out union workers who were non-violently blocking the entrance to the Staley plant. Even though we live in a violence-jaded age, the scene that resulted (captured, of course, on videotape) was a horrible thing to behold, perhaps because one realizes that if this could happen to these people it could happen to anybody: masked and gloved cops methodically assaulting people who are *sitting,* arm in arm, *with their backs to the police.* The viciousness that ensued was repulsive not only because the workers were visibly incapable of having provoked the attack but because the police involved seemed to derive such obvious joy from discharging their weapons on the helpless, cringing protesters. Officers in the rear reach enthusiastically past their comrades so they too can spray their gas on the screaming, coughing pickets, who are by now rolling on the ground and covering their faces; one officer even turns a helpless man on his back, waits for the opportune moment, and then sprays the stuff directly into his face.

According to the management theorists of the global age, this shouldn't be happening. The business regime that enjoys such total allegiance is said to be a benevolent one. It promises to look after all of us, all the people who will never make it into upper management, the people who will never pile up enough to invest heavily, the people who just work. As anyone knows who's ever worked in an office, read one of the various best-sellers by Tom Peters, or picked up an airline in-flight magazine, today's executive is obsessed with the mystical idea of "empowerment," the secret ingredient by which the (Japanese) competition may be beaten.

"Empowerment" has brought about a corporate revolution, at least in the public-image realm: the Taylorism of prewar years, the efficiency-crazed process that conceived of workers as automatons, has been abandoned, replaced by a softer system in which workers are referred to by evasively sentimental terms like "stakeholders," management and workers join forces in "quality circles," and supervisors subscribe to the cult of "leadership," according to which management is not merely the whip hand of capital but an association of natural-born "motivators," people whose God-given task it is to relate the needs of production to those whose God-given task it is to produce. Our corporate masters now value workers as people, they treasure our information about how to do things (what some would call "skills"), and they will look out for us.

But labor unions are a different matter. As a standing rejoinder to the doctrine of the eternal benevolence of capital ("empowerment" had a wholly different meaning in Pullman in 1894), organized labor is just about as antithetical to the business-utopia ideology of Gingrich, Drucker, Microsoft, et al., as it's possible to be. Not only do union wage scales cut deeply into manufacturing profits, but unions challenge business at a basic level, a level on which capital feels it needs no longer tolerate challenges: the level of ideology. Repentant professional union buster Martin Levitt depicts management's animosity toward unions in his recent *Confessions of a Union Buster:* "Today there are more than seven thousand attorneys and consultants across the nation who make their living busting unions, and they work almost every day. At a billing rate of $1,000 to $1,500 a day per consultant and $300 to $400 an hour for attorneys, the war on organized labor is a $1 billion-plus industry."

At worst, unions are portrayed by management theorists and their devotees in politics, journalism, advertising, and TV as nests of demagogues, as quasi-criminal obstacles to the warm friendship and cooperation that would normally exist between owners and employees. At best, unions are obsolete remnants of the distant past struggling to maintain the power of no one but themselves. Either way, their day is done. As a December subhead in the *Indianapolis Star* characterized the Decatur battle, "Experts [management experts, they mean] see simultaneous strikes in Decatur as last big union fight in new global economy."

Amid the great tides of capital sweeping the world, places like Decatur are becoming increasingly redundant and obsolete. While global business demands total flexibility, instant change, and an environment of permanent flux, Decatur (and most other industrial towns) is rooted far too securely in the political and cultural values of the past. It's easy for the doltish TV commentators of Illinois to portray Decatur's resistance as a wrongheaded rejection of the glories of progress. And clearly the language and the feeling of desperation in this once prosperous town are straight out of the '30s.

But the significance of the three battles in Decatur is far greater than platitudes would have it appear. In Decatur, quite by chance, all the various economic forces and trends that make up the New World Order have come together and, in broad daylight, dealt a sledgehammer blow to the ways of ordinary working people. In Decatur the myth of global prosperity under the benevolent rule of multinational "competitiveness" has debunked itself, publicly and forcefully. And in Decatur there has finally been a spark of resistance, a whispering of innovation in the tired ranks of dissent. While the fight here began over the fate of a small local union, the national labor movement increasingly realizes that its meaning and credibility are somehow on the line. And thus in Decatur, finally, have come the first hints of a long-awaited reawakening.

In 1988 the facts of the global economy were brought home to Decatur. After decades of more-or-less local ownership, the A.E. Staley Manufacturing Company, one of the city's largest employers, was acquired as part of a hostile takeover of its holding company by the British sweetener conglomerate Tate & Lyle, PLC. To make matters even more portentous, much of the dirty work was done by that paragon investment banker of the decade, Drexel Burnham Lambert. The move was a good one for Tate & Lyle, a company that owns a number of sugar brands, among them Domino. One of Staley's primary businesses has always been "corn wet milling," the process of breaking corn down into a variety of chemical components, primarily starches and sugars, which are then developed into industrial ingredients. And the star performer of these ingredients during the 1970s was high-fructose corn syrup, which virtually replaced cane sugar in the U.S. and other markets as the soft drink sweetening ingredient of choice. To maintain a share of the world sweetener market, it was imperative that Tate & Lyle get a piece of the corn wet milling industry.

The international logic of capital may come cloaked in palaver about "competition," but its fundamental impulse, particularly with respect to agribusiness, is toward conglomeration. In an extremely capital-intensive industry like corn wet milling, the barriers to entry are correspondingly high. In other words, it would have been next to impossible for Tate & Lyle to compete with the likes of Staley by setting up its own operation: the costs of doing so would have been too great. The only way for the company to "compete" in the sweetener business was to acquire one of its competitors.

It is difficult to imagine that such dealing can take place without fundamen-tally changing the relationship between a company's owners and its employees. The management decisions of roving transnational capitalists are governed by a different set of values and imperatives than those of a company that grows organically over a long period of time, whose management and directors remain rooted in the community and are subject to the sanction or opprobrium of that community.

According to Local 7837 of the United Paperworkers International Union (which has represented workers at Staley's Decatur plant since the UPIU subsumed the local's former international union, the Allied Industrial Workers, in September 1993), inklings of these new imperatives appeared shortly after Tate & Lyle's takeover. In a 1993 report called "Deadly Corn," the Staley workers' local union charges that their company's change of ownership brought with it "a big change in management's attitude toward safety." Among the dangerous new practices alleged are an increased reliance on poorly trained and incompetent subcontractors and a practice of shifting hourly workers into jobs in which they have little experience. The accidental death of mechanic James Beals in 1990 underscored for the union what it claimed had been a general, noticeable deterioration in plant safety. And sure enough, at the conclusion of a detailed investigation in 1991, the Occupational Safety and Health Administration fined Staley $1.6 million for a total of 298 health and safety violations.

Even more disturbing to Staley workers was a series of actions taken by the new multinational management in the year and a half before their contract was due to expire that seemed calculated to anger the workers. They say management became much more rigid in matters of discipline, verging on what longtime local bargaining committeeman Dan Lane calls "Gestapo tactics." Work rules were changed, incorporating harsher punishment for minor infractions. Managers started threatening workers with discharge on a more regular basis. Workers were often subject to discipline for conduct as innocuous as reporting to first-aid stations after minor injuries—a strategy, in Lane's opinion, calculated to intimidate those who might otherwise file grievances.

Then, in the first months of 1992, as workers remember it, Staley management began asking union laborers in the Decatur plant to compose detailed written manuals describing the operations and techniques of their jobs. Even though the company had long sponsored various labor-management cooperation schemes, this manual-writing push immediately rang alarm bells. Workers met it with the same skepticism and resentment with which they'd viewed Staley's past attempts to court the participation of workers in "quality circles" and the like.

However, managers cast the effort as part of a company-wide "job safety analysis." "The company's plan all along," says Royal Plankenhorn, a senior process operator with 20 years at Staley, "was to force a strike. They'd hand your 'safety manual' along to the next guy, the scab that replaces you. You've told him how to do your job, and there's no glitch in production. They don't miss a beat."

By the end of 1991, the local union membership was tense. They sensed that Staley was grinding an ax, and they wanted to prepare for a fight. Through a regional union organizer, the local leadership arranged to have Mark Crouch, a professor of labor studies at Indiana University, come to the union hall to advise the membership on their situation and their options. Before visiting Decatur, Crouch asked the local to compile a file of information relating to their concerns. As he went through the data, Crouch was struck by what he terms "clear signs" that Staley management was planning to provoke a strike. Especially clear was the attempt to prepare operations manuals. "Anytime an employer is going to get involved in a strike or a worker replacement strategy," Crouch says, "he has to know either that there is a readily available supply of people out there with the skills he needs, or that he has a way to capture the skills his workers have so that he can transfer them to somebody else."

Crouch tried to impress on the local's members his belief that the company was counting on them to react confrontationally, that it was simply waiting for a pretext to replace them. It was important for the workers to come up with a strategy that would allow them to fight on their own terms. The fact that this warning came almost a year before the contract was due to expire gave the union time to reenergize its shop floor communication network and to prepare psychologically for a fight, Crouch believes. The local set about making a budget for the fight the members saw coming, and raised its monthly union dues from $18 to $100.

That almost every union member voted for the increase—and that there was almost complete compliance—reflected the grim reality of recent labor struggles in central Illinois. The members of Local 7837 recalled the recent quashing of a large strike by Caterpillar workers, and they were determined not to succumb to the same fate. "We'd seen just around this area," explains veteran power systems operator Art Dhermy, "that strikes don't get you anything but lost pay."

The contract that was ultimately proposed by Staley's new management, in September 1992, seemed designed to force a strike. According to what the company called its "best and final offer," workers would have to abandon important elements of the seniority system and settle for a less hospitable grievance process. Most objectionable of all, workers were to begin a 12-hour rotating schedule according to which each of four shifts would work a month on a 12-hour night shift, then a month of 12-hour days.

The benefits to the corporation were obvious: an entire shift would immediately be eliminated. But for workers, the demand was an outrage. The struggle for the eight-hour workday is one of the sacred stories of American labor, a cause for which a vast number of people have fought and died (it was this radical idea, among other things, that precipitated Chicago's infamous Haymarket riot). The eight-hour day allows workers a life and a humanity outside the factory, and this is precisely what Staley's demands seemed designed to take away.

The 12-hour day "takes these people out of anything and everything that is a community-based activity, related to anything outside of work," says Crouch. "That's everything from bowling leagues to little league to church to running for public office. You wind up living to work rather than working to live. People who work in these places don't even have the same schedules. If you want to see the destruction of the American family, there is no better way than to put the heads of the household on a rotating shift."

Again the actions of Staley management typify the direction, with all its apparent contradictions, of contemporary business thought. Even as it made demands that it knew its unionized workers could not accept, Staley still talked the "empowerment" line. It sponsored cooperative programs between workers and management, issued statements about "elimination of we/they perceptions," and mouthed standard workplace pieties like "trust, confidence, and pride at high levels." While these two aspects of management behavior might seem contradictory, there is in fact no real dissonance between Staley's "empowerment" patter and its apparent disregard for workers' safety and expertise. Both are arms of the fundamental management drive to rid their factories of the alien union presence.

The contract that Staley offered its union workers may have guaranteed their right to remain unionized, but workers believe management's intent was quite the contrary: provoke a strike, hire replacements, and thus achieve the much sought after union-free workplace. "There's no way the workers will accept it," is how Don Rhodes, a feed dryer operator with 20 years experience at Staley, summarizes management's thinking. "Their second thought was, 'If they don't accept it, they're striking. If they strike, we'll permanently replace them.'"

As both sides of the conflict are aware, the years since 1980 have been extraordinarily bad ones for organized labor, and, based on their knowledge of events like the bitter Hormel strike of 1985–86 and the failed Caterpillar strike of 1992, Staley management could count on a victory in case of a walkout. Labor writer David Moberg summarized the situation in 1993 in the *Chicago Tribune:* "It may seem odd that an employer, not labor union members, would want a strike. Yet during the past decade, many companies have seen a strike as their opportunity to permanently replace longtime workers with nonunion strikebreakers."

The Staley workers' union could not agree to the company's "best and final offer," but neither could they back up their own position with traditional methods. As Art Dhermy puts it, workers could "either go on strike, accept their conditions, or find the other way. We decided to go the other way." As Staley management proceeded to impose its contract, including the hated 12-hour day, the union turned to a number of innovative strategies that had been suggested by a pair of labor consultants who were brought in early on.

In June 1992, Dave Watts, president of the Staley local, then 837, invited labor activist Ray Rogers to pitch the local on the idea of running a "corporate campaign." Rogers, a partner in a firm called Corporate Campaign, Inc., is widely acknowledged as one of the pioneers of the strategy. The basic principle of a successful corporate campaign, according to Rogers, is to bring irresistible economic and political pressure to bear on the targeted company, which can be most readily achieved by alienating the company from the financial and other corporate partners that are its lifeblood.

The local union was suitably impressed, and Rogers was hired on as a consultant. With the help of Corporate Campaign's printing capabilities and mailing list, the local was able to raise money and disseminate literature telling its side of the story. Mailings were sent to union members and labor activists all over the midwest instructing them to boycott not only Tate & Lyle–owned sugar brands, but a couple of bank chains on whose boards two Staley executives served as directors. The banks quickly buckled, and to the exultation of the union, the Staley executives resigned from their boards. Similarly, the Miller Brewing Company, a substantial customer of Staley, severed its relationship with the company when attention was turned to it.

Despite these victories, the extent to which the pressure on Staley's corporate associates will succeed is still to be seen. Currently the union is trying to pressure Coca-Cola and Pepsi-Cola, Staley's largest sweetener customers, to decline to renew their contracts with the company. Judging from the statements of spokespeople for these companies, neither is willing to change its business relationship with Staley at this time. Nor is the State Farm Insurance Company, which was made a target of the UPIU corporate campaign because of its large stake in Archer Daniels Midland, the largest shareholder in Tate & Lyle.

In January 1995, UPIU 7837 reluctantly terminated its relationship with Rogers, although not because the members felt he was ineffective. "He got us on the map," said local spokesman Ron Van Scyoc. "We owe him a lot of allegiance." But many members weren't happy with the effort being made by the AFL-CIO and even their own international union to help their cause, and they suspected the presence of Rogers was the reason.

Why? Rogers had a history of confrontation with some of the leadership of organized labor itself, most notably during the United Food and Commercial Workers' acrimonious strike against a Hormel meat-packing plant in Austin, Minnesota. That nine-month strike ended in 1986 when the international went over the heads of the more militant Local P-9, agreed to a new contract with Hormel, and put P-9 in trusteeship. Rogers's corporate campaign, while overwhelmingly sanctioned by P-9's membership, was one of several points of contention between the local and the international.

At the same time Rogers was advising Local 7837 on its corporate campaign, members were preparing for a "work to rule" campaign. The latter, a tactic invented years ago by the Industrial Workers of the World, has been popularized of late through the efforts of Jerry Tucker, the leader of a reform movement in the United Auto Workers. Effectively executed, a work-to-rule campaign can cripple productivity more effectively than a strike, with the added benefit that the rank and file remain on the company payroll. Advised by Tucker, union workers began to follow instructions for every task to the letter, adding no initiative or know-how that was not explicitly stipulated in job specifications. Suddenly workers had to be instructed in the basic operation of machines they had run for years—in some cases, machines they understood much better than did the supervisors who had been brought in by Tate & Lyle.

"When they imposed their 'best and final offer,' then we chose to work to rule," remembers Don Rhodes. "To let them know that we do do more than just our jobs. We didn't just go out there, adjust something, and walk off. We adjusted it, checked it, did this, did that, make sure everything runs properly. So we decided, if they're so smart, we're so stupid, we'll do only what they tell us to do."

"Work to rule is an innovative tactic in labor, a new way of fighting back when you feel the corporation wants to throw you on strike, and you're just not strong enough to withstand a strike," explains Steven Ashby, labor historian and member of a Chicago solidarity committee for the Staley workers. "You slow production down by doing only what you're told to do. You don't use all the skills and experience that—what is the average in that plant, 28 years?—you don't bring that to work with you. You leave it at home. They [at Staley] had cut production significantly; the estimates were at least from a third to a half."

Working to rule may sound like jolly high jinks, but workers emphasize that it can be difficult to implement. "The work ethics and the knowledge of this group of people are probably some of the best in Illinois...so that was really hard for a lot of people to do," says Dick Schable, a sheet metal worker with 27 years' experience in the Staley plant. "We're all law-abiding citizens, pretty much; we're all, pretty much, over the age of 40. So this isn't some rebellious young group that just came to the work force and are trying to make waves. These are people that have been well-established in this plant for a number of years."

What makes work to rule so effective is its vivid political implications. By working to rule, laborers strike at the heart of the above-mentioned contradiction in current doctrines of "empowerment." Suddenly all those cherished notions of worker-manager cooperation evaporate, all those "quality circles" are broken, "leadership" seems not to reside in the "leaders" after all. Workers know how to run the plant; management doesn't. And by simply withdrawing that knowledge, workers provide a maddening reminder that workers are empowered already, that they understand "cooperation" better than any MBA can ever imagine, and that they will approach management on their own terms.

"One of the powers that I think work to rule gives you," continues Don Rhodes, is this: "For years you went out there and you did your job, see, and the companies really didn't have to do that much except for making sure you're there. They didn't have to make any decisions. I think the thing that scared the company the most was when they realized that to work to rule, we started using this [our heads] instead of this [our backs]. They looked over and said, 'Hey, they're using their minds. We have lost control. If they start using their mind and target it towards us, we've lost control of that plant.' And they'll spend millions of dollars [getting it back]—that's what this is all about, control. And we took that power and control away from them."

Working to rule was a political attack on the theories so beloved by Staley's multinational management. And it seems to have been understood as such at Staley headquarters. By June of 1993 plant efficiency had been seriously reduced; and, charging its union work force with "sabotage," management resorted to perhaps the only technique for dealing with labor that will still put you on the wrong side of American public opinion: the lockout.

The crucial third part of a successful labor struggle, according to Steven Ashby, is community outreach. "We have to show that we can overcome our differences; we have to reach out to the African American community, the clergy, and so forth. That's the meaning of the slogan, 'It's our solidarity against theirs.'" Shortly after the Staley workers were locked out, Ashby, his wife C. J. Hawking—a minister—and two colleagues formed a Chicago solidarity group. One of their first activities was to hold a demonstration outside the State of Illinois Building to advocate full unemployment benefits for the locked-out workers. Their demonstration, which coincided with a demonstration by a group of workers at the state capitol, apparently sent the point home to state legislators: for the first time in Illinois history locked-out workers were granted unemployment benefits. The Chicago group has pitched in mightily, raising over $125,000 and organizing a number of benefits, including one by the Chicago Symphony Orchestra.

While Ashby and Hawking are willing to put their years of organizing experience to work, they express deep admiration for the members of UPIU 7837 who have made of their adversity an opportunity to transform labor politics. And that has meant tackling the difficult issue of race relations. Black members of the local invited white members to join them in Decatur's 1994 Martin Luther King Day parade, and together they marched carrying labor placards in defiance of a city ban. Not only were they the largest marching party in the parade, they also put on what turned out to be the largest interracial demonstration in the city's history. Jeanette Hawkins, one of the march's organizers, a few months later became the first woman and the first African American elected to the local's bargaining committee.

Men and women who have spent decades as hourly laborers are now being sent around the country, to union halls and to Ivy League business schools alike, raising funds and relating the experiences of the Staley workers to anyone who will give them a sympathetic ear. "I know I'm not fluently educated in English," admits Frank Travis. "But people in America are getting tired of people getting up and fluently speaking, fluently cynical and full of bullshit. They're tired of it and they want to hear honesty."

Travis has a witness in the person of striking rubber worker Dave Frasier. In July, in 1994 Frasier's union, the United Rubber Workers, went on strike against six Bridgestone/Firestone tire plants, including the one in Decatur, for many of the same reasons that have caused the Staley workers to be locked out. Like Staley, Bridgestone/Firestone wants to impose rotating work shifts. Its "best and final offer" also cuts premium pay for holiday work, increases employee health-benefit contributions, institutes a two-tier pay scale, and ties pay increases to company-set productivity targets. "These guys saw the handwriting on the wall," Frasier says of the UPIU local. The URW is in a relatively weaker position, having been lured into a strike few outside the union think they can win. "You could see what was going on with the labor movement, that they were doing their best to break us. And our people did not respond; their people did."

For its part, management explains its position toward its workers by using the language and logic so commonplace in this era of global conglomerates: "competitiveness." The Decatur plant, according to Staley spokesman J. Patrick Mohan, is just not efficient enough. "Decatur was being subsidized by our other plants, and returns were inadequate," he explained to Britain's *Guardian*. (Mohan would not return our phone calls.) "As we modernize, we need modern labor agreements."

An official Staley newsletter puts it even more explicitly: "To succeed in business, companies must constantly work to improve efficiency and competitiveness. Staley is no different. We are changing the way we work in our Decatur plant to make it a strong, efficient operation that can compete effectively in today's tough marketplace."

This line of argument will be familiar to observers of public policy debates raging all across the country. Premonitions of damaged competitiveness cut a lot of ice with timid state and local politicians, who quake in fear of creating— or, more realistically, being accused of creating—the buzz-killing "bad business climate." Meanwhile, large corporations blithely threaten workers at facilities in Rust Belt states that they can easily relocate in the land of "right to work"—places like Bill Clinton's Arkansas.

If state and local officials are intimidated by the taint of diminished competitiveness, UPIU Local 7837 denies that it threatens Staley's operation in the least. Says Royal Plankenhorn: "Today, the average grain mill worker makes $200 an hour in pure profit for his company. That's after you pay for the materials, the power, the taxes, the building."

As part of its preparation for the long fight ahead, the union consulted in 1992 with Professor Laurie Clements, director of the Labor Center at the University of Iowa and a scholar with experience analyzing the wet corn industry. His findings are a startling refutation of Staley's official line. The average value added, per worker per annum, in the wet corn industry grew from $353,367 in 1988 to $425,783 in 1989. The figure for 1991, the most current available, reflects an average value added of $526,758, a towering figure for any industry. Furthermore, average revenue growth from 1973 to 1991 in the corn wet milling industry sailed along at an average rate of 8.8 percent per annum. Of 141 industry groups surveyed, only one—audio/visual equipment—experienced such a high rate of growth. In fact, only 11 of the 141 industries even sustained half the growth rate of corn wet milling over the same period.

Certainly, overall trends in an industry may not necessarily reflect the fortunes of every company that operates within that industry. But when an industry exceeds the norms of business in general to the extent that corn wet milling has, it is difficult for any single player to fail. And Staley certainly has not. In recent years, Tate & Lyle's most profitable sectors have been in the North American corn processing industry. In an open letter to the mayor of Decatur, union officials stated as much, declaring: "Before we can give up any of the things that our members have earned over the years, we must have proof that the Staley Decatur plant is not competitive. The union's bargaining committee has repeatedly asked the company to show exactly how Staley has lost its competitive edge, and never received any information."

If the logic of competitiveness were as all-important as it is said to be, Staley's chief rival would be agribusiness giant Archer Daniels Midland (ADM), which is also based in Decatur. Instead, as the locked-out Staley workers frequently point out, the two companies constructed a slurry pipeline between the ADM and Staley plants in Decatur during the tense months leading up to Staley's labor negotiations. Workers are convinced that this was an intimidation tactic designed to show that ADM would come to Staley's aid in the event of a work stoppage. They further point out that ADM holds the largest ownership stake in Tate & Lyle (7.3 percent), giving its competitor considerable control over the fate of Staley and its work force.

"Narrow business logic says that if one of them is economically in trouble, its competitor should be in a position to take advantage of that in the market," Clements points out. "What we have here is the direct opposite. They can move the slurry across the city to keep whatever plant going. The notion of open competition sounds very dubious to me."

Never in our lifetimes have labor unions constituted a force of real opposition to the order—economic and philosophical—of corporate America. Sure, as students of history we were aware that trade unionism was once a dynamic political force, and so on. But in the years since World War II, labor had settled into the comfortable, complacent pattern that is now referred to as "business unionism." It was forever proclaiming its partnership with big business, affirming the foreign policies of Republican presidents, protecting its own interests as sedulously as any investment banker. But in Decatur, this has slowly begun to change.

On October 15, 1994, some four months after the violent gassing of the Staley workers appeared on national TV, over 7,000 union members, their families, and supporters from across the country gathered in Decatur. The vacant lot next to the UAW hall teemed with people in red. "We'll NEVER Forget Labor War of '94," read one T-shirt. "Union spouse with attitude," announced another. A speaker instructed the vast audience in the tactics of nonviolence. "Injury to one," he shouted at the conclusion of his speech. "Injury to all!" the crowd responded—the slogan of the old IWW, for years but a dead memory. The podium even made a reference to Joe Hill.

As the workers marched out onto one of Decatur's main streets, orderly, well organized, and bearing a profusion of American flags, they were watched at every step by worried police who scrambled ahead of the parade to radio which way it was turning, which streets it was going to be blocking. Their concern was justified, since the workers carried banners with such menacing legends as "Corporate Greed Is Tearing Decatur Apart," and "Labor Rights Civil Rights." And yet there was no question of gassing this time, the throng was too immense. The enforcers of order could do little more than get out of the way and keep the good people of Decatur at least a block from the parade, at one point even abandoning a police cruiser, its flashing lights left turning inconsequentially, in the middle of an intersection where it was quickly engulfed by the marchers.

The parade mounted an enormous viaduct that passes over the Staley plant and stopped in the very middle. Below on all sides were the Staley buildings, and the odor from the chemical processing within was intense, a graphic illustration of why the Staley workers' concerns about job safety were so urgent. People could barely breathe. Everywhere they were clamping handkerchiefs over their noses and mouths. High up on a catwalk inside the plant a lone uniformed figure videotaped the parade, which now stretched far into the distance, red shirts, placards, and American flags challenging, just for this one day, the country's official corporate order. The tableau put one in mind of a Capra movie, with portly old corporate men (of course they are in fact tanned, slim, well tailored, and completely assured in their righteousness) cowering in their offices as the People reclaim the geography of their town for themselves. Father Martin Mangan of the Saint James Catholic Church in Decatur came forward and did the honors, rechristening the bridge "Workers' Memorial Viaduct" in honor of Jim Beals, the man who died on the job at Staley in 1992.

The march came to an end about an hour later in an enormous intersection near the Caterpillar plant, where operations had been called off for the day. On the way we were videotaped by uniformed paramilitaries on the grounds of the Firestone plant, videotaped by uniformed men in the backseats of slowly moving police cruisers, and probably also videotaped by the noisy state police helicopter (perhaps the noisiest they could find) that droned in circles overhead all day. The powers-that-be in Decatur were doing their level best to make these people feel like criminals.

Everything we saw that day put us in mind of the labor radicalism of the 1930s and before, the years of labor's great accomplishments. The lethargy and complacency of the postwar years were nowhere to be found: they had dissolved in the clouds of pepper gas back on June 25. What we saw was a new phenomenon, a social movement that had no place in the orderly world of people who had been born since the war.

In his study of the landmark Hormel strike of 1985–86, Peter Rachleff suggests that after years of disheartening defeats, labor may be on the verge of one of its periodic resurgences. While "business unions," top-heavy with bureaucracy, seem to be capable of little more than slowly negotiating their own extinction, elements of a new labor movement are emerging in response to the hostile climate of the 1980s. Echoing many of the tactics and slogans of the old IWW, this new unionism involves a much greater role in decision making for the union rank and file, as well as an ideological commitment to the working class as a whole, rather than limiting their efforts to their own immediate interests. Both ideas have been manifested powerfully in Decatur.

Locked-out Staley workers that we talked with noted again and again the participation of the membership as a whole in the making of important union decisions, and were careful to describe this involvement of the rank and file as a crucial element of their battle with Staley. "Dave [Watts, president of UPIU 7837] realized that a fight of this magnitude is not won and fought by the leadership," agrees Royal Plankenhorn, speaking to us at a packed solidarity meeting. "It takes the whole union to fight back. And if they don't have the knowledge of what's going on they can't fight back. Unions at the local level are more democratic than at any other level…'cause we are the union. Not those guys sitting up front. It's us sitting here at this table and everybody else sitting out here in the audience tonight. We're the union. We run this show."

In fact, as its proponents point out, the union's work to rule strategy is impossible without the near-unanimous participation of the membership. "You don't do work to rule successfully unless the ranks take it up," says Steven Ashby. "They went unit by unit, department by department, and took the contract and discussed it line by line. They'd talk about it in groups, and in the bars after work and in the plant. And they did this until everybody understood…. The idea of work to rule definitely came from the ranks. They had advisers giving them suggestions, but it was taken up wholeheartedly and the tactics were devised very creatively on the shop floor.

"You can't do work to rule from the top down, by definition," Ashby continues. "If you don't have the membership involved, leading the campaign, then it won't work. It's exciting that it's being brought up, but at the same time it's very threatening to many traditional trade union leaders that do not encourage membership involvement."

There has been a similar change in the language and ideology of labor in Decatur. In opposition to management's talk about "competitiveness," the striking and locked-out workers speak of "solidarity." In Decatur one sees and hears the word everywhere: on T-shirts, on bumper stickers, as graffiti on overpasses. But while "competitiveness" has been emptied of meaning, the events in Decatur have done the opposite to "solidarity," giving new significance to what was, until quite recently, a cliché, a slogan that leaders might throw around when rousing the troops for strike action, but that was forgotten as quickly as demands were met.

Don Rhodes offers a succinct example of the word's new meaning when he says that the only way to combat multinationals is by "uniting in solidarity." The fight is "for all working people all over the world. Not just union people." If the events in Decatur have any greater significance, ideas like this one are where it begins: the rediscovery of the working class. The workers in Decatur have realized that what has happened to them is part of a global pattern—a pattern that can only be successfully resisted by the united action of all working people, regardless of race or nationality, of what union they belong to, of whether they belong to a union at all.

"This struggle is about winning a fair contract," observes Steven Ashby, "but it is also about uniting a divided and forlorn working class, which is...divided along racial lines and gender lines and age lines and so forth. And it is about reinvigorating and reforming and mobilizing a labor movement, which is a big task about the future of the country."

But while the concept of class seems simple on the surface, it is in fact a political mine field, as commentators from Paul Fussell to James Loewen have recognized. For decades it has been high-school-civics orthodoxy that America is a "classless society," that our fabled prosperity has made virtually everyone a member of the Great Middle. And just watch as politicians wiggle this way and that to avoid uttering the dreaded words "working class." Although sociologists and historians use notions of class quite routinely, it is considered vaguely treasonable in politics and other public forums to talk about class at all.

For years, class has even been a taboo subject for American workers. Class is, of course, the fundamental activating principle of organized labor. The primary weapon of labor unions, the strike, depends on class consciousness—either overt or latent—to succeed: it can only be effective if other working people, recognizing that the victory of the union is a victory for everyone, refuse to cross a picket line. But in the aftermath of the great victories of the '30s and '40s, union leaders insisted on describing their followers as "middle-class." Measured strictly by income, this was clearly true, and organized labor could justly pride itself on the fact that it had singlehandedly democratized American prosperity, made the comforts of life available to working people.

As they abandoned the idea of the working class, though, American unions fell into the complacent pattern for which they are so often criticized today. Organized labor became satisfied and sectarian, concerned narrowly with improving the wages of particular workers in particular industries and largely forgetting about everyone else. Some assert that union weakness today is a direct product of labor leadership's unwillingness to grapple with issues of class. After World War II, Steven Ashby observes, "They...gave up this class consciousness, class struggle perspective of 'all workers everywhere.' They took what they could get for themselves, the union leaders at least. And that led to significant isolation, and that is still something we're struggling with today."

As the workers in Decatur are realizing, today such a limited perspective is rapidly becoming impossible. Since no single union acting alone can prevail against a multinational, labor must rediscover the principle of class not just for reasons of politics but simply to stay alive. And this perhaps is what makes the Decatur events so portentous: with the concept of solidarity the strikers there are addressing themselves to the entire working population. They aren't just looking to get back to the more-or-less comfortable ways of the past while the rest of the country's workers are slowly forced into longer hours and lower wages.

"We have to get back to the concept of the IWW," locked-out Staley worker Royal Plankenhorn maintains. "One big union. Because we built these walls of internationals and locals and stuff, and it's worked against us. It's been, 'Well, that's his fight. Don't bother me. He's the one going through that. I've got a job.' We can't do that anymore. The fact is, we have to break down the walls that divide us because his battle is my battle, my battle is his battle, and your battle is my battle. We can't succeed any other way."

Speaking on the same theme, Mike Griffin, another locked-out Staley worker, insists that the complacency of recent union leadership, its abandonment of the all-encompassing working-class vision of people like Big Bill Haywood, has enabled the multinationals to roll back workplace gains that everyone assumed had been won for all time. "Big business needs an alternative work force, and that's the scab," Griffin says. "The scab is stealing your standard of living. But he's also stealing your heritage, what the generations of workers before you fought to give you. And he's stealing what you can give to your children and your children's children. We went to sleep in the '60s and '70s, the labor leadership. We forgot our heritage, we failed to teach our kids. And now we're paying the price. We're fighting for the eight-hour day. Do you understand what that means? We have to fight a battle labor fought a hundred years ago! We've pissed away a legacy. Damn us!"

The rediscovery of class has had a profound effect on the Decatur workers' vision of society and politics. When the Staley workers entered into their battle, most no doubt expected a fair shake from media, politicians, and police. They regarded themselves, after all, as patriotic, law-abiding citizens engaged in a self-evidently just cause. Instead they have seen their struggle ignored, distorted, and (especially in the case of the police and local politicians) attacked outright—in the classic 19th-century pattern. The concept of class provides an explanation for these otherwise baffling anti-labor biases in the nominally "objective" fields of government and media: they are economic constructs like anything else, and they serve the needs of their creators.

"These are average American workers who have become politicized in their struggle," Ashby says. "It's been an education to find that the courts and the judges and the city council and the police and the company work hand in hand and are working against the workers. And the media as well….There are not tens of thousands of Marxists running around Decatur, but there are a lot of people waking up to the fact that there are two classes and that the corporate class has a lot of institutions on its side. You'll hear in very everyday language radical things said that come directly out of people's experience, including when they got gassed by the police. This was a big shock to them, and it took a lot of education and discussion to figure out that the police individually may be nice people here and there, but ultimately they do the bidding of the corporation."

The frustration was evident at the Staley workers' union hall a few weeks ago, when, speaking from the floor, one locked-out worker told his colleagues, "Solidarity is the working-class politics. Not the Republicans, not the Democrats. Solidarity's your politics." Solidarity is "the ultimate answer for turning this thing around. Workers, black and white, men and women, are going to have to be shoulder to shoulder."

Another man rose to speak. "The system is crooked and corrupt, totally corrupt," he said. The only reliable politicians are the ones that "come from working-class backgrounds, that are working-class people." Striking rubber worker Dave Frasier was even more blunt. "The rich have got two parties," he told us. "We need one."

Attitudes toward the police have changed dramatically in Decatur since last June's pepper-gas incident. Before, the unions had gladly cooperated with the local police. According to one locked-out Staley worker, "Up till June 25, we had always talked to them about what our plans were—we're going to do this demonstration on this day at this time—and that was all well and good until they pepper-sprayed us. This floor [the members of UPIU 7837] said, 'That's enough. We will no longer talk to the police. This is how they treat us. We will not put up with it anymore.' So when [the rally on] October 15 rolled around, they didn't know what we were doing because we didn't tell 'em. And it drove 'em nuts." Workers think differently about the police now. "They're hired thugs," one man told us. "They're not police."

Workers have also perceived an antilabor bias from the Decatur media. Again, the pepper-gas incident was instructive. As locked-out Staley worker Art Dhermy remembers: "The Decatur station had their camera people there. In fact, their reporter got sprayed with pepper gas. They had the six o'clock news, she's still got the runny nose, watery eyes, and the whole bit, and she reports about children being sprayed, this, that, and the other. Ten o'clock news—no mention of it."

Nor can the media be relied upon to communicate the facts of the Decatur struggle to workers elsewhere. "You can't base your life on the media," one worker told us. "Because the media's not gonna do us any favors if we're not gonna do it ourselves."

The workers in Decatur have set about spreading the gospel of solidarity, sending teams of "road warriors" around the country to speak to whatever groups will listen, to tell the story of the Decatur battle, and to "educate" workers every-where. They have discovered that multinationals use similar strategies against labor wherever they do business, while workers remain fragmented and isolated in their individual unions.

"I've covered everything in the northern quarter of this country," says Royal Plankenhorn. "I've been from Minnesota down to Missouri, and I've been all the way up the east coast.... And every time I go out and tell the story about what's happened to us, these guys say, 'You know, that's happened to us, too.' Everywhere we go."

Without communication and solidarity among workers, though, the multi-nationals cannot be resisted. "Until somebody came and told them what was going on," Plankenhorn continues, "they didn't see what was going on. The same way we didn't see what was going on until somebody came and told us what was going on. It's education. We go out and educate these people. And they go out and educate somebody else. Somebody has come and said, "Hey, this is what has happened to us. You need to look for these warning signs."

American labor is only beginning to comprehend the size and power of the forces arrayed against it, only beginning to understand the ramifications of capital's international scope. "This goes beyond Decatur, Illinois, and beyond our national borders," observes Mike Griffin. "What you're looking at here is an all-out effort...to destroy the labor movement. They're doing the same thing in France and Honduras and Canada and Haiti—I met with labor leaders from those countries two months ago in San Francisco. In order to generate this new world order—you're looking at the IMF, the World Bank, the World Trade Organization, trying to create a worldwide two-class system. What is happening in Decatur is the cutting edge of a class struggle worldwide. They have to take out organized labor to get what they want....We had better wake up as workers, union or nonunion, in America or elsewhere around the world. They have to destroy those that have the means to fight back and organize.... It has biblical proportions."

As the strategies of the unions in Decatur have been designed to confront the business theories of the global economy, so has their discovery of solidarity confronted the prefabricated consciousness that is such a pervasive part of "information age" capitalism. The war in Decatur has been as much about conflicting ideologies as it has been about workplace conditions. As such, it strikes at the heart of the new international business order.

The single most remarkable business fact of recent years is the rise of the entertainment industry to national preeminence. Beneath the continual flood of busi-ness articles about this movie-giant merger and that cable-and-telephone system buyout lurks one simple unspoken premise: sometime in the last 40 years or so consciousness became the foremost product of American busi-ness. And as information technology has washed away the local and particular in matters of production, sweeping unhindered across national boundaries, so it has done in matters of culture as well. The TV, movies, and popular music that are produced for us by the various culture industries have become the stuff of real life for most Americans. The imperatives of corporate America now dominate our thoughts as well as our working hours.

The genius of such a culture-intensive economy was made clear last November: it is a system without opponents. Unlike previous forms of capitalism, the obvious excesses of this one have energized no muckrakers, no populists, no socialists or anarchists. It has brought with it a politics in which even the feeble concessions to compassion of the Great Society are beyond the pale of acceptable discourse. So despite the rule-breaking fantasies of *Wired* magazine and the awestruck 20-something rebels whose images promote the IBM OS/2 Warp, the Information Age, it seems, is a regime without dissenters.

More depressing still is the sense of the absolute futility of doing anything about these changes that pervades intellectual discourse. The consolidation of power by the new class of Information Age executives is a fait accompli, and, as

Christopher Lasch wrote, they have already quietly abandoned things like cities, public services of all kinds (especially schools), and even national identities. For common people the world is changing dramatically for the worse, but since the wealth of the new elites is secure, nothing—absolutely nothing—will be done. Our duty is not to ponder such matters, but to sit placidly in front of the TV, enjoy its 90-channel bounty, and let Schwarzenegger fight our battles for us.

Against such a backdrop, the rediscovery of the working class in Decatur is a remarkable thing, an awakening that could easily become the first step in a wider movement. At the October 15 rally, folksinger Anne Feeney singled out consciousness as the great difference between the victimized workers of the 1990s and their forebears of ages past. "In the '30s, people had nothing and they knew it. Today, people have nothing and they don't know it. They're sitting at home and they're anesthetized." But Jack Spiegel, a veteran of the labor battles of the 1930s, says, "The spirit is coming back." By insisting on the hard, undeniable realities of class and exploitation, by refusing to forget the bitter struggles and the bloody victories of the past, the Decatur workers have put an ugly crack in the smooth, banal facade so recently perfected by the consciousness industry. In addition to the fight for jobs and conditions, the people of Decatur are struggling to reclaim the populist myth at the heart of the American imagination, the idea of a country organized around the real needs of its vast working population.

Perhaps it would be asking too much of mainstream media to report on the growing disaffection with the world they themselves have built. But the media are only too happy to present to you the world according to United Airlines (hard-working, satisfied executives returning in slow motion from strange but prosperous lands to Hometown USA in time to see little Caitlin in the school play), or the world according to General Motors (cars doing stunts and hardworking, satisfied executives sighing heartily in slow motion, dealing with people from strange but prosperous lands and looking out over this great country that they have built). This, then, is precisely the workers' problem, as a veteran dissenter like Noam Chomsky never tires of pointing out: giving union representatives "equal time" to express their views on television (not that this is ever done, of course) can never allow them real parity. Capital controls the terms as well as the immediate content of the televisual discourse, and it is the myths of capital, not the stories of the Ludlow martyrs or the sainthood of Joe Hill, that are drummed into viewers' heads 24 hours a day. To offer a spokesman for labor a few minutes (or a few seconds) in which to dispel the vast edifice of fable and ideology that is built up on television all day long is a farce that not even the most sympathetic and liberal-leaning network newscasters come anywhere close to redressing.

As Royal Plankenhorn observes, the media are not out to do labor any favors. If the newfound truths of the Decatur war are to survive and grow, they will have to be carried by the workers themselves, discussed in local union halls and on shop floors across the country. What is going on is fundamentally outside both the ideology and understanding of official American discourse. It cannot be made understandable or sold as a prepackaged life-style, and no matter how it progresses it will never be speakable on TV.

In the development of their thoughts and experiences, the workers in Decatur have followed a classic trajectory that some would call "radicalization." Suddenly finding themselves on the receiving end of the grotesque, brutish demands of the new global business order, they have begun to perceive the system in ways that had been literally unthinkable. What were once normal, routine aspects of American life are now strange and menacing. Those who have experienced the war in Decatur will never again be able to watch the news without suspicion, to marvel innocently at the doings of Rambo, or to sit through the monotonous banquet of business fantasy that constitutes American mass culture without an overpowering sense of disgust. The doings of A.E. Staley, the media of central Illinois, and the Decatur police force have accomplished what a century of modern art could never do: they have transformed ordinary people into outsiders.

We wondered if, as such, the locked-out Staley workers were worried about being labeled "radicals" for the ideas and strategies they were using. Red-baiting has, after all, played a large and ignominious role in labor history. But what Decatur's owners would no doubt denounce (if the sorely missed cold war was still on) as dangerous Red subversion is understood by the workers themselves as their patriotic, community-minded duty.

"Right now, a 'radical' is somebody that stands up and says enough's enough, we ain't taking no more," says Art Dhermy. "Instead of taking what they give you and run. Standing up for what you believe in, standing up for what your grandparents and parents have fought for 50 years to be able to give you as an inheritance. Is that too radical? It's up to me now to stand up for my kids, and my grandkids. In fact, it's almost too late for my kids. Its time for me, really, to stand up for my grandkids, so they have somebody for them to look up to and say, 'My grandfather saved this and gave this to me as an inheritance gift,' like my grandfather did for me when he fought the coal mine wars here in central Illinois.... If we don't do it, where's it gonna stop? It's gonna stop when my grandkids are working for a dollar and a quarter an hour like I did when I was first married."

"This is the resurgence of the labor movement. It's not the end," Plankenhorn says to those who perceive in the Decatur struggle a relic of the distant, benighted past. "Those people will fall by the wayside. Because they don't have the guts to fight back. They've taken it so long and given the concessions to keep jobs, where they've forgot what we learned in the '30s and the '40s: that nothing was given to us, it was fought for. We didn't fight for it; we've done our damnedest to give it away. Now it's our turn. And if we don't do it, then the middle class as we know it in this country will die. There will be two classes, and it will be the very very poor and the very very rich."

Since the article was written in January 1995, at least one of the more ambitious organizing strategies of Decatur's unions has come to fruition. Union-backed candidate Terry Howley defeated the conservative, business-oriented incumbent in the city's mayoral election, and other pro-labor candidates were elected to city offices. Nonetheless, all three unions have been driven closer to the breaking point. Staley's paper workers narrowly rejected another company proposal in a vote forced by a dissident faction of the local. In May, facing the possibility that their local would be decertified by replacement workers, Bridgestone's rubber workers voted to end their strike and return to work with no contract.

A SUSTAINABLE ECONOMY FOR THE TWENTY-FIRST CENTURY

JULIET SCHOR

THE FAILED PROMISE OF A DEMOCRATIC ADMINISTRATION

The slaughter of the Democrats in the 1994 midterm elections was in many respects a transformative moment. The inability of President Clinton and other Democrats to get any credit for an expanding economy was striking. Business was good, unemployment was down. The electorate was in a surly mood.

Gender and race explain a great deal. The gender gap in November 1994's voting ranged from 6 to 10 percent. Men are leading the stampede toward the Republicans, and toward the definition of the nation's woes as welfare, crime, and taxes. Men, especially young white men of low educational status, have suffered a tremendous decline in their economic position and status. They are feeling insecure and inadequate. Demagogic politicians find it easy to stoke the flames of insecurity, especially among white voters, with simple-minded slogans on welfare, crime, and immigration. The "mean season" predicted a decade ago has arrived.[1]

In 1992, Clinton ran for President with a rhetoric which spoke to some of these concerns. He noted the failure of the economy to meet people's needs. He stressed the urgency of economic change and renewal. Millions of working Americans and significant segments of the business community coalesced around the hope that Clinton could provide the leadership necessary to "rescue" the U.S. economy.

Despite more than four years of "official" recovery, Clinton has not been able to convert economic expansion to political support. One interpretation is that the effects of the recovery have been negligible for most Americans. The Census Bureau recently reported that median family income has fallen since 1987. The real unemployment rate (corrected for discouraged workers and involuntary part-timers) is about twice the official rate.[2] Downsizings and the stagnation of real wages have created widespread insecurity and pessimism. People are working harder and feeling poorer. It is now widely believed that today's young people will not match the standard of living of their parents.

These feelings stem from the profound changes the U.S. economy has been undergoing in the last 15 years. These include rapid technological change, increased domestic and international competition, a shifting mix of products and occupations, and increased concentration in many industries. The effects for many Americans have been disastrous: two decades of worsening inequality of income, stagnant wages, chronic unemployment and under-employment, rising work hours for full-time employees, and heightened levels of job stress and insecurity.

For most people, the deterioration in their economic situation is connected to changes in the employment system. The system of employer-employee relations which was in place for the first three decades after the Second World War brought an unusual degree of stability to a large percentage of Americans. Corporations accepted the idea that workers would share in productivity gains, and passed them along in annual increases in real wages. Corporations also tolerated the existence of unions, and worked with them, rather than against them. For white collar workers, and a segment of the blue collar ones as well, the corporation also maintained a tacit kind of employment security; not as extensive as that in Japan certainly, but nevertheless a quasi-permanent system of employment. The watchword in employment relations was stability.[3]

True, this system never extended to everyone. People of color and women continued to be disproportionately represented in low-wage or so-called secondary labor markets with inferior wages, benefits, job security, and job conditions. Nevertheless, aspects of the "golden age" system did work their way down to the secondary labor market. The point is perhaps made by contrast with what is happening today: the breakdown of the previous regime has left workers at all levels with fewer and fewer protections, less of a share in productivity gains, and with a deteriorating job situation. It's the "scramble to survive" system. And it's no surprise it is creating fear, insecurity, and anger. The destructuring of the employment system (i.e., scramble to survive) lies at the heart of the failure of economic recovery to improve the lives of many Americans, and the inability of the Clinton Administration to garner credit for what it sees as positive economic news. A majority of Americans are working longer and harder, earning less, and living with more uncertainty. It's a recipe for political disaster.

The Administration seems not to have understood this reality. The shift from campaign rhetoric to policy implementation partially explains why. The "putting people first" theme which dominated the campaign, and spoke to Americans' needs, has been replaced by the "putting corporations first" policies of a thoroughly establishment, pro-business administration. Half of the Administration's worldview can be found in Robert Reich's writings on the global economy. In *The Work of Nations* Reich argues that our future depends on accepting and even welcoming the growth of increasing corporate power and reach, especially with multinational companies.[4] He, and the Administration more generally, believe the globalization of the economy is both inevitable and positive. The best we can do is to make our country the place where corporations will want to put their corporate headquarters and hire sophisticated technological and managerial personnel. That's where the good jobs are supposed to come from. The other half of Reich's vision—the "human face" of concern for income inequality and low wages—is the half that has disappeared. In its place are solicitation of the bond market, deficit cutting, limiting welfare, and punitive approaches to crime.

Ultimately, Clinton's economic policy differs only marginally from that of his Republican predecessors. His instincts are more humane, but his long term vision is not much different. His goals are stimulating higher growth, enhancing international competitiveness, and creating more jobs. But a truly democratic and humane economic policy needs to ask more probing questions. What kind of growth does the country need? And for whom? The Clinton Administration argues that the market knows best, which is to say that corporations know best. Clinton's team sees the government's proper role as aiding the aims of commercial enterprises, rather than helping to set priorities. As a result, they balk when it comes time to intervening in markets in ways that business dislikes; in the public or environmental interest. But will entrusting even more control and power to our large corporations serve the interests of the public or benefit the environment? Increased attention to international competitiveness may well further undermine our quality of life—by creating even more pressure to increase working hours, lower wages, and weaken environmental standards. The passage of GATT, with its undemocratic World Trade Organization, suggests as much. Maybe what we want most from our jobs are satisfying work and employment security, not the anxiety produced by an ever "freer" market.

The promise is that growth will bring new products and more of them. But will they necessarily make us better off? How important are HDTV, computer-driven households, inflatable sneakers, and yet another silk blouse? Are we still finding happiness in the consumerist lifestyle? Might we not be better served by upgrading the quality of public goods, such as schools, parks, and culture? Perhaps what we want is more time to be with our children, safer streets, better schools, and environmental preservation. The resumption of high levels of industrial growth will also intensify ecological contamination, imbalance, and decay.

The debate between Republicans and Democrats on economics has narrowed to a marginal one. Both sides now worship at the alter of the market, differing mainly on whether it should be marginally regulated in the public interest or not regulated at all. Both defend the sanctity of the existing distribution of income, wealth, and power. And both Republicans and Democrats turn their backs on democracy to genuflect to the twin Gods of "growth" and "free trade." We think we've got a better idea.

THE NEW PARTY'S VISION
OF A TWENTY-FIRST CENTURY ECONOMY

The New Party has an optimistic economic vision. We want to transform the economy in such a way that it is finally responsive, not to concentrations of wealth and power, but to the needs of ordinary people. Why this optimism at a time when common sense might dictate a gloomier prognosis, given the growth in multi-national capital, increasing levels of inequality and the evident deterioration in economic performance?

Our optimism stems in part from an assessment of public opinion. Large majorities of people care about problems which cannot be solved with existing approaches. They articulate a set of basic values which are at odds with current Republican/Democratic policies and economic outcomes. Americans want a healthy, clean environment, and laws that protect the land, air, and water. Americans have a strong sense of fairness and equity. They do not believe they should be slaves to their jobs. They put peace, meaningful work, and basic values above affluence. We read the evidence as saying that people want a decent quality of life and they do not want to pay the price that global capitalism is threatening to exact.

The purpose of the economy should be to provide a good quality of life for all Americans in an ecologically sustainable way. That means reasonable employment security, security in material standard of living, sustainable family and community life, and environmental sustainability. The New Party believes that Americans can design a set of economic policies which can achieve these goals—based on principles of sustainability, democratic control, equality, and efficiency.

ENVIRONMENTAL SUSTAINABILITY. Year by year, the environment becomes more degraded. We are fiddling while Rome burns. If current trends continue, we may find that it is too late to save the planet from wholesale ecological deterioration. Relying on the market—economists' preference—will not work. If we contaminate and despoil the planet today, the costs will be borne by our children and grandchildren, who have no voice in today's decisions. Nor can we assume, as the Administration sometimes implies, that environmental regulations will be costless. The tradeoffs are real: autos versus clean air, housing development versus habitat preservation, nuclear power versus an unradiated biosystem, meat-centered diets versus sustainable soil and water use. We cannot continue to think about economics and the environment separately. We need to develop new ways of living and to encourage them now through education, debate, institutional restructuring, and democratic policy. Neither life, nor liberty, nor the pursuit of happiness are possible in a diseased and dying environment.

DEMOCRATIC CONTROL OF THE ECONOMY. The salient principle driving economic decisions is that money talks. This is true for the corporations who relocate plants at a moment's notice, leaving communities high and dry. It is true in the financial sector where buyouts and the resulting debt burdens destroy productive companies in a few short years. And it is true in the government, where the rich and powerful "buy" politicians who enact economic policy in their interest.

Right-wing ideology, and increasingly Democratic party ideology, argues that the "money talks" principle is efficient, that democracy is too messy for the economy and that centralization of money and power creates good economic performance. But for almost two decades we have been ceding power and resources to corporations. They have gotten tax breaks. They have gotten regulatory relief. They have gotten cheap resources from the government. We have opened our schools and cultural institutions to corporate propaganda. The influence of unions has been nearly eliminated. Despite all these concessions, long-term economic performance continues to deteriorate. We might have saved ourselves the trouble by looking at the many examples of successful economies (Western Europe, Japan, and Korea) in which business is more tightly regulated and controlled. It's time we read the handwriting on the wall: giving more power to business is not the way to cure the nation's ills. If the economy is to serve the people, it needs to be controlled by the people.

EGALITARIANISM. The U.S. economy is structured by hierarchy and in-equality. Within the enterprise power flows from the top, through numerous layers. In the labor market, arbitrary and rapidly changing patterns of job loss, wage reduction, and access to working hours have created new sources of inequality and insecurity. Inequality still reigns in many families, where the revolution in gender relations is far from complete. (Despite egalitarian ideologies, women still do most of the childcare and household work, even if they have jobs. And women are still responsible for children, despite their significantly lower incomes.) The global distribution of wealth and resources still heavily favors the industrialized North, which has a standard of living many times that of the South. And these poor countries have been funnelling capital to the rich ones for more than a decade, causing untold misery and degradation among the poor.

In the end, everyone loses from inequalities. Corporations suffer because the talents of the people below are wasted. Workers suffer stress because they are over-supervised. More egalitarian families are better for both women, children, and men. And with a more equal global economy, jobs in the industrialized countries will be less in jeopardy from low-wage competition. We believe that any truly progressive economic policy must put a very high priority on the elimination of arbitrary inequalities based on sex, race and ethnicity, sexual preference, and nation.

EFFICIENCY. Progressive economists have been dramatically outgunned in recent years, as the economic discourse has lurched to the right. Part of the problem is that we have clung to outdated paradigms. The Keynesian approach of big government redistributing the fruits of growth is no longer credible. We need to abandon the old tradeoff between efficiency and equality for a new vision of economic activity. We must begin by restoring nature, rather than stripping and looting it. We need to support a new business paradigm which is participatory, economically and socially responsible, flexible, and forward looking. We need to identify and articulate new efficiencies which will make a democratic economy actually work. We need reform of corporations to make them less top-heavy and more accountable. We need more democratic control of government spending, and re-regulation of the financial sector. We need to solve social problems in cost-effective ways (e.g., by prevention rather than after-the-fact-intervention). We need to be for change, but in a way that guarantees people security.

TIME, WORK AND MONEY: CREATING QUALITY OF LIFE

The problem of time is central to the deterioration of this nation's quality of life. The American worker has been working a progressively longer schedule for twenty-five years, with increases in overtime, moonlighting, weekly hours, weeks of work each year, and a dramatic decline in vacations and paid holidays. Compared to the late 1960s, the average worker is working about an extra month of work per year. The U.S. experience stands in sharp contrast to Western Europe, where workers enjoy four to six week paid vacations, and declining weekly hours. Fifty years ago the United States had substantially shorter hours than Europe. Today, we stand with Japan as the world's workaholics.

Most economists explain these trends by people's desire to consume more, failing to see the complex forces which are leading to longer hours. Americans are working more in large part because employers are not making it possible to do otherwise. Downsizing, falling real wages, fierce competition for jobs, mandatory overtime, and a lack of decent "short hour jobs" have all contributed to the phenomenon of "the overworked American." Families are experiencing a sharp time squeeze, as the hours of both men and women rise. There's no one left to watch the children, cook the dinner, or clean the house. The rich can hire servants. But for almost everyone else, the expansion of worktime is taking its toll. Our economic program needs to give people control over their time. And we can do that.

1. NEW WORK SCHEDULES

Part of the worktime problem is that we are still operating with a "male" model of employment—full-time hours and full-time dedication to the job. A take-it-or-leave-it option. As women have entered the workforce in large numbers, they have had to conform to this model to succeed. But this causes serious problems, because women still retain primary responsibility for and attachment to childcare and household work. And increasingly, men want time off the job too, often to be with their children. (If they had enough money to live as comfortably as they'd like, only 23 percent of adults say they would work full time, with 29 percent choosing part-time work, 19 percent volunteer work, and 25 percent work at home caring for family.)[5]

One solution to the time problem is to use productivity growth to reduce hours. Rather than automatically channeling productivity growth into higher wages and salaries, as they have done for 50 years, employers should give workers the option of taking shorter schedules. Through a combination of regulations and tax incentives, employers can be induced to offer worktime options, such as the choice of trading off income for time, job-sharing, the upgrading of part-time work. In addition, the Fair Labor Standards Act (FLSA) should be amended to prohibit mandatory overtime, to forbid discrimination in pay and promotion to workers who choose to work short hours, to substitute compensated time for overtime premia, to include salaried workers, and to give all American workers a guaranteed four week vacation. Over time, these measures will undermine the increasingly archaic divide between full and part-time work. Employees will be able to make their own choices about the number of hours they work without undue job and career penalties. And as a society, it will be possible for us to use our "productivity dividend" differently—to "buy" more time, rather than more things.

2. UNEMPLOYMENT AND WORKTIME

In the twenty-five years that worktime has been rising, so too has unemployment and underemployment. At each business cycle peak, unemployment and underemployment rose—from 7 percent in 1969 to 14.5 percent in 1989, before the last recession began. This is no coincidence. Employers are hiring fewer workers in part because they are using their existing workforces for more hours. Factory overtime has now reached its highest recorded level, in the midst of a recovery which was long dubbed "jobless." In the automobile industry, where tens of thousands of workers have been laid off, daily overtime has become standard. In the Detroit area the average workweek is 47.5 hours, Saturn workers have a regular 50-hour week, and in some plants, workers are doing 60 hours a week. The United Auto Workers (UAW) estimates that 59,000 automobile jobs would be created if the plants were on a 40 hour week.[6] High per person costs of fringe benefits, especially medical costs, are a big part of the problem. Those will only be solved with publically funded health care. The Clinton plan would have made the problem worse by covering more people through their employers, instead of doing the sensible thing, which is to separate health insurance and employment altogether. (Why should GM be in the business of "selling" health insurance to its employees?)

It is now very unlikely that the U.S. economy can generate large numbers of jobs without reducing the hours associated with each job. The measures advocated above (especially job sharing, trading income for time, guaranteed vacations, and the abolition of mandatory overtime) should have a major impact on job creation. Beyond this, we need special attention to the high unemployment found in inner cities and in some regions of the country. We advocate two approaches: government subsidies for job creation among groups and geographical areas with high unemployment rates and direct employment programs by local governments.

3. CONSUMERISM, THE ENVIRONMENT AND THE PRODUCTIVITY DIVIDEND

Looking back over the past fifty years, the U.S. experience raises troubling questions. We have more than doubled our productive potential, as a result of rising productivity. Had we channeled this "productivity dividend" into leisure time, Americans would have already reached the twenty hour week. But instead we used all of our economic progress to produce more goods and services, and to consume more. So Americans of all income classes got a higher material standard of living—about twice as "high"—but not many got more leisure time. On the contrary, those of us with jobs have lengthened our hours.

We have gotten more things, but there is growing evidence that consumerism is not giving us satisfaction and peace of mind. Americans are neither happier nor more satisfied. Measures of social health show decline, not progress. Millions feel trapped in a cycle of working and spending, running faster and staying in place. Might it not be time to hop off that treadmill? As a society, we have achieved affluence as measured by average income; nonetheless, an increasing number of Americans are impoverished. But if we choose, which we should, to distribute our wealth more equitably, everyone in this country could live well, indeed handsomely, by historical comparison. However, even for those who have achieved a middle class standard of living, quality of life is problematic. Now it's time to figure out how the consumerist lifestyle relates to true well-being.

One thing we do know is that consumerism is disastrous for the environment. The United States, with its big malls, fast food, and lots of private (versus public) consumption, has the most ecologically damaging pattern of consumption in the world. The last half-century of growth has been the most ecologically destructive in human history. How can we reconcile our needs for material comfort, adequate time, and a healthy planet?

A SUSTAINABLE ENVIRONMENT

Our economic activity must become sustainable. This will involve new ways of living. There are areas of waste (packaging, failure to conserve energy), which need to be eliminated. The U.S. military, the world's single-largest polluter, must be brought under control. Nuclear power must be eliminated and the environment spared from more radioactive waste. Much environmental degradation can be prevented by changing our basic systems of production and consumption. On the production side, factories and offices have been built and designed with the assumption of free or low-cost natural resources. We need to move to closed-loop systems, where waste, toxic chemicals, radioactive materials, and pollution resources are not produced in the first instance. On the consumption side, we need to design new systems of housing and transport which are sustainable. Although these prescriptions may sound politically infeasible today, we believe there is a strong reservoir of support for sustainability. In a recent poll 37 percent of respondents strongly agreed and 40 percent agreed somewhat that "American over-use of resources is a major global environmental problem that needs to be changed."[7]

1. GREEN QUOTAS AND TAXES

As we destroy more and more of the planet's clean air, water, habitats, and ecosystems, the underpricing of these resources becomes an increasingly calamitous practice. We need an economic system which values "natural capital," in addition to physical, financial, and human capital. First, we propose incorporating natural resource accounting into the Gross National Product. (A preliminary step has just been taken in this direction, which we applaud.) This would provide the basis for setting limits or quotas on polluting and degrading production activities. For example, industries would be restricted to producing fixed amounts of toxic wastes, airborne or waterborne pollutants. On the consumption side, we advocate the introduction of a national value-added "green" tax. This tax would be levied on consumers at the retail level, so that they pay the true social costs of their consumption activities. Examples of commodities which might be taxed are gasoline; household, lawn, and pool chemicals; air conditioners; meat; furniture; jet travel; and disposable products. The tax should be clearly identified, so that consumers are informed about the environmental consequences of their purchases.

2. INDUSTRY-WIDE ENVIRONMENTAL STANDARDS

One barrier to sustainable practices is competition among businesses. If every toothpaste manufacturer feels a cardboard box is necessary to entice the consumer to buy, moral appeals to reduce packaging will not be powerful. By contrast, industry-wide standards have the potential to reduce costs without adversely affecting individual producers. We propose the introduction of industry-wide standards in areas such as packaging; energy efficiency for appliances, heating units, vehicles; and household construction.

3. ALTERNATIVE HOUSING AND TRANSPORTATION

A key environmental problem is that current systems of housing and transport are unsustainable. In American suburbia, houses are large and costly to build. They are energy inefficient and cannot be kept cool without air conditioning. They have large lawns, often with ecologically destructive landscaping. Because of the distances and the land-use patterns, automobile travel (extremely damaging) is virtually imperative. We need to initiate a long-term shift to smaller, differently designed houses, with new transportation systems and new conceptions of land use. Ultimately, we believe these changes will improve the quality of life as well. With mixed land-use patterns, people can work, shop and live in a close geographic area, a lifestyle we believe is becoming increasingly popular. Walking, bicycling, and public transportation become feasible. Community is easier to maintain. And, in this era of time-stressed, dual-earner couples, freedom from the large time commitment required for maintaining suburban homes and lifestyles will be increasingly appealing to people.

RESTRUCTURING THE ENTERPRISE

Our major economic problem is not the government, as conservatives claim, but the American enterprise itself. GM and IBM are only the most visible examples of how this once mighty institution has gone awry. Large U.S. corporations became arrogant, complacent, and unresponsive. They are not rooted in basic values of accountability to people they serve—employees, consumers, communities, or stockholders. The biggest dinosaurs are crumbling before our eyes, and many more companies have serious problems.

Small business is not a panacea. They typically pay less and have fewer benefits than their larger cousins. Indeed, the problems of the enterprise may ultimately be less an issue of size than of restructuring. We need new structures of governance, new models of behavior and new sets of incentives.

1. PROMOTING SOCIAL ACCOUNTABILITY

This country already possesses a growing sector of socially innovative companies. Some are small, some large. What ties them together is that they are able to combine enviable conditions for their employees with principles of social accountability, such as environmental sustainability, community revitalization, or global equity. They subject their products to standards of social usefulness. Many are employee-owned although many have traditional ownership structures. Some of these companies are well known, such as Ben & Jerry's or the South Street Bank in Chicago. Together they represent a range of new models of corporate structure, behavior, and performance which we need to take a careful look at.

We need to expand this sector of the economy. Government should provide significant incentives for democratically controlled enterprises, such as consumer cooperatives, employee-owned firms, and municipally and community-owned enterprises. These include tax incentives, regulatory encouragement, financial schemes, preferential buying, and technical aid. We call for the establishment of a demanding Federal code of social responsibility. Companies which abide by it should be eligible for "most favored company" status, with attendant benefits.

2. CORPORATE GOVERNANCE

The failure of corporate America is a failure of governance. Corporations are not sufficiently accountable either to their stockholders or to their "stakeholders"—the employees, customers, suppliers, and communities who comprise and depend on the corporation. We propose a comprehensive Corporate Democracy Act. Its centerpiece would be a mandate for newly constituted Boards of Directors. These would be filled from outside the ranks of management and include not only representatives of stockholders, but stakeholders as well. Directors would be elected by the various stakeholder groups. The Corporate Democracy Act would also erode the legal fiction of the corporation as person, thereby creating increased civil and criminal liability for individual managers. The Act would also transfer corporate chartering to the Federal government and set minimum standards for tax subsidies, pollution, and unfair labor practices, thereby avoiding destructive state-against-state bidding to attract investment. Finally, we call for amendment of ERISA to allow worker-owners more control over the $2 trillion of pension assets about which they currently have no say.

3. RESTRUCTURING LABOR RELATIONS

The labor market has been undergoing restructuring for over a decade. Long-term job security is being substituted with temporary and casual employment, the use of consultants, outsourcing, and a variety of other techniques which erode commitments to employees. This is the "scramble to survive" system. In this regime, our productivity will be zealously monitored, our pay continuously adjusted. We are told this is what is necessary to keep afloat in the global capitalist economy. We reject the "scramble to survive" model. Not only is it inhumane, it's bad economics. Insecurity undermines efficiency. It creates stress and erodes loyalty. The dismal results from downsizings bear this out.

We can do better. Our vision of restructured employment relations also contains an imperative to become more efficient, but contends that we can do so by restructuring authority relations and giving employees a genuine voice in the running of their companies.

We would begin by eliminating management layers, sharply curtailing the number of supervisory personnel, and creating new structures of power and authority. The United States has been devoting about 13.5 percent of its non-farm employment to administrative and managerial personnel, as compared to ratios of less than one-third that among our competitors—3.3 percent (France), 3.3 percent (Germany), 4.2 percent (Japan).[8] While some of this wasteful staffing has been eliminated recently, U.S. corporations are still too top-heavy. In restructurings what matters most is how the process occurs. Simply cutting personnel, as companies have been doing, creates overwork and stress for the remaining employees. The flow of work and decision-making authority itself must change, giving more latitude to teams and people farther down the hierarchy. People must be allowed more freedom of self-management. This will reduce stress and increase productivity. Skill levels will rise—one requirement for the twenty-first-century economy everyone can agree upon. The millions of workers whose skills are already under-utilized will have a chance to see what they can do.

Ultimately, employees can only be "empowered" (another contemporary buzzword) if they have organizations through which to exercise their voices.[9] The precipitous decline of union membership means that U.S. workers are now virtually unrepresented, despite the fact that polls show a significant unmet demand both for unions per se, and for other forms of collective representation. We propose changes in labor legislation which will increase the fraction of the workforce which belongs to unions, and foster other forms of employee organization (in both union and non-union settings). Reforms which would facilitate unionization include card check certification for the choice of bargaining representative, the legalization of minority union membership and activity, stronger penalties for employer unfair labor practices, and extension of the right to unionize into the ranks of exempt employees.

4. CHANGING CORPORATE CULTURE

Of course, most of the nation's management would be bitterly opposed to most of the aforementioned changes. They would see them as unworkable and disruptive. But before we let them do away with our jobs, we should assess how well they are doing theirs. Isn't their stewardship increasingly a failure? The times clearly call for innovation and change. But the so-called pro-business vision of change is not much more than a return to the nineteenth century—anti-union, anti-worker, anti-safety, anti-leisure. Their narrowmindedness is leading them, and the nation, backwards. Let's try to take them forward, to a new democratic model of work relations and enterprise.

POVERTY AND INEQUALITY

The distribution of income in the United States is now the most unequal among the industrialized countries of the world. Between 1973 and 1993, the income share of the bottom fifth of families fell a full percentage point, from 5.5 to 4.2 percent. The share of the top fifth rose from 41.1 percent to 46.2 percent. The top 10 percent of the population now own just over 72 percent of the nation's total privately held wealth, and wealth is also becoming more unequally distributed.

The decline in income for the bottom fifth has led to increasing rates of poverty. By official measures, just over 15 percent of the population was poor in 1993. But official definitions are sorely out of date; one more recent estimate puts actual poverty at one quarter of the population. Not only are there more poor people, but they are getting poorer—their incomes are falling even farther below the poverty line. More than twenty percent of all children in this country are now poor.[10]

Much of the poverty problem can be laid at the feet of sex and race discrimination. Nearly 40 percent percent of female-headed families are poor. That's largely because 40 percent of women earn wages (in 1993 dollars) of $7.60 an hour or less. With a 40 hour week, that's an income of only about $15,000 a year.[11] And despite all the attention to women's economic progress, these women are earning less per hour than they did 20 years ago. The income gains have all gone to the highly-paid. About half the nation's women workers still cannot manage a decent standard of living without the help of a man. This is a basic and sobering fact of economic life for women. The closing of the gender wage gap in the last ten years (from the famous 59 cent figure to the most recent estimate of 78 cents) has been mainly due to falling wages for men. The story is similar for racial minorities. Among African-Americans, 36 percent of workers did not earn an hourly wage sufficient to lift them out of poverty. Among Hispanics, the comparable fraction was 45.5 percent.[12] Affirmative action notwithstanding, African-Americans and Latino/-as are still concentrated in the economy's least desirable, lowest paying occupations.

1. RAISING LOW WAGES: COMPARABLE WORTH AND THE MINIMUM WAGE

The first step to solving these problems is to recognize that they are based on an implicitly discriminatory valuation of the work that people do. Research has shown that women's work is paid less, *just because women do it*. Women and non-whites are far less rewarded for their education, skills, and experience. Comparable worth programs aim to root out these often-subtle discriminations. The programs use existing compensation methods to recalibrate the worth of various jobs, in the absence of discriminatory effects. They are instituted by employers, and they have been very successful, particularly in rectifying inequities against the lowest paid, who are often employees of color. We recommend that all places of employment be required to institute comparable worth programs. We envision this being phased in over a three year period.

A second, long overdue step is to raise and index the minimum wage. Almost two-thirds of minimum wage workers are women, and the vast majority are adults. As compared to the 1960s and 1970s, the real value of the minimum wage has fallen 20 percent. We suggest a phased-in increase to $7.00 an hour for adults, with subsequent pegging of the minimum to the median wage in the economy. Although the conventional wisdom is that a higher minimum will cause unemployment, new evidence disputes this view. If a higher adult minimum is instituted with productivity-enhancing measures, it is affordable.

2. THINKING BIG

The current debate on welfare, with its mixture of Dickensian and Orwellian qualities, is a sobering reminder of how close Democrats and Republicans have become. The facts and realities of welfare programs have been lost in a frenzied attack on women, people of color, and the poor. But scapegoating the least powerful among us will not address the underlying dissatisfactions being pandered to by politicians. Neither will cutting welfare spending, which is quantitatively negligible.

We believe that the entire thrust of the welfare debate must be transformed. We say, let's think about "welfare" the way we think about social security. It should be a "universal entitlement": everyone contributes and everyone is eligible. This welfare program would be run with a minimum of bureaucracy—basically as a check printing service, with no social workers or administrators. It is called a Basic Income Grant (BIG), and is being discussed in Europe. The idea is that every citizen would be eligible to receive a minimum income from the government, which would be sufficient to provide a modest standard of living. A BIG would allow people to opt out of the labor market for a while, to raise their children or pursue activities that are not lucrative (the arts, community work, or social services). It would enable them to retire when they feel ready, or to pursue schooling or retraining. Eligibility would be tied to a work requirement: the length of eligibility for receiving BIG would be tied to past work and participation in unpaid community service, as well as child and elder care.

In America, the introduction of a basic income grant would be a radical departure from historic practice. But we think it's worth beginning to think about. The likelihood of further job loss, the growing desire of people to pursue activities outside their jobs, and the crisis of inadequate family time all point to something like a BIG. As labor market status and family composition become increasingly precarious, our basic systems of providing income (income from work and income transfers within the family) are proving inadequate. We need a comprehensive social security system which guarantees stability in the face of family breakup, labor market displacement, and other unpredictable events which disrupt people's access to income. BIG could be that system. We're not sold on it. But we definitely think it should be on the table.

THE GLOBAL VILLAGE

The twenty-first century will make good on the promise of a global village. Communication, migration, and commerce will grow. But the global village raises the problem of inequities between countries and relations among them. Today, the United States has 5 percent of the world's population, but consumes 30 percent of its resources. Eight percent of the world's population own cars, as compared to about 90 percent of Americans. The American child's annual pocket money—$230 a year—exceeds the income of the world's half-billion poorest people.[13]

The problem of global inequities is complex. On the one hand, how can the conditions of life be raised for those in poor countries? On the other, with increasing international competition, how can we in the North avoid having our living standards dragged down to the level of Mexico, Brazil, or China? Progressives have argued that the answer lies in raising wage levels in places like Mexico, Brazil and China, rather than letting international competition bring down U.S. wages. Fair enough. But for environmental reasons, we cannot simply "raise living standards to our own." The earth cannot support five billion people (or twice that, by the next century) who are driving cars, eating meat, turning on the air conditioning when it gets hot, and throwing away a can every time they drink a soda. But what else have development and rising incomes meant but emulating the American way of life?

Our vision of the global economy is based on two principles. First, neither free trade nor protection is the answer. We advocate instead a world trading system whose foundation is a series of international agreements guaranteeing basic rights and protections for workers and citizens. Second, those agreements must safeguard the environmental health of a planet in a globally equitable way. Those of us in the developed world, because we account for the bulk of the world's pollution, have a special responsibility to change our lifestyles and methods of production.

1. A NEW WORLD TRADING SYSTEM

The problem with an international "free market" is that it can drag down wages, environmental regulations, and social welfare programs to the level of the worst-off country. This is the basis of much of the opposition to NAFTA. U.S. companies can move or threaten to move their production to Mexico if American workers don't take wage cuts. Similarly, the government can be coerced into rescinding environmental regulations or social programs if employers oppose them. It becomes impossible to regulate business if capital is free to move to countries without such regulation.

On the other hand, protectionism is not the answer. Ultimately, protectionism has helped employers, not workers. Jobs are rarely saved permanently. And prices rise for consumers. Furthermore, protectionism pits U.S. workers against workers in other countries, who often want and need jobs as desperately, or more, than we do.

How can we steer our boat between the Scylla of free trade and the Charybdis of protection? We can be for world trade, but in a framework of minimum standards. Countries would have to abide by international codes of conduct on workers' rights and environmental protections which would stipulate basic protections such as minimum wages, maximum hours of work, rights to representation, and non-discrimination by race and sex, as well as the regulation of air and water emissions, toxic wastes, etc. (The green quotas and taxes we proposed above would be the national versions of such agreements.) The codes would be sensitive to the situations of poor countries, and would allow for initial differences in some of the standards to which countries are held. They would also contain provisions which allow poor countries access to "clean" technologies.

In a world trading system built on such cooperative agreements it would no longer be possible for Japan to gain advantage because workers are forced to put in unpaid overtime. Or for companies to cross the border to Mexico to avoid environmental regulations. When countries violate or refuse to sign on to these agreements, their products would be subjected to "social tariffs" which would be set to compensate for the deviation from the code. If Brazil was a dollar below the global minimum wage, a Brazilian product taking one hour to make would carry a $1.00 tariff. If Korea has cheaper steel because its plants are more polluting, or its workers get no leisure time, the social tariff would make up the difference so that the Korean steel would no longer have a cost advantage. Over time, the tariffs become a powerful incentive for companies to improve environmental performance and their treatment of employees. Where the tariff revenue goes (to the consuming country, or into a global facility) is a matter open for discussion.

If this sounds utopian, remember that the International Labour Organization has already developed codes of labor rights; the problem now is enforcement. And global environmental protections such as the Montreal Protocol and the treaties emanating from the Rio Summit are already being enacted. What is lacking is the political will and leadership to move forward.

BUDGET, TAXES AND FINANCE

So far we have said very little about the budget, taxes, and spending, the issues which usually dominate the economic discourse. On the all-consuming question of the Federal budget deficit, we side with those who believe its importance has been overstated. *When properly calculated,* it is much less a problem than is usually assumed. The deficit has become a political tool, frequently used by conservatives to cut social spending they do not like. We need to reduce the Federal deficit, but we oppose further cuts in social spending in the name of deficit reduction.

1. TAX REFORM

Despite all the talk of tax and spend Democrats, the fraction of national income going to Federal taxes has hardly budged in fifty years.[14] However, regressive payroll taxes have taken up a larger share than the more progressive income tax. And the corporate tax burden has fallen significantly. State and local taxes, comprised largely of the more regressive sales and property taxes, have risen. We believe that continued reform of the tax system is necessary, both to continue the path to simpler taxes and to create a fairer tax system. We advocate reinstating progressive measures into the tax system. For Federal income taxes these include the expansion of exemptions at lower income levels and higher rates at the top; eliminating income caps for payroll taxes; and bringing corporate profits back into the taxation system. At the state and local levels we advocate greater reliance on income taxes. We also propose much higher inheritance taxes, so that unfair economic advantage does not carry through from generation to generation.

2. REDUCING FEDERAL SPENDING

Like many conservatives, we favor reduced Federal spending. But we believe in military downsizing, eliminating subsidies to agribusiness, cutting fewer agricultural subsidies to agribusiness, cutting subsidies to fossil-fuel and nuclear energy sources, and fewer dollars in interest payments. In conjunction with the tax reforms we advocated above, these changes will bring down the Federal deficit. We advocate splitting the Federal accounts into consumption and investment components. In the long run, we advocate the elimination of any "structural" deficit in consumption spending. With respect to investment spending, deficits are not a problem because they generate increased revenue in future years.

3. REREGULATING FINANCIAL MARKETS

The current administration has shown little inclination to reassume the control over financial markets which was ceded through deregulation and the failure to keep up with innovations in finance. No surprise then, that Clinton has been the "darling" of the bond market. But pandering to the financiers will not bring us economic health. By now it is widely recognized that deregulation has had disastrous effects: the savings and loan scandals, a possible coming banking crisis, and the growing influence, corruption, and income of financiers. The federal government, in conjunction with international regulatory agencies, needs to reassume a modicum of control over financial markets. We need reregulation to reintroduce prudence and eliminate the incentives for reckless behavior which currently exist. The principles of regulation should be that *all* financial institutions are regulated equivalently (i.e., the so-called level playing field); that regulations *raise,* not lower the field (unregulated financial institutions are a recipe for disaster); and that a financial social contract be introduced in which the privilege to be a lending institution with Federal deposit insurance carries with it responsibilities to poor and urban communities and small businesses which are starved for funds.

Financial reform should also address the structural position of the Federal Reserve, which is insulated from democratic pressures and mainly accountable to large banks and financial institutions. This accountability is in large part responsible for the high real interest rates of the past decade and a half, and the attendant negative effects on investment and productivity. The Federal Reserve should be brought under more Congressional control, and appointments to the Board of Governors should be restructured to introduce citizen influence. Finally, we favor reforms which will decentralize finance, and increase availability of funds for socially worthwhile projects which traditional bankers will not support. We applaud the Clinton Administration's advocacy of new, local community financing vehicles. These could be federally supported, and devoted to providing alternative sources of finance.

SOLVING THE PRODUCTIVITY PROBLEM

Many of these reforms will require new economic resources. Cleaning up the environment, raising the wages of the bottom half, giving ourselves more leisure time, or instituting a basic income grant are all costly proposals, in their own ways. Yet the prevailing reality is that we are living in a world of increasing scarcity of resources and that we are getting poorer, not richer.

New resources can be found by organizing our economy and society more rationally. For example, unemployment deprives the economy of the productivity of the unemployed, and creates costly social problems such as poor health, crime, and family dissolution. So too have we been dealing with crime in an inefficient way (locking people up at a great cost to society). There has been a tremendous growth of "unproductive" employees in our society (excessive numbers of security guards, paper-pushers, and supervisors). A more equitable and participatory economy could do away with many of these functions, thereby freeing up resources. But ultimately, new resources will have to be created through productivity growth: becoming more efficient in our methods of production and distribution.

The recent U.S. record on productivity growth has not been good, in comparison to our competitors. And herein lies much of the concern about the decline of the U.S. economy. Economists don't have a very good understanding of why productivity growth has been so meager, but the likely culprits are low investment, heavy-handed labor management, declining quality of education and training, the short-term perspective imposed by financial markets, and distorted resource use due to uncounted environmental costs. We also believe that the growing inequities of our society are having an impact: unemployment, poor schools, crime, drugs, homelessness. All these problems take their toll.

Productivity growth in manufacturing has been far better than in services, where more than 70 percent of Americans are employed. The productivity problem is in many ways a service sector problem caused by low wages, high turnover, low capital intensity, low levels of education and training. Much of the service sector is an "economic backwater" in need of upgrading. The policies of the Republican Administrations have encouraged low-wage, low-cost labor, allowing businesses to get by without investing in new technologies or organizational innovations. We need policies which stimulate innovation, technical change, and upgrading. We need to encourage (or force) companies to invest in their employees' "human capital," knowing that when they do, they are paid back handsomely. In a global economy, to do otherwise is to court disaster. If we do not raise our productiveness in services, our wage levels *will* be dragged down the international scale, from Britain to Spain to Turkey and finally Mexico and Brazil.

Many of the reforms mentioned above will help, such as comparable worth and raising the minimum wage. So too will reform of labor relations. We also advocate the maintenance of a highly valued dollar, rather than allowing continued depreciation. Similarly, we need federal help in upgrading public schools and a comprehensive program to make college educations available and affordable for all. And we also need direct incentives (for example, loan programs and tax credits) for service sector businesses, particularly small ones. Government could institute tax reductions for companies which achieve high productivity growth, thereby encouraging the most productive businesses and penalizing the least.

These ideas rest on the historical evidence that there are two paths to economic growth. One is the high-wage, high-productivity route. The other is with low-wages, least-costs, and low productivity. This country got rich with the first, and is now getting poor with the second. We think it's time to change that.

ECONOMIC POLICY IN THE AGE OF GLOBALIZATION

Looking over the economic policy debates of the past fifteen years, the steady demise of progressive economic ideas is striking. A Democratic President dares not even speak out for strong side agreements on labor and environment in NAFTA, regulation of financial markets, or an effective approach to joblessness. The absence of a progressive voice is in no small part due to the powerlessness that people feel in the context of a globalizing economy. We have been taught— by liberal Democrats and Republicans alike—that our nation is *subject* to global trends, not a creator of them. We have been taught that other nations, especially Japan, cause our economic problems. And we have been taught that the "free market" is the only rational economic institution available to us.

These views are ideology, not reality. They represent the interests of the world's most powerful economic actors, the large transnational corporations who are making an increasingly successful bid to free themselves from even modest levels of social accountability. If it did nothing else, the fight over NAFTA identified whose interests lie where. Globalization is mainly a process being carried out by the giant transnationals, among whom U.S. transnationals are the most numerous and powerful. If ordinary people and national governments are becoming powerless in the face of globalization, it is because we are granting our own corporations too much power. The market is not impersonal, it is not too big to regulate, and most of all it is not free. It is created and maintained by concentrations of corporate and governmental power. The urgent task of the New Party in the area of economics is to confront the myth of economic powerlessness perpetuated by America's archaic political system, and to mobilize alternative visions for a sustainable economy in the twenty-first century.

How We Might Unite

JOEL ROGERS

What follows is based on a talk given at a national meeting of U.S. progressive activists in May 1994. Thanks to Noam Chomsky and participants in the May meeting for comments, and to Josh Cohen and Gerry Hudson for the same, as well as for countless discussions of these themes.

When you look at American society what do you see? Falling wages and rising inequality, retreats from racial justice, destruction of inner-city neighborhoods, environmental degradation, violence against women, the agonizing problems of urban youth, more new prisons than schools. The business dominated media celebrates it all. But for the rest of us, the inventory of destruction and unnecessary pain recalls that current policies fail to "promote the general welfare" or to ensure "liberty and justice for all"—and why we are saddened and outraged by how we now govern ourselves as a people.

What can we do about it?

We can in fact do better. Neither circumstance nor our nature prohibits improvement. America remains blessed with abundance, free of external military threat, and populated by a spirited and resourceful people no more stupid or corrupt than any other. Our problems arise from how this particular society is now organized, how power within it is now exercised, the fact that that power is not now exercised in sufficiently democratic ways. And all these things are within our power to change.

By "we" I mean progressives, a different breed from the corporate liberals with whom they commonly ally. Progressives actually believe in democracy. We believe that people of ordinary means and intelligence, if properly organized and equipped, can govern themselves, and that if we do, the results will be better than if we do not. Liberals lack such confidence in ordinary people, and so put less emphasis on popular democratic organization. They favor the "kinder, gentler" administration of people, usually done through the state, as the best means to social improvement.

The present moment should be especially inviting to progressives, if they really understand their commitments to democracy, because the limits of a liberalism not so essentially committed are increasingly apparent. Without organized popular support, liberals cannot do the heavy lifting against entrenched and resourceful actors—almost always corporate interests—that is often needed to enact desired policy outcomes. Without the monitoring, enforcement, and trust-inducing capacities of socially-rooted organizations, they often cannot administer policies effectively. When it comes to fighting opposition, they don't have the troops. When it comes to solving problems inside schoolrooms or communities, their government programs are "all thumbs and no fingers." As problems of both kinds become more evident, as they are today in everything from health care reform to education and public safety, so too do the limits of liberalism. Popular awareness of these limits creates an enormous opportunity for developing a viable alternative: uniting for a change and building a progressive movement in America. A movement of more popular democratic governance and the organization to support it.

This opportunity must be seized, however, which is where progressive problems start. While progressives recognize more clearly than liberals the need for democratic organization, we face a problem of our own—the right kinds of organizations do not arise naturally. They need to be built, and revised and built again in light of changed circumstances, through political projects of mass appeal that energize and consolidate our own ranks. And the ability to do that has recently been made more difficult by all sorts of developments, from the erosion of neighborhoods to the decline in urban manufacturing to the rise of issue and "identity" concerns different from the class concerns that once unified progressive politics.

To find our way to a new practice, we need to take account of these difficulties and then, recognizing them, figure out what the appropriate projects are today. To a degree and with an urgency that I cannot recall since the late 1960s, there is considerable demand inside the progressive community for some common program of action, and considerable demand outside that community among the general population, most of whom would never describe themselves as "progressive," for the sorts of demands such an action program might naturally provide. What is needed is some clarity and honesty about our present situation, and a willingness to break with old habits in improving it. Are we up to it?

WHY WE ARE WEAK

U.S. progressives today are organizationally and ideologically fragmented. And so they are weak—missing opportunities for mutual gain, scale, and public coherence only available through coordination. Weakness confirms their fragmentation, and thus further weakness, by inspiring a narrow and defensive politics, particularist in the extreme and lacking popular appeal. In the limiting case, widely reached today, the self-identified "progressive community" does not even aim at such appeal. It does not mount broad programs of social moment, much less aggressingly compete for power based on them. It seeks not to rule, but only to be tolerated, as a hodgepodge of essentially single-issue groups possessed of more grievances than ideas. For some, the resulting isolation from "the people" confirms illusions of saintliness. Its most immediate and obvious effect, however, is to guarantee political irrelevance.

How did this sorry state of affairs come to pass? Why are progressives so divided when it is clear they would be stronger together than apart?

One obvious answer is that progressives have legitimate differences of opinion and emphasis; different groups simply respond to the needs or interests of different constituencies. Only slightly less obvious is the fact that differences beget differences. An institution that forms to address X because it feels X is not addressed well by existing organizations often comes over time to be less capable of addressing the related issue Y—because of turf considerations, the natural hardening of institutional arteries, or the narrowing of activity, given scarce resources, to "signature" concerns. Also obvious, if rarely stated, is that the past practice of the left itself plays a constitutive role in present division. Many of the groups and movements that now find it hard to talk to one another originally formed because their members were not heard in conversations with the broader left.[1]

None of these observations is very satisfying as an answer to our question, however, since all of them basically just redescribe the problem. A better answer, I think, begins by looking at what progressive movements and organizations need to do to flourish, and then indicates how the conditions of their doing that have eroded in recent years.

WHAT PROGRESSIVES NEED TO FLOURISH

Progressive organizations/movements advance when they put forth practical programs of action that benefit their members or potential members, solve problems in the broader society (often, perhaps surprisingly, problems for capitalists, on whose well-being the rest of the society unfortunately depends), and by doing both these things get the political and social respect needed to advance their own interests in general and to secure supports for their own organization. Projects of this kind, uniting the particular with the universal, are at the core of stable progressive politics; they give progressive organizations something to do other than complain. Unions in the postwar period, for example, redistributed income toward their members, thereby helped stabilize mass markets for consumer durables, and thereby inspired investment, which increased productivity, which lowered the real costs of consumer goods for everyone. By doing something for their members that also, distinctively, helped the broader society, they gained social respect.

One problem for progressives today is that most of their old projects of this sort have run out of steam. The claim might be argued in different ways, most directly perhaps by considering the relationship between progressive organizations and their members. With rare exceptions—and suggesting that whatever it is that their organizations are doing, members don't find it very compelling—this relationship barely exists. Of course, members may give their organization a little money—because they are forced to, or out of nostalgia, or even conviction. But they usually won't use their own energies to build the organization and they are not readily mobilized by its leaders. Unions are able to collect dues money and some PAC contributions but can't put 16 million people in the street. U.S. Greenpeace has 1.4 million members but can get only a tiny fraction of them to do more than contribute. And so on.

But if members or potential members aren't really turned on by current progressive appeals, why don't progressive make different appeals?

Two related reasons. On the one hand, the conditions of getting progressive agreement on projects have gotten more demanding. On the other hand, most progressives have just stopped looking; they've given up on mass politics.

GOODBYE SOLIDARITY

Social projects, especially oppositional ones, require some measure of solidarity among their members—and then of a sufficiently encompassing kind that it can provide the fuel for mass action. Sometimes this is supplied by "organic" solidarities—arising "naturally" from common race or ethnic background, common neighborhoods or friends, or common conditions of work. Sometimes it is supplied by a shared ideology—a common view of the world and one's place in it. Most often it is supplied by both, through ideologies that connect the organic with some general theory—usually elevating the interest attributed to that organic group to some universal status. For generations, working-class solidarity was fueled both by the fact of a distinctly working-class life marked by spatial proximity, common employment, intermarriage, and shared formal restrictions on mobility and by the view that workers had shared interests as a class which also happened to be the true universal interests of society.

Today, however, progressives cannot rely on encompassing organic solidarities, and certainly cannot rely on agreement to elevate any single interest, connected to any particular solidarity, as the universal interest. They also lack a common ideology or framework for discussion, which makes it hard to settle disagreements or set new directions.

For example, even in America (which has never been big on working class solidarity), even among whites (who have always been, well, white), there was until recently at least some civic culture, rooted in relatively stable face-to-face communities, relatively stable jobs (located near the home), and an array of local public goods (schools, libraries), political organizations (local political machines, party clubs, good government associations), civic associations (churches, trade unions, PTAs, Kiwanis Clubs), sources of information (lots of local newspapers, even a little labor press), and diverse quasi-public meeting places and practices (sports leagues, taverns). Within the working class proper, moreover, shared interests were spotlighted by the institutions of mass production. In a vast assembly-line factory churning out cars or refrigerators, with each worker doing some numbingly simple task overseen by layer upon layer of oppressive management, it wasn't too hard to figure out which side you were on.

But this world is long since lost. Today, most people commute several hours to work. They work in relatively small organizations that are far more heterogenous (if no more satisfying) than those of old, and that often (sometimes only rhetorically, sometimes in practice) blur the lines between managerial and non-supervisory personnel. When they get home from work, they don't talk much to their neighbors, and aren't much involved in local community life. Shopping and watching TV are their principal leisure activities, usually pursued alone. The quality of their local neighborhood life seems to be—largely is— decided somewhere else.

Even among the non-white population, where the level of solidarity and community feeling generally remains immeasurably higher than in the white population, there is obvious fraying. The last generation of African-Americans, Asian-Americans, and Chicano/Latino/Hispanic-Americans, for example, have seen major changes in their lives in part because of progress made in civil rights. As a consequence, their communities are more fractured than they once were—fractured spatially, with members no longer living exclusively in racially-defined areas; fractured in terms of class, because with new opportunities has come greater class stratification; and increasingly fractured by intense ethnic and cultural divisions within communities which only white progressives casually lump together as undifferentiated "people of color."[2]

If encompassing organic solidarities have declined, only the sectarian are prepared to elevate any one progressive interest—in race, or class, or gender, or the environment, or whatever—to the status of universal interest.[3] Progressives deal with this "decline of the universal" by making lists and assuring each other of their sincerity in embracing all these values and concerns. But ideology is not about lists or civility. It's about giving different people enough of a common view of things that they are willing to do things with each other. And at this level, the left sorely lacks a common ideology.

Indeed, progressives today seem even to lack a shared framework for discussing problems—a common sense of relevant facts, conventions on evidence, and so on—out of which a new analysis and strategy might come.

One consequence of this is that the sheer quality and distinctiveness of left discussion, as compared to the general population, is lower than it once was. Ask the typical hardened leftist in 1970 what the U.S. was doing in Vietnam, and you got a whole rap on imperialism, offshore oil leases, geopolitics, and the rest. It may have been rough in parts, but at least it was news to the consumer of the mainstream press and TV. Ask the same person today if she thinks the deficit matters, if training is the solution to the country's economic problems, whether single-payer is really more efficient than other health insurance systems, what unions should be doing, and whether community policing works, or what to do about public housing and you usually get warmed-over opinions from someone else, maybe even the editorial board of the *New York Times*.

But the more immediate consequence of the absence of a shared framework is simply to make common left discussion more difficult. Adding to the fact of very different organizational concerns and the imagined fact of differences arising from innocent differences in language,[4] the absence of a shared framework makes discussion hard to get going and easy to abandon before substantive engagement.

If shared ideologies help underwrite shared projects, projects help underwrite shared ideologies. The lack of a common project here in the United States is part of what we're trying to explain. In explanation of it, however, we should note the collapse of foreign projects that have in the past helped orient domestic discussions.

In the 1960s, the left here (old and new) in some measure saw itself as precisely what the right accused it of being—the agent of a global revolutionary struggle.[5] While it did not, contrary to the right's fantasies, draw actual material support from foreign powers, it drew political capital from the fact that current U.S. governance was contested abroad by those powers. And if relations between the U.S. left (new and old) and the giant pole of opposition to U.S. global dominance—the Soviet Union—were at best deeply ambivalent, there was little ambivalence about the importance of revolutionary struggles—including those relying heavily on Soviet support—to our own practice. During the anti-war movement, for example, "ho ho, Ho Chi Minh, NLF is gonna win" was not just a chant. It was a fact offered as evidence for the plausibility of our convictions, as well as a source of inspiration for the task of defining their local application. And long after Third World revolutionary struggles ceased to be seen as appropriate evidence of much of anything of relevance to the United States (a change itself qualified by Sandinista Nicaragua[6]), progressives looked to the functioning social democracies of Western Europe as models of what they were about at home.

Today, this world too is gone. The Soviet Union has collapsed. Third World revolution appears as a thing of the past. European social democracy, while hardly dead, is in deep crisis. Today then, U.S. progressives from very different perspectives share the absence of any "model" they can point to. This makes getting a common framework of analysis that much more difficult.

Nor is the absence of a solidaristic presence or ideology relieved by the presence of some issue of compelling importance for a critical mass of people. While there are many issues that are important and even compelling (not to mention fatal) for one population or another, there is nothing that similarly affects a critical mass in ways manifest to those in it. There is no Great Depression or Vietnam. Our depressions are now "silent," our wars are "bloodless." The sources of our degradation are complex, obscure, distant ... and thus not easily identified and contested.

Current American progressives thus find themselves in a difficult, even unique circumstance. They can neither rely on some particularistic ideology or "found" solidarity nor on any obvious external source of popular mobilization. They need, in effect, to construct solidarities and campaign for issues, since neither are handed to them. And doing this will require that they be more cosmopolitan and deliberate than most of their predecessors about the terms of their coordination that they look squarely at their own fragmentation and construct organizations and projects designed to relieve it. Merely invoking the happy memories of times when the left was more together than it is now will not do the trick, because the conditions of internal left deliberation have fundamentally changed.

GOODBYE MASS POLITICS

Partly for these difficulties in talking to one another, partly because of their shared experience of defeat over the last 20 years, progressives have forsaken even the ambitions of mass politics. They are generally no longer in the business of aiming at truly mass democratic organization, of mounting programs of action speaking to actual majorities (or functioning pluralities) of the people. Abandoning mass politics, they have opted instead for a more or less dignified marginality, or a life of elite "good works." They no longer really reach for governance.

Just when this change occurred is debatable. It was in any case more process than event. Pressed for a date (mostly, I acknowledge, for the white left), however, I'd pick the first Wednesday of November 1972. Until the McGovern campaign, those manifestly shaped by the upheaval of the 1960s had not fully participated at the leadership level of a national campaign. McGovern's capture of the Democratic presidential nomination promised in some sense the first "fair" election, the first real test of "our" values against "theirs," in our lifetime. And we were completely wiped out.

After that, until Clinton, the self-identified left was never really a presence in the campaign of any Democratic nominee. There was the Carter weirdness in 1976. The Mondale shutdown in 1984. The Dukakis fiasco of 1988. There were always unsuccessful candidates favored by that racy Hollywood Democratic elite (Hart the most important). And there remained the still undeciphered, and certainly not "decharismatized" Jackson, alive (if wounded) after enduring a decade of attacks from Democratic and media elites, and the memory of his spectacular campaign in 1988.[7]

None of this gave much general sense that Democratic Party politics at the presidential level was in any way a metaphor for our generation's taking power.

Until, of course, our generation did take power, at which point we weren't running our generation anymore. All progressives voted for Clinton in 1992, with a greater degree of excitement and hope than they liked to admit, but with the self-understanding of the merely tolerated. Among whites, those who had really protested the invasion of Vietnam had long since lost out; it was time to turn things over to the friendly student government types who had occasionally come to demonstrations and tell us how very troubling they found the whole issue. Time to hand it over to the foundation hands, the FOBs, and an entirely new generation of power-hungry children who had somehow grown up in our absence from the scene. It wasn't 1972.

Among African-Americans, Clinton offered the possibility of some advance in race relations, and an ease and familiarity in dealing of the sort acquired by successful Democratic politicians in the South. But he did so according to a DLC picture of the world that had room for anti-poverty efforts but not employment, sympathy for the devastation of our cities but no money for urban reconstruction, solid support for anti-discrimination efforts but not economic organization or real political power. The Clintons were people far more comfortable with African-Americans than any previous presidential couple, but no more accountable to their needs, and quite prepared to engage in public humiliation rituals of Jackson to show their "independence" of concern.

The early 1970s also commenced the 20-year decline in American living standards, the "silent depression," which inevitably gnawed at general impulses to radical action; a sharp drop in union density, which removed all sorts of resources from potential progressive use; the "defunding" of the left by conservatives actively funding a radical right; all manner of other changes in policy, starting during the Carter administration, that permanently changed the terms of progressive organization (e.g., the deregulation of major unionized industries, exposing them to non-union competition) and increased the immediate needs of progressive constituencies (and thus the time progressive organizations needed to spend on servicing those constituencies rather than strategizing their seizure of power); and so on.

At some point, in any case, the scope of progressive ambitions changed. The fear permanently lodged that they were in the minority. And as a minority they did best to hunker down, hopeful only that the storm might one day (not their day) pass. And as that happened, progressives found themselves increasingly drawn to desperate oppositionism or liberalism, to denunciations of all exercises of public power or to the belief that it could not in fact be popularly exercised. For the realization of progressive values, of course, these are equivalent defeats.

STUPID!

And a terrible mistake. Despite the peculiar organizational difficulties progressives face now (and for the foreseeable future), despite the need, arising from those difficulties, for them to "construct" a future for themselves (solidarity and all the rest) rather than wait to inherit it, the present moment is ripe with opportunity. All manner of forces are now conspiring, as they have for close to a generation, to put on the table of American politics the only issues that make it even more uncomfortable than race: democracy and class. All around us we see the wreckage of an unregulated, not-popularly-controlled economy: falling living standards, families strained to the breaking point, rising inequality. All around us we see the alternating feebleness and corruption of formal government incapable of solving problems, not even trying, in hock to monied interests, almost incapable of rational debate, certainly incapable of doing the heavy lifting needed to put the country right.[8]

These observations, moreover, are not the privileged insights of progressives. Everybody knows this. Everybody—well, almost everybody—knows that "the country's in a mess," that government as we know it cannot solve the problem, that "the people" need to get organized, and that greater popular control needs to be exerted over an economy that is killing us. Most Americans are sick to death of "save yourself, not your brother" politics of greed and striving. Most Americans desperately want more control over the lives they see continually disrupted and degraded by current economic governance.

There is, in short, huge demand for precisely what progressives have been arguing for forever: greater social control of the economy and the democracy of which it would be one instance. Not a bad demand to satisfy. Nothing could more readily advance the general welfare, while consolidating distinctive progressive (as against liberal) nostrums for current disorder. And nothing would do more to relieve current progressive organizational difficulties.

But the opportunity must be explicitly seized.

HOW TO GET OUT OF HERE

These truths seem self-evident, or very nearly so.

Progressives will not measurably increase their power in American society merely by working harder at the same things. We are already working desperately hard and getting nowhere.

Progressives will not measurably increase their unity merely by expanding the list of concerns that provide a base for one-time coalitions. Nor will the relevant unity be achieved by getting deeper agreement among themselves that all these concerns are shared by all progressives on an ongoing basis. Such agreement is welcome, but already evident. The question is how to utilize it organizationally—how to get everyone who shares these concerns, however unevenly, to support something together.

Progressives cannot pretend the world has not changed in certain material ways that affect their strategies of organization. The economy is more competitive, and simple redistributive strategies are no longer enough. Unless we are involved in the actual organization of the economy on the "supply" side, we are doomed. The conditions of organizing are less favorable: the dispersion of communities, the lure of privatizing consumer electronics, the increased exit threats of capital, the weakness of political parties, the literal capitalization of electoral politics, the decline of public libraries, schools, parks, streets, business districts, spaces.

And again, progressives cannot make their appeals only to those who already identify themselves as such. We need to accept the discipline of doing something with broad appeal. Not because we are worried about a fight, or think it can be avoided, but because we realize that we cannot win any important fight alone. We need others to join us, many others, if our values are to be realized in any substantial way.

In brief, we need a project, of benefit to our existing base, solving a larger and current problem in the society, that would mobilize those not now moving and organize those already in motion in directions potentially congruent with our own. Given our own divisions, this project must be sufficiently obvious, and obviously of some potential benefit to all of us, that its statement and debate are possible according to some shared terms.

A project. Or several such projects. Here are three that meet these conditions.

PROJECT I: DEMOCRACY NOW

Some 75 percent of Americans think government is "run by a few interests that don't care about me." Made clear by the mobilization of Perot, evident among middle class liberals as well as progressives, is widespread popular concern that the people don't "own" or "control" their government anymore. Why not put such ownership and control of social governance, such democracy itself, on the table as an issue? Certainly it would be good for us. Certainly we could agree at least on this as a basis of our own coordination?

Imagine a "Democracy Campaign" initially targeted to states, eventually providing the basis for federal reform that would aim to equip all citizens with the"tools" (rights, remedies, organizational resources) they need to practice democracy under 20th century circumstances.

An immediate goal might be reform of our corrupt system of campaign finance and voter and party rights. Despite the fundamental nature of the reforms proposed, this part of the campaign would appeal to individuals in their more or less conventionally recognized social role as citizen/voters. But the campaign would also include, and from the outset be framed as including, reform aimed at enhancing opportunities for democratic action in other core social roles that is, as workers, consumers, taxpayers, and shareholders of private and public wealth. A democratic toolkit offered, explicitly, as a way of rebuilding the whole of the civic infrastructure on which a vibrant democracy depends. Democracy itself, not just some part of it, being the issue.

How to do this? Perhaps by developing and publicizing and winning some new "Bill of Rights" for each of the "roles" just mentioned. Here's a brief set of ideas on each offered as a way to get discussion going, not to set the limits of that discussion.

> Citizen/Voter Bill of Rights: It shall be the right of each citizen to participate freely and equally in an electoral system in which candidate access is not determined by money, party competition is open and fair, and rights to referendum, recall, and initiative are secure.

Enactment of this bill would require universal or same day voter registration, a serious exploration of alternative voting systems designed to represent minority electoral sentiment more effectively than "winner take all" rules currently do, a revival of the "fusion" option in party politics, lowered barriers to third (and fourth) party qualification and maintenance requirements, universal referendum, recall, and initiative rights, a right to "none of the above" balloting, and no doubt more. Strikingly, virtually all of the above enjoy majority political support.

> Worker Bill of Rights: It shall be the right of each employee to form associations at the workplace free of the interference of employers.

Without a genuine right to organize on the job, workers cannot form independent organizations. Without independent worker organizations, sensible labor market policy, and equality, and rising living standards, are virtually unimaginable.

> Shareholder Bill of Rights: Individual and collective shareholders shall enjoy rights of effective control over their assets.

The "owners" of corporations have very little control over them, and this separation of ownership and control has a good deal to do with the lack of corporate accountability. The most pointed and immediate case is that of private pensions $2 trillion in assets beyond the control of its worker-owners. We need to give workers, consumers, local communities, shareholders and other "stakeholders" some say in corporate decision-making.

> Consumer Bill of Rights: All consumers of goods and services shall have the right to form associations to monitor, bargain over, and lobby for the regulation of the integrity and sale of such.

From the experience of the Nader-inspired Citizen Utility Boards, established in a few states in the 1980s, we know that it is possible for consumers to be organized very effectively on a mass scale. There is no reason why the CUB model might not be extended to the likes of the U.S. Post Office, Social Security and Veterans administrations, public housing authorities, insurance companies and banks, and other government agencies and private producers. The model is voluntary, self-financing, and effective as consumer protection.

> Citizen/Taxpayer Bill of Rights: Citizen/taxpayers shall have convenient facilities for banding together in order to shape the priorities of the public purse and the management of public assets, including the public lands, airwaves, public works, government data, and other common assets of our heritage and creation; the information necessary to exercise their sovereignty; and the access to government decision-making necessary to implement it.

Establishing these rights would entail such things as set-asides of public revenues from private use of public lands to fund citizen watchdogs on such use; the requirement that all data collected by the government be made available, for free and in accessible form, to citizens; vastly increased taxpayer standing rights in administrative and judicial proceedings bearing on the disposition of public assets or monies; a restoration of public regulation of the airwaves (particularly with regard to citizen access, more diversified ownership, etc.).

If Americans had these rights and supports, what might be the result? The honest answer is that nobody knows for sure, since they have never had them in the past. But it seems likely that the results would include: a much livelier and engaged civic culture; almost infinitely higher rates of voter participation;

a significant reduction in corporate and government fraud, abuse, and waste (with certainty, we can say that none of the really major scandals of the last several years, e.g., the S&L fiasco, pension defaults, nuclear weapons cleanup disasters, slum lead poisoning, massive securities fraud, continued redlining of inner-city neighborhoods would have occurred if these sorts of monitoring arrangements were in effect); a more disciplined programmatic approach to problems affecting the public welfare; a stronger and more effective party system for the processing of citizen demand into effective governance; and better enforcement of statutory commands, with less bureaucracy.

Sounds pretty good. How to operationalize it initially? By taking back from the right the control of the initiative process, and running a left-wing answer to "term limits USA" in the 20-odd states with initiative rights. Couple that with legislative campaigns, lots of direct action and citizen petitioning, in the non-initiative states. Again, consider a major coordinated national campaign on campaign finance reform to kick the whole thing off.

PROJECT II: SUSTAINABLE AMERICA

Some 85 percent of Americans think the economy is "moving in the wrong direction." Why not turn it around?

What is most basically wrong with current economic policy is its failure to block (and, in fact, to promote) the "low-wage option" on industrial restructuring the option that seeks profit and increased competitiveness achieve via downsizing, temporary workers, job insecurity, environmental degradation, and cutbacks in social spending, regulation, training, and taxes. Instead of a rising tide to lift all boats, American corporate and governmental elites are draining the pool even while they cling, shortsightedly, to their privileged position on the top of the ladder.

We need a campaign to foreclose the low-wage option and to harness the productive energies of workers and communities in a more satisfying restructuring path. We need a "Sustainable America" because we need an economy that will truly support and sustain us, and build for the generations that come, in full awareness of the interdependence of all life on this planet. We need an economy that moves from ruinous low-wage sweating and competition to one marked by greater control of production, exerted with competence and verve, exerted by ordinary citizens.

Flowery rhetoric, to be sure, but the campaign itself could be quite concrete. It would combine national policy campaigns against "low-wage" policies with a series of local organizing efforts in major urban centers, aimed at actually asserting productive popular control over the economy.

At the national level, a campaign on the minimum wage would be a good fit, or an "our money, our jobs" campaign targeted at "subsidy abuse" by government, or better rules on the use of dislocated worker training monies, or a gigantic summer youth jobs effort, or an attempt to put conditions back on Congressional approval of GATT, all might be ways to tap into natural constituencies. Less important than settling such issues right now is agreeing that we want to settle them in the future. Merely announcing our intention to oppose what we see as this economically stupid and morally stupid low-wage option—making that itself an issue—is enough for the moment.

But we must be more than nay-sayers, and offer some positive ambitions. We would need as a group to say something like

> Diverse as we are, we stand together in declaring that ruinous low-wage restructuring must and can stop, and we hold our elected officials and ourselves accountable to stopping it and starting something better a high-wage, low-waste, more democratically controlled economy. We oppose anything (NAFTA, GATT, etc.) that furthers current destruction. We support policies aimed at raising social standards on wages, production conditions, environmental sensitivity and developing popular capacity to enforce them. We want public policy to support a new social contract, with supports for firms complying with its terms and punishment of those defecting from it. The terms of this contract are...

We would then need to fill in the blanks for a positive alternative to present carnage. There are lots of ideas available about what might be in that alternative. The point here, however, is to see the need to state an alternative, specifically an economic alternative, and to have a variety of groups and constituencies not classically identified with economic concerns declare them as their own.

Whatever is done on national policy on labor market regulation or trade however, needs "legs" organizing projects on the ground that both carry the national message locally and act constructively in local arenas to show what taking it seriously would mean there. What might this look like?

Consider Milwaukee. There, the labor leadership of Progressive Milwaukee, joined by environmentalists, housing activists, women's groups, black ministers, and local elected officials, has initiated a process to develop, publicize, and then implement a program for a Sustainable Milwaukee—a plan for the metro area that would produce family-supporting jobs, invest heavily in low-waste production and transport, generate popularly controlled investment, and more. Most fundamentally, the project is about declaring and enforcing a new social contract, with double-barreled support for "good" firms that comply with the terms of the contract and punishment for "bad" firms that do not.

The planning process is itself understood as an organizing, educating, and outreach effort. Issue groups on each of the above issues have formed, led by community leaders with special expertise in the area, doing outreach complementary to the overall planning effort. The bus drivers union leads on transportation concerns. Low-income housing organizers pore over mortgage data. Inner-city manufacturing unions consider how to prevent firms from even thinking about relocating, and how to bring young people into union apprentice programs. And so on. Real people, actual organizations, beginning the process of defining their own vision of what the economy of southeast Wisconsin should be.

The kinds of people who are driving the Sustainable Milwaukee project are to be found in every major metro region in the country. If encouraged and supported, they could provide both the local face of for national campaigns and a consolidating, forward-looking, this-is-what-we-want-to-do-right-here force for local economic restructuring.

PROJECT III: NEW PARTY

Some 50 percent of voting Americans (and, presumably, more non-voters) say they would like to have a "new political party" in the United States. Why not give them one?

The reasons we would want to have some independent progressive electoral presence are clear enough. It's a way of mobilizing support that will never be mobilized through direct action. It's a way of sustaining discussion of positive alternatives. It's a way of uniting, in the electoral arena, progressives who basically agree with one another, even if they don't work that often together, and of expressing that agreement in ways accessible to those not already in the loop of movement work. And, of course, it's a way of pressuring the Democrats and Republicans toward actually representing the interests of ordinary Americans.

Discussion among progressives has always recognized this fact, but also recognized the formidable barriers of entry to third parties in the United States

These typically make votes for independent candidates "wasted" votes or "spoilers," which reduces support for third parties even among those who agree with what they have to say. The basic position of the non-sectarian progressive community, exercised since the New Deal, has been to avoid third party efforts and instead work for progressive reform inside the Democratic Party. Jackson is the most important recent example of this, but there are many, many others.

Such work should certainly continue. But the time is ripe for diversifying the portfolio of progressive strategies to include independent politics, i.e., the establishment of a political party structure distinct from the Democratic Party.

It goes without saying that this structure must be internally democratic (the party should be governed by members, not money); value-centered (standing for something, not just unaccountable candidates); broad in its vision (green, consumer justice, feminist, committed to racial justice, pro-worker, but not exclusively identified with any one of these concerns); and willing to do those non-electoral-campaign things (education of members, support for non-electoral issue campaigns) needed to give electoral efforts real context. Most immediately, however, it must have a way of avoiding the wasted vote syndrome that destroys most third party efforts.

The New Party is/does all these things. On the last, most vexing, issue, it simply does not run its own candidates for office where they do not have a serious chance of winning. Instead, it does nothing, or works with the most progressive major party candidate (nearly always a Democrat, of course) it can find. Thus far, this strategy appears to be working. Active chapters are building in 11 states, and their win-rate on candidates is nearly 70 percent. Third party politics appears possible. It just takes some patience and time and self restraint.

As a broad progressive third party that doesn't waste votes, and that works both inside and outside the Democratic Party, the New Party is a natural electoral vehicle for a more consolidated progressive movement built in part through greater national coordination, in part from the ground up. It offers a natural outlet, at the local level, for consolidating an electoral presence around a common progressive agenda. It thus gives national campaigns local bounce. It gives local efforts at independent electoral politics a connection to a national effort at the same, in part through the medium of shared non-electoral work.

But I care much less about the New Party per se than the idea that it stands for independent progressive politics with a practical intent. The left is not going to be heard inside the Democratic Party until is has a credible "threat of exit" from that party. The relationship between progressives and the Democratic

Party is an abusive relationship. They take our votes, and we get little back. As in any such relationship, to end the abuse you need the ability to leave. And the Democratic Party, at least as presently constituted, is simply not the popular organization needed to wage the sorts of battles described here. We need an alternative. We need a progressive version of GOPAC or the Christian Coalition—something to push our values in electoral space.

SOME SORT OF A PROJECT: INVESTING IN OURSELVES

All the projects just described look outward—to a possible mass politics inspired by but not confined to the left. Getting serious about them, however, recommends that we also look inward, to the infrastructure and culture of our own organization.

Just as a modern economy relies on all sorts of public goods—roads, sewers, telecommunications networks, etc.—a modern left (even more than the left of old[9]) needs to make investments in organizational infrastructure to facilitate its own coordination and impact. We need, for example, to be more self-conscious and ambitious in the use of electronic communication among ourselves; to harness the energies of what are now highly scattered and largely inaccessible sources of technical expertise through shared networks of information diffusion and technical assistance of use to activists; to establish our own financial intermediaries and common sites of deposit; to take care of our own through explicitly sheltered labor markets (keeping people well-funded as they move from one project to another, rather than throwing them onto the external market), and common (permitting transfer across projects) retirement and benefit plans that we control; to organize our recruitment and validation of our values (while giving parents a break) through summer camps and other sorts of shared recreational activity; and more. Above all, perhaps, we need to train our activists in more advanced ways than the usual "here's how to run a meeting" leadership training.[10] We need shared schools—a hundred Highlanders!—that teach people the arts of practical politics in this age, and give them a safe place to talk about and puzzle through the meaning of their activism.

In the 1970s the right got together and said, "hey, let's run the country." They invested millions in their own coordination, including just such infrastructures of training, policy analysis, technical assistance, TV schools, and more. Their destructive project continues to bear fruit today. If we ever expect to run the country, we too must invest directly not just in projects, but our own coordination and capacity.

As some of the examples may suggest, some of this recommended infrastructural investment would contribute to the development of part of what we now lack—a shared analysis or ideology. It would do so by building a more common organizational culture, with more possible points of entrance by more people, and better supports for conversation among them—conversation that would plausibly go somewhere constructive and common. The character of our shared culture itself, however, needs to be directly attended.

As already suggested, I think it is important that the culture of the left should be a learning culture—one that supports wide-ranging discussion, rewards attempts to advance understanding, is resolutely non-dogmatic in its willingness to confront changed circumstances, and to test any theory of what we're about by its ability to define viable projects of our advance. But both as a good in itself, and to be this, our culture must also be kind, forgiving, and fun. At a time recent enough in everyone's memory to be recalled, to be "left" meant—if again often only within too narrowly defined communities of interest—to be associated with the most loving, funny, informed people around.[11] Now, for too many, it means simply going to boring meetings for another round of assignments and abuse. It is not very informative. It's not much fun. As a result, it's not very inviting to any but those whose principles already bar them from not participating.

We need to correct this. We might begin simply by better accommodating within our own practice the demands of our lives outside it,[12] but we can get more adventurous than that. As remote a prospect as this may sound, we need to find ways of genuinely enjoying, not just respecting, each other's company again. That doesn't require that everyone do the same thing in common—a giant left sing-along—though common activities also have their place. It does require that we build into our organizational plans some explicit space for quiet, for informal get-togethers, for family activities and parties (sedate and rowdy), for discussion groups, rock bands, softball teams, street theater ... or whatever other zany nonviolent things that political people might like to do together. This isn't rocket science. We need something other than heavily structured meetings, something that's fun and rewarding, that involves us but doesn't require that we always be "on." Just as solidarity now needs more to be constructed than found, culture needs to be aimed at. We need to take more care, beginning with ourselves.

SO WHAT'S THE MOVE?

Imagine that the above organizational suggestions were taken seriously. Imagine that in a few years time we had radical campaign finance and voting reform. Imagine that we targeted states with significant urban populations, and that within those populations we had mass projects of reconstruction up and running. Imagine that those projects hit head-on into local power elites, and that they decided not to stop at protest but to establish themselves as the base of a new independent politics. Imagine that all this were done while articulating a credible economic alternative to the "neoliberalism with a human face" propagated by the better of the major parties. Imagine that this mix was organized politically to the point of being politically threatening to those who now only offer cities abandonment—that it did not wait or hope for but effectively required their attention as a practical matter of their own survival. Imagine that while all this was happening the left was busy getting sharper, tighter, and more enjoyable.

All this is more or less immediately within our reach, and would change the face of American politics. Presidential hopefuls as soon as 1996 would need to take account of the weird development. A vast array of progressive forces would find a new organizational lease on life. They would be joined by millions of others, newly awakened to the possibilities of a more benign, hopeful, and rational politics. A left pole on national policy discussion, rooted in actual mass constituencies, finding voice in many movements and campaigns but also speaking between them, would be established.

Within our reach, but not yet grasped. Progressives can again emerge as a powerful force in American national politics, but their doing so will require a real decision, a choice against habit. Politics as usual—most immediately the sectarian politics of "wreck and split, divide divide, soon we'll have nothing!" or our increasingly liberal politics of "let's all agree to love one another but do nothing serious together"—will not save us. And nothing on the horizon promises to force salvation on us. We are all long past any fantasy of making history under circumstances of our own choosing. The question before us—best answered after a bloodless gaze at the failures of our present organizing as well as the depravity of present policy, the uniqueness of our historical position as well as our discomfort with one another, our own worried faces as well as the ignorant beauty of our children—is whether, knowing that to do so requires a break from our recent divided practice, we are prepared to make any history at all.

We should be. Let's get to it.

Notes

1. Among other examples, despite its vital leadership support for civil rights, the labor movement of the 1960s (not to mention the 1950s, 1940s) was a profoundly unwelcome place for most black workers—not to mention women, those concerned about the environment, or those opposed to U.S. imperialism abroad; the deep sexism of the leadership of the student and anti-war movements of the time had to be experienced to be believed, and the general left was almost as homophobic as the rest of society; the environmental movement was for a long time almost wholly indifferent to (if not exacerbating of) race and class distributional concerns; the intolerance of any number of left sects and the devolution of much left practice toward sectarianism are too well known to require comment. For many good people who've at one point or another found themselves on the far side of any of these lines of exclusion, "the left" is not an unambivalently appealing, or sometimes even useful, source of identification.

2. In the group properly most identified with the civil rights struggles—African-Americans—these conditions yield three very different impulses in contemporary politics. One is a straightforward continuation of the civil rights strategy, though again its past success, and the fractioning that has followed on that, undermine it as a unifying theme for further advance toward racial justice. Another is toward a more or less nationalist, exclusivist politics, particularly among those who didn't reap the material benefits of strengthened civil rights. This has deep cultural appeal, but under current electoral rules, and the class, spatial, and other fractioning just mentioned, it is ultimately a dead end as a viable mass politics. A third is some sort of race-conscious class strategy. This is directed toward broad economic benefit, but insistent on the core prominence of racism in disabling the American working class from getting that. Structurally (given all that was said above about majoritarian politics, and all that we know about the need for an economic program), this last approach seems most promising in the long run. Given the decline in white working-class fortunes, it is also increasingly possible—at least if some sort of white proto-fascism doesn't beat us there first. At present, however, it doesn't have anywhere near the organizational base or leadership focus of the other two.

3. Or, in Lani Guinier's wonderful phrase, as the certified winner of the "oppression sweepstakes."

4. I know language is never innocent. But people often are. Without disputing the importance of language, we can mourn the fact that too many discussions today run to ground on differences in what only amounts to linguistic style—different ways of describing or analyzing what all parties recognize as reality. "Actually if pressed I would agree with you, but I don't like the way you're putting it because it hurts my feelings or makes me worry that on some other point where we might

disagree (not that I know yet that we will) you won't hear my objection clearly, and so I don't want to talk any more, it's just too much hassle" is an extremely common move, the frequency of which is partly driven by the ease with which it can be made. Needless to say, it limits the range and depth of conversation.

5. This self-conception was—and this was part of its strength as well as of its eventual vulnerability—often expansively inclusive (at least at the level of cultural referents). In some weird way, even after King got killed, everyone from Cesar Chavez, Frank Church, Jean-Luc Godard, and Jane Fonda (she was learning!) to Wayne Morse, Ho Chi Minh, Fidel Castro, and the Isley Brothers all seemed to be on one side, trying to do some good, against the corporate suits running America, which was trying to run the world.

6. For many, especially among the new left, this was the real thing—an effort not just to throw off neocolonial/neo-imperialist bondage and aggression, but to do so in ways not sacrificing of democratic pluralism. The defeat of the Sandinistas was, for the new left, as depressing as the utter collapse of the Soviet Union was for some sections of the old.

7. To a degree that I think remains uncomprehended among whites, the sheer amount of disrespect shown Jackson in 1988 may have made that election in some ways equivalent to what the defeat of McGovern was to whites. For a group that never had any illusions about its arithmetic "minority" status, the issue in formal electoral politics has always been the degree to which alliances with whites could be genuinely non-racist with regard to leadership—whether whites would ever accept being led by blacks. Vividly, the failure of liberal and even progressive whites to rally around the Jackson candidacy made clear the grounds for doubt on this point. While the temptation to an exclusive nationalism has always, and understandably, been alive in the African-American population, this fueled the temptation in obvious ways.

8. Editorial pages don't like to admit it, but any genuinely popular program of social reconstruction implies a significant measure of in-your-face conflict between "the people" and "the powers that be." And that conflict will not just be about values. It will be about power. Most Americans, for example, would like a greener economy, higher and more equal wages, fewer bombs and better health care, some time with their kids, cities that function, and better relations between the races. But you can't construct an environmentally sound economy without reduction in the sources of pollution inside privately owned firms. You can't bring more equality to labor markets without some measure of wage regulation, secured either through the state or unions. You can't convert to a peace economy, or get national health insurance, without eliminating at least some firms entirely. You can't work out a significantly improved relation between work and family without assigning real value to things that are not now valued in

markets, and getting people some time away from work while continuing to pay them. You can't find the funding base needed to rebuild cities to pay for cops and parks and education without taxing those who have the funds. And you can't get clear of the wreckage of 400 years of racism through love alone. For any of these things to happen, people with power and resources need to accept constraints or reductions in their relative standing. And that is not something that is ever done without some conflict.

9. Not to split hairs or reinvent the wheel, much of what is recommended in what follows could, with slightly different referents, be said of much successful left practice in the past, which was almost infinitely more sophisticated in its targeting of projects and in the richness of its cultural life than the left at present (although, again, commonly in ways that by current moral sensibilities would be offensively exclusionist). The "more" in the text is meant only to reprise what has already been said regarding the decline of organic and other solidarities. So split apart are we that the need to pay attention to common terms is greater.

10. One glaring deficiency, noted at the meeting, was the quality of present training on how to be more effective in appearances in mass media.

11. True, there were always humiliations, unnecessary fights, sectarian stupidities, and more. But there was also a fairly deep sense of something at least available to people—before they chose to muck it up with any of the above—that was pretty inviting to those initially accepted by those communities.

12. For example, well into the third decade of the modern women's movement, well after all that we have learned about the ways different organizational practices are "gendered" and how resistant the division of labor inside the household is to formal labor market and political freedom outside it, how many organizations have a rule that membership meetings will not be held without provision of child care?

CONTRIBUTORS

TOM ATHANASIOU lives in San Francisco and is on the technical staff of Sun Microsystems. He is the author of *Divided Planet: The Ecology of Rich and Poor* (New York: Little, Brown, 1995).

JEREMY BRECHER is a historian and coeditor of *Global Visions: Beyond the New World Order* (Boston: South End Press, 1993).

NOAM CHOMSKY, long-time political activist, anarchist, writer, and professor of linguistics at MIT, is the author of numerous books and articles on U.S. foreign policy, international affairs, and human rights. His most recent books are *World Orders, Old and New; Deterring Democracy; Year 501;* and *Rethinking Camelot.* His efforts are instrumental to movements for peace, political justice, and greater democracy worldwide.

MARC COOPER writes articles for many U.S. and foreign publications, ranging from the *Nation* to *Rolling Stone.* He is a staff writer for the *Village Voice* and *Spin* magazine.

KRISTIN DAWKINS is a senior fellow at the Institute of Agriculture and Trade Policy. She worked for sixteen years in community development and public policy research in Philadelphia, including nine years as the executive director of the Philadelphia Jobs in Energy Project. She has a master's degree in city planning from MIT.

DAVID DELLINGER has been an activist for more than half a century. He lives in Vermont, where he still works on issues of peace and justice. He speaks frequently on college campuses and is author of *From Yale to Jail* (New York: Pantheon, 1993).

TOM FRANK holds a Ph.D in American history from the University of Chicago. He is the founder and editor-in-chief of *The Baffler* magazine, and his writing has appeared in the *Washington Post*, the *Village Voice*, the *Chicago Reader*, and other publications. His book on advertising in the 1960s will be published next year by the University of Chicago Press. He lives in Chicago.

BELL HOOKS is a writer and professor who speaks widely on issues of race, class, and gender. Her books include *Killing Rage, Feminist Theory, Yearning,* (with Cornel West) *Breaking Bread: Insurgent Black Intellectual Life,* and *Art on My Mind.*

HARVEY J. KAYE is the author of *The Education of Desire: Marxists and the Writing of History* (winner of the Isaac Deutscher Memorial Prize) and the Ben and Joyce Rosenberg Professor of Social Change and Development at the University of Wisconsin, Green Bay.

NANCY C. KRANICH is associate dean of New York University libraries. She is also a member of the American Library Association's Executive Board and Council, Committee on Legislation, and Ad Hoc Subcommittee on Telecommunications, and chair of the committee's Subcommittee on Government Information.

WINONA LADUKE is a member of the Mississippi band of Anishinaabe from the White Earth Reservation. She presently serves as Campaign Director of the White Earth Land Recovery Project. After graduating from Harvard, LaDuke received her M.A. in community economic development from Antioch College and received the International Reebok Human Rights Award in 1988.

MANNING MARABLE is director of Columbia University's Institute for Research in African-American Studies. His column, "Along the Color Line," appears in more than 170 periodicals in the United States and abroad.

SEYMOUR MELMAN is professor emeritus of industrial engineering at Columbia University and chairs the National Commission for Economic Conversion and Disarmament. He has long been involved in developing strategies for conversion from a military to a civilian economy. His latest books are *The Demilitarized Society* (Montreal: Harvest House, 1988), *Profits Without Production* (Philadelphia: University of Pennsylvania Press, 1987), and *The Permanent War Economy* (New York: Simon and Schuster, 1985).

DAVE MULCAHEY is senior editor of *The Baffler* magazine, and assistant managing editor of *In These Times*. He lives in Chicago.

LAURA POWERS recently served as field director of Libraries for the Future. In cooperation with the Benton Foundation, she established the Strategy Group on Technology, Public Spaces and the NII and is a founding member of Access for All, a New York-area coalition concerned with the future of community media.

JOEL ROGERS is a professor of law, political science, and sociology at the University of Wisconsin—Madison and director of the Center on Wisconsin Strategy.

HERBERT SCHILLER is a professor emeritus of communications at UC—San Diego and a visiting professor at New York University. His works include *Mass Communications and American Empire* (1969), *Communication and Cultural Domination* (1976), *Culture Inc.: The Corporate Takeover of Public Expression* (1989), and *Beyond National Sovereignty: International Communications in the '90s* (1993). Public intellectual par excellence, he writes and lectures extensively about the obesity of corporate power and its increasing control of public space and democratic culture.

JULIET SCHOR is the author of the best-selling book, *The Overworked American: The Unexpected Decline of Leisure* (New York: Basic Books, 1992). Schor earned her B.A. from Wesleyan University and her Ph.D. in economics from the University of Massachusetts at Amherst. She has been teaching at Harvard University since 1984, where she is currently a senior lecturer on economics and the director of studies in the women studies program.

CORNEL WEST is an author, lecturer, and professor of African-American studies and philosophy at Harvard University. He has written many books, including the acclaimed *Race Matters*.

THE ZAPATISTAS are an indigenous insurgency movement demanding political and economic democracy in Mexico. Their guerrilla activity began on January 1, 1994, as a global protest to NAFTA. Their movement demands fair elections and basic human liberties for all Mexicans.

HOWARD ZINN, professor emeritus at Boston University, is one of America's most distinguished historians. Professor Zinn is a decorated World War II bombardier. He was an active figure in the civil rights and anti–Vietnam War movements. His seminal book, *A People's History of the United States,* is widely used in college and university classrooms throughout the country. His latest book is *You Can't Be Neutral on a Moving Train,* published by Beacon Press.

More Information

MEDIA REVIEW

ACTION AGENDA
Produced by Media Watch & Media Action
Alliance, *Action Agenda* aims at "challenging
sexism and violence in the media through education and action." A damaging indictment of
the mass media and the sex industry it helps to
perpetuate, *Action Agenda*'s incisive articles are
complemented by boycott lists, tear-out political postcards, and popular culture reviews.

P.O. Box 618, Santa Cruz, CA 95061-0618
Tel. (408) 423-6355

EXTRA!
Published by Fairness and Accuracy in
Reporting (FAIR), *Extra!*'s articles reveal the
extent that the profit-motivated mass media
bias information and manipulate the public.
Many issues are devoted to a single theme, and
meticulously cited articles provide strong
source material for media research. Essential
reading. Sample copy—$3.50; yearly subscrip-
tion—$30.

130 West 25th Street, New York, NY 10001
Tel. (212) 633-6700 Fax. (212) 727-7668

MEDIACULTURE REVIEW
MCR is an excellent bimonthly review of television, radio, print, and electronic media, advertising, information, and telecommunications
politics. Interesting, informative, and hip.
Subscriptions: $16/yr. Institutions: $36/yr.

77 Federal Street, San Francisco, CA 94107
Tel. (415) 284-1420 Fax. (415) 284-1414
email: alternet@alternet.ors

QUARTERLY REVIEW OF
DOUBLESPEAK
QRD documents the flow of lies, doublespeak,
misinformation, and propaganda spewed from
the mouths of politicians and corporate executives. Subscriptions: $8/yr. Payable to:

National Council of Teachers of English
1111 Kenyon Road, Urbana, IL 61801

PROGRESSIVE POLITICAL
PUBLICATIONS

COVERT ACTION QUARTERLY
Covert Action Quarterly investigates, documents, and exposes many dimensions of secret
U.S. intervention and manipulation at home
and abroad. Published quarterly, it has featured
important research by Jane Hunter, Noam
Chomsky, Diana Reynolds, Clarence Lusane,
Mike Davis, and many others. Sample copy—
$6. 4-issue subscription—$22.

1500 Massachusetts Avenue, NW #732,
Washington, D.C. 20005
Tel. (202) 331-9763 Fax. (202) 331-9751
email: caq@igc.apc.org

INDEX ON CENSORSHIP
Index on Censorship has been covering international developments in free expression for
twenty-two years. It covers political prisoners
in all regions of the world and publishes news
analysis, debates, banned literature, and
personal witness.

Lancaster House, 33 Islington High Street,
London N1 9LH England
Tel. (071) 278-2313 Fax. (071) 278-1878
email: indexoncenso@gn.apc.org

IN THESE TIMES
Published weekly by the Institute for Public
Affairs, *In These Times* presents alternative
analysis and background on a wide range of
foreign and domestic issues. 13 issues / $19.95.

2040 N. Milwaukee Ave., Chicago, IL 60647
Tel. (800) 827-0270 email: itt@igc.apc.org

THE NATION
Founded in 1865, the *Nation* offers weekly
sociopolitical reporting and commentary. Every
issue brings together a collection of terse edito-
rials, essays, and political tracts that keeps its
readers on the frontlines. The cover price simply
can't be beat. 24-issue subscription—$21.95.

P.O. Box 10791, Des Moines, IA 50340-0791

PEACE & DEMOCRACY

Published by the Campaign for Peace and Democracy, this magazine is dedicated to promoting a new, progressive, and nonmilitaristic U.S. foreign policy—one that renounces power politics and uses cooperation, aid, and political support to encourage democratization and social change throughout the world. Edited by Joanne Landy and Jennifer Scarlott. U.S.: $3.50/copy; Foreign: $7.50/copy.

P.O. Box 1640, Cathedral Station, New York, NY 10025
Tel. (212) 666-5924 Fax. (212) 662-5892
email: camppeacedem@igc.apc.org

THE PROGRESSIVE

With regular columns from social critics Molly Ivans, Peter Dykstra, June Jordan, Nat Hentoff, and Elayne Rapping, the *Progressive* offers penetrating insights into contemporary U.S. politics. Critical of left and right politics, yet receptive to environmentalist, feminist, and anarchist insights, the *Progressive* provides an essential forum for multicultural, democratic social movements. Subscriptions in the U.S.: $30 for 1 year; $55 for 2 years; Foreign: $36 for 1 year; $67 for 2 years.

P.O. Box 421
Mt. Morris, IL 61054-0421
Tel. (800) 827-0555

THIRD WORLD RESOURCES

Third World Resources maintains a documentation clearinghouse and computer-accessible databank on Third World–related organizations, books, periodicals, pamphlets, audiovisuals, and other education/action resources. Their journal, *Third World Resources,* is published quarterly to alert concerned educators and activists to new resources related to Third World regions and issues. Two-year individual subsriptions: U.S. & Canada— U.S. $35/2 years; Foreign—U.S. $45/2 years.

464 19th Street, Oakland, CA 94612-2297
Tel. (510) 835-4692 Fax. (510) 835-3017
email: tfenton@igc.apc.org or
datacenter@igc.apc.org

VILLAGE VOICE

Despite being an unashamedly commercial paper, the *Voice* consistently publishes some of the best in-depth investigative journalism produced today. Feature stories on the elections, activism, and media bias—to name a few— far outlast the one-week shelf life of each issue. A bastion of free thought and uninhibited commentary. One-year subscription—$47.95; Foreign—$79.20.

36 Cooper Square, New York, NY 10003
Tel. (800) 825-0061

WORLD CITIZEN NEWS

Newsletter of the World Government of World Citizens. Founded by Garry Davis, who renounced his citizenship in 1948 because he believed nationhood was outmoded in an era of instant communication, global economy, and potential nuclear holocaust. Articles cover human rights, government misinformation, and electronic communications. Subscriptions: U.S. $12/6 issues.

NWO Publications, 113 Church Street, Burlington, VT 05401
Tel. (802) 864-4656 Fax. (802) 864-6878
email: 76507.2343@compuserve.com

Z MAGAZINE

Z Magazine presents in-depth assessments of the political, cultural, social, and economic life of the United States. Each issue is packed with articles, essays, reviews, updates, and networking information supporting a diverse range of resistance efforts and projects for social change. A potent and indispensable source of information and activist contacts. $5.00 an issue.

18 Millfield Street, Woods Hole, MA 02543
Tel. (508) 548-9063 Fax. (508) 457-0626

RADIO AND TELEVISION RESOURCES

ALTERNATIVE RADIO CASSETTE SERIES

Alternative Radio Cassette Series presents a seminal audio-archive of many of today's most vital scholars, dissidents, historians, and activists. Programs in the series confront issues that are systematically ignored by mainstream media—issues like sustainable economics, global corporatism, labor, foreign policy, institutional racism and sexism, Native American resistance, and media bias. Produced by David Barsamian, the series features lectures and interviews with Noam Chomsky, Barbara Ehrenreich, Edward W. Said, Angela Davis, Howard Zinn, Elaine Bernard, Manning Marable, and many others. Send a self-addressed stamped envelope for a free catalog listing all available cassettes:

2129 Mapleton, Boulder, CO 80304
Tel. (303) 444-8788   Fax. (303) 546-0592

FREE RADIO BERKELEY

Using low-watt "micro" broadcasting to promote social activism, Stephen Dunifer aims to liberate the airwaves from corporate control. His organization, Free Radio Berkeley, is returning the airwaves to the people through "pirate" broadcasts, court battles with the FCC, seminars, and information on how to assemble your own transmitter.

1442 A Walnut Street #406, Berkeley, CA 94709
Tel. (510) 464-3041 email: frbspd@crl.com

PAPER TIGER TELEVISION

Paper Tiger video programs lift the veil of Oz from the communications, media, and information industries. Their subject catalog ranges from art, women, and information politics to international affairs and business. Send $2 for their superb catalog:

339 Lafayette Street, New York, NY 10012
Tel. (212) 420-9045 Fax. (212) 420-8223

PUBLIC RADIO SATELLITE SYSTEM

The Public Radio Satellite System enables grass-roots organizations and individuals to have their own audio-programs uplinked to a communications satellite and made accessible to over 400 public radio stations nationwide. Uplink fees for 1 hour of satellite time are shockingly inexpensive. Free brochure with detailed information available upon request:

2025 M Street, NW, Washington, DC 20036
Tel. (202) 414-2610

TV TRANSCRIPTS— JOURNAL GRAPHICS

Journal Graphics provides transcripts of ABC's *Nightline*, CNN programs, and other mainstream television programs.

267 Broadway, 3rd Floor, New York, NY 10007
Tel. (212) 227-7323

ALTERNATIVE BOOK PUBLISHERS

AK PRESS

Distributor and publisher of anarchist and antiauthoritarian books, CDs, cassettes, and ephemera. Free catalog.

539 Divisadero Street, San Francisco, CA 94117
Tel. (415) 923-1429 Fax. (415) 923-0607
email: akdis@aol.com

COMMON COURAGE PRESS

Founded in 1991 as an activist publishing house, Common Courage books present perspectives and strategies for social change. Manning Marable, Noam Chomsky, and Ward Churchill are among the authors Common Courage has recently published. Write for a free catalog of all available titles:

P.O. Box 702, Corner Route 139 and Jackson Road, Monroe, ME 04951
Tel. (207) 525-0900 Fax. (207) 525-3068

LEFT BANK BOOKS

The Left Bank Distibution collective makes available a huge collection of countercultural, antiauthoritarian, anarchist, and movement pamphlets, leaflets, chaps, books, zines, how-to manuals, and manifestos. A guidebook to political counterculture not to be missed. Free catalog.

4142 Brooklyn NE, Seattle, WA 98105
Tel. (206) 632-5870 Fax. (206) 622-0195

PATHFINDER PRESS

The publisher of more than 250 titles by Karl Marx, V. I. Lenin, Leon Trotsky, Rosa Luxemburg, Che Guevara, Fidel Castro, Malcolm X, Farrell Dobbs, James P. Cannon, Joseph Hansen, George Novack, Evelyn Reed, Nelson Mandela, Thomas Sankara, Maurice Bishop, Carlos Fonseca, and others.

410 West Street, New York, NY 10014
Tel. (212) 741-0690 Fax: (212) 727-0150
email: pathfinder@igc.apc.org
compuserve: 73321.414

SOUTH END PRESS

A nonprofit publishing house, South End Press presents an invaluable compendium of books addressing the most pressing issues of our times. In every area of radical social change— race, class, gender, economics, media, ecology, national security, activist strategies, and foreign policy, South End Press books are a resource to both the lay reader and the researcher. Readers can order books over the phone or join South End's membership program. Members are entitled to two free books and a 40 percent discount on all titles. Write for a free catalog:

116 St. Botolph Street, Boston, MA 02115
Tel. (617) 266-0629 Fax. (617) 266-1595
email: sep@world.std.com or epress@aol.com

ALTERNATIVE CULTURE

ALTERNATIVE PRESS REVIEW

APR informs its readers of a plethora of zines and magazines exploring culture, community, critique, econlogy, sexuality, and humor. *APR* also includes informative articles by and about the independent, do-it-yourself small press. One-year, surface-rate subscriptions: U.S.— $16; Foreign—$24.

C.A.L. Press, P.O. Box 1446, Columbia, MO 65205-1446

THE BAFFLER

The Baffler is dedicated to exposing the endless fraudulence of what passes for "culture" in America; to articulate resistance to the Official Styles of the day; to sabotage the great machinery of mindmaking. Every issue is filled with searing articles, satirical cartoons, and poetry. Single issue: $5; Subscription: 4 issues/$16.

P.O. Box 378293, Chicago, IL 60637

CENTRAL PARK

Central Park magazine is one of America's most thought-provoking literary journals. Each issue features a wide selection of theory, photography, fiction, poetry, experimental writing, and reviews that touch on everything from new models of perception and learning to scathing critiques of advertising and commodity culture. A veritable think tank of pioneering and provocative works. Not to be missed at $7.50 a copy.

P.O. Box 1446, New York, NY 10023

DREAMTIME TALKINGMAIL

Dreamtime Talkingmail is dedicated to the pursuit of the intentional community living in the temporary autonomous zone. Issues explore permaculture, hypermedia, natural healing, experimental poetics, gardening, and anarchism.

Xeroxial Endarchy, Rt. 1, Box 131, LaFarge, WI 54639

FUSE

Each issue of *Fuse* is an active mixture of arts, journalism, investigative features, and regular reviews of visual art, conferences, film and video, alternative press, independent music, and performance. Insightful articles provide essential information exchange and prove that a vital and internationally diverse arts culture exists outside of the major museums and galleries. Subscriptions: $20/year.

183 Bathurst Street, Toronto, Ontario, Canada, M5T 2R7
Tel. (416) 367-0159 Fax. (416) 360-0871

ND

ND magazine reviews art and interviews artists who have overcome established frameworks and conventions and speak forth with substance and honesty. This magazine serves as an essential forum for artists, musicians, writers, and other culture workers. Subscriptions: 2 issues/$7; 4 issues/$12.

P.O. Box 4144, Austin, Texas 78765

PLAGUEWATCH

Plaguewatch magazine breeds a healthy disrespect for corporate capitalism and the passive consumerism it infects. Articles cover electronic network accessibility, pirate radio, privatization, advertising, permaculture, and community empowerment. $20 for 5 issues.

Plaguewatch, P.O. Box 6, Buchyrus, MO 65444-0006
email: demigalt@well.sf.ca.us

PAIN MAGAZINE

A neo-Luddite guide to low-tech living and promoting more meaningful relationships to earth and its people. Issues provide a forum for environmental issues, intentional communities, and anticorporate, chemical-free living. Subscriptions: $18/6 issues.
Subscription Office:

P.O. Box 200, Burton, OH 44021

SITUATIONIST ANTHOLOGY

Edited and translated from the French by Ken Knabb, this 392-page opus makes available in English many of the writings of the insurgent art collective, the Situationist International. Laced with a biting sense of humor and at some points theoretically obtuse, the S.I.'s insurgent cultural critique continues to provide penetrating insight and radical tactics for subverting our "society of the spectacle." Fifteen dollars and well worth it.

Bureau of Public Secrets, P.O. Box 1044, Berkeley, CA 94701

THE UNDERGROUND FOREST

The Underground Forest is a bilingual, hemispheric publication devoted to the dissemination of informed opinions and good writing. Its poetry, articles, interviews, and documents plunge deep into investigative poetics and issues of political conscience. Subscriptions: U.S.—$12/4 issues.

1701 Bluebell Avenue, Boulder, CO 80302

WHOLE EARTH REVIEW

The famous guidebook of tools for sustainable living in an endangered world, *Whole Earth Review* catalogs new books, magazines, and resources on the cutting edge of learning, ecology, alternative energy, spirituality, communications, sexuality, politics, technology, etc. An invaluable resource, always interesting. $20 for 4 issues.

27 Gate Five Road, Sausalito, CA 94965

PROGRESSIVE ECONOMIC RESOURCES

CENTER FOR POPULAR ECONOMICS

CPE offers training workshops and programs for community and labor organizers who have not had formal economics training. Classes are designed to demystify economics and provide a framework for understanding the economy and alternatives to mainstream and conservative analyses. For publications, contact:

P.O. Box 785, Amherst, MA 01004
Tel. (413) 545-0743 Fax. (413) 549-2921
email: cpe@acad.umass.edu

CITIZENS TRADE CAMPAIGN

CTC is a national coalition of consumer, environmental, labor, family farm, religious, and other civic groups promoting a citizens' agenda in U.S. trade policy. Engaging 60 national groups and 45 million U.S. citizens, CTC lobbies Congress as a coalition against GATT and NAFTA. For more information contact:

600 Maryland Ave, SW, Washington, DC 20024
Tel. (202) 879-4298

DOLLARS AND SENSE MAGAZINE

D&S offers progressive economic analysis accessible to people with no formal training. They publish annual editions of *Real World Macro*, an anthology of D&S articles organized in a textbook format. Ten issues a year. Individual: $22.95/yr.; $39/2 yrs. Institution: $42/yr.; $84/2 yrs.

One Summer Street, Somerville, MA 02143
Tel. (617) 628-8411

INSTITUTE FOR AGRICULTURE & TRADE POLICY

IATP was organized in 1986 to alert the public to the impact of global policymaking on our daily lives. From monitoring GATT, NAFTA, and UNCED developments to providing "win-win" solutions to trade conflicts, IATP is invaluable to all people working for a balanced, sustainable future.

1313 Fifth St. SE #303, Minneapolis, MN 55414
Tel. (612) 379-5980 Fax. (612) 379-5982
email: iatp@igc.apc.org

INSTITUTE FOR INTERNATIONAL COOPERATION AND DEVELOPMENT

IICD offers 12-month Global Education programs, including volunteer work projects in Africa and Latin America. Course brochure and quarterly newsletter are available.

P.O. Box 103, Williamstown, MA 01267
Tel. (413) 458-9828 Fax. (413) 458-3323

LABOR NOTES

Labor Notes is a monthly newsletter for union activists promoting democracy and creative strategy within labor. Individual subscription: $20/yr.; Institutional: $30/yr.

7435 Michigan Avenue, Detroit, MI 48210
Tel. (313) 842-6262 Fax. (313) 842-0227
email: labornotes@igc.apc.org

NATIONAL COMMISSION FOR ECONOMIC CONVERSION AND DISARMAMENT

ECD was established in 1988 to educate the public about why the orderly transfer of military resources to civilian uses through conversion is necessary for reversing the arms race and restoring the nation's economic health. *The New Economy* pioneers how defense cuts can be invested in infrastructure, civilian R&D, and other productivity-enhancing investments that will create new jobs and promote sustainable economic growth.

1801 18th Street NW, Suite. #9, Washington, DC 20009

CIVIL RIGHTS ADVOCACY GROUPS

AMERICAN CIVIL LIBERTIES UNION (ACLU)

A national civil rights advocacy and litigation group that publishes a free biweekly newsletter and annual list of cases.

132 W. 43rd Street, New York, NY 10036
Tel. (212) 944-9800

THE CENTER FOR DEMOCRATIC RENEWAL

Formerly known as the National Anti-Klan Network, CDR organizes opposition to hate-group activity and bigoted violence, through education, activism, and action. CDR provides programs in education, research, victim assistance, community organizing, leadership training, and public policy advocacy. The organization is multiracial, multiethnic, interfaith, and nonprofit. For information and a free copy of CDR's journal, the *Monitor,* write:

P.O. Box 50469, Atlanta, GA 30302-0469
Tel. (404) 221-0025 Fax. (404) 221-0045

MALCOLM X: THE FBI FILES

Carroll & Graf has published the comprehensive FBI files on Malcolm X, edited by Clayborne Carson with an introduction by Spike Lee. Since 1955, the FBI followed Malcolm with a special detachment employed to record and transcribe his speeches and movements. These are considered some of the best transcriptions of Malcolm X's work. 512 pp. $23.95 cloth; $12.95 paper.

260 Fifth Ave., New York, NY 10001
Tel. (212) 889-8772

MARTIN LUTHER KING, JR., CENTER FOR NONVIOLENT SOCIAL CHANGE

Established in 1968, the center preserves and advances Dr. King's unfinished work through teaching, interpreting, and advocating the nonviolent elimination of poverty, racism, and violence. For free information and literature write:

449 Auburn Avenue, N.E., Atlanta, GA 30322

NATIONAL ALLIANCE AGAINST RACIST AND POLITICAL REPRESSION

Since 1973, the NAARPR has organized a national multicultural coalition of labor, church, educational, activist, and women's groups. Confronting racism, anti-Semitism, police crime, and the presence of political prisoners in the United States and South Africa are central among the alliance's concerns. Send a SASE for a complimentary copy of the *Organizer,* the alliance's newsletter:

11 John Street, Room 702, New York, NY 10038

NATIONAL ASSOCIATION FOR THE ADVANCEMENT OF COLORED PEOPLE

The NAACP is the oldest and largest civil rights organization in the United States. The NAACP presently has 1,800 branches, 300 youth and college chapters, and a membership of over 500,000 people. For more information write:

4805 Mount Hope Drive, Baltimore, MD 21215

SOUTHERN ORGANIZING COMMITTEE FOR ECONOMIC AND SOCIAL JUSTICE

SOC is an interracial network of southern activists and organizers who work with their local communities against racism and war. The group is involved with community-labor coalition building and has organized a major conference devoted to improving human health, safety, and the environment. For a free copy of their newsletter, *Southern Fightback,* write:

P.O. Box 811, Birmingham, AL 35201

NATIVE AMERICAN— COUNTER-QUINCENTENNIAL

ALLIANCE FOR CULTURAL DEMOCRACY

National network of artists, educators, and organizers committed to grass-roots cultural expression. The Alliance has been working on counter-Quincentennial projects since 1988 and publishes a newspaper that is available free by writing to:

P.O. Box 7591
Minneapolis, MN 55407

ECOLOGY RESOURCES

ECODEFENSE

Committed to environmental preservation, this book guides readers through an array of step-by-step strategies that involve direct action, civil disobedience, and nonviolent sabotage. Topics cover everything from billboard removal to disabling logging and earthmoving equipment. Available for $12.

Ned Ludd Books, P.O. Box 5871, Tucson, AZ 85703
Tel. (602) 628-9610

THE ECOLOGIST

The *Ecologist* features timely and incisive articles on the state of world ecology. Issues investigate the pernicious effects of IMF-sponsored "development," international trade, nuclear power, and tourism among other issues. Subscriptions: $34; current issue: $7.

Agriculture House, Bath Road, Sturminster Newton, Dorset
DT10 1DU England
Tel. 25-847-3476 Fax. 25-847-374
email: ecologist@gn.apc.org

FRIENDS OF THE EARTH

Friends of the Earth is an independent, global advocacy organization that works at local, national, and international levels to protect the planet; preserves biological, cultural, and ethnic diversity; and empowers citizens to have a voice in decisions affecting their environment and lives.

218 D Street, SE, Washington, DC 20003
Tel. (202) 783-7400 Fax. (202) 783-0444
Telex. 650-192-5483 email: foedc@igc.apc.org

GREEN LETTER

Green Letter is a national quarterly newspaper reporting on the development of the Green movement in the United States and abroad. Each issue covers international, national, and indigenous organizing with news, analysis, and resources linking social justice and environmental movements. $5 per issue; $20 per year.

P.O. Box 14141, San Francisco, CA 94110

GREEN PERSPECTIVES

Green Perspectives is a collective, eco-anarchist, social ecology newsletter, edited by Janet Beihl, Murray Bookchin, Chuck Morse, and Gary Sisco. Covers issues of radical ecology, social ecology, communities, and natural ecologies. 10 issues for $10.

Box 111, Burlington, VT 05402

LEFT GREEN NETWORK

The Left Green Network is a continental organization devoted to "Greening the Left and Radicalizing the Greens." The principles of the Left Green Network and info on how to participate in the network are available from:

P.O. Box 366, Iowa City, IA 52244

$10/yr. subscriptions to *Left Green Notes* are available from:

825 East Roosevelt, Suite 178, Lombard, IL 60148

ROCKY MOUNTAIN INSTITUTE

Considered to be the world's leading energy analysts, Amory and Hunter Lovins founded (1982) and continue to run RMI. A nonprofit resource policy center, RMI's eco-wisdom is sought by corporations and governments worldwide. *Least-Cost Energy* (U.S.—$15 ppd., add $7.53 postage for foreign orders), as well as a catalog of related materials, can be obtained from:

1739 Snowmass Creek Road, Snowmass, CO 81654-9199
Tel. (303) 927-3851 Fax. (303) 927-4178

SEED LINKS

Seed Links is developing solidarity networks among activists dedicated to an ecologically sustainable future. This newsletter sounds the clarion call to resistance against the G7, the IMF and the World Bank, and their instruments of planetary control. Its pages abound with reports on actions staged to end corporate profiteering from the destruction of the earth's precious natural and human resources. Suscriptions: DM 15 (U.S.$10).

EYFA, Post Box 566, 6130 AN Sittard, Netherlands
Tel. 31-46-513045 Fax. 31-46-516460
email: gn.eyfa

WORLDWATCH—STATE OF THE WORLD REPORT

The primary environmental intelligence report for many countries, the *State of the World Report* is an excellent source of environmental data and analyses.
Send a check for $11.95 to:

1776 Massachusetts Avenue, Washington, DC 20036
Tel. (202) 452-1999 Fax. (202) 296-7365
email: worldwatch@igc.apc.org

ZAPATISTA UPRISING

AZTEC HARVESTS COFFEE COMPANY

Aztec Harvests Coffee Company is a gourmet coffee importer collectively owned by small farmer cooperatives in Chiapas, Oaxaca, Veracruz, and Guerrero. Peasant farmers formed the company in response to the tough economic conditions they faced to sell their best beans for better prices. Write for a catalog:

1480 66th Street, Emeryville, CA 94608
Tel. (510) 652-2100 Fax. (510) 652-2636

BASTA!

In *Basta!,* George Collier, an authority on Chiapas who is fluent in Tzotzil, and Elizabeth Lowery Quaratiello, a journalist, look beyond romantic images and superficial explanations. They outline the local, national, and international forces that created a situation ripe for a violent response. Includes a forward by Peter Rosset. ISBN: 0-935028-65-X; 130 pp. $12.95 + $4 shipping & handling.

Food First Books, P.O. Box 160, 265 5th Street, Monroe, OR 97456

DIOCESE DE SAN CRISTÓBAL DE LAS CASAS

The Diocese of San Cristóbal has been acting as a center for information about the Zapatistas, especially during the Dialogue for Peace and Reconcilliation. They are also a good way to send support to the Zapatistas.

20 Noviembre, Esquina, Calle 5 de Febrero, Colonia Centro
29200 San Cristóbal, Chiapas, Mexico
Tel. 011-52-967-80053 Fax. 011-52-967-83136

FIRST WORLD, HA HA HA!

The Chiapas uprising is a new kind of challenge to a developing global economic system that threatens to impoverish communities and individuals around the world. In this collection, writers, activists, and political theorists from Mexico and the United States respond to the Zapatistas' bold attack on the New World Order. Included are Efrain Bartolomé, Blanche Petrich, Guillermo Gómez-Peña,

John Ross, Elena Poniatowska, Leonard Peltier, Ward Churchill, Noam Chomsky, M. Annette Jaimes, Juan Bañuelos, Eraclio Zepeda, Leslie Marmon Silko, Alberto Blanco, Antonio García de León, Jack Hirschman, and Elva Macías. ISBN: 0-87286-294-1; $10.95.

City Lights, 261 Columbus Avenue, San Francisco, CA 94133
Tel. (415) 362-8193 Fax. (415) 362-4921

MEXICO-U.S. DIALOGOS

Mexico-US Dialogos was founded in 1988 as a program to promote an ongoing interchange between social constituencies in the United States and Mexico directly affected by economic integration. An information resource for social organizations in both countries. Contact: Dave Brooks.

103 Washington Street, Suite 8, New York, NY 10006
Tel. (212) 233-0238 Fax. (212) 233-0155
email: dialogos@igc.apc.org

NATIONAL CENTER FOR SOCIAL COMMUNICATION

Centro Nacional de Comunicación Social or CENCOS (National Center for Social Communication) is a Mexican NGO and vital center for Zapatista solidarity. They are a good source of information, and letters of solidarity could also be sent to them:

Calle Medellín No. 33, Colonia Roma Delegación Cuauhtemoc, 06700 Mexico, DF
Tel. 011-525-533-8476 Fax. 011-525-533-6475

PROTEST THE POLICIES OF THE PRI

Write letters to President Zedillo asking the Mexican government to respond to the demands of the indigenous people of Chiapas in a spirit of peace, justice, and democracy. These could be sent to Mexican consulates in the United States or to the President himself.

Via Olmos #1, Fraccionamente del Bosque, Camino Sta Teresa 480 Tlalpan, Mexico, DF, 14060

REBELLION FROM THE ROOTS

John Ross chronicles the Zapatista revolution through the recent elections, vividly encapsulating their unfolding struggle for justice. With powerful narrative skill, Ross, a journalist, social activist, and poet, covers the history of indigenous and agrarian popular efforts of the Mexican poor, and asks, "Do the elections represent a step toward democracy or the promise of further strife?" ISBN: 1-56751-042-6; 424 pp. $14.95 + $2.50 shipping & handling.

Common Courage Press, P.O. Box 702, Monroe, ME 04951
Tel. (207) 525-0900 Fax. (207) 525-3068

SHADOWS OF TENDER FURY

Shadows of Tender Fury is a collection of the letters and communiqués of Subcomandante Marcos and the Zapatista Army of National Liberation. Introduced by Mexico City journalist John Ross, *Shadows* presents an impeccable translation by Frank Bardacke, Leslie López, and the Watsonville, California Human Rights Committee, and includes and "exclusive" prologue by Subcomandante Marcos and his speech to the Democratic National Convention of August 1994. ISBN: 0-85345-918-5; 288 pp./$15 paper.

Monthly Review Press, Order Dept., 122 West 27th Street, New York, NY 10001
Tel. (212) 691-2555 Fax. (212) 727-3676
email: mreview@igc.apc.org

ZAPATISTAS! DOCUMENTS OF THE NEW MEXICAN REVOLUTION

This essential reader contains over 100 of the EZLN's and Subcommandante Marcos's interviews, manifestos, and communiqués documenting the daily struggle of the indigenous campesinos and their numerous attempts to bring social justice to all of Mexico. The book covers the story from January 1 to June 12, 1994, and includes a major events timeline, an informative glossary, a brief contact list of solidarity groups, and a thorough list of electronic resources. $12 paper, $2 postage. ISBN: 1-57027-014-7.

Autonomedia, P.O. Box 568, Brooklyn, NY 11211-0568; Tel. & Fax. (718) 963-2603

CITIZEN EMPOWERMENT

THE COUNCIL OF CANADIANS

The Council of Canadians is a public interest group working for social and economic justice, and popular sovereignty. They're allied with progressive organizations across Canada, the U.S., and Mexico. Council provides a base for community-based resistance to human rights violations, globalization from above, and publishes a newsletter, *Canadian Perspectives*.

904-251 Laurier Avenue West, Ottawa, Ontario K1P 5J6 Canada
Tel. (613) 233-2773 Fax. (613) 233-6776

EQUIPO PUEBLO

Founded in 1977, Equipo Pueblo works closely with popular movements and citizen coalitions in the promotion of democracy, the defense of human rights, and the advancement of economic justice. Their news bulletin, *La Otra Cara de Mexico/The Other Side of Mexico,* appears 6 times a year. Yearly subscriptions are U.S.$10 for Latin America & U.S.$15 for North America and Europe.

Apartado Postal 27-467, 06760 Mexico DF
Tel. 011-525-539-0015
Fax. 011-525-627-7453

GOVERNMENT ACCOUNTABILITY PROJECT

A nonprofit organization, GAP provides legal and advocacy assistance to concerned citizens who witness dangerous, illegal, or environmentally unsound practices in their workplaces and communities and choose to "blow the whistle." For a $35 annual subscription to *Bridging the Gap,* or a catalog of titles, contact:

810 First Street NE, Suite 630, Washington, DC 20002-3633
Tel. (202) 408-0034 Fax. (202) 408-9855

THE LEARNING ALLIANCE

The Learning Alliance provides alternative educational resources and cassettes on Native American issues, ecology, social justice, community health, arts, feminism, economics, and culture. For a free catalog write:

324 Lafayette Street, New York, NY 10011
Tel. (212) 226-7171 Fax. (212) 274-8712
email: alliance@blythe.org

THE NEW PARTY

The New Party is working from the bottom up to provide a viable, pragmatic, third-party alternative to the two-wing business party that rules the American political arena. They believe that the key to a fair economy and a new democracy is to change the rules of the campaign game—to make people rather than money the decider of elections. For more information contact:

227 W. 40th Street, Ste 1303, N.Y., NY 10018
Tel. (212) 302-5053 Fax. (212) 302-5344
email: newparty@igc.apc.org

PUBLIC CITIZEN

Public Citizen is a nonprofit citizen research, lobbying, and litigation organization. Since 1971, Public Citizen has fought for consumer rights in the marketplace, for a healthy environment and workplace, for clean and safe energy resources, and for corporate and government accountability.

215 Pennsylvania Ave SE, Washington, DC 20003
Tel. (202) 546-4996 Fax. (202) 547-7392
email: pcctw@igc.apc.org

RESOURCE CENTER OF THE AMERICAS

The Resource Center of the Americas works to connect people in the United States with people and issues throughout the Americas. They provide community access to information from electronic networks, the Latin American press, the U.S. press, and first hand accounts. Contact: Larry Weiss at

317 17th Ave SE, Minneapolis, MN 55414
Tel. (612) 627-9445 Fax. (612) 627-9450
email: rctamn@maroon.tc.umn.edu

INFORMATION SUPERHIGHWAY

ALLIANCE FOR COMMUNITY MEDIA

A national membership organization representing local public-access cable stations, their programmers and volunteers, ACM advances democratic ideals by ensuring that people have access to electronic media, and by promoting effective communication through community uses of media.

666 11th St. NW, Suite 806, Washington, DC 20001-4542
Tel. (202) 393-2650 Fax. (202) 393-2653
email: alliancecm@aol.com compuserve 71420.2554

CENTER FOR CIVIC NETWORKING

A nonprofit organization serving civic networking practitioners and promoting policies, products and services that can support the sustainable development of local economies and communities in the twenty-first century.

91 Baldwin Street, Charlestown, MA 02129
Tel. (617) 241-9205 Fax. (617) 241-5064
email: ccn@civicnet.org /sadelman@civicnet.org

CENTER FOR MEDIA EDUCATION

A nonprofit public interest policy and research organization dedicated to promoting the democratic potential of the electronic media.

1511 K Street NW, Suite 518, Washington, DC 20005
Tel. (202) 628-2620 Fax. (202) 628-2554
email: cme@access.digex.net.

COMPUTER PROFESSIONALS FOR SOCIAL RESPONSIBILITY

"The mission of CPSR is to provide the public and policy makers with realistic assessments of the power, promise, and limitations of computer technology." CPSR has 21 chapters in the U.S. and affiliations with similar groups worldwide. Send for their invaluable report *Serving the Community: A Public Interest Vision of the National Information Infrastructure.*

National Office: P.O. Box 717, Palo Alto, CA 94301; Tel. (415)322-3778
email:cpsr@csli.stanford.edu

LIBRARIES FOR THE FUTURE

A national organization dedicated to supporting grass-roots and national citizen advocacy for libraries; to fostering opportunity and innovation in public libraries across the United States; and to representing the community of users of public libraries.

521 5th Avenue Suite 1612, New York, NY 10175-1699
Tel. (212) 682-7446 or (800) 542-1918
Fax. (212) 682-7657
email: lff@phantom.com

LIBRARY AND INFORMATION TECHNOLOGY ASSOCIATION

The division of the American Library Association concerned with the planning and application of technology within libraries. "LITA envisions a world in which the complete spectrum of information technology is available to everyone."

50 E. Huron Street, Chicago, IL 60611-2729
Tel. (312) 280-4267 Fax. (312) 280-3257
email: tl.aviv.barbee@aoa.org

NATIONAL TELECOMMUNICATIONS AND INFORMATION ADMINISTRATION

The coordinating body of the nation's tele-communications and information policy. Contact them to obtain government information about the NII and related projects.

15th Street and Constitution Avenue, Washington, DC 20230
Tel. (202) 482-1840 Fax. (202) 482-1635
email: nii@ntia.doc.gov

TAXPAYER ASSETS PROJECT

Founded by Ralph Nader to monitor the management of government property including information systems and data, government-funded R&D, spectrum allocation, and other government assets.

12 Church Road, Ardmore, PA 19003
Tel. (610) 658-0880 email: love@essential.org.

COMMERCIAL-FREE CULTURE

ADBUSTERS
Adbusters magazine attacks the various ways that commercial media sell ownership as identity and consumption as a way of life. Each issue decodes the images and illusions generated by advertising and reports on constructive strategies toward the liberation of public space. Sample copy, $4.75; subscription, $16.

1243 West 7th Avenue, Vancouver, British Columbia, V6H 1B7 Canada

CENTER FOR THE STUDY OF COMMERCIALISM
CSC seeks to limit the influence of advertising on our lives by establishing commercial-free zones, developing media literacy curricula, and campaigning against advertising's intrusion into our public and private spaces. Their book, *Marketing Madness,* documents the insidious role of advertising and commercialism in America. To become a member and receive their quarter newsletter, *AdVice,* write:

1875 Connecticut Avenue, NW Suite 300, Washington, DC 20009-5728
Tel. (202) 332-9110 Fax. (202) 265-4954

UNPLUG
A national, youth-run coalition conducting a coordinated campaign against Whittle Communications' Channel 1 and other attempts to commercialize the classroom. "We stand for community-controlled, free public education." Send for their excellent newspaper *With a Growing Voice.*

360 Grand Avenue Box 385, Oakland, CA 94610
Tel. (800) UNPLUG-1 email: unplug@igc.org

ELECTRONIC COMPUTER NETWORKS

ACTIVIST MAILING LIST
The Activist Mailing List regularly posts news stories/analyses on a vast array of activist issues. To get a once-a-day index of articles available, send the command "set activ-l index" to the address "listserv@mizzou1.missouri.edu." Activ-l's discussion group is on USENET and has the name "misc.activism.progressive."

ALTERNET
AlterNet is the Institute for Alternative Journalism's on-line computer wire service, which distributes articles from the independent and alternative press on a wide range of subjects. Individuals can subscribe to AlterNet for $25 per month. Subscriptions include a weekly hard copy of the index of story abstracts and varied information on important reports and upcoming events.

77 Federal Street, San Francisco, CA 94107
Tel. (415) 284-1420 Fax. (415) 284-1414
email: 71362.27@compuserve.com

LBBS— LEFT ON LINE UNIVERSITY
Nearly 3,000 people have logged on to the foreign policy, economy, sexuality, telecommunications, vegetarianism, and other engaging conferences of this exciting bulletin board run by *Z Magazine*. LBBS also features a Left On Line University with online courses and weekly discussions run by professors Noam Chomsky, Stephen Shalom, Mike Albert, and others. Tap into LBBS for $2 per hour or $10 per month for unlimited hours of political education.

18 Millfield St., Woods Hole, MA 02543
LBBS Sysop: (508) 548-9064
Lydia Sargent: (508) 548-9063

PEACENET COMPUTER NETWORK
Through computer modems, Peacenet links together media, environmental, and human rights activists in over 70 countries. The net opens access to more than 600 electronic conferences that provide everything from timely

information on world events to open discussions, activist tactics, and media strategies. Initial set-up fee is $15; monthly subscription fee is $10; on-line rates $5–$10/hr.; Internet access from universities—$3/hr.

18 De Boom Street, San Francisco, CA 94107
Tel. (415) 442-0220 Fax (415) 546-1794
email: support@igc.apc.org

THE WELL COMPUTER NETWORK
Organized by the folks at the *Whole Earth Review,* The Well provides on-line conferences on a multitude of subjects including art, media, and hacking. For more information:

The Well, 27 Gate Five Road, Sausalito, CA 94965-1401